by Susan Sontag

FICTION
The Benefactor
Death Kit
I, etcetera

ESSAYS
Against Interpretation
Trip to Hanoi
Styles of Radical Will
On Photography
Illness as Metaphor
Under the Sign of Saturn

FILMSCRIPTS
Duet for Cannibals
Brother Carl

A
Susan Sontag
Reader

A
Susan Sontag
Reader

INTRODUCTION BY

ELIZABETH HARDWICK

Farrar / Straus / Giroux

NEW YORK

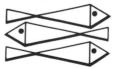

Library of Congress Cataloging in Publication Data
Sontag, Susan. / A Susan Sontag reader.
I. Title.
PS3569.06547A6   1982   818'.5409   82-9259
AACR2

The essays in this volume first appeared, in a somewhat
different or abridged form, in *The New York Review of Books,*
Evergreen Review, Partisan Review, The Seventh Art, Aspen,
and *The New Yorker.* The stories were originally published
in *The Atlantic, American Review,* and *The New Yorker*

appropriately, for Roger

Contents

Introduction

Essays lie all over the land, stored up like the unused wheat of a decade ago in the silos of old magazines and modest collections. In the midst of this clumsy abundance, there are rare lovers of the form, the great lovers being some few who practice it as the romance this dedication can be. And romance for us, the readers, when certain names appear on the cover of periodicals. Susan Sontag: the name is a resonance of qualities, of quality itself. The drama of the idea, the composition, a recognition from the past that tells us what the present may bestow when we see her name. The term "essay" itself is somewhat flat as a definition of the liberality of her floating, restless expositions. *A Susan Sontag Reader,* a choice from her criticism and fiction, is in no way scant, but it interested me to note that one could regret the omission of almost any piece of her writing, any square of the mosaic that is in the end an extraordinarily beautiful, expansive, and unique talent.

Her writings are *hers,* intimately and obsessively one might say. They bear, each one, the mark of a large and coherent sensibility, the mark of her *interests,* her sense of the aesthetic and moral world around us. Almost none of her work comes out of the mere occasion, the book published, the film released, or the fad acknowledged. I suppose her theme is the wide, elusive, variegated sensibility of modernism—a reach of attitude and feeling that will include great works of art, the modern disturbance of the sense of self seen in "camp" and in pornography, and account for the social, historical disturbance represented by the contemporary glut of photographic images. Modernism is style and the large figures of culture she likes to reflect upon leave in their styles the signature of wishes, attractions, morals, and, always, ideas.

Susan Sontag is not drawn to her themes as a specialty, as one might choose the eighteenth century, but rather as expressions of her own taste, her own being, her own style perhaps. Her imagination is obstinate, stubborn in its insistence upon the heroic efforts of certain moving, complex modern princes of temperament such as Walter Benjamin, Artaud, Roland Barthes, Lévi-Strauss, Canetti, and the tragic moral philosopher Simone Weil. The modern sensibility in her view is democratic; it embraces the aristocratic spirit of the films made by Godard, Bresson, Bergman, and Syberberg. The listing of her "interests" shows an almost spendthrift openness to example and precept and vivacious practice. But her thoughts surprise. Films, writers, philosophers are, as it were, excavated, brought up to the topsoil to be viewed in the round. This is a particular vision, the defining glance of cultural history in which each thing is itself, unique and to some degree "against interpretation"—and yet reflecting a disjunctive modern consciousness that is historical. On this theme and its fascinations each of her essays has a profound authority, a rather anxious and tender authority—the reward of passion.

"Writing Itself" is the title of an essay on Roland Barthes. This essay, her last in point of sequence, is a complicated discourse that may be called "formal" in its inclusiveness. And yet in the purest sense it is a long, excited aside, free of pedantry, personal in its elevated attentiveness. It is an absorption, a saturation, indeed an infatuation arising from the mind laid bare in the writing, Barthes's writing. There are his themes, his manner, and since no mind lives alone there are other philosophers, other writers, the period, and France itself. In the midst of all that, the style, the being who undertook his creative enterprises, cannot be understood apart from intuitions that see creation as a private destiny. This sense of the person is the text within the text in Susan Sontag's essays; the man himself is a sort of interpolation to be arrived at by the critic's imagination and feeling. She writes of Barthes: "He speaks of the quiver, thrill, or shudder of meaning," and his intention is to give "pleasure."

As I read over her work about figures from France and Germany, it occurs to me to remark what a "good European" is this completely American woman who grew up in Arizona and California, attended North Hollywood High, went to the University of Chicago and to Harvard. If I understand the phrase, to be a "good European" means to be international, respectful of the cultures and peculiarities of nations, to be rooted but not small or provincial or too native for curiosity. With Susan Sontag the ocean-spanning curiosity has been a kind of quest, an obligation to culture as well as the expression of a singular and brightly colored personality. The writers she has chosen to reflect upon are somewhat daunting and I do not think she would place herself among the undaunted. The tone of her writing is speculative, studious and yet undogmatic; even in the end it is still inquiring. There remains what Henry James called the "soreness of confusion," the reminder of the unaccountable and inexhaustible in great talents. This remnant of wonder is her way of honoring the exceptional, the finally inimitable.

I do not wish to suggest too great a degree of the ambassadorial in her career, to make of a free and independent intelligence a bringer of news or even of *the new*. She is too much of a New Yorker for that, too much at home here where you cannot tell anyone anything. What I see as the urbanism of her spirit is the fluency that includes Paris, Berlin, and Rome, and thoughts about the fate of the photograph in Peking and curious aesthetics in Tokyo. She is patient about the mysteries of foreign cultures and patient with our own; her fluency extends to our streets with their pornography and politics, their theater and psychoanalysis. Style is everywhere; it is by patience and intuition that intentions are uncovered.

There is here the essay on style as an abstraction, on form and content as a question of philosophy and moral aesthetics. "Whenever speech or movement or behavior or objects exhibit a certain deviation from the most direct, useful, insensible mode of expression or being in the world, we may look at them as having a 'style,' and being both autonomous and exemplary." In my view, *useful* is the most interesting word here; to be beyond the useful and the necessary is to seek authenticity for the urgently invisible threads of cultural experience.

Style is to some degree a decision but it is most importantly a fate, growing out of the unconscious and exemplified, or partly exemplified, in the solutions of craft. This matter, style, which is always her theme, is the opposite of decoration and instead is a consuming essence from which morals, politics, vices, and virtues cannot be expunged. Style, often wishing to hide, is a constant exposure. The "spiritual style" of Robert Bresson's films is cool, impersonal, and reserved; the "fascist style" of Leni Riefenstahl is dramatic, grandiose, orderly, communal, and tribal. Thus, you have not only creators and their achievement, you have character itself. The inner life revealed in style is quite apart from biography in the conventional sense, the biography of dates, ancestry, traumas, and endings. Although Susan

Sontag's work is rich in the sense of the artist as a living person, or as one who has lived, there is very little of the biographical.

On Photography is one of the truly notable books of our period. It is a prodigality, an acceleration, a *rapido* which carries an immense accumulation of thought, interpretation, history, and detail as lightly as eggs in a basket. Photographs, the idea of photography, the familiarity of it explode in a dazzle of light. Susan Sontag has made three remarkable films and is herself a sort of pictorial object, as the many arresting photographs of her show. But her book ends on a wistful imagining of an ecology to limit the exploitation, the strip-mining of reality by the greedy photographic image.

"Whatever the moral claims made on behalf of photography, its main effect is to convert the world into a department store or museum-without-walls in which every subject is depreciated into an article of consumption, promoted into an item for aesthetic appreciation." The camera, then, is a huge repository of secrets, aggressions, evolutionary usages. It is too relishing perhaps and the result of her fervent, eloquent, and learned exploration is to discover for us—and it is a discovery—that there is a chill in it. The design of cultural phenomena, the design of attitudes, postures, creative acts, the design of a great career—this is the landscape of her talent and dedication. "Behind their obtrusive verbosity, Godard's films are haunted by the duplicity and banality of language."

She, like Barthes and Benjamin, chose philosophy as a student. It is easy to imagine her as a prodigy at the Ecole Normale and no accident that, being an American, she turned up at sixteen at the University of Chicago. Her metaphysical vocabulary retains this habit of mind and she has Nietzsche and Plato as readily at hand as bits of memorized poetry. "The powers of photography have in effect de-Platonized our understanding of reality . . ." Conceptualization from instances gathered from afar is her method. There is seldom anything whimsical or indulgent in this far-flung patterning. The structure is genuine, convincing, and the gathering-in is an illumination.

She practices delicately and lightheartedly the aphoristic summation, rather than the aphoristic interruption. About sadomasochism: "The color is black, the material is leather, the seduction is beauty, the justification is honesty, the aim is ecstasy, the fantasy is death." Her style, her prose language, is clear, fresh, not meant to tease or to confound. However, the extremity of her subjects will often demand that the expositor by a gymnast. Waywardness attracts her and in waywardness there is humor, outrageousness, the unpredictable, along with extremity. In that sense her work is sensual and many of her essays are about heroic insatiability, as in the instance of the brilliant "Syberberg's Hitler."

"Notes on Camp" is an early, exhilarating work about "style" at an ineffable outpost of sensibility. "Camp" is parochial in that it can only be fulfilled in the city with its infinite byways. "Camp is the answer to the problem: how to be a dandy in the age of mass culture." If the word is beyond definition, it is not beyond reflection, example, listing. The essay is amused, a sophisticated precondition for a pose that elevates the amusing to a criterion. The camp sensibility is not a text to be held in the hand. The only text is finally this essay, with its incorporation of the exemplar of the camp mode—the epigrams of Oscar Wilde. The essay is intuition, observation, tolerance for the inverted, the willful. "Camp is a woman walking around in a dress made of three million feathers."

In her novels and stories we discover what we have learned to expect from Susan Sontag; that is, that all is unexpected. Her fiction is angular, devious, and yet I would call it ruled by a special rationalism, and when we read we are trying to bring these aspects into harmony. Form, the narrative challenge, must be, will be, made to yield; it is a battle, but a lighthearted, good-natured battle. In *The Benefactor* the domestic is the stuff, the furniture of solitude and dreams have the willed complicity of actions: "This dream was my first immoderate act." *Death Kit:* the railway tunnel of death is bursting with life; it is crammed with quotations, messages, visions of firemen, Civil War veterans, football players, those who wear the uniforms of function. Space is overwhelming, determining.

The fictions are not fantasies; they are inventions chained to the normal, even to some possible average. Dalton Harron in *Death Kit* is "a mild fellow, gently reared in a middle-sized city in Pennsylvania and expensively educated. A good-natured child, the older son of civilized parents who had quietly died." "Debriefing," laid out in a random and episodic manner, is finally about sequence, cause and effect. From the flow of the consuming debris of consciousness in the street, in the national life, from books in the head, cleaning women, metaphysics, diet, and music, you have the "cause" of Julia's suicide. Julia, a wayward, retreating young woman, is very far from being "unmotivated." She can be seen as disastrously locked in the idea of final consequence—and the end is suicide. The narrator, who will live, finds life in the recognition of the absurd. She will, as she says, roll the rock up the hill, again and again. "Nothing, nothing could tear me away from this rock."

In the story "Unguided Tour," the surface is conversation, question, response, musing statement, drifting comment. Everything is swept over rapidly, none of it quite fulfilled. There is a plot and the lovers are on a trip to the cities of the beautiful, famous things, the objects of cultural reverence. Or they will consume scenery of aesthetic acclaim, mountains and lakes. They quarrel, falter with fatigue, they buy things, they are forced into the inescapable utterances of travel, which will inevitably be clichés. The young people are not caricatures, not "innocents abroad," but nevertheless they will suffer, as we all do, from the inexpressible because there is no language, no spoken definition of feeling equal to the experience of the things seen, the places visited. The openness of the world and history inspires greed and an immense weariness. The infinite is exhausting and there is no relief from "the great longing for another place."

Finally, availability is an illusion. The restaurants, the churches, the monuments, the centuries, the ruins can yield only a sameness. They are still there, but the present is tinged with loss. The ancient streets are filled with automobiles. There is a crack in the cloister wall and what a pity one could not have seen it all a hundred years ago, when it was *more itself.*

In 1966 a number of essays by Miss Sontag which had appeared in magazines were collected into a published book, *Against Interpretation.* "Appeared" is to the point in this case since it leads to the personal, the noticeable, the theatrical element in taste and in "point of view" when the observer is a foraging pluralist. This first book of essays was provoking, meaning to unsettle by an insistent avant-gardism, by aesthetic irregularities such as "camp," science fiction, and the film *Flaming Creatures,* "the poetry of transvestism," closed on the ground of obscenity by the police. These diversions are bright, poisonous poppies, flaming about Simone Weil, Lévi-Strauss, Camus, and others. There is an anarchic, intrepid stretch to the book. In it we are invited to a "new sensibility," in which the "beauty of a machine or of the solution to a mathematical problem, of a painting by Jasper Johns, or a film by Jean-Luc Godard, and of the personalities and music of the Beatles is equally accessible." Youthful, brilliant, and so ardently interesting and unmistakably hers. And a mood that would at last disappoint, or if not disappoint, fall into familiarity and thereby ask of her intelligence some steadier and more difficult refinement.

Her essays gradually became longer, and perhaps more serene, and certainly less imploring. The labyrinthine perfectionism, the pathos of a "dissatisfied" spirit like Walter Benjamin came to her, I think, as a model, and certainly as an object of *love,* the word in no way out of bounds. It is love that makes her start her essay on Benjamin by looking at a few scattered photographs. Benjamin is not an image to us; his is one of those faces that dissolve. It would seem that his body and soul are not friends. And so we can never be surrounded, illuminated as we are by the face of Kafka, a face of absolute rightness. The wish to find Benjamin as a face is touching, subjective, venerating. And this is the mood of much of her recent work, particularly the majestic honoring of Barthes and the homage to Canetti, himself a great and complicated "admirer" of his own chosen instances of genius.

Thinking about Susan Sontag in the middle of her career is to feel the happiness of more, more, nothing ended. An exquisite responsiveness of this kind is unpredictable, although one of the intentions of her work is to find the central, to tell us what we are thinking, what is happening to our minds and to culture. There are politics, fashions, art itself, and of course the storehouse of learning to be looked at again and again in her own way. I notice that in her late work she stresses the notion of pleasure in the arts, pleasure in thinking. Only the serious can offer us that rare, warm, bright-hearted felicity.

Elizabeth Hardwick

The Benefactor

One

My childhood and university career.

I find friends and become independent.

My resolutions.

On the difficulties of this narrative.

Je rêve donc je suis

If only I could explain to you how changed I am since those days! Changed yet still the same, but now I can view my old preoccupations with a calm eye. In the thirty years which have passed, the preoccupation has changed its form, become inverted so to speak. When it began, it grew in me and emptied me out. I ignored it at first, then admitted it to myself, then sought consolation from friends, then resigned myself to it, and finally learned to exploit it for my own wisdom. Now, instead of being inside me, my preoccupation is a house in which I live; in which I live, more or less comfortably, roaming from room to room. Some winters I don't turn on the heat. Then I stay in one room, warmly wrapped in my leather coat, sweaters, boots, and muffler, and recall those agitated days. I have become a rather cranky old man, given to harmless philanthropies. A few friends pay me calls because they are lonely, not because they greatly enjoy my company. Decidedly, I have become less interesting.

Even as a child, there were traits which distinguished me from my playmates. My origins themselves are unremarkable: I come from a prosperous family which still resides in one of the larger provincial cities. My parents were well into middle age when I was born, much the youngest of three children, and my mother died when I was five. My sister was already married and lived abroad. My brother had just come of age and entered my father's business; he married young (shortly after my mother died) and with equanimity, and soon had several children. I have not seen him for many years. Thus, I had ample opportunity to be alone as a child, and developed a somewhat premature taste for solitude. In that large house, from which my father and brother were chronically absent, I was thrown upon myself, and early evidenced a seriousness, tinged with melancholy, which youth did not dispel. But I did not seek to be different. I did well at school, played with other children, flirted with young girls and brought them presents, made love to the maid, wrote little stories—in short, filled my life with the activities normal for my class and age. Because I was not particularly shy, and never sullen, I managed to pass among my relatives as a somber but likable child.

It was when I completed my schooling and left the town of my birth to attend the national university that I first became unable to suppress the sense of being different. In everything, one's surroundings are of great importance. Up to now I had been surrounded by my nurse, my father, relatives, friends, all of whom were easily pleased with themselves and me, and lived in comfortable agreement with each other. I was fond of their society. The only one of their traits I found distasteful was the ease and complacency with which they assumed a posture of moral indignation; otherwise, they were to me no more and no less than people might sensibly be expected to be. But when I moved to the capital I soon realized that not only did I not resemble the stolid provincials among whom I had been reared, but I was also unlike the restless cosmopolitans among whom I now lived and with whom I expected to have more in common. Around me were young men and women of my own age, some like myself from the provinces but most from the metropolis in which the university was situated. (I omit the name of this city, not to tease the reader—for I have not excised from this narrative certain words and the names of local institutions known to every would-be tourist, so that the reader will soon be able to identify in which city I lived—but because I wish to indicate my conviction that where I lived was not of importance in the matters I shall relate; I make no complaint against my homeland or against this city in particular, which is no worse and perhaps better than most places, a center of culture and the residence of many interesting and gracious people.) At the university, then, were gathered the ambitious youth of my country. Everyone was preparing for accomplishment, some in medicine, the law, the arts, the sciences, some for the civil service, and some for revolutions; while I found my heart empty of personal ambition. Ambition, if it feeds at all, does so on the ambition of others. I did not come into this sort of relation, part conspiratorial and part envious, with my peers. I have always enjoyed being by myself, and the company of others is more pleasant to me when interspersed with large quantities of the refreshment which I find in myself, and in my dreams and reveries.

Genuinely, I believe, lacking all the usual motives of ambition such as spurred my fellow students—not even the ambition to displease my family, this being a time of great strain between the generations—I nevertheless proved myself a capable and enthusiastic student. Inspired by the prospect of becoming learned, I enrolled in the most varied courses of lectures. But this very thirst for inquiry, which led to the investigations that subsequently preoccupied me, did not find a proper satisfaction in the divisions and faculties of the university. Do not misunderstand, it was not that I objected to specialization. On the contrary, genuine specialization—the neat and sensitive marking off of a subject, and its accurate quartering and adjacent subdivisions—was just what I looked for and could not find. Neither did I object to pedantry. What I objected to was that my professors raised problems only in order to solve them, and brought their lectures to a conclusion with maddening punctuality. My stubborn commitment to learning was comparable to that of a hungry man who is given sandwiches and eats them in the wax paper, not because he is too impatient to unwrap them, but simply because he has never learned or else has forgotten how to remove the paper. My intellectual hunger did not make me insensible to the unappetizing fare of the university lecture rooms. But for a long time I could neither peel off the tasteless wrappings nor eat more moderately.

I studied in this way for three years. At the end of this time I published my first and only philosophical article; in it I proposed important ideas on a topic of no great importance. The article was controversial and excited some discussion in the general literary world, and because of it I was admitted to the circle of a middle-aged couple, foreign-born and newly rich, who had an estate in the suburbs and collected stimulating people. On weekends, the Anderses provided horseback riding in the afternoon, chamber music in the evening, and long formal meals. Besides myself, the regular guests included a professor who had written several books on the theory of revolution, a Negro ballet dancer, a famous physicist, a writer who had been a professional boxer, a priest who led a weekly forum on the radio called "Confessions and Remedies," and the elderly conductor of the symphony orchestra of a neighboring city (he came sporadically, but he was having an affair with the young daughter of the house). It was Frau Anders, a plump sensuous woman in her late thirties, who really presided, her husband's presence being irregular and his authority nominal; he was often away on business trips; I gathered that their marriage was one of convenience rather than sentiment. Frau Anders insisted on punctuality and deference, but was otherwise a generous hostess, attentive to her guests' idiosyncrasies and skillful in drawing them out.

All of Frau Anders's guests, even the vain and handsome ballet dancer, were virtuoso talkers. At first I was irritated and bewildered by the looseness of their conversation, by their readiness to express an opinion on any subject. These exchanges over a sumptuous dinner table seemed to me no more responsible intellectually than the acrimonious café debates of my fellow students. It took me a while to appreciate the distinctive virtues of the salon. Having opinions was only part of it. The more serious part was the display of personality. Frau Anders's guests were particularly accomplished at this display; no doubt, that was why they had come together. I found this emphasis on personality, rather than opinions, restful. Already I had detected in myself a certain paucity of opinions. I knew that entering the estate of manhood meant purchasing a set of more or less permanent opinions, yet I found this more difficult than others apparently did. It was not due to intellectual torpor nor, I hope, to pride. My system was simply too busy receiving and discharging what I found about me. And in Frau Anders's circle I learned not to envy others because I had less certitude than they. I had a great faith (it seems a little naïve in retrospect) in my own good digestion, and in the eventual triumph of patience. That there is order in this world still appears to me, even in my old age and isolation, beyond doubt. And I did not doubt that in this order I would find a place, as I have.

I ceased attending lectures at the university after acquiring this new circle of friends, and soon after officially resigned. I also stopped writing the monthly letter to my father. One day my father visited the capital on business and took the opportunity to see me. I assumed he meant to reproach me for neglecting my epistolary duties, but I did not hesitate to tell him immediately that I had abandoned my formal studies. I thought it better to deal with his reproaches in one interview than to have him hear the news, which he would interpret as truancy, indirectly. To my great satisfaction, he was not angry. According to his view, my older brother had fulfilled all the hopes he had for a son; for this reason he declared himself willing to support me in any independent path I might choose. He made arrangements with his banker to increase my monthly allowance, and we parted warmly with assurances of his continued affection. I was now in the enviable position of being entirely at my own disposal, free to pursue my own questions (the treasure I had accumulated since my childhood) and to satisfy, better than the university had done, my passion for speculation and investigation.

I continued to spend many hours of each day in rapid voracious reading, though I fear that as I read I did not think much. Not until years later did I understand that here was reason enough to abstain from reading. However, I did stop writing: except for a film scenario, my journals, and numerous letters, I have written nothing since that youthful philosophical article on a topic of no importance. Nothing, that is, until now, when with difficulty I again take up my pen. After reading, my chief pleasure at that time was conversation, and it was in conversation at Frau Anders's and with a few ex-comrades at the university that I occupied those first fledgling months of independence. Of my other interests there seems no reason to speak in detail. My sexual needs were not unduly clamorous, and periodic excursions into a disreputable quarter of the city sufficed to satisfy them. Politics interested me no further than the daily newspaper. In this I resembled most of my generation and class, but I had additional reasons of my own for being unpolitical. I am extremely interested in revolutions. But I believe that the real revolutions of my time have been not changes of government or of the personnel of public institutions but revolutions of feelings and seeing, much more difficult to analyze.

Sometimes I have thought that the perplexities I encountered in my own person were themselves symptoms of such a general revolution of feeling—a revolution not yet named, a dislocation of consciousness not yet diagnosed. But this notion may be presumptuous on my part. In all likelihood, my difficulties are no more than my own; nor does it distress me to claim them as mine. Luckily, being of a sturdy constitution and serene temperament, I did not endure my inquietude passively, and have extracted, through struggle, crisis, and years of after-meditation, a certain sense from it. However, I wish at the start to warn the reader that while I endeavor conscientiously to present a just selection of those events, it is with no more than the eye and mainly the ear of recollection. It is easier to endure than to change. But once one has changed, what was endured is hard to recall.

"Strangeness becomes you," my father said to me that kind May afternoon.

I was, in fact, not as eccentric then as many of the people I knew—in Frau Anders's salon, on the boulevards, in the university—but I did not contradict him.

"Let it be so, Father," I said.

One word more. From my earliest schooling, I was exposed to the secular intellectual ideals of my country: clarity, rigor, education of the feelings. I was taught that the way to treat an idea is to break it into its smallest component parts, and then to retrace one's steps, proceeding from the most simple to the complex—not forgetting to check, by enumeration, that no step is omitted. I learned that reasoning itself, apart from the particular demands of whatever problem it is applied to, has a correct form, a style, which may be learned as one learns the right way to swim or to dance.

If I now object to this style of reasoning, it is not because I share the distrust of reason which is the leading intellectual fashion in our century. My old-fashioned teachers were not in error. The method of analysis does solve all problems. But is that what is wanted always: to solve a problem? Suppose we reverse the method, and proceed from the most complex to the most simple. To be sure, we will be left with less than we started. But why not? Instead of accumulating ideas, we might be better occupied with dissolving them—not by a sudden act of will, but slowly, and with great patience. Our philosophers teach that "the whole is the sum of its parts." True. But perhaps any part also is the sum of the whole; perhaps the real sum of the whole is that part which is smallest, upon which one can concentrate most closely. To assume that "the whole is the sum of its parts" is to assume also that ideas and things are—or can be made to be—symmetrical. I have found that there are symmetrical ideas and asymmetrical ones as well. The ideas which interest me are asymmetrical: one enters through one side and exits through a side which is shaped quite differently. Such ideas rouse my appetite.

But the appetite for thinking must be regulated, as all sensible people know, for it may stifle one's life. I was more fortunate than most in that, in my youth, I had no settled ambitions, no tenacious habits, no ready opinions which I would have to sacrifice to thought. My life was my own: it was not dismembered into work and leisure, family and pleasure, duty and passion. Still, I held back at first—keeping myself free of unnecessary entanglements, seeking the company of those whom I understood and therefore could not be seduced by, yet not daring to follow my inclinations toward solitary thought to their conclusion.

During this period of my youth, in the years immediately following my resignation from the university, I took the opportunity to travel outside my native country, and to observe the manners of other peoples and social classes. I found this more instructive than the wordy learning of the university and the library. Perhaps because I never left the country for more than a few months at a time, my travels did not demoralize me. Observing the variety of beliefs in different countries did not lead me to conclude that there is no true right and wrong but only fallible human opinion. However much men disagree about what is forbidden and what allowed, everyone aspires to order and to truth. Truth needs the discipline of custom in order to act. I do not deny that custom is usually narrow-minded and ungenerous. But one has no right to be outraged when, in self-defense, it martyrs the partisans of extreme acts. Any discipline, even that of the most sanctimonious custom, is better than none.

While I was occupied with my initial investigations into what I vaguely thought of as "certitude," I felt obliged to reconsider all opinions which were presented to me. Consequently, I felt entitled to none myself. This open-mindedness raised certain problems as to how my life was to be guided for the interim, for while I questioned content I did not want to lose form. I drew up, for the duration of this period of inquiry, the following provisional maxims of conduct and attitude:

1. Not to be satisfied with my own, or anyone else's, good intentions
2. Not to wish for others what they did not wish for themselves
3. Not to spurn the advice of others
4. Not to fear disapproval, but to observe as much as is feasible the rules of tact and discretion
5. Not to value possessions, nor be distracted by ambition
6. Not to advertise myself, nor make demands on others
7. Not to wish for a long life

These principles were never difficult to follow, since they accorded with my own disposition anyway. Happily, I can claim to have observed them all, including the last rule. For although I have had a long life, I have not gone out of my way to provide for it. (I should mention, to give the reader a proper perspective, that I am now sixty-one years old.) And this life, I must also add, I do not recount because I consider it an example to anyone. It is for myself alone; the path I have followed and the certitude I have found would be unlikely to suit anyone but myself.

The traditional metaphor for a spiritual investigation is that of the voyage or the journey. From this image I must dissociate myself. I do not consider myself a voyager, I have preferred to stand still. I would describe myself rather as a block of marble, acceptably though crudely shaped on the outside, inside which there is a comely statue. When the marble is hewn away, the freed statue may be very small. But whatever the size of the statue, it is better not to endanger it by moving the marble block frequently.

For this effort of hewing away the marble which enclosed me, no experience, no preoccupation was too small. I found nothing to despise. Take, for example, the group of people collected by Frau Anders. It would have been easy to dismiss them as vain and frivolous. But each of them had some perspective on life which was of interest, and something to teach me—the most satisfying grounds for friendship. Sometimes I wished that Frau Anders were not so solely concerned to please and to be pleased. She could have set herself up as a counter-force to her guests' pursuit of their own individualities. Then, instead of revolving around our hostess with compliments and attention, we could have spied on her. She might have asked us to perform and to create in her name, which everyone would have refused. She might have forbidden us to do things, like write novels or fall in love, so that we might have disobeyed her. But good manners forbade that I should have asked more of this woman than she was capable of giving. It was enough that the society I found at her house amused me, without arousing in me many expectations.

As evidence of my friendly conduct as a member of this society, I submit the following anecdote. One day Frau Anders asked me if the lack of financial privation in my life did not open opportunities for boredom. I replied, truthfully, that it did not. I then realized that this rich and still handsome woman was not asking me a question but telling me something, namely, that she herself was bored. But I did not accept her discreet complaint. I explained to her that she was not bored; she was, or was pretending to be, unhappy. This little comment instantly lifted her spirits, and I was pleased to see in subsequent visits to the house that she had become quite gay. I have never understood why people find it so difficult to speak the truth to their acquaintances and friends. In my experience, the truth is always appreciated, and the fear of giving offense is greatly exaggerated. People fear to offend or hurt others, not because they are kind, but because they do not care for the truth.

Perhaps it would be easier for people to care for the truth if they understood that truth only exists when they tell it. Let me explain. The truth is always something that is told, not something that is known. If there were no speaking or writing, there would be no truth about anything. There would only be what is. Thus, to me, my life and my preoccupations are not the truth. They are, simply, my life, my preoccupations. But now I am engaged in writing. And in daring to transpose my life into this narrative, I shoulder the dreadful responsibility of telling the truth. I find the narrative which I undertake a difficult task, not because it is hard for me to tell the truth about myself in the sense of reporting honestly "what happened," "what took place," but because it is hard for me to speak the truth in the more pretentious sense, truth in the sense of insisting, rousing, convincing, changing another.

Sometimes I cannot help pursuing various ideas I have of the character and preoccupations of my readers. This weakness I hope to conquer. It is true that the lessons of my life are lessons only for me, suited only to me, to be followed only by me. But the truth of my life is only for someone else. I warn the reader that I shall try henceforth not to imagine who that someone else is, and whether he or she is reading what I have written. This I cannot, and rightly should not, know.

For to speak the truth is one thing; to write it another. When we speak, we address someone else. When we speak what is best—which is always the truth—still it is to a person, with the thought of a person. But if there is any chance of writing something that is true, it will only be because we have banished the thought of another person.

When we write the truth, we should address ourselves. When in writing we are didactic and admonitory, we must consider that we instruct and admonish only ourselves, for our own failings alone. The reader is a happy accident. One must allow the reader his liberty, his liberty to contradict what is written, his liberty to be distracted by alternatives. Therefore, it would be improper for me to try to convince the reader of all that is in this book. It is enough that you imagine me now, as I am, with the companionship of my recollections, in comparative peace, desiring the solace of no one. It is enough that you imagine me now, elderly scribe to my younger self, and accept that I am changed, and that it was different before.

Two

I have a dream,

the "dream of two rooms."

Jean-Jacques and I discuss it.

I don't know how soon it was after the commencement of my visits to the Anders house that I began having a series of dreams that moved and upset me. It was a year, I think, perhaps more. I recall that I had just returned from a brief trip abroad. And I remember how I spent the evening before the first dream. With some others of her circle, I had accompanied Frau Anders to a concert; afterwards I joined a university friend at a café, where I drank somewhat more than was usual for me and argued for the unseemliness of suicide. Toward morning I returned to my rooms in a mood of buoyancy, and without undressing flung myself in bed.

I dreamed that I was in a narrow room which had no windows, only a small door about thirty centimeters high. I wanted to leave and bent down. When I saw that I could not squeeze through the door, I was ashamed that someone might see me conducting such an investigation into the obvious. There were several chains hanging from the wall, each of which terminated in a large metal band. I tried to fasten one of the chains first to some part of my body, but the band was too big for either my hand or my foot and too small for my head. I was in some prison, although apart from the chains the room did not have the appearance of a cell.

Then I heard a noise which came from the ceiling. A trap door opened, and a large man wearing a one-piece bathing costume of black wool peered down at me. The man lowered himself by his hands, hung for a moment, then jumped to the floor. When he stood up and walked, he limped a trifle and grimaced. I assumed he had hurt himself in the jump. I thought it possible that he was already lame; but then it seemed odd for him to have attempted such a feat, for the ceiling was high. And being lame did not suit the acrobatic fitness of his shiny muscular limbs.

Suddenly I became afraid of him, for I knew I had no right to be in this room. He said nothing, and merely indicated by signs that I was to pass through the small door which I had previously investigated. The door was larger now. I knelt down, and crawled through. When I stood up, I was in another room which looked exactly like the first. The man in the bathing suit was behind me, holding a long copper-colored instrument which looked like a flute. He signaled me to dance by doing a few steps and turns himself. I was afraid again, and asked him why I had to do this. "Because in this room he dances," he said in an even, placating voice.

"But I am not 'he,' " I replied, delighted to be able to reason with him. "I am Hippolyte, a student at the university, but I do not dance." These last words I said more emphatically than I meant to, with perhaps a touch of rudeness. I only meant to appear firm.

He answered with a threatening gesture aimed at my stomach, and the words "That's a mistake. He dances."

"But why? Tell me why," I protested. "It can't give you pleasure to watch a clumsy man dance."

He made another peremptory gesture, this time not simply a threat of violence but a hard blow across the calf of my leg with his flute which made me leap with pain. Then, in a tone of great mildness which seemed to contradict the blow, he said, "Does he want to leave this room?"

I knew that I was in the hands of someone stronger than myself, and that I could not afford to challenge the man's peculiar way of addressing me. I wanted to please him. "Can't he leave, if he doesn't dance?" I asked, hoping he would not think I was mocking him.

With that, he hurled the instrument at my face. My mouth filled with blood. I felt very cold. "He has lost his chance to dance," he said. I fell to my knees in fear, closed my eyes; I smelled the damp odor of his woolen bathing suit, but nothing happened.

When I opened my eyes the other person in the room was a woman sitting in a tall wicker chair in the corner. She was dressed in something long and white, like a communion dress or a wedding gown.

I could not keep from staring at her, but I knew my gaze was discontinuous, broken, composed of hundreds of frozen gazes, with a tiny interval between each as long as the gaze itself. What interrupted my gaze—the black intervals between the frames, as it were—was the consciousness of something loose in my mouth, and of a painful swelling of my face, which I feared to know more about, as one fears to look at oneself because one doesn't want to discover one is naked. Since, however, the cordial look which the woman turned on me did not reveal any antipathy, I tried to master my embarrassment. Perhaps my look went on and off because it was changing, and the only way I could convey the illusion of a smooth transition from one stage of my gaze to another was precisely by slicing into the gaze, whereas if it had remained continuous there would have been a blur, and a dissolving of my features, and she would have had a disagreeable impression of my face.

I thought of an ingratiating way to approach her. I started to dance, turning around and around. I jumped, and slapped my knees, and waved my arms. But when I stopped to catch my breath I saw that I had not moved nearer. My face felt heavy. She said, "I don't like your face. Give it to me. I'll use it as a shoe."

I wasn't alarmed by this, because she did not get up from her chair. I only said, "You can't put a foot in a face."

"Why not?" she answered. "A shoe has eyeholes."

"And a tongue," I added.

"And a sole," she said, standing up.

"Why do you make silly jokes?" I cried, beginning to be alarmed. I asked her the purpose of the chains on the wall, this room being furnished as the other was. Then she told me a story about the house I was in and why I had been put in the room. I have forgotten this part of the dream. I remember only that there was a secret, and a penalty. Also that someone had fainted. And that because someone had fainted, and others were busy caring for him, I was being neglected, and had a right to demand better treatment.

I told her it was I who fainted.

"The chains are for you," she said. She came toward me. I took off my shoes hastily, and went with her to the wall, where she fitted the chains around my wrists. Then she brought me her chair to sit in.

"Why do you like me?" she asked. She was sitting opposite me in another chair. I explained to her that it was because she didn't make me do anything I didn't want to do. But as I said this, I wondered if it were so.

"Then there's no need for me to like you," she replied. "Your passion for me will maintain both of us here happily."

I tried to think of a tactful way of telling her that I was happy but that I still wanted to leave. I was happier with her than I had been

in the company of the man with the flute. The chains felt like brace-
lets. But my mouth was sore, my feet were perspiring, and my gaze,
I knew, was insincere.

I stretched out my legs and placed my feet in the lap of her white
dress. She complained that I was soiling the dress and told me that I
would have to go. I could hardly believe my good fortune, and so
strong was my feeling of relief that the desire to leave the room was
now less urgent than the need to express my gratitude. I asked her
if I could kiss her before I left. She laughed and slapped my face.
"You must learn to take things before you ask," she said sharply,
"and dance before you are bidden, and surrender your shoes, and
compose your face."

Tears came to my eyes. In my distress I implored her to explain
further. She didn't answer. I threw myself on her, with the intention
of taking her sexually, and at that very moment awoke.

I got out of bed in a state of elation. After making myself coffee I
cleaned my room thoroughly and put everything in order. I knew that
something had happened to me which I wanted to celebrate, and for
this purpose the gestures of orderliness are always most satisfying.
Then I sat at my desk and considered the dream. Several hours passed.
At first the dream intrigued me because it was so clear; that is, I
remembered it so well. Yet it seemed as if the very explicitness of the
dream barred the way to any fruitful interpretation. I persisted. I devoted the entire morning to puzzling over the details of the dream,
and urged myself to apply some ingenuity to their interpretation. But
my mind refused to cavort about the dream. By mid-afternoon, I suspected that the dream had, so to speak, interpreted itself. Or even
that this morning of mental sluggishness was the real dream, of which
the scenes in the two rooms were the interpretation. (I do not hope
to make this thought wholly clear to the reader at the present moment.)

Certain features of my own character in the dream—my crafty humility, my propensity to shame, my posture of supplication and fear,
my desire to placate and cajole and endear myself to the two personages of my dream—recalled to me the way many people speak of
their childhood. But I was not a fear-ridden child: I don't remember
my mother, and my father never hit or frightened me. "This is not a
dream of childhood," I said, perhaps prematurely.

I paused over the man in the bathing suit and his flute, and his
antagonism to me. I savored my attraction to the woman in the white
dress, and her refusal of me. "I have had a sexual dream," I said.
And I could make little more of it than that, before the evening.

That evening I had an appointment at a café with the writer friend I have already mentioned to you, the one who had been a professional boxer when he was in his early twenties. I had become more intimate with this man, who was about ten years older than myself, than with any of the others whom I met at Frau Anders's, despite the fact that he led a life with many compartments and a costume for each, a life difficult to grasp in its entirety. By day he sat in his room, dressed in boxing trunks, and wrote novels which were well received by the critics; for the aperitif hour and the early evening he put on a dark suit and went to the opera or to Frau Anders's house; and in the late evening he roamed the boulevards of the city soliciting men, for which purpose he donned various exotic costumes of an aggressively male character, like that of a hoodlum, a sailor, or a truck driver. Since none of his novels had sold more than a few hundred copies, it was through prostitution and petty thievery that Jean-Jacques earned a modest living. Because he spoke quite openly of his "job" as he called it—he called writing his "work"—I had often asked him to tell me of his experiences. He confided more in me, I supposed, because he sensed something neutral in my attitude, something which was neither disapproval, nor attraction, nor anything like the respectful fascination with which his other friends regarded his "job." His indiscretion and my attentiveness, up to the time of my first dream, had been the basis of our friendship.

That night, however, it was I who talked first, he who listened. I told Jean-Jacques of my dream, and it interested him. "Have you ever feared for your sanity?" he asked.

I wondered why he said that, since I understood that the license of dreaming permitted us the most irregular and cryptic fantasies. And I was surprised that this unusual man should find anything in my plain life to stir him to wonder.

"You see," he continued, "I don't dream. I find intolerable the slow leakage of my substance in dreams, so I have staged my life to incorporate the energy that is usually diverted in dreaming. My writing forces from me the dream-substance, prolongs it, plays with it. Then I replenish the substance in the show of the café, in the political intrigue of the salon, in the extravagances of the opera, in the comedy of roles which is the homosexual encounter."

"Up to now I have not dreamed, either."

"But now that you have started," he said, smiling, "you are not going about it in the right way. Your dream contains so much talk, at least as you have related it to me. If you must dream, silence is best. You must be silent if you are absorbed in anything." He laughed. "Perhaps I myself am too talkative to dream."

Jean-Jacques was not only very talkative but restless, too. He walked and moved rapidly and always seemed to want to go somewhere, yet never seemed in a hurry to be off. His manner of speaking was similar: he talked quickly, hurriedly, but with assurance and conceit. His pronunciation was, if anything, overdistinct. I wondered to myself if he did anything silently—if he wrote in silence, if he made love in silence, if he stole without words.

We ordered two more cognacs. "Do you think I will ever explain this dream?" I asked him.

"You can explain one dream with another," he said thoughtfully. "But the best interpretation of your dream would be to find it in your life. You must outbid your dream."

Finally he reminded me that it was getting late, and that pleasure and business called him. As I paid our bill, he waved and walked away, and I saw him take a golden bracelet from his pocket and attach it to his wrist.

This conversation with Jean-Jacques encouraged me to pursue my dream more intently. In the suspension of all preconceptions which I had adopted as my path to certitude, I could hardly ignore so singular a visitation.

I suppose I had dreamed before my "dream of the two rooms." Perhaps I had dreamed every night. But I did not remember my dreams. If there were shadows of people and situations in my mind when I awakened, as soon as I arose from bed and washed, the shadows vanished, and the day and its tasks appeared to me untrammeled and continuous from the night before when I had lain down. No counter-images waylaid me as I slept.

I had often wondered why I did not dream. Perhaps my personality was assembled late. Nevertheless, the advent of my dreams did not take me completely by surprise. From books and conversations with friends, I was acquainted with the usual dream repertoire: dreams of being trapped in a fire, dreams of falling, dreams of being late, dreams of flying, dreams of being followed, dreams of one's mother, dreams of nakedness, dreams of murdering someone, dreams of sexual conquest, dreams of being sentenced to death. Neither this dream, nor any of those which followed it, failed to include some of these standard dilemmas of dreams. What was odd, and memorable, about the dreams was not their originality but the impression they made on me. My previous dreams, if I had had any, were easily forgotten. This dream and its successors were indelible. They were written, as it were, by a firmer hand, and in a different script.

As I have said, my first recourse was interpretation. It seems that from the beginning I did not accept the dream as a gift but as a task. The dream also provoked a certain reaction of antipathy in me. Therefore, I sought to master the dream, by understanding it. The more I thought of the dream, the greater I felt the responsibility. But the various interpretations I conceived did not relieve me. These interpretations, instead of reducing the pressure of the dream on my daytime life, added to it.

The verbosity of the dream, which Jean-Jacques had pointed out to me, alone gave it an entirely different character from what I understood dreams generally to be like. Most dreams show. This dream said.

My vanity was not wounded because the dream, speaking in the accent of command, showed me as without force and pride. I knew that the dream was both voluntary, in that I had imagined it, and involuntary, in that it issued a command I could not understand or answer.

I labored with my dream.

Once, during my travels, I was staying in a mountain village and had observed a woman in difficult childbirth. One wondered how love could ever become her. She was obviously bewildered that by any act of her own she could have brought herself to such great pain. She refused all help—rather, she no longer understood what her relatives and the neighbors and the midwife wanted from her when they tried to help her. She was drowning in herself.

Her husband approached the iron bed and tried to take her hand. She did not push him away. But her senses were turned in an inward direction; only the nerves in the interior side of her skin registered. She was alone in the crammed shell of herself.

There was a period after this first dream when I felt as I have described this woman: weighty, interred. I did not know how to deliver myself. Interpretation was my Caesarean operation, and Jean-Jacques my complaisant physician. Most of this time, you understand, I was quite calm. I was not in pain. This dream was not a nightmare. Nevertheless, this dream changed me. The even tenor of my investigations into the world and its opinions was broken, when I turned to investigate this dream.

The woman who suffered in childbirth had already committed an extreme act: she had slept with her husband and conceived a child. The pain she now suffered was only the logical result of that act. But I seemed to bear fruit without planting anything. This dream was unwanted. It procreated itself.

This dream was my first immoderate act.

Three

Aftermath of the first dream. I accept a

musician's hospitality.

"Dream of the unconventional party."

I become the lover of Frau Anders.

It is hard to explain what happened in the next months. For a long time, no night passed without presenting me some variation on this original dream. Sometimes the woman surrendered to my embrace. Sometimes it was I who played the flute, and struck the bather. Sometimes the woman told me I could go, on the condition that I continued to wear the chains. Sometimes I would not dance for her. Sometimes the bather remained with the woman and made love to her before my guilty eyes. But always at the end of the dream I wept; and always I awakened with a driving empty elation which ruled the whole of my day.

I did not make much progress in my morning's meditation of the dream. These generous variations on the original scenario made the task of interpretation even more difficult. I no longer knew whether I was master or slave in my dream. Too much was being given for me to understand.

The dream of my imprisonment in the two rooms narrowed my life, so that I thought more, and went out less. Thus, when my father visited the capital again for a few days, I forgot to go to see him. Of this absorption by the dream, I do not complain: blessed is the mind with more to occupy it than its own dissatisfactions. But the mind needs the occasional reward of understanding. I was exhausted by my futile efforts to understand the dream, and wondered if I would even know how to act once I did understand. Finally, I began to take seriously the advice of Jean-Jacques, and thought less of how the dream might be interpreted and more of what I should do with it. Since the dream haunted me, I would now haunt the dream. I considered the exercises and prohibitions commanded in the dream. I bought a black bathing suit, and a flute which I painted the color of copper. I walked around the bedroom barefoot. I learned the tango and the fox-trot. I conquered the affections of several reluctant women.

The bridge which I built between my dream and my daytime occupations was my first taste of an inner life. I was not surprised to discover that the claims of an inner life modify one's attitudes to the world, and particularly to other people. The small gallery of characters in my dream now took their place alongside my relatives and my friends. They were perhaps more like the members of my family, whom I no longer saw but whose image I still carried in my head, than my friends in the capital. (For do not the personages of the past have a status similar to the personages of one's dreams? That they existed is confirmed only by turning inward, or by consulting a photograph album or looking at old letters. This autobiographical narrative serves the functions of a photograph album or a collection of letters: already I reread what I have written, and only so far as I confirm by memory that I dreamed these dreams do I recognize what I wrote as constituting my past.) But even the people I knew in the present took on another aspect. I saw them superimposed upon the personages of my dream, or I superimposed the man in the black bathing suit or the woman in white upon them.

Then, one weekend at Frau Anders's, the elderly conductor who came there sporadically to visit the daughter of the house invited me to spend a fortnight with him in the city where he had his post with the municipal orchestra. I accepted the invitation, for it occurred to me that a change—I had not been out of the capital for months— might provide the stimulus that would crown my efforts of self-mimicry and even dispel the dream. Later I learned that the Maestro had extended this invitation at Frau Anders's request. She was distressed by the mood of thoughtfulness (which she took to be melancholy) I could not conceal during my recent visits and by my increasing abstention from that large ration of shameless flattery which it was necessary at all times to supply her with.

We went by train. When we arrived at his house, the housekeeper showed me to my room; then she served tea, and the Maestro, after the most elegant apologies, left for a rehearsal, which I imagine he expected me to ask his permission to attend.

I spent the evening playing records and looking at scores. Although I do not have that facility with a score which allows me to hear with my inner ear the full orchestration as I read, I was sufficiently entertained, and not at all bored.

I went to sleep early, and was rewarded with a new dream.

I dreamed that I was in a crowded city street, hurrying toward some appointment. I was anxious not to be late, but was not sure of my destination. I was not discouraged, though: I thought that if I continued with sufficient energy and display of certitude, I would recognize the place I was to go. Then there was a man walking beside me and I asked him politely for directions.

"Follow him," he said.

The voice was familiar. I turned to inspect my companion and recognized the flute player in the black bathing suit from my other dream. In exasperation I struck him with what, I believe, was his own flute. He groaned and fell, and rolled down the steps of a Metro entrance. Then I remembered he was lame and regretted my fury, for I could not claim that this time he had menaced me or seemed to intend me any harm.

Fearful that he would emerge brandishing his flute in anger and pursue me, I began to run. At first I had to exert myself, but soon the running became easier. My panic subsided, for it was as if someone were helping me. I was running on a large black disk, which was revolving faster than I could run, so that I was losing time. I felt my hair becoming stiff and heavy on my scalp. I jumped off the disk, and stood in the street again. At first I was extremely dizzy; then I felt quite calm. I must have had, at this point, that semi-awareness of the dream state itself, common in dreams, which inspires a complacent passivity before events. At the same time that I stood in the street looking for an address which I had forgotten, I saw myself very clearly farther down the conveyor belt of the dream, safely at my destination.

At some point in this part of the dream I bought some cigarettes. I remember that the brand I requested was "face cigarettes," and that the proprietress of the *tabac* told me she had only "musical cigarettes." I assured her that these would be equally satisfactory, and paid for them with some warm unfamiliar coins which I had in my pocket.

Then I was arriving somewhere, a large atelier where a rowdy party was in progress. The red tile floor was littered with still-burning cigarettes. I stepped carefully for fear of burning myself. I was barefoot.

The hostess was Frau Anders, who was sitting on a stool and leaning with her elbows on a slanted drawing board. She was overseeing the party, and did not seem to mind that some of her guests were breaking glasses and others scribbling on the walls with lipstick and pieces of charcoal. She did not see me come in and I avoided meeting her eyes, for I owed her some debt which I was afraid she might confront me with and demand that I pay. Someone proposed a game, and I accepted with the idea that by joining the game I should show myself cooperative and of good character and at the same time be more inconspicuous.

I understood we were going to play charades. But all we were asked to do was to bend over from the waist and touch the floor with our hands, "making an inverted U," as the leader of the game described it. Vaguely indecent thoughts passed through my mind—rising to a definite state of sexual excitement—but I could find no grounds for legitimate embarrassment, since I saw that all around me the other guests had already assumed the difficult posture, and were playfully chatting with each other between their legs.

There was a concert going on in the next room, and I was saying something about it to my neighbor in the game, the Negro ballet dancer. As we were talking, he began to spread, to unfold until he was prone upon the floor. He closed his eyes and sighed. Others near me followed suit, sliding to the floor, their bodies touching and over-lapping, everyone sighing; they all looked so happy, I felt suddenly peaceful and happy myself. A feeling of great lightness maintained my body above the others.

"Hippolyte can hold the position longest," I heard Frau Anders de-clare. "Hippolyte has won the game." Her voice interrupted my mood of tranquillity, and for a moment I was annoyed. I did not see why in so pleasant a game anyone need be designated as the winner. This seemed to me just the virtue of the game, that there were neither rules nor goal. But after all, if it is a game, it must end, I then thought, and was pleased that, still somehow in keeping with the spirit of this mysterious and delightful game, I had won inadvertently, without striving. So warm was the love I felt for my prostrate companions on the floor that I was not embarrassed over my winning and their los-ing, nor did I fear that they would think I had not deserved to win. I felt quite clearly that they all wished me to win, or at least—since their eyes were closed and they did not register any awareness of Frau Anders's announcement—that they wished to be where they were. Their heavy contented position on the floor was as apt and desired by them as my weightless approval, suspended above them, was by me.

Of course, I had thus attracted Frau Anders's attention despite my efforts to avoid it. But now, I knew, she would be pleased with me.

And so she was. She put her arm under my stomach to raise me to a standing position, led me to a couch, and then sat on my lap.

"Frau Anders," I said into the space between her heavy breasts. "Frau Anders, I love you." She embraced me tightly. "Let those mock who will," I cried, caught up in a mounting enthusiasm. "I am not like the others, who accept your hospitality only for the celebrities whom they can meet at your house, for I am not ambitious. I do not care for your money, for I am rich. I will not touch your daughter, for I have you. Come away with me."

She held my neck more tightly. "Tell me you will always love me," I said, forcing her to look at me. "Tell me that you will do all that I wish."

"Now," she whispered.

"Not in front of all your guests!" I replied. I could hardly believe that I had aroused this proud woman so quickly, or that she could be so thoughtless of her duties as a hostess.

She pointed to the drawing board. We tiptoed across the floor. She leaned backwards on the hard table. For a moment I was numb with embarrassment. "Draw me," she whispered, pulling my head toward hers. Then I recovered myself, and told her it could not be done here. I told her we would go to my room. I had only to find my shoes.

We both squatted and began to search for them on the floor among the bodies of the guests. We did not find them. I now regretted that I had placed any conditions upon this happy sexual encounter which had been so imminent only a moment before, and began looking for my shoes less conscientiously, as if by this means the search might be abandoned without regret. But now it was Frau Anders who insisted, crawling on the floor, that I must have them.

"Look," she said. "I have found some of your hair." In her right hand she held a piece of my black hair which seemed congealed and shiny. I begged her not to distract herself with that.

"And here is another piece," she said loudly, lifting up a larger tuft. Again I implored her not to concern herself about my hair. At the same time, I did not believe it was mine. I felt my head. Everything seemed perfectly normal.

But when she told me that it couldn't have come from any of the other guests, because no one had hair as black as mine, I thought she might be right. And since she insisted that she would not have this mess on her floor, I had to help her. Still squatting in the middle of the floor, we collected a small pile of it, she remarking continually at the blackness and quantity of my hair in a way which conveyed an unmistakable tone of disgust.

"You have spoiled everything," I shouted, feeling my cheeks flush with shame. I decided not to stay in this place another minute, clambered to my feet, ran to the door, and awoke.

When I awoke from my dream, my room was still dark, and the black sky outside my window just starting to purple. Nevertheless, I dressed and went downstairs where I saw a light under the door of the conductor's study. Emboldened by the bizarre liberations I had lived through in my dream, I knocked without hesitating and found the Maestro at his desk.

"Come in, Hippolyte," he said cordially, removing his spectacles. "I am not working, only writing a letter since I cannot sleep."

"Perhaps the rehearsal has overstimulated you," I ventured politely.

He ignored my comment and said, "Hippolyte, will you give me your opinion, as a friend and as a younger man to one much older? Do you feel that a great difference in age between two people who love each other is important? You no doubt know," he continued, "of my attachment to young Lucrezia Anders, and you may have guessed—if you are indeed as sensitive as I believe you to be—that it is to her that I am writing."

I sensed that I had the Maestro's permission to pause lengthily before making my reply, and that any answer, however wise, if delivered quickly, would be offensive to him. I paused, thinking how I should reply.

"Well, Maestro, I have had a dream," I finally said. "I learn very much from my dreams, and in this dream I saw that both attraction and repulsion exist between youth and age. If an older person pursues too shamelessly, the younger will be repelled. Youth must woo and age must yield."

He frowned. "I take it you are advising me to be less ardent. But frankly I am afraid to visit the Anders's house less often, or to write fewer letters to my shy darling. The only respect in which I am confident I can outdo a younger man is in the tenacity of my wooing. Reserve is a great gamble for an older man. It can be misinterpreted as debility."

"Perhaps there's no chance you will be misinterpreted," I said, trying to be helpful. "May I ask if you are her first lover?"

"Alas, no," he said. "Our estimable hostess has seen to Lucrezia's education long before my advances were sanctioned."

"And do you think that at the present moment you alone enjoy her favors?"

He paled and I could observe that the question was distasteful to him. "I do not know my rivals," he said. "And surely these are unnecessary questions from someone who frequents the household more than I do. Although"—he collected himself—"Frau Anders tells me that you have been acting strangely of late, that you withhold yourself and do not call as regularly as before. Is there some young woman who occupies your time? I should not burden you with an old man's problems." He put on his glasses again. The lenses were thick, and made his eyes look round and empty. "You must have problems of your own that you would like to discuss with me," he continued. "In fact, my little remarks just now—which I know you will treat in the strictest confidence—were less an expression of my own thoughts and problems than they were—I hope you are not offended—directed to make you repose an absolute confidence in me and promote a more intimate atmosphere between us. I had intended to bring this up tomorrow, perhaps at lunch, though I really should not be distracted before the concert, so perhaps this is a more propitious occasion. There is something troubling you, Hippolyte. And if I can be of any . . ."

His thin monotonous voice stopped. I had been watching the dawn break through the window behind the Maestro's desk.

"No sir," I said. "There is nothing. Except, perhaps, too much solitude."

"But it is your solitude which is the result, I am sure, of some inner unhappiness; and not the solitude which causes your present manner, a manner which distresses all your friends. Allow me to . . ."

"My solitude is entirely voluntary, I assure you."

"I beg your pardon but . . ."

"Let me tell you, Maestro," I exclaimed, "that I am having experiences of a purity, albeit of a great narrowness, such as cannot be shared. Only in myself—only in himself I might say, if you permit the locution—do I savor them."

He tried to soothe me, and only succeeded in being patronizing. "My young friend, ever since I first saw you in Frau Anders's drawing room I have felt you had the makings of an artist. But we artists"—he smiled at his generous gift, this "we"—"we artists must avoid the temptation to isolate ourselves, to lose contact with the . . ."

"I am no artist, dear Maestro. You mistake me." I decided to patronize him in return. "I have no inner burden which I wish to unload upon a passive audience. I do not wish to contribute one jot to the fund of public fantasy. Perhaps I have something to reveal, but it is of so intensely private a nature that it could not possibly interest anyone else. Perhaps I will reveal nothing, even to myself. But I know

I am on the trail of something. I am crawling through the tunnel of myself—which takes me further and further from the artist's base craving for applause." Since he refused to be offended at my pointed words, I continued. "I am looking for silence, I am exploring the various styles of silence, and I wish to be answered by silence. You might say," I concluded gaily, "that I am disemboweling myself."

I detest what are called looks of understanding. "Dear Hippolyte," he said, without even trying to understand what I had said, "all young artists go through a period of . . ."

I stood up and walked to the door, determined to take this very morning's train back to the capital. I became inexcusably hilarious at that moment; it was the excitement of the new dream. "Maestro," I shouted at him as he rose to follow me, "Maestro, does Lucrezia give you pleasure? Does she make you jump?" He scowled with disbelief at my rudeness, and stood still. I sped down the hall and took the stairs two at a time, roaring with laughter. "Does she make you dance, old man?" I called over my shoulder. "Do you wave your baton? Do any of the instruments play for you alone?"

Once back in the city, I unwearily went about my new project, the seduction of Frau Anders. The source of energy tapped in my new dream, which I fondly denominated "the dream of the unconventional party," was not illusory. That zest which had begun inauspiciously with my rudeness to the Maestro continued. I felt more lively than I had in months. And I had need of much energy. For while I was courting my patroness with all the smiles and winning words I could muster, she professed to see only the evidence of my recovery from melancholy. It took the most shameless, the least subtle glances to refine her neutral complicity into a state of sexual awareness of my intentions. Flattery had become for my mistress a drug administered in such large doses that her system had become immune to anything else. To convert flattery into seduction, it was not enough merely to sleep with her. The sex act itself was to her like the gift of a rare *objet d'art* or a bouquet of flowers or a verbal compliment. Only with difficulty, with the crudest insistence, could she be brought to understand the sex act as a gesture different from these. The point had to be made again and again that she was not being flattered, not being given anything at all. The despair of my campaign was that she did not believe anything had changed between us!

I realize there was something contradictory in the management of our affair. I wished to make Frau Anders realize that my love for her was not something that was her due. Nothing was more frustrating

to me than that she should take my feeling for her, the surprising
and unexpected command of my dreams, for granted. The only way
in which I could shake her exasperating self-assurance was by insin-
uating to her that she was not altogether desirable to me. I dropped
remarks on the difference in our ages, her tendency to gain weight,
the stridency of her laughter, her color blindness, the imperfections
of her accent—none of which in fact was the least unattractive to
me. I did not wish to humiliate her. Therefore, I only insinuated these
things, always short of the point of conviction. You see my dilemma.
I am not an unkind person. But I regretted that she was deprived of
the pleasure of knowing herself the recipient of a love different from,
and stronger than, what she wanted to arouse.

I did not wish gratitude from Frau Anders, you understand—only
seriousness. It was not enough that she pleased me in bed. I hardened myself against her easy responsiveness. Thus in the newly
opened but complacent arms of my mistress I found a portion of pleasure but not happiness, and she found in me happiness but little
pleasure.

You may conclude that our affair did not take me outside the curious questions which preoccupied me, but rather provided me with
new material. My feeling for Frau Anders was an exploration of myself. Our affair ran parallel to the successive editions and variations
on my second dream, "the dream of the unconventional party."
Sometimes I lost the bending-over game, sometimes I never reached
the party, sometimes the irate man in the bathing suit pursued me,
sometimes Frau Anders gave up the search for my hair and lay, voluptuous and adorable, in my arms. In order to wait for the secret
and unpredictable cues from the dreams, I had to impose a rigid discipline on our liaison. It was only by keeping some reserve with Frau
Anders that I managed to continue my feelings at their height. The
art of feeling, as of erotic performance, is the ability to prolong it; in
my case, duration depended on my ability to refresh my fantasies. To
insure privacy, I did not let her do me favors. Neither did I move into
a house on her estate, as she wished me to do; and in all I insisted
on discretion and tried to maintain as correct an exterior as possible.
The role of the lover of a married woman has its conventions, like
any other role, and I wanted to observe them. Unconventionality for
its own sake does not attract me. Such differences from other people
as I do display force their way to the surface of action from the depths
of my character without my being particularly pleased at the result.

My mistress's unconventionality was, by contrast, entirely superficial. The lies entailed by her frequent adulteries had been perfunc-

tory; nothing except truth could disturb the life of the salon and its incessant conversation. Having the fortune to live in a milieu where unconventionality was encouraged and appreciated, she was, outwardly, unconventional. Inwardly she was full of respect for society's law; only it hardly ever applied to her. No wonder that consistency always surprised her, the arbitrary never.

Thus, she was not surprised by the ebb and flow of my desire for her, according to the secret tides of my dreams. Nor did she complain when for a week or more at a time I occupied myself in the city, and endeavored not to think of her. These activities often kept me in my room, where I felt most at liberty. Besides reading and meditating on my dreams, they included various exercises which I practiced for the care of my body, and such cerebral amusements as tracing hieroglyphs, memorizing the histories of the two hundred and ninety-three Popes and Antipopes, and corresponding with a Bolivian mathematician on a logical problem on which I had been at work for several years.

The dream life which was never absent from my thoughts subsided into curious variations on my nights with my mistress—no new dream yet, but a lengthy entr'acte as it were. I found that the excitement of my dreams surpassed that of my meetings with Frau Anders. It was never she who aroused my sexual feelings. Such feelings were born in me and perished in her. She was the vessel in which I deposited the substance of my dreams. But this did not make her any less important to me. To me she was unique among women. The puzzles and variations in erotic technique proposed by my dreams were solved on her body—on hers, and on no other. This I took as a good omen for our affair, which, however, I had determined would last no longer than it should.

When, finally, the energy of my dreaming was attenuated and it occurred to me to break off our connection, I found myself with less energy to be cruel than I had counted on. I even contemplated leaving the city without telling her. Luckily, just at this time, Frau Anders's husband returned from one of his long business trips abroad and—to her surprise—asked her to accompany him on the next. She urged me to forbid her to go. This was the first of her infidelities, she told me, in which she wanted to tell her husband everything. But I, pleading respect for her reputation and comforts, declined to rescue her permanently from her conjugal bonds.

Thus I was entirely at liberty in my adopted city, for the first time in six months. I returned to the seduction of Frau Anders in my dreams, until one night a new dream revolved into my view.

Four

Third dream,

"the dream of piercing the roof of a cathedral."

Conversation in the park with a priest.

I exchange a rosary for a ball.

In the dream I was standing in the cobblestone courtyard of some building. It was noon, and the sun was hot. Two men, wearing long pants and naked to the waist, were violently locked together. At times they seemed to be fighting; then it seemed to be a wrestling match. I wanted it to be a wrestling match, even though there were no spectators other than myself. And I felt encouraged in believing this by the fact that the two men were of equal strength; neither could force the other to the ground.

To insure that this was sport and not private violence I decided to wager some money on one of the wrestlers, the one who looked somewhat like my brother. But I couldn't find a booth where I could place my bet. Then both men suddenly fell. I was frightened. I suspected that this had been a personal fight, even a fight to the death. There were several other spectators now. One of them, a child, nudged the prostrate men with a stick. She poked her stick in the face of the one who resembled my brother. Both men, pale and motionless, had their eyes closed.

I realized that I knew a secret of which the other spectators were ignorant and tried to compose my face, lest I give the secret away. The effort made my face very warm, and I decided I was doing myself an injury by being so discreet. I wanted to tell my secret to another person, and looked about for someone I knew. I recognized the man in the black bathing suit, and it seemed to me that he was my friend. Reassured, I smiled and beckoned to him. He approached me, but made no gesture of salutation. But he was only pretending not to know me.

"The outcome remains quite clear," I whispered into his ear. I felt as if we were fellow conspirators. Although his head was turned away from me, I was sure he was listening.

"That's because they are dead," he said.

"The contest was unfair." I replied. There was an idea which I was struggling to express. "At least one of them must be alive. The other may or may not be dead, as he chooses."

He turned and put his face next to mine. "In a moment," he shouted, "I am going to dispose of the bodies."

"Don't shout," I answered boldly. "Shouting has never made me understand anything."

He yawned in my face. I reflected that I had no right to demand courtesy from this man, and should have been grateful that he did not abuse me.

He had something with him that looked like a large drum. He slit open the skin of this drum with a knife. Then he lifted the wrestlers one at a time and stuffed them into the drum, hoisted the drum on his back, and carried it out of the courtyard. I watched his efforts, and saw that the load was much too heavy for one man, lame at that. But I determined to let him labor alone since he would not acknowledge me.

When he was gone, however, I regretted not offering to assist him. I felt I had been harsh and spiteful. The fault swelled to the size of a sin, and I wanted to be absolved of it. No sooner had I entertained this thought than I was entering a small building with bronze doors and a low roof. I was surprised at how easy it was to find a church. Inside, I looked about for the man in the black bathing suit, in order to apologize to him. I could not find him.

I went to a side altar, with the intention of lighting a candle. On the altar there was a statue of the Virgin, and astride or rather straddling the shoulders of the Virgin sat a priest who was nodding gravely and blessing the people who passed in the aisle with a pink flower he held in one hand. I noticed the flower particularly because ever since I entered the building I had been aware of a strong sweetish odor, and I now supposed that the smell came from the flower. Then I saw that it could not, because the flower was artificial, made of alabaster. More curious than ever, I left the altar and went looking, without success, for the choir boys swinging their brass incense holders. It then occurred to me that the smell was not provided for the pleasure of the worshippers but to conceal a bad odor which I could not yet detect. I decided to remain in the church until I discovered where the smell came from. I should have liked to sit quietly in a pew, but I felt that I should be more useful to the church if I moved around and acquainted myself with the monuments and statues, for I dimly remembered that this was an ancient building and contained much that was worth seeing for anyone, like myself, who is interested in architecture.

At some point later in the dream, I discovered that the smell came from the central sanctuary, where, lying in state, was the corpse of a bearded man wearing a gold crown. People milled about the coffin and bent down to kiss the king's nostrils. This is why there was no one to watch the wrestlers, I thought. I approached the coffin respectfully, and tried to imitate the others. But when I bent over, I was felled by a great weight in my body. As I rolled and turned on the floor, unable to get up, an old man sternly admonished me. "There is a room for that sort of thing," he said. He conferred with the others briefly. "Put him in the room," another said, "before he does it here." I thought they meant they were going to take me to the confessional.

Someone else said, "Put him in the chair." I was seized forcibly and seated in a black electric chair such as I had seen in American gangster films. With horror I realized this was not for a confession. But while I waited, trembling, for the switch to be thrown, the chair seemed to rise with me in it. I dared to look down and saw that the chair was still bolted to the floor. It was I alone who was soaring, rising higher and higher in what was now an immense cathedral with rose and blue windows. I was rising toward an opening in the vault still far above me, buoyed up by a dense wet substance which lapped about my face.

"It's only a dream," I called to those below me, who were now tiny black figures on the great cruciform stone floor. "I'm having a religious dream." I rose still higher until, just as I had pierced the cathedral roof, I awoke.

This dream, arriving as I reposed from my calculated felicity with Frau Anders, informed me that I was not to have rest also from my labors of investigation. In certain ways, I found the dream puzzling. This new dream, perhaps because it was the most recent, seemed to offer matter more challenging than the torments and delights of what I had interpreted as my erotic dreams of the past year. Was not my first dream, "the dream of the two rooms," about two species of love and domination, in both the masculine and the feminine style? And did not my second dream, "the dream of the unconventional party," furnish me with a direction for my erotic life in the person of Frau Anders? But what did this third dream—the wrestlers, my old friend the bather, the king, the cathedral, the ascent—dictate for me to do?

Certainly, this dream was no less enigmatic than its predecessors, despite the odd fact of my having shouted into the dream, as it were, an interpretation before I awoke. This could not be what the dream really meant, but must be interpreted along with what else lay within the brackets of the dream.

Still, the remark could not be denied a certain privileged position in the order of dream thoughts. Besides, it was, so clearly, "a religious dream," the dream of a devout person, lame with guilt, hungering for absolution.

I did not wish to deny an obvious erotic sense to all the dreams. But in this dream the sexual was joined with more abstract longings for union and penetration. The sexual was acted out with scenes of death and with palpable images of excrement—for how else could I interpret that hidden smell, and that repulsive substance which enveloped me at the close of the dream? A distasteful conjunction, I admit! But while I shall try to put the matter decorously in order to spare the reader any undue embarrassment, it is necessary to write unsparingly and truthfully.

The widening thematic range of my dreams plunged me into a new melancholy. The enterprise which I had undertaken was, I now saw, enormous. You understand, my dismay did not arise from the fact that I barely recognized the oppressed principal actor in the dreams as myself. I was not looking for my dreams to interpret my life, but rather for my life to interpret my dreams. But I now saw this was a more formidable undertaking than I had anticipated. I had acted on my dreams, well and good. But the mere execution of the dream images, the process whereby I inscribed them on my life, was not enough. Perhaps, I thought, the dreams not only instructed me to do something—like seduce a woman; but also to do nothing—except concentrate on purging myself of some impurity, which might be the dreams themselves. I could no longer single out the erotic in my interpretation and acting out of the dreams.

Here I took my cue from the setting of this latest dream. After all, where throughout history have the indescribable longings and anxieties of man been invested? Surely not in the communion of bodies, but in the exaltations of the spirit. No doubt the first religious men were as perplexed as I, since they knew no name for what they experienced.

It was in this manner that I conquered the sentiment that my dreams had marked and defiled my daytime life. I concluded that my dreams, being susceptible to many interpretations, were no less susceptible to the religious one: namely, that something which one might, for want of a better name, call religious had erupted within me. This did not in itself afford me pleasure, for I am not a credulous person nor given to postponing my happiness to another world. Neither do I crave the dubious prestige of the name "religion" to make my spiritual efforts respectable in my own eyes. Nevertheless, I know that I am a person capable of devoutness. Yes, definitely, I would say that, in certain circumstances, I enjoy nothing better than being devout.

I have said that my first reaction to the dream was melancholy. Further reflections promptly turned my melancholy to thoughtfulness, and I experienced a marvelous calm. One of my reflections was about thoughtfulness itself: I realized that I had never really thought except when I wrote or talked. Now I resolved to become more silent, without becoming morose. This was easier without Frau Anders about; she had the habit of interrupting my silences to ask me what I was thinking. Being at times a sociable person, however, I continued to frequent my café and attended some parties, but certain friends, heirs to the solicitousness of Frau Anders, remarked the difference and judged that I was again unhappy.

One of my friends, the priest who conducted the radio program, undertook to cure my melancholy by taking me on long walks in the famous woods which lie on the outskirts of the city. He was a kindly alert man whose conversation I esteemed, for the clergy in my country is better educated than it used to be. (There is always something touching in the tardy efforts toward self-improvement of an institution or a feeling in decline.) I accepted his ministrations with interest, because of the recent turning of my thoughts toward religious schemes. What he told me, after a series of talks, was that my dreams represented the revolt of my conscience against a religious vocation which I had suppressed.

"I do not mean," said the good Father Trissotin, "that I believe you should aspire toward the priesthood." I blushed and assured him that I would not take his words other than as he meant them.

"What I mean," he continued, obviously relieved, "is that you should go to confession. Our talks are only a preparation for that step, for which you already yearn in your dreams. It is there that you will find yourself purged."

I must explain that I have always respected the church which baptized me and which only a million and a half citizens of my country disavow to the extent of belonging to another religious community. There is no doubt that the Church has performed much good, and even today when I see the little priests hurrying through the city on motorcycles, their black cassocks trailing in the wind, I generally pause to watch them. They cannot harm those souls in distress to whom they minister: the dying; the pious housemaids; the pregnant girls, abandoned and remorseful; the criminal, the insane, the intolerant. I have a congenital susceptibility, some might call it a weakness, for those who profess the cure of souls.

Also I enjoy religion aesthetically. As my dream indicates, I am attracted by the slow ceremonies of the cathedral. I respond to incense, stained glass, genuflection. I like the way the Spanish kiss their thumbs after making the sign of the cross. In short, I welcome gestures which are repeated. I suppose that part of the reason my dreams intrigued me was that every dream was a recurrent dream. Thus, every gesture in the dream gained the status of a ritual.

But I do not see how one gesture can suppress another. And I did not want to be appeased.

"Confess rather than express, my son." Father Trissotin's rosy face was set in a look of concern.

I have already said that I was prepared to admit that something religious had erupted within me. But I did not like Father Trissotin's well-meaning assumption that my dreams were something of which I would necessarily want to rid myself. However, I thought it best to keep this objection to myself, and decided to challenge my friend on the appropriateness and efficacy of the confessional.

"Do you really think," I said finally, "that a confession would rid me of my dreams?"

I did not intend to take up with him the question of the value of my dreams. But he seemed to anticipate my inward reservation. "I believe," he said, not at all portentously, "that you are possessed, if not by God, then by the devil. You have freely admitted to me the perverse and arbitrary impulses by which you have lately been governed, and you attribute these to your dreams. But you cannot simply hold your dreams responsible. What if they are sent by the devil? It is your duty to combat them, not yield to them."

When I did not reply immediately, I could see that he took my silence as a good omen for the success of his counsel. "All dreams," he added gently, "are spiritual messages."

"Perhaps these dreams are a message," I said. "I have often thought so myself. But I believe they are a message from one part of myself to another." Father Trissotin shook his head disapprovingly. I continued. "How dare I *not* answer the sender of these messages with my own body? I say my body, since the dreams are grossly, indecently preoccupied with the fate of my body. How dare I employ an intermediary instead? Especially the one you propose, a priest, someone trained in the arts of neglecting the body."

"Don't trust your own clarity," he said. "The body is more mysterious than you think."

I was silent again. It would have been ungracious of me to challenge Father Trissotin on these grounds, his vocational disavowal of his own body giving him immunity from embarrassing rejoinders. Though he might proselytize in intimate libertine circles, like Frau Anders's, as well as over the radio to the mass of his countrymen, most of whom cared far more for the outcome of the annual bicycle race than for the salvation of their souls, he risked nothing. He always spoke across the unbesiegeable moat of his own chastity.

"You have been given a message which you cannot read," he continued with marvelous confidence. "If you were illiterate, you would not hesitate to appoint a scribe to conduct your correspondence."

"Ah," I answered, "in such a case it would be I still who dictated the letters. But when I accept the advice of priests, I accept a form letter. And while I admit my dreams may not be as original as they seem to me, I cannot yet give up the idea that an answer that is different, that is mine alone, is expected of me."

With that, Father Trissotin looked at me with pity, and said: "You are being naïve. The illiterate peasant never knows if the scribe really puts down his words exactly as he dictates them. It must often happen that the scribe thinks he knows better than his client. He has, after all, more experience in anticipating the reactions of those who read letters." He went on: "You are just such an illiterate in spiritual transactions, and the priest an experienced scribe. All letters are form letters, are they not? Letters of hope, of love, of spite, of hypocritical solicitude . . . Why not seek out the most expert form your message can take, since your purpose is not just to be understood but to have a certain effect on the person receiving your letter?"

"Perhaps," I replied, "I do not want to have any effect at all." I could not restrain myself from explaining to him. "You assume, Father, that I wish to rid myself of the dreams, and you recommend to me the agency of the confessional for this purpose. But, no! What I want, if anything, is to rid my dreams of me."

He seemed almost defeated by my obstinacy, for he delivered, in a troubled tone, a most impersonal answer. "God gave you your soul to be saved."

I would not permit this evasion. "Father, let me continue my explanation," I said, directing my steps to a bench by the fountain. We sat in a gloomy truce-like silence for a moment and watched the children playing. Then I roused myself and said: "What I mean is this. I see the confessional as a devious means to answer a message which comes from myself. It is the long way around, like stepping out of one's front door onto the highway to reach the back door. Or going to the airport to hire a plane to travel from the attic to the basement." He stared with displeasure. I went on: "It's not the distance, you understand, which I object to in these maneuvers. For in an oddly designed house it could indeed be very far from the front door to the back door, from the attic to the basement. But why go out of the house?"

Hearing my own words, I doubted my ability to convince Father Trissotin, for I have observed that the most direct path for one person appears intolerably roundabout to another.

"To choose a priest to answer my own message, seems to me . . ." I paused, not wishing to be indelicate. "It reminds me—if you will permit my frankness, Father—of the not entirely rational conventions of sexuality. I mean," I concluded, somewhat anticlimactically, "that I cannot altogether see the reason for coupling when anyone can procure for himself an equally intense and purer pleasure alone."

With that he was, after all, shocked, and recalled an appointment with his bishop or with someone at the radio station, I do not remember. The afternoon was almost over, but I sat for a while in the park, thinking of what we had said.

Perhaps I should have recounted some of my earlier meetings in the park with Father Trissotin; but this to me is the most interesting because it was the least doctrinal. In earlier sessions, Father Trissotin had assumed I needed theological instruction, and had expounded the claims and glories of the Church. He had even given me a rosary, which I always took with me when we had an appointment, but otherwise kept in a drawer with my cuff links. For all my good will, however, I had not listened too patiently to Father Trissotin. I did not believe in his form letter, nor understand how he could believe in it. Which form? The proliferation of religions throughout the world irritates me. How can one worship the divine in so many postures? While Buddha reclines on his side on one elbow, Christ strains at the cross. They cancel out each other.

While these thoughts were wrestling in my mind, I was watching a little girl playing with a large rubber ball. Ever since I have been myself no longer a child, I have enjoyed the company of children. I felt it would relieve me to talk with a child, and since this one was nearest to hand, I began to watch her movements more attentively. When the child's ball rolled down the pathway a good distance away from her nurse and she toddled after it, I got up and followed her.

I shall not insult my reader's character by reassuring him as to the purity of my motives. For the fact was that I did not know what I would say to the child or do with her.

She was a pretty child in a pink frock, about four years old. I walked behind her in order to watch her run. When she reached her ball, she hugged and talked to it. But again it slipped out of the grasp of her short plump arms and rolled away. This time I went ahead of her and picked up the ball.

"It's mine!"

"I know," I replied. "What do you think I'm going to do with it?"

"Give it back to me?" she said doubtfully.

"Don't cry, little one. Of course I shall give it back to you. But what do you suppose I shall do with it first?"

"Eat it."

"And then?"

She giggled. I was delighted. I longed to toss my fantasies at her, like the ball, and hear them bounce back at me in her childish accents. But I did not want her to take the ball from me, as she was at that moment trying to do.

"No, no. Not yet." I held it out of her reach. "Tell me, little one, what is the first thing you remember?"

"I want my ball."

"Do you remember anything?"

"Once I went to the zoo."

"Anything else?"

"I remember my name. Do you want to know what it is?"

"No."

"I remember where I live, too. Do you want to know that?"

"Do you remember your mother?"

She laughed heartily. "Silly! How can I? She's at home!"

"I don't remember my mother, either," I said.

"Is she at home?"

"No, she's dead."

"I know lots of dead people," the child replied. "Millions. Millions and millions. Millions of them."

"Where are they?"

"My father keeps them in his office. He goes every day to talk to them."

"Is he a doctor, your father?"

"No, he makes money. That's what he does."

"Does your mother often scold you?"

"No. Only my nurse. She scolds me when I go away from the bench."

"Would you like your ball back?"

"Aren't you going to eat it? Is it too big?"

I wanted to please the child, so I said, "No, I breakfast on bigger things than this every day. I eat tigers and acrobats and doorknobs. This morning I ate a black chair."

It was better than any confessional to see her laugh. "Did you? I don't believe it. You're pretending."

"No, I swear. It's true. Would you really like me to eat your ball?"

"Can I have it back then?"

"Perhaps. Look." I took out my pocketknife and made a small incision in the fleshy rubber of the ball. The ball crumpled in my hand. Then I crammed the rubber in my mouth and made the motions of chewing.

"Oh, you did! You did! Let's tell the nurse."

"No, you must go now." I turned so she could not see me, and spit the rubber into my hand.

"I want to eat the ball, too."

"No, you must get another one."

"Is the ball dead? Did you kill it with your knife?"

"No, the ball is inside me. It will take a long time for it to come out, so you must get another in the meantime. But I have a present for you." I saw the nurse looking anxiously up and down an adjacent path.

"A present!"

"Yes, it's a rosary. A good priest gave it to me. And now you can pray for your ball." I put it into her hands. She took it hesitantly, and then smiled when she looked at it more closely.

"I think I would like to have my ball, too."

"Goodbye, little one."

"The rosary is black," she said in a puzzled tone.

"Goodbye, little one." And I left her, in the middle of the path, peering between the beads.

Five

I spend more time with Jean-Jacques.

His ideas, his world.

I came to spend more time with Jean-Jacques. He seemed to understand better than others what preoccupied me. But I did not encourage him to interpret my dreams. He had his life, which I assumed to be suitable for him; I had mine. To keep myself alert to his influence, I began a notebook in which I recorded some of our meetings and conversations. Here are several entries.

"May 21. It is Jean-Jacques's cheerfulness that attracts me most to him. He tells me, 'I hate plots that illustrate the death of love, the failure of talent, the mediocrity of society.' This refusal to be dreary is admirable. Why, for instance, are there so many novels about parents—the giants of our childhood who cut off our feet and shove us, limping, into the world? He is right: the writer may celebrate or mock, he must not stare or whine. I am rereading his first two novels, and I find them very good, although a little overwritten. The one about the boxer is especially fine. He has made something sublime out of the agonies of the arena."

"May 23. No wonder Jean-Jacques is so prolific; he writes five or six hours a day, and rewrites very little; that baroque style of his dictates itself to him in the first draft, he tells me. But why does he never draw upon his exploits of the night as the subject for a novel? Not out of prudence. I have never known anyone so careless of his reputation . . . I think I understand this seemingly uncharacteristic reticence. Because he keeps the day and night separate, his acts are not hectic. His life is not dismembered, because he has found the seams in a piece of whole cloth and calmly unstitched them. Thus I find all his acts mysterious and graceful . . . I, too, want my life not to be dismembered. But I am not willing to separate the day from the night. 'You wish to unify,' Jean-Jacques says to me. 'I practice the arts of dissociation.' "

"July 13. I am methodical, secretive, honest. Jean-Jacques is lavish, indiscreet, dishonest. This contrast is the basis of our friendship."

"August 4. I am annoyed with Jean-Jacques for bothering to tell me I am not a writer, and inform him that I have never thought that I was. But his reasons for thinking this of me are not the obvious ones. You can't write, he says, because you are a born specialist, the sort of person who can do only one thing. Writing is not that thing, he concludes. Is it dreaming? I ask, somewhat facetiously. He does not reply, he only smiles."

These are several journal entries of that period. Although I realized that, in Frau Anders's absence, I should not neglect my sexual needs, the pleasures of spectatorship came to interest me more than my own performance. From spending only my late afternoons with Jean-Jacques, I began to accompany him on his nightly rounds. It was a mild spring and a voluptuous summer.

We would meet at his café at aperitif time. He would have just emerged from his regimen of writing, and always greeted me with a vacant and distracted look. I soon understood that this merely signified the slow return of his attention from its lunar voyage of withdrawal. By the second vermouth he would be chatting gaily about old furniture or the opera, or I would be leading him into the maze of my latest reflection about my dreams.

When his energies had returned, we would leave the café and go to his hotel. Jean-Jacques was permanently and comfortably installed in a large, atelier-sized room on the top floor. For a while I liked just to sit on the bed and watch him shave and dress. He was very conscious of clothes, perhaps because he was plain-faced, lean, and even a little nondescript. "I have the face of a stockbroker," I once heard him mutter to his image in the mirror. The choice of his apparel for the evening was as carefully considered as if he were an actor making up in his dressing room, which in a way he was. Sometimes he felt boisterous, and assembled a real costume, such as the red kerchief, striped shirt, and tight black pants of an *apache*. Generally the choices were more delicate—it was a question of the slimness of the pants; leather jacket or turtleneck sweater; rings, military or dandyish; the boots or the pointed shoes.

Later, when the fascination of his dressing had become more familiar to me, I used to amuse myself looking among the objects in his room. Jean-Jacques was a collector. On tables, and on the floor, under the bed and in corners of the room, were boxes of strange treasure. In one box were hundreds of turn-of-the-century picture postcards of music-hall dancers. There were files of newspaper clippings about prizefighters and wrestlers, autographed photos of film stars, and confidential police reports (I never found out how he got hold of these) on cases of armed robbery committed in the capital in the last twenty years. In other boxes there were fringed scarves, fans, seashells, feather boas, cheap jewelry, miscellaneous carved chessmen, wigs. It seemed that whenever I came he had installed something new in his room—another Epinal print, a Boy Scout hat, an Art Nouveau mirror with a snake design, a beaded lamp, a piece of cemetery statuary, a circus poster, a set of marionettes representing Bluebeard and eight wives, a white-and-green wool rug in the shape and design of an American dollar bill. When I tired of looking and touching, he would play records for me: an aria from an obscure melodramatic opera of the last century, or an old java. I did not share these enthusiasms. Since I knew Jean-Jacques to have the most scrupulous judgment in all the arts, his love of these exaggerated, trivial, and vulgar artifacts was a mystery to me. "My dear Hippolyte," he would say, "you will never understand, but sometime I will explain it to you anyway." I do not think of myself as a solemn person, but Jean-Jacques made me feel so.

When he had finished dressing we would go down, past the deaf old concierge who never failed to shout some cheerless obscene compliment to Jean-Jacques. Once in the street, Jean-Jacques walked stealthily but steadily, and I followed at a distance. Usually he had to wait no more than a half hour before someone, silently, joined him. If he were concerned solely for his own pleasure, it might be a truck driver, an immaculate Italian businessman, an Arab, or a student; the main requirement was that his partner be evidently manly in his appearance and tastes. For this purpose, he could venture almost anywhere in the city and might remain with whomever he found for the entire evening. But if he were out to be paid, he was confined to certain neighborhoods and cafés where he would find the confirmed homosexuals, invariably middle-aged or elderly, to whom he appealed as a rough type, and who would be eager to pay him for some minutes of his virile company. He and his companion would merely go off to the quais and disappear beneath a bridge; or if the financial prospect were more promising, Jean-Jacques would take the man to his own room, and would not return to the route he patrolled until an hour or two later.

I therefore cannot speak with much knowledge of what Jean-Jacques did for his own pleasures; on these excursions, understandably, he went alone. But on the several nights a week which he would set aside for business, I would often accompany him through the entire evening. While he was off with a client I would wait for him in various cafés which were the specialized territory of the male prostitute—of the delicate-featured young boys, the toughs and bandits like Jean-Jacques, and the transvestites. Gradually I, too, became known and came to sit at tables of the waiting, gossiping sisterhood of men, the peroxided and beringed friends of my friend. They did not talk to me much, although their regard was always amiable; polite conversation in that circle, conversation that was not about their vocation, was unthinkable. Their sentences were expletive, never expository. They had no opinions. They knew only two emotions, jealousy and love, and their talk, which was often spiteful, was only of beauty. *Folles de nuit,* madwomen of the night, was what they jokingly called themselves. A genuine whore is rare; most whores are businessmen. But these whores really loved their clients. They had gone too far in demonstrating their love for the bodies of their own sex to feel the detachment which a female prostitute customarily feels toward men. They were so proud of their ability to give pleasure that they did not allow themselves to feel rejected when, after making love, their clients reviled them.

When I was not sitting in such cafés the nights of that summer, I too walked the streets—observing further how men employ themselves for their pleasure. I frequented the other public stations of this transient lust, where I learned to recognize the more disguised homosexuals who sought each other in the urinals and the back rows of cinemas. I cannot think of a more perfect example of understanding without words than these faultless encounters. Not a word was exchanged, but some mysterious chemistry of attraction drew them together to grasp each other in public places—they never seemed to make a mistake—and to consummate the sex act with such swiftness that it was as if each man worked singly at a task which could only be performed alone, the other invisibly assisting.

Once I came upon such a scene already in process, among a number of men in a *pissoir.* There was perfect silence. A tall Arab in an ill-fitting blue suit had seized the member of the man urinating beside him. That man seized that of his neighbor, and so on down a line of men, none of them in the least effeminate-looking, all responding as though to a prearranged signal. It was like a dream, in that the strange had become easy, the willed merely necessary. And then, as quickly, the line was broken, the dancers abandoned the rhythm; it was over and the men walked out, hitching up their pants.

Another time, in a Metro lavatory, I witnessed the scene from the beginning. It started with jokes, and a fight between an African and a dark, well-dressed man over an insult which I had not heard. They began to grapple with each other and others gathered around shouting words of encouragement, until the fight—which I soon realized was a delicate pretext—spread to the spectators and each man was pushing and shoving his neighbor, calling out obscene insults. One cried, "You wouldn't dare!" and another, "I challenge you to repeat that outside!" and another, "Let me out of here!" But no one left. The shoving and shouting continued at the same level—the African and the businessman were already on their knees—and I joined in, taking care neither to exceed nor to fall short of my neighbors in vehemence. I wondered why the shouting prolonged itself since it was so repetitive, and they seemed to be growing less rather than more angry. Then another man dropped to his knees, then another. Now the spirit of the encounter had taken over, flushing away the dark uncertain scraps of each man's personality. Silence came to each in turn, like the serial extinguishing of candles. And on the cold tile floor the act of love was performed in haste but dexterously, with economy and professionalism.

When I began to accompany my friend the writer, I had no opinions about his activities, and even if I had felt licensed to urge him to a less perverse and promiscuous life, I would have held my tongue. Jean-Jacques, however, would not allow my silence. Though I did not attack him, he was resolute and ingenious in his own defense, or rather the defense of the pleasures of disguises, secrecy, entrapments, and being-what-one-is-not.

Several times that summer, he tried to overturn my unspoken objections. "Don't be so solemn, Hippolyte. You are worse than a moralist." While I could not help regarding this world of illicit lust as a dream, skillful but also weighty and dangerous, he saw it simply as theater. "Why should we all not exchange our masks—once a night, once a month, once a year?" he said. "The masks of one's job, one's class, one's citizenship, one's opinions. The masks of husband and wife, parent and child, master and slave. Even the masks of the body—male and female, ugly and beautiful, old and young. Most men, without resisting, put them on and wear them all their lives. But the men around you in this café do not. Homosexuality, you see, is a kind of playfulness with masks. Try it and you will see how it induces a welcome detachment from yourself."

But I did not want to be detached from myself, but rather in myself.

"What is a revolutionary act in our time?" he asked me, rhetorically, at another meeting. "To overturn a convention is like answering a question. He who asks a question already excludes so much that he may be said to give the answer at the same time. At least he marks off a zone, the zone of legitimate answers to his question. You understand?"

"Yes, I understand. But not what bearing it has—"

"Look, Hippolyte. You know how little audacity is required today to be unconventional. The sexual and social conventions of our time prescribe the homosexual parody."

I could not agree. "It takes courage to parody the normal," I said. "Courage and a great capacity for guilt. I don't see the humor in these proceedings that you do, my friend. Surely it would be easier for them—I exclude you, Jean-Jacques, because you're not like the others—if things were as you say."

"You're wrong," he replied. "The price is not as exacting as you think."

"Doesn't the transvestite who roams the streets yearn for his family whom he can no longer face because he has plucked his eyebrows?"

"Hippolyte," he said in an exasperated tone. "I am very angry that you speak of them—and exclude me. And thus you try to please me!"

"But you aren't like them, Jean-Jacques. You choose. They are obsessed."

"So much the worse for me," he said. "No," he continued, "to pretend one thing is only not to pretend something else. But to be obsessed is not to pretend at all. The sun does not play at rising every morning. Do you know why? Because the sun is obsessed with its tasks. All that we admire in nature under the name of order, and the basis of the confidence we repose in her regular movements, is obsession."

The idea struck me as true. "Then obsession, not virtue, is the only sensible ground for trust."

"Right," he said. "Which is why I trust you."

Then I thought, that is why I cannot trust you, Jean-Jacques. But this I did not say.

You see, even if I did not trust Jean-Jacques I honored and admired him as a mentor and companion in the search for the self. But so much of taste and habits of character separated us. Because he was absolutely committed to his work, writing, he could afford to be unreliable in every other way—and to ornament his life with games, strategies, and artifacts. These strange rites he practiced with himself were not mine.

"You and I are very much alike," he explained to me on another evening of that ambulatory summer.

I expressed surprise.

"Only," he continued, "you will not succeed and I will. I am prepared to carry out my character to the extreme—"

"So am I," I interrupted.

"I am prepared to carry out my character to the extreme, which is a variety of character. You know nothing of varying yourself. You wish your character to be concentrated and clear, but you will find that when you have boiled away the water you have reduced yourself to an acid that is too strong for your own nostrils, not to speak of the world's. You will burn away, while I—I am diluted through and through."

Of course I protested.

"I know," he went on, "that you think my life adventurous. How little you know of risk! You are the adventurer, the one taking risks, because you are not clear about what territory you are surveying, your body or your mind. If you mistake one for the other, you will stumble."

I listened intently. Although not a vain person, I enjoy hearing my friends talk about me.

"My life is bizarre but tractable," he went on. "Yours is too resolute and full of dangers . . . It's well to be serious, but not to understand seriousness as making a demand on you."

"If you mean," I replied, "that I do not have your catholicity of taste, that is true."

"There are many demands," he said. "Seriousness is only one of them. But I like you, Hippolyte," he added, smiling, and put his arm around me. "You have character, like an American temperance tract or the great unfinished cathedral in Barcelona. Everything you do is you. You are incapable of being otherwise. That is why I . . . collect you."

Whatever I wanted from Jean-Jacques, it was not for him to find me merely amusing. I suppose this was the first moment I resented him.

"I *want* to be myself, more than anyone else in the world," I declared firmly.

"And so you are, dear Hippolyte," he said, smiling and propelling me toward the door of the crowded café where we sat that August evening. And just to show me that he could act out of character, that he could surprise me as I could never surprise him, that night he took me home with him to bed.

This impromptu sexual encounter did not change our relationship. We parted as friends. But although the experiment was never repeated, I was dismayed at Jean-Jacques's flippancy and vowed to be more on guard against him.

I was never tempted to discuss Frau Anders with my friend, but then it is natural for me to be discreet. Jean-Jacques, however, was most indiscreet with me. He always had a new story to tell me about his latest conquest, or his latest enthusiasm. He discussed his sexual escapades—as well as his impoverished childhood, his boxing career, his thefts, everything except his writing—prodigally, without reserve; and I learned to my surprise that he was often impotent. Throughout these confidences I forbore remonstrating with him about his unnatural tastes and exaggerated life, for while I did not agree with Jean-Jacques's curious theory that homosexuality was both guilt and humor, revolt and convention, it has never been my aim to interfere with other people's happiness. This, you will remember, was one of the maxims I had decided upon early in my intellectual adventures. And Jean-Jacques seemed to me a happy man.

Perhaps, though, I should have guessed that his cynical virility was partly sham. There was something in Jean-Jacques's small eyes and high forehead, a look of ill health—but no, this was misleading. He was in perfect health. I, in contrast, have the look of good health that derives from a well-fed childhood, and the reliable body that makes the appearance true. The reader may have gathered that I do not experience difficulties of Jean-Jacques's sort, however bizarre the situation, though I would not be surprised to learn that I miss certain peaks of satisfaction in the course of my unruffled potency.

Neither have I ever suffered during long periods of sexual abstinence. In Frau Anders's absence, I busied myself with reading and correspondence, with an occasional participation in the life of Jean-Jacques's night, and in continued meditation on my dreams.

I made an inventory of my possessions. I had a modest acceptable wardrobe—nothing to pare away there. I thought of selling my books, but I had not freed myself from the habit of reading a good part of each day. The furniture was another matter. All but the most necessary furniture—a bed, a chest of drawers, bookshelves—I gave away to student friends. Even the chair went, for I could sit on the bed. I also disposed of the few paintings which I owned, and the flute which I had purchased after my first dream. Eventually I got rid of the bed, too, and slept on a mat which I rolled up and put in the closet in the daytime.

I was also concerned with the proper maintenance of my body, which I do not neglect and am never tempted to despise. Then I liked to take long walks, and found that any change of scene revived my too easily depleted energies. To supplement my walks, Jean-Jacques suggested a program of exercises of the type practiced in the Orient which I could do in my own rooms. The purpose of these exercises had nothing to do with the vain purpose of strengthening the body. They had nothing to do with the body, apart from the aim of reaching perfect control over it. They aimed, through the body, straight to the mind, to produce an alertness without content, a state of shimmering weightlessness. But it was mainly the idea of the exercises which attracted me; perhaps this is why I did not become proficient at them. I never did succeed in attaining control over my digestion and anal sphincter, so that I could vomit, excrete, and increte at will. Even after I stopped doing the exercises, however, I often imagined myself doing them, wearing a close-fitting bathing costume of black wool.

I did practice regularly one less strenuous exercise, of my own invention, in which I performed on an invisible electronic instrument. I sat very still, trying to find the right posture, the right disposition of my arms and legs—in order to touch all the invisible nodes and start the current flowing. Sometimes it was not an electronic instrument which I played but an impalpable wind instrument, such as a flute: then I had to search for where I was to put my mouth, where the stops were, and what to play.

A less successful expression of my concern for my body was with diet experiments. I knew that some religious sects forbid their members to eat sour, pungent, or spicy foods, and all meat and intoxicating drink. I decided to see if these rules applied to me. Some weeks I would eat nothing but rice and fruit, while for certain periods I would eat only the forbidden foods. In neither case did I notice any significant change in my body's sensations.

It then occurred to me that there was no reason to reproach myself for not doing all the exercises. After all, what is their function? The exercises are a method of eliminating thought, of devoting oneself to the utmost void. But was not this the purpose that was served by my meditation on my dreams? The substitution was confirmed by what the exercise book, which Jean-Jacques lent me, recommends to the adept after the body is mastered: to be perfectly still, select a spot, and concentrate on it. This act of concentration is the real climax of the exercises. Concentration upon a particular spot rules out other thoughts; the mind is opened, and the light shines within. According to the exercise book, the concentration spot may be either a small, centrally placed part of one's own body or a small object in one's room. But was not this what I had been doing? I had something better than my nose or my navel, or a landscape on the wall. I had my dreams.

I now turned back to my dreams with a new demand. If I was to concentrate on my dreams as an analogue to fasting or exercising, I wanted them to be bare and taciturn. But in this I was disappointed; they were not laconic but full of conversations. I wondered what I might do to curb the loquacity of my dreams.

I dared to hope that one day my dreams would be altogether silent, as Jean-Jacques had once suggested. But for this large improvement, I felt I needed models. I found such a model in one of my favorite recreations, the temple of public dreams, the cinema. Films had already begun to talk at this time, but in out-of-the-way theaters I could still see old movies which were blessedly silent. The reading of medical books provided another model, in the chapters on aphasia. I wanted to emulate those who hear the voice, the sound of speech, but not the words; to an aphasiac, the words do not pronounce themselves. Though I was far from being able to put this into practice in my dreams, I came to understand that words coerce the feelings they attempt to embody. Words are not the proper vehicle for a general upheaval which destroys the old accumulation of feeling.

I suppose I could be considered a stubborn person, but my stubbornness is not superficial or ostentatious. It lies deep down, and behaves like deference and humility. At least I was not entirely literal-minded, the most common cause of stubbornness. If I were, I would not have continued to talk with my friends.

"Hippolyte, my dear," Jean-Jacques said to me one early evening, as we walked along a boulevard, "you have taken a vow to be absurd. Not just one vow, even. Many vows. You make vows like a greedy pauper buying recklessly on the installment plan. You're becoming more and more deeply in debt to yourself, and you are already bankrupt. What's the point of encumbering yourself so?"

I explained to Jean-Jacques how misleading was his metaphor. "I am not interested in buying or possessing anything," I said. "I am only interested in postures."

"Then I tell you to break your posture and dance. You look at yourself too much. That's the beginning of all absurdity. Look about you. The world is an interesting place."

I replied that I waited for my dreams to be explained to me.

"There are no explanations," he said, "just as there should be no vows and promises. To explain one thing is to make another thing—which only litters the world the more. What blank useless things your explanations will be when you finally settle on them!"

"But you, Jean-Jacques, your life is filled with useless passions and contradictory pleasures."

"It's not the same," he said. "Let me tell you a story which will explain. I know two pacifists. One is a man who believes that violence is wrong and acts in a way that accords with his beliefs. He has committed himself to being a pacifist, and so he is. He acts as a pacifist because he is one."

"And the other?"

"The other man abjures violence in all situations and therefore knows he is a pacifist. He is a pacifist because he acts like one. Do you see the difference?"

I did not, and it is never my habit to claim more understanding than I have.

"Look," he said. "I am a writer, yes? You know that I write every day. But I might not write tomorrow, from tomorrow on I might never write again. I am a writer because I write. I do not write because I am a writer."

I thought I understood then, and was disheartened by the distance which Jean-Jacques was putting between us. "But you said you were going to tell me a story," I said, pushing aside my melancholy thoughts. "You have only introduced two characters."

"Oh, the story is that the man who was a pacifist because he acted like one killed his wife yesterday. I was in court this afternoon when he was arraigned."

"And the other?"

He laughed. "That one, he's still a pacifist."

"And you find some . . . beauty . . . in the murderer who violated his principles?" Again I was baffled.

"No beauty. Only life. Don't you see, that man had never acted out of principles. He had taken no vows—and neither have I. Therefore, nothing I do is useless or contradictory, as you thought a moment ago. It is you who are scattered and dismembered."

"Language does that to me," I murmured, half to myself. "My dreams are too talkative. Perhaps, if I didn't speak—"

"No, no, don't tamper with yourself any more than you have! It's much simpler. All you have to do is speak without trying to prolong the life of your words. For each word that is spoken, another word must die."

"Then I must learn to destroy."

"Not destroy either!" He was becoming exasperated with me. "Life will take care of itself, unless it is diluted by too much life."

"I want to improve the mixture, but you tell me I am brewing an acid."

"Exactly," he said. "But I know it does you no good to tell you these things. Oh, I could tell you many things . . . Listen, if I tell you something, will you promise not to seize on it as a candidate for your damned set of rules for yourself? Please."

I promised.

"One should always be submerged. But never in one thing." He paused. "Now, doesn't that sound like a rule?"

I acknowledged that it did.

"But it isn't, it needn't be. Imagine that submergence is not a rule or a vow on which you act, making you diversify your tastes and affections, but something you discover each day about yourself. Each day you—rather, I—discover that I am engrossed, submerged, in something or someone."

"But don't you think about what to do with your discoveries? Doesn't it happen that one overwhelms the rest and makes you want to change your life?"

"Why should I change my life?" he said. "Why can't I have everything I want? You see"—he smiled roguishly—"how the bees come straight to my honey."

Was this another scene of seduction? Better to change the subject! "And I believe," I spoke slowly and solemnly, "that one should always be submerged. Like you, Jean-Jacques. But the rest cannot be decided. My temperament is more serious than yours, as I think we both agree, but do not caricature me as a man who decides everything while feeling nothing. I assure you I am a man of feeling." I thought tenderly of Frau Anders.

"No, little Hippolyte, you do not decide anything. You linger atrociously over your dreams. You let them influence your acts, only because you have decided to be the man-who-dreams. You are like a man who discovers a log across his path, and instead of pushing aside the log he calls in a construction company to widen the entire road."

"You will trip," he called after me as I left him.

Six

My mistress and I take a trip

to the city of Arabs. We enjoy the city and

I abandon her to a merchant.

N o," I said to myself one day. "It's very clear, I have not yet done with Frau Anders. I am waiting for her."

Frau Anders returned, strangely irritable, from accompanying her husband on the business trip which had evolved into a world tour and second honeymoon. I had never known her like this. "How dead the world is," she cried, "how dreary the people in it! I used to be so gay, so eager for life. Now I can barely lift my head from the pillow in the morning." I urged her to come away with me, to leave her husband and his money, her daughter, and her salon.

Perhaps it was the intensive company of her husband with whom she had spent so little time in the past years: she agreed. Frau Anders wanted a final interview with her husband so she could denounce him for driving her by his neglect into her various adulteries, but I forbade melodrama. She would not at first be dissuaded, but I pressed the point, for I realized that if we were to live together I had to assert my authority at once. Eventually and somewhat to my surprise—she was by nature an imperious woman—she agreed to this as well. We waited until her husband left on another trip. She told her daughter she was visiting a relative in the country where she was born. Our exit from the city was clandestine. No one except Jean-Jacques knew I accompanied her.

When we began to travel, I learned that my mistress had an unlimited capacity for boredom. She required continual entertainment, and took up cities like facial tissues, to be used once and thrown away. Her appetite for the exotic was insatiable, for her only purpose was to devour and to move on. I did my best to keep her amused, and at the same time worked at refashioning her idea of our relationship. Before her trip I had been, as I have already indicated, extremely frustrated. Frau Anders did not understand our affair, or my feeling for her. I knew that our relationship was more serious than she thought it was—and I regretted not being able to give pleasure when it cost me nothing but the truth, an easy premium. She must have been aware of my lack of romantic interest in her, but I wished she had been aware of how deeply, though impersonally, I felt her as the embodiment of my passionate relationship to my dreams. Through my willful matchmaking dreams, she had stirred me sexually as no woman had ever done before and, perhaps, since.

After some months of hasty expensive touring, Frau Anders was sufficiently appeased and confident in me to rest for a while. We settled in a small island, where I spent the days near the boats talking with the fishermen and sponge gatherers and swimming in the warm blue sea. I am very fond of islanders, who have a dignity which city dwellers have lost and a cosmopolitanism that country dwellers can never achieve. In the late afternoon, I returned to the house we had rented to take the waning sun with my mistress. In the evenings we sat by the dock, at one of the three cafés on the island, drinking absinthe and exchanging comments with the other foreign residents about the splendor of visiting yachts. Occasionally a policeman, wearing his cape and patent-leather cockade hat, strutted past, and the foreigners' conversation halted in order to admire his vanity. My senses became very acute on the island, with this reliable diet of sun, water, sex, and empty talk. My palate, for instance: the evening meal, soaked in olive oil and crushed garlic, came to have an exquisitely varied tang and odor. And my hearing, too. When at ten o'clock the island's electricity was turned off and kerosene lamps were lit, I could distinguish at a distance of many miles the sounds of the different bells, the heavier bell worn by the donkey from the shriller ring of the goat bell. At midnight, at the final tolling of the monastery bell from the hill behind the town, we would retire.

Away from the ingenious conversation of her guests in the capital, and discovering (and at first resisting) my own need for solitude, Frau Anders was openly bored. I suggested that she try to meditate, now that there was silence. The idea seemed to revive her spirits. But a few days later she confessed to me that the effort was not bearing fruit, and begged my leave to write. Reluctantly I agreed. I say reluctantly because I had little confidence in Frau Anders's mind, and considered that her best qualities—her sweetness, her stubbornness—flourished only because they had escaped her own detection. I feared that the effort of assuming the identity of a writer might deprive her of the scant realism about herself which she possessed. "No poetry," I said firmly. "Of course not," she replied, offended at my insinuation. "It is philosophy alone which claims my interest." She decided to communicate her insights to the world in the form of letters to her daughter, who, at the time we left the capital, had discarded the elderly conductor for the middle-aged physicist.

"Dear Lucrezia," she would sigh on the veranda as we lay sunbathing. This was the signal that her epistolary efforts were about to resume. She would go indoors to take up her scented note paper and fountain pen with red ink, and set down several pages of her reflections. Upon finishing, she would come outside again and read the letter aloud to me. Generally she refused all my sincere efforts at emendation.

"Dear Lucrezia," began one letter I remember. "Have you ever noticed that men feel called on to prove that they are men, while women do not have to assert their femininity in order to be counted as women? Do you know why this is so? Permit me, with a mother's and a woman's wisdom, to instruct you. To be a woman is to be as human beings were meant to be, full of love and serenity"—here she stroked my thick hair consolingly—"while to be a man is to attempt something unnatural, something that nature never intended. The task of being a man overstrains the machine"—I beg the reader to note how she confounded the natural and mechanical metaphors—"which is continually breaking down. The violence and rashness and schemes, all pathetic pretenses, by which a man persists in his vain enterprise of proving himself are known and esteemed as 'acts of manliness.' Without them he is not a man. Of course not!"

I will admit that if I am to be patronized as a man, I would rather it were by Jean-Jacques, whose haughtiness was at least tempered by the habit of irony that is second nature to all who play games with their sexual identity. Yet how could I be angry with Frau Anders? Her impudence was so naïve, so endearing, so funny. And even if I had been angry I would have forborne, thinking I had no right to judge this woman, having never known my own mother.

"Money, dear Lucrezia, clogs the spirit. False values begin with the worship of things. It is the same with reputation. What should we ask of society more than indifference, more than the freedom to pursue our pleasures?" This was the theme of another letter, which charmed me by its attempt to emulate my own indifference to possessions and reputation, which I had by this time often demonstrated to Frau Anders.

"Do not be afraid of your body, dear Lucrezia, the loveliest body in all the world. Dare to cast aside all false prudery and seize your pleasures as your wise mother counsels you. Oh, that mothers always instructed their daughters thus! What a garden the world would be, what a paradise. Do not let the dead hand of religion inhibit your sensations. Take, and it will be given to you. Disregard all those around you who measure themselves out, saving and spending! Dare to ask for more."

As she read these lines to me, I recalled that placid blond girl whom her mother imagined as a great courtesan. I felt sorry for Lucrezia, and angry at her mother for continuing at a distance to play the procuress for her, if only with theories. But in this quick judgment I was subsequently to be corrected, for in later years I learned that Lucrezia had never been an innocent girl corrupted by a worldly mother. If anything, as Lucrezia later explained to me, it was the other way around: it was the daughter's libertine adolescence which had incited her more affectionate, innocent mother into her own career of erotic freedom. At the time about which I write, however, I saw Lucrezia only through the eyes of her mother's hectic admonitions, as before I had seen her through the elderly conductor's desire. I judged her accordingly, as the victim of both.

"There is only one communion, dear Lucrezia, the communion of instinct. For two thousand years instinct has labored under the pretentious dictates of the spirit, but I see emerging a new nakedness which will free us of the old chains of legality and convention. Our senses are numbed by the heavy weight of civilization. The dark people of the world know this wisdom; our pale race is finished. Man with his machines, his intellect, his science, his technology will give way before the intuition of women and the sensuous power and cruelty of black men."

But enough—I shall not tire the reader further. And I do not wish to give the impression that my feeling for Frau Anders was totally dissipated by our living together in greedy proximity. In the privacy of the bedroom I tested her theories and found her more compliant than ever. I was a vigorous lover (despite my pale flesh), though, as I have said, I found her ardors too easily satisfied. I began to complicate our relationship. There was a young fisherman on the island who followed my mistress around like a lost dog, and I made my absence of jealousy very clear to her. Once she began to doubt her hold over me, she doubled her solicitude, and I basked in the peace of the flesh if not of the spirit.

After one winter on the island, I proposed one day that we decamp.

Soon we headed farther south to the exotic lands Frau Anders professed to admire. Along the way there were many purchases of "native goods," but I wanted to travel as much as possible unencumbered by baggage, and suggested that they be mailed to my rooms back in the capital. I took these packages, elaborately wrapped by Frau Anders, to the post office myself, and sent them to a nonexistent address.

One day we arrived in a city of Arabs, and on my urging prepared to settle there for a time. We toured the native quarter with a fourteen-year-old boy who had accosted us outside our hotel. It was in the annual month of abstinence prescribed by their religion, during which all believers are required to be sexually continent and to fast between sunrise and sunset. The boy watched without expression as we drank glasses of delicious mint tea in the sultan's palace (now open to tourists) and consumed the sticky honey cakes sold in the marketplace. Frau Anders tried, unsuccessfully, to coax the boy into eating them. To divert her attention from this impiety, I suggested that she get the boy to give us a prohibited pleasure, since he would not allow us to give him one. She asked him where we might procure some of the narcotics for which the city was noted. He looked cheerful for the first moment since we had engaged him, and led us to the native equivalent of a pharmacist's shop, where we purchased two clay pipes and five packets of coarse green powder, which we took back to the hotel and sampled. I do not approve of narcotics—at least I have not known the need for them, never having appraised my senses as jaded—but I was curious to see what effect they would have on my mistress. Promptly she lay down on the bed and began to giggle. The sexual invitation was unmistakable. But I wanted to see something new, and seizing her by the arm, I told her that we must go out, that the city would be her lover tonight, that it would appear to us distended, in slow motion, more sensuous than any city she had known. She allowed me to raise her from the bed. After putting on her best frock and fussing over my tie, she went slowly, partly leaning on me to steady herself, to the elevator.

The sunset gun was sounding. We hired a carriage to take us to a shabby wooden building by the harbor which housed a bar where sailors and the more disreputable foreign tourists gathered. The barman, a tall well-built Arab, pressed my hand as I paid for our first round of drinks. The band played flamenco, polkas; we sat at a table and watched the dancers. An hour later, the barman came over and introduced his wife to us. The woman, also Arab, but red-haired as well, put her arm around Frau Anders's bare shoulder and whispered

something in her ear. I noted the sly embarrassed look which my
mistress gave the woman, followed by a vacant, slightly smug glance
directed at me.

"They have invited us to have a drink with them after the bar closes,
dear Hippolyte. In their apartment above here. Isn't it delightful?"

I agreed that it was.

So, after the noise ended and the last chalk sums written on the
wooden surface of the barman's counter were added up and paid for
or charged, we retired to the dark lodging upstairs. More drink was
offered, which I refused. I did not assist in the seduction of Frau
Anders by the barman's bulky pockmarked wife. It was an easy task.
All I did was to give my consent at a crucial moment when my mistress wavered, out of fear, I suppose, that I might be jealous and
reproach her with our adventure in the morning. The barman and I
sat in the parlor and he recited some poetry to me, accompanying
himself on the guitar. I could not give his performance my full attention, my ear being repeatedly diverted by the sounds that I thought
came from the adjacent room. Perhaps I was a little jealous, after all.

Next morning—or rather, afternoon—Frau Anders was claiming a
satisfaction with her adventure which I could see was less than sincere. As usual, in moments when she was aspiring to an emotion she
did not altogether feel, she thought of her daughter. "Dear Lucrezia,"
she began at the narrow hotel writing table. "Love transcends all
boundaries. I have long known, and encouraged you to discover for
yourself, that the love between two persons of widely differing ages
is no barrier to the mutual fulfillment of both. Let me add to that
counsel, dearest child, that love knows no boundary of sex either.
What is more beautiful than the love of two manly men, or the love
of a refined woman of our northern climate for a slim dark girl of the
pagan world? Each has much to teach the other. Do not be afraid of
such leanings when you find them *genuinely* in your heart."

This letter I burned the next day while Frau Anders was out shopping. I wrote to Jean-Jacques, a letter full of tiresome dissection of
my mistress's character, but thought better of it and tore it up. A
letter for a letter. I repented of these fits of censoriousness to which
I was subject still, despite all my good resolutions. Once again I tried
to think of what was beneficent in Frau Anders's nature, to herself
and to me.

That she was thriving, there could be no doubt. It even seemed to
me that she was more attractive. For a woman of about forty (she
would never tell me her exact age) she was good-looking in any case.
Now she was blossoming under the southern sun and the heat of her

narcotic fantasies, becoming artless in her dress and allowing me to see her without cosmetics. This did not make me desire her more, for I found her compliance to my every whim fatiguing. But I became more fond of her, as my passion depleted itself.

I thought I would give my passion one last chance by making her privy to my dreams. She listened in lazy silence, and after I had related several of my treasures, I regretted what I had done. "My darling Hippolyte," she exclaimed. "They are adorable. You are a poet of sex, you know. All your dreams are mystically sexual."

"I think," I said gloomily, "they're all dreams of shame."

"But you have nothing to be ashamed of, darling."

"Sometimes I am ashamed that I have these dreams," I replied. "Otherwise, there is nothing I am ashamed of in my life."

"You see, darling!" she said affectionately.

"Prove to me that I may be proud of my dreams."

"How?"

"I shall tell you something," was my calm answer. "What would you think if I told you that every time I embrace you my care is not for your pleasure, or even for mine, but only for the dreams?"

"Fantasy is perfectly normal," she said, trying to conceal her hurt.

"And what if I told you that my share in the fantasy is no longer enough, that I need your conscious cooperation in my dreams, in order to go on loving you?"

She agreed to do what I asked of her—had I hoped otherwise?— and I showed her how to enact the scenes from my dreams when we made love. She played the man in the bathing suit, the woman in the second room, herself as the hostess of the unconventional party, the ballet dancer, the priest, the statue of the Virgin, the dead king—all the roles of my dreams. Our sexual life became a dream rehearsal, instead of a dream reprise. But, for all my careful instructions and her willingness to please me, something did not work. It was her very willingness, I think; I needed an opponent rather than an accomplice, and Frau Anders did not act toward me with the certainty demanded by my dreams. This theater of the bedroom did not satisfy me because, while my mistress lent me her body to carry out the varied roles of my fantasies, she no longer knew how to patronize me.

But can another person ever participate in one's dreams? Surely this was a foolish, youthful project on my own part, and I cannot blame Frau Anders for its failure. I have also thought since, in reflecting on these events, that in her own way Frau Anders did become engrossed in my preoccupation. It is true she suffered from it—

knowing herself loved not as a person but as a *persona*—yet she did not defend herself by finding me ridiculous. She had come to love me too much. And the fact I was not afraid of her ridicule does not diminish the credit due her for transcending her storehouse of clichés to accept, if not understand, me. Fortunately I am not the kind of man who fears ridicule, at least outside my mysterious dreams; but I know enough of the world to recognize it.

Since she had consented to take my dreams seriously, I thought it only just to repay her in kind. But I must confess that I could not match her naïve seriousness; my own efforts to convert her fantasies into deeds made me laugh sometimes. I cannot excuse the morbid levity that possessed me then. You must understand that I did not mean to be cruel, though my acts might be so interpreted.

We began, largely at the initiative of Frau Anders, to spend our evenings in the native quarter. It was now summer, and even an afternoon at the wide handsome beaches which adorned the city did not keep us cool through the evening. Since my mistress dispensed money lavishly at bars and cafés, we were always warmly received. She continued to occupy her days with the erotic good-naturedness induced by kif and with her exuberant letters to Lucrezia, who was now having an affair with the Negro ballet dancer, and presiding over her mother's salon with a success she only modestly hinted at in her own letters. Frau Anders was not that out of touch that she was incapable of being piqued at the news, and it seemed to make her restless and occasionally irritable.

I decided it would be good for her to taste more fully the exotic passions she rhapsodized over. There was a merchant who accosted me one evening as I was returning to the hotel with a new purchase of kif.

"Your wife, monsieur?" he began. "My son has greatly admired her. He will not touch a morsel of food."

"My wife would be delighted," I said somewhat nervously. The man's candor—a quality which I admire above all others—disarmed me, but his utter lack of ceremony suggested an unseemly impatience which hinted at violence should his wish be thwarted.

"How much?" he said.

"Sixteen thousand francs," I said, having no idea of an appropriate figure. The reader must think of the value of the franc as it was thirty years ago.

"Oh, no, monsieur," he replied, backing away and gesticulating eloquently. "That is too much, much too much. You Europeans set too high a value on your women. And besides, I make no commitment as to how long my son wishes to enjoy the company of your wife."

I decided it was well to adopt the firmest tone, since it was impossible not to bargain with these people. "I must tell you," I said, "that in exactly one week I intend to leave this city to return to my country. Should I depart without my wife, I shall count the eight thousand francs which you shall pay me tonight, when my wife and I visit your house, as a down payment on the balance of eight thousand which you shall pay me one week from today."

He drew me into a white doorway. "Five thousand now—and—perhaps—if all goes well—another five thousand in a week."

"Seven thousand now, and the same—if all goes well," I replied, pulling my arm from his grasp.

We settled at seven thousand that night, and six thousand in a week. It seemed to me fair that a week or less with my mistress should be more expensive, being tiresome, than the indefinite purchase of her person. Nevertheless, I protested gallantly that her worth was far greater than this insignificant sum.

"Assure me that you will make your son promise not to hurt her."

"I promise," he said genially.

It seemed to me obvious at the time that there was no son at all. My merchant friend was merely being gallant himself; seeing my attractive but aging mistress in the company of a reasonably good-looking young man, he wished to assure me that she would not be making a disadvantageous exchange. I, however, thought it improbable that a young Arab would desire an expensive middle-aged European woman, no matter how earnestly his dark flesh yearned to triumph over white. I assumed, then, that the stout graying merchant wanted her for himself. Why was I so sure? The month of abstinence being over, who knows what strange fantasies demanded to be executed. I already knew well there is no predicting sexual tastes: had I not wanted Frau Anders myself? Had she not proved attractive to as unlikely a person as the barman's wife? So it was that on the boat home I decided that it was a virile white-toothed Arab youth who desired Frau Anders, and that she had yielded with joy, relieved to be rid of her tiresome Hippolyte with his dreams and dissatisfactions. At least I hoped so. I did not like to think that there might have been violence and terror and rape and mutilation of that ever-hopeful body.

When she did not return to our city immediately after my own return, I liked to think that she was happy—there is later evidence for this—and that she learned the truth of the brash sentiments in her letters to Lucrezia. For nothing that she wrote was untrue. But Frau Anders had the ability to make truths untrue when she said them. Her letters were rhetoric; I had enabled her to act.

Perfumed and in ignorance of her destiny, I delivered her to the merchant's door. She stepped in before me, and the door closed silently behind her. I wondered if this would prove a lesson to her as to the true worth of those ceremonial courtesies to women which falsify the relationships of European men and women. If men preceded women through doorways, or if there were no order of precedence, it would not have been so simple.

I waited on the cobblestoned street before the house. In a half hour the merchant came out bearing a discreet-looking envelope containing the seven thousand francs and kissed me on both cheeks. I lingered a few moments after he went in again. There was no sound.

Apparently, all went well. In a week my friend was at the dock with another envelope, more kisses, reassurance as to Frau Anders's health and contentment, and poetic compliments to her person.

I sailed directly for home.

Seven

I return to the capital.

"Dream of an elderly patron."

Professor Bulgaraux acquaints me with

the doctrines of the Autogenists.

After returning from the city of Arabs, I thought only of how best to make use of my freedom. I wished for a powerful desire or fantasy, which could be fulfilled as I had fulfilled that of Frau Anders. I wanted to shed my skin. In a way I had done this, by disposing of my mistress; but I had accomplished more for her good than for my own. The sale of Frau Anders was, perhaps, my own altruistic act. And, as with all altruisms, I suffered from certain twinges of guilt. Was the act correct? I asked myself. Was it well-performed? Did I not have some secret, self-serving motive?

I thought of resuming my old diversions with Jean-Jacques. We met, and he inquired, "What has happened to our amiable hostess?" I had made the mistake of confiding in him before my departure, but I was determined not to repeat the error. He received my silence playfully. "You surprise me, Hippolyte. I would have predicted it would be Frau Anders who would return, and you who would stay." I did not allow myself to be provoked into explanations. "Will you share with me none of the fruits of your southern journey?" he said finally. His irony troubled me. I dreaded our incipient intimacy.

Fortunately, the following dream intervened.

I dreamed I was at a garden party. The grade of the hill on which the party was being held made the tables and chairs stand somewhat crooked. I remember best an extremely small wizened old man who sat in an infant's high chair, drinking tea out of an earthenware jug, spilling it on his shirt, and mumbling inaudibly.

I asked someone who the old man was, and learned that he was

R., the multimillionaire tobacco king. I wondered how he had become so small.

Later I was told the old man wanted to see me. Someone guided me up the hill, through the stone gates, down a gravel path, and into a side entrance of the large house. I was led through a series of deserted basement passageways. The only person we encountered was a servant stationed by a door which interrupted a long, wide, institutional-looking corridor. He wore a green visor and sat reading at a small table, which held a lamp and some magazines. As we approached him, he jumped to his feet and opened the door for us with a bow. The door was not heavy, nor was it locked.

I was impressed with this ostentation, and envied the luxuries which the old man's fortune could provide for his family. We entered the old man's room, which had all the trappings of a sickroom. I stood at the foot of his bed, in an attitude of respect, thinking of the bequest which he might make me when he died.

"Send him around the world," he said to the youth standing beside me, the one who had led me into the house, and who I now understood was his son. "It will do him good."

The son beckoned to me. I thanked the old man profusely and followed the son out into the garden, where he told me to wait, and left. I stood there alone for a while, not in the least impatient, for I was relishing the sense of being cared for, of being deployed by some benevolent power. I thought of Frau Anders, and that I would tell her, if I met her on my travels, how well I had been understood by the old man.

A gray cat came by, which I picked up in my arms and fondled. I was repelled by the cat's strong odor. I flung it on the ground but it remained by my side, so I picked it up again and put it in my pocket, thinking I would wait until I found a place to dispose of it.

A score of people had collected near me, and I joined them. We were all waiting for a doctor to arrive, who was to question us. "We do this every Sunday afternoon," one of the party explained to me. The doctor came down the slope, and we sat down on the grass in a circle. He passed around sheets of paper for each of us to fill out— name, identity-card number, weekly earnings, profession—and to sign. I was dismayed at this requirement, for I did not have my papers with me, and I had neither profession nor salary. Watching the others busily filling out their forms, I realized my presence was illegal. I was sorry to miss whatever was to happen, but I was afraid of being detained or perhaps even refused a passport. I left the group.

I decided to return to the house and was heading in that direction when I met the millionaire's son. He told me to adjust the large bath towel which I realized was all I was wearing, and led me to another part of the garden, where I was given a shovel and told to dig. I began earnestly enough, though the towel which was knotted around my waist kept coming loose. The ground was hard and the digging strenuous. And when I had dug a fair-sized trench, water began seeping into it. Soon the trench was half filled with muddy water. There seemed no point in continuing, so I stopped digging and threw the cat in.

Somehow though, I seemed to have kept the cat with me and carried it from the garden. Then I met Jean-Jacques and gave him the cat, which he tossed away in disgust. "Dogs!" he shouted at me.

"Don't be angry," I answered.

"Have you forgotten it's time for your operation?" he said. I became afraid, for I now did recall something about an operation, though it seemed to come from a previous dream.

"Everything is too heavy," I said, to distract him. "Besides," I added ingratiatingly, "I'm asleep."

"Shark balls!" he said, and laughed coarsely.

I could not understand how I was continuing to provoke him. "There's nothing unhealthy about that," I continued. "I get up very early."

"Go on your trip and leave me alone," he said.

But instead of leaving me, as I expected, Jean-Jacques became very large, and I faced an enormous pair of feet and could barely see the head which soared above me. Alarmed and perplexed, I considered how I might cajole him to return to normal size. I threw a rock at his ankle. There was no response. Then I looked up at the giant, and saw he was no longer Jean-Jacques but a malevolent stranger who might step on me, and I did not dare continue trying to attract his attention.

At that moment I was aware that something was wrong with my body, and looking under the towel I saw to my horror that, from the middle of my ribs to my hip, my entire left side was open and wet. I couldn't understand how I had failed to notice it before. This butcher's view of myself was revolting. I wrapped the towel around me even more tightly and, with both hands pressed against my side to prevent my entrails from falling out, I started to walk. At first I felt dignified and brave, and I determined to ask help of no one.

It was dusk now. People were hurrying home through the streets, on foot and on bicycles. It grew darker. I had to find a hospital, for I felt weak now from the loss of blood and could barely walk. I also thought of trying to find the mansion of my aged patron, where I would lie down in the garden, for I dared not go inside and tell the little old man how I had failed to carry out his advice. There was a doctor there, I remembered, although I was not sure that he was not a consul or some passport official. Yet finding the mansion seemed out of the question. I was lost. There was no one to ask directions from; night had fallen and the unfamiliar streets were empty. I pressed my left side, holding back my tears of humiliation. I wanted to lie down, but I was reluctant to dirty my white towel on the pavement. The feeling of heaviness on my left side increased. I was draining away and struggled to lean toward the right. It was then that I died. At least, it became completely dark.

"This dream is too heavy," I said to myself when I awoke, in an effort to be cheerful. Whenever I woke up still submerged in a dream, I would try to recover my equanimity as quickly as possible. It was not easy, for this dream told me all too plainly how burdened I was and how I despised myself. Who am I to aspire to being free? I thought. How dare I go about disposing of others, when I cannot even dispose of myself? Yet I am free, except for the languishing captivity of my dreams. I cursed my dreams.

After a melancholy morning, I managed to slough off my heaviness, but it was only through the most extreme posture of resignation to the dream. I said to myself: If I am burdened, so be it. And I was reluctant to consider a more hopeful interpretation of the dream.

But someone to whom I related this dream, Professor Bulgaraux, a scholar whose special field of study was ancient religious sects, thought differently. "According to certain theological ideas with which I shall acquaint you," he said, "this may be interpreted as a dream of water. You dug a ditch and it filled with water. And in the end, you were not heavy. You were—how shall I say?—liquefying."

It was a comforting thought, but I was not convinced. "Do you think I should travel, as the old millionaire advised?"

"You have been traveling, have you not?"

I nodded.

"Now you must digest what you have learned, and then expel it. There is guilt in your bowels."

I did not answer, but considered sadly that he might be right.

"You credit yourself with a detachment which you do not yet possess. You are right in listening to your dreams and accepting them— how could you refuse?—but wrong in condemning the self that is revealed in them. I could show you, if you will listen to me."

At first I did not understand this invitation, and felt wary of revealing myself once again. I may have made a mistake in telling my dreams to this man. God knows what he believed! I had been told that he practiced incantations and tried to summon dream-sending demons, all of which is repugnant to any person of sense. However, I would not convict him of charlatanry without giving him a full hearing. I respect an authentic mystery, while I deplore the attempt to mystify. I had to find out whether Professor Bulgaraux really believed in what preoccupied him.

"It is rumored," I told him one day over a glass of sherry in his book-lined apartment, "that you are not content with the vocation of a scholar, but in your private life actually subscribe to the beliefs you study."

"Yes, it's true. Or partly," he replied. "I do not believe, alas. But I know how these beliefs truly apply. I am prepared to carry them out, and to teach others how they may be carried out."

"To teach me?" I asked.

He looked at me thoughtfully for a while. "You say your dreams concern you more than anything else?"

I nodded.

"Let me read you the theogonic myth of a sect about which I am lecturing and writing a paper at the moment. It occurs to me that their doctrines apply particularly well in your case."

He took down several volumes bulging with paper slips, opened one, and began to read in his dry, rather nasal voice. I will summarize as best as I can. According to this sect, there was originally one god, a self-sufficient male deity named Autogenes. He was not entirely alone, though. In creating himself, by a superabundance of the creative gesture he had also brought into existence a certain number of angels and powers. But he created no world. His own being, and that of the angels and powers who reinforced his being by knowing and acknowledging him, was sufficient. He only was; he knew nothing of himself. Then it happened that this all-sufficient god came to know one thing—that he was known. And then he wanted to know himself; he became dissatisfied with merely being. This constituted his fall. He united with one of his female attending angels, Sophia. The issue of that union was a child who was both male and female named Dianus.

The sect which adhered to this myth flourished about two thousand years ago. Its earliest devotees regarded Dianus as a usurper, a pretender, an evil god whose birth signified the corruption of the original godhead. But when the sect began to spread and win converts, the newer members tended to regard Dianus as the principal god, and to relegate Autogenes to the status of an ineffectual guarantee of the divinity of Dianus. More and more it was to Dianus that they turned. To him they could pray, in the hope of their salvation, while Autogenes remained distant and inaccessible. Dianus, unlike Autogenes, was not an altogether aloof god. But he had some of the traits of his father. Most of the time he slept on top of a mountain. Periodically he ventured forth among human beings to be worshipped, assailed, and martyred by them. Only in this way could he continue his divine sleep.

"Of course," observed Professor Bulgaraux, "I do not give credence to the magical arts which this sect practiced. Members of the Autogenist fellowship used to brand each other inside the lobe of the right ear. You may examine my right ear, Hippolyte. You will find only a small mole which I have had since birth."

Not understanding the application of this myth to me, I challenged the value of myth itself. "Such tales are just a sop for the credulous, picturesque concessions to those who cannot stand the shock of a naked idea."

"Are your dreams merely allegories?" returned Professor Bulgaraux. "Do you believe that they present themselves to you as stories because you can't bear the shock of a naked idea?"

"Certainly not! My dreams are no more or less than the story they tell."

"Would you be content to regard your dreams as poetry, if poetry be opposed to truth?"

"No."

"Then reflect, Hippolyte, and see if you do not find more than attractive poetry in this obscure mythology."

I agreed to try, and found that there was as much truth, and a truth quite similar in content, in the Autogenist myth as in my dreams. Were not my dreams about the ideal of self-sufficiency, and the inevitable fall into knowledge? If I had begun to feel martyred by them, was this not ingratitude? However painful they were, I needed my dreams—the metaphor for my introspection—if I was ever to be at peace. I liked very much that part of the myth which explained that the periodic martyrdom of Dianus was necessary, not for the salvation of men, but for the comfort and health of the god. Here was godmaking in its most dignified and candid form. Similarly, I was learning to regard my dreams not as producing any knowledge useful for others, but for myself, my own comfort and health alone. Here was dream interpreting in its most dignified and candid form.

In the Autogenist account of the creation of man, I found another clue to my dreams, particularly this last one, which I called "the dream of an elderly patron." The Autogenists believed that the human race is not created by the aloof father-god, nor by the somnolent and lovely Dianus. Rather, man owes his generation and allegiance to Sophia, the female agency, who took the form of a serpent; and as proof of this their teachers pointed to the shape of the human viscera. Our internal configuration in the form of a serpent—that is, the shape of the intestines—is the signature of our subtle generatrix. I was delighted with the idea. I would not have thought that among the body's juices and bones and crowded organs churning and pumping there was room for such an extravagant symbol—much more imaginative than the banal identification of the brain with thought, or the heart with love. When, in this last dream, I dreamed that my entrails were falling out, was I not dreaming that I was losing the signature of my humanity? It was a warning to me—of the guilt in my bowels, as Professor Bulgaraux put it.

I decided to lay aside my intellectual reservations, and hear further what Professor Bulgaraux had to say. If I was to escape the insupportable view that the dreams were an ultimately senseless burden foisted on me by my own malice toward myself, I would have to be purged of any residual attitudes by which I stood condemned in my own eyes . . . No matter that this was another "religious" interpretation. At least Professor Bulgaraux, unlike the good Father Trissotin, did not urge me to submit my dreams to judgment, but encouraged me to go on as I had been doing—grooming my life for the judgment of my dreams. If this was heresy, so be it. The most exacting forms of spirituality are usually found among heretics.

I thought I was already acquainted with all the heterodox movements available to the searcher for truth in this city and, as I have already indicated to the reader, I am not addicted to group enthusiasms. There are too many ill-thought-out sects in our century, too many partial revolutions inspired by little more than the vogue of being revolutionary. Yet I do not condemn heresy as such, if it be sincere enough, and I came to believe that Professor Bulgaraux really meant what he said.

On his invitation, I visited his apartment several times in the next month to hear him expound the views of the Autogenists. He had in his possession an ancient codex which had been found in an urn buried in a cemetery in the Near East. For many years he had been deciphering and preparing it for publication; these private seminars were, ostensibly, about the contents of the codex. Though there were always other auditors, a few curious academics and some middle-aged women with foreign accents whose occupation I could not determine, the meetings had a very different character from the university lectures I had once attended with such naïve zeal for enlightenment. A few simply took notes. But to those who listened eagerly to Professor Bulgaraux's words without paper and pencil in their hands, he made a point of interspersing personal remarks, showing his auditors how these ideas applied to each of them. As I looked about the room, I saw women who reminded me of Frau Anders. It stirred me to realize that Frau Anders might well—if she had ever heard of this group—have become one of Professor Bulgaraux's disciples. What was he expounding if not the idea of being liberated through contradicting one's settled life and unleashing one's deepest fantasies—the very thing which I had done when I disposed of Frau Anders?

I don't mean to give the impression that he sent the ladies off to murder their husbands, or eat candle wax, or steal from church poorboxes, or drink the semen of their poodles. However, the incitement to action which he offered was not a subtle one. I found it in remarkable agreement with my own instinct in these matters.

"Moderation is the sign of a mixed spiritual state," he said. But any act, he continued, might be performed moderately or immoderately. There are moderate murders and immoderate walks along the river.

You see, the Autogenist cosmology and plan of salvation entailed a whole code of conduct, or rather anti-conduct. Man was created by Sophia, the subtle generatrix, out of dark matter in which only a spark of Autogenes's pure light remained. But man, whom the Autogenist scripture calls "the subjacent dregs of matter," nevertheless can, by various rites of purification, ascend to heaven. Man can return to the bosom of Autogenes, if he becomes "light"—meaning, Professor Bulgaraux explained with a glance intended just for me, as much the absence of weight as luminousness. This purification does not take place through self-denial but through total self-expressiveness. Thus the Autogenists held that men cannot be saved until they have gone through all kinds of experience. An angel, they maintained, attends them in every one of their illegal actions, and urges them to commit their audacities. Whatever might be the nature of the action, they would declare that they did it in the name of the angel, saying: "O thou angel, I use thy work! O thou power, I accomplish thy operation." "They called this perfect knowledge," continued Professor Bulgaraux, "performing such actions as their critics blushed to name."

"There is no need to name them," cried one of the ladies of the enrapt circle. "Or to blush at naming them," I added to myself.

The Autogenist view that good and bad are only human opinion had nothing in common with the familiar modern disenchantment with morality. They intend this view as a means of salvation. As the result of moral distinctions is that, through them, we gain a personality, that is to say a weight, so the purpose of defying the moral law is to become weightless, to free the person from being only himself. Individual personalities must be neutralized in the acids of transgression.

Looking at Professor Bulgaraux's broad bespectacled face, his unkempt beard, his egg-stained vest, his baggy wrinkled suit, I could not determine whether I saw before me a paragon of anonymity or merely an unsuccessful zealot in all his picturesque and particular squalor. But if he had something true to teach me it did not matter what he was himself. "What is this personality that you advise us to lose?" I asked him at the last meeting I attended in his apartment. This was the only time that I dared to allude publicly to his more than scholarly attachment to the beliefs of the Autogenists, to take for granted that these were indeed his own beliefs.

"Lose it, and you will understand."

"Tell me how," I asked.

"Do you still dream?"

"More than ever."

"You've lost it," he cried, and each of the dozen or so other auditors rose from their upholstered chairs to shake my hand and congratulate me.

Yes, I still dreamed. Would that it were as simple as that! Nightly I lay in the sarcophagus of sleep, the man in the black bathing suit carved in stone on the coffin lid. But, like Dianus, I awoke restless, expectant. Sometimes it seemed as if my dreams were a parasite upon my life, other times that my life was a parasite on my dreams. I wanted to find the heart of my preoccupation. I wanted to escape from this personality which hedged me in, and clashed so sorely with my dreams. The divorce between my life and my dreams I came, through Professor Bulgaraux's instruction, to see precisely as a result of this thing—call it personality, character—which everyone around me seemed to cultivate and take pride in. I concluded that "personality" is simply the result of being off-balance. We have "characters" because we have not found our center of gravity. A personality is, at best, a way of meeting the problem of imbalance. But the problem remains. We do not accept ourselves for what we are, we retreat from our real selves, and then we erect a personality to bridge the gap.

Is not to have a personality just to define our points of vulnerability and strength? A personality is our way of being for others. We hope that others will meet us halfway or more, gratify our needs, be our audience, soothe our fears.

But how to escape having a personality? I should have liked to be Chinese for a while, to see if their fabled impassivity feels different, lighter, on the inside. But I could not change the color of my skin or the geography of my heart. Narcotics were equally out of the question. They had never supplied me, even temporarily, with this sense of imperturbability and lightness.

There is one well-advertised way of experiencing this loss of personality—the sex act. For a time I went often to prostitutes because I expected they would not pretend to be persons; at least their calling forbids it. In the carnal maneuvers of two people who have not been and will not be introduced to each other, a certain silence and lightness may prevail. But one may not count on it. The odor of personality—a photograph on the wall, a scar on the woman's thigh, a certain print dress in the closet, an appealing or contemptuous look on her face—is always seeping in. I learned not to expect too much from sexuality. Nevertheless, I understood why sexuality, like crime, is an imperishable resource of the impersonal. Properly performed, these acts do blunt the sense of self. It is, I think, because the end is fixed: in sexuality, the orgasm; in crime, the punishment. One becomes free precisely through those acts which have an inescapable end.

But for this purpose there is something even more valuable than sexuality and crime—and I testify from the experiences which I relate to you of a life at times libertine, a life in some respects criminal. That is the dream. Could it be that my dreams, which had been often a source of anguish and heaviness to me, were in fact the transparent medium whereby I would lose my tiresome personality? I had thought of the dreams as a foreign body in my flesh, against which I fended as best as I could. Now I was inclined to see them as a blessing. The dreams were grafted on my life, like a third eye in the middle of my forehead. With this eye, I could see more clearly than I ever had before. Jean-Jacques had warned me against my dreams, and my seriousness. Father Trissotin had urged me to confess and rid myself of them. Frau Anders had submitted to my dreams, but had understood them only as fantasies. Now Professor Bulgaraux had suggested to me that I might be proud of them. If I was losing something in the dreams, it was something I should be happy to lose. I was losing myself—losing the serpent that is inside, as shown in my last dream, "the dream of an elderly patron," which ended so graphically with the loss of my very entrails. I was becoming free, if only to be more exclusively a man-who-dreams. I knew that I did not yet understand the nature of freedom, but I had hopes that my dreams, with their painful images of enslavement and humiliation, would continue to elucidate it for me.

Most people consider dreams as the trash bin of the day: an occupation that is undisciplined, unproductive, asocial. I understand. I understand why most people regard their dreams as of little importance. They are too light for them, and most people identify the serious with what has weight. Tears are serious; one can collect them in a jar. But a dream, like a smile, is pure air. Dreams, like smiles, fade rapidly.

But what if the face faded away, and the smile remained? What if the life on which the dreams fed withered, and the dreams flourished? Why, one would really be free then, really lightened of one's burdens. Nothing can compare with it. We may wonder why we seek so meager a daily portion of that divine sensation of absence and soaring which rises from the commerce of the flesh to erase the world. We may well say of sexuality: what a promise of freedom it is, how astonishing that it is not outlawed.

I am surprised dreams are not outlawed. What a promise the dream is! How delightful! How private! And one needs no partner, one need not enlist the cooperation of anyone, female or male. Dreams are the onanism of the spirit.

Eight

I become an actor.

Lucrezia: another friendship.

Later news of Frau Anders.

On the proper narration of dreams.

I started keeping a journal in which I wrote down my dreams, ventured to interpret them, spun reveries around them. This work was made possible by the new leisure I obtained by giving up reading. I had discovered that the taste for print, and the ability to read rapidly, depend on a trained mental passivity. It would be an exaggeration to say that the bookish man does not think. But he thinks only up to a point; he must arrest his thoughts or else he could never pass beyond the first sentence. Because I did not want to miss even the faintest whisper or echo of my dreams, I determined to discontinue the habit of crowding my mind with the printed dreams of others. One day I cleared my room of most of my books and donated them to the public library of my native city. I retained as souvenirs some *lycée* textbooks on the inside of whose covers classmates had scribbled various affectionate or insulting messages. I also kept a Bible, a handbook on semaphore signals, a history of architecture, and the inscribed copies of his works which Jean-Jacques had given me.

I was no longer so ingenuous or so eager to share my ideas with others. You must not imagine that I had entirely lost the capacity to confide in my friends. But I had lost the confidence that they might teach me something I did not already know. Thus, I saw less of Jean-Jacques, who continued to treat me as a novice in any matter we discussed.

Young Lucrezia had succeeded her not greatly lamented mother as my companion and prospective mistress. (No one, not even her husband, exerted himself greatly over Frau Anders's disappearance.) I

worried about my growing tendency to irascibility, and made a considerable effort to be less demanding of Lucrezia than I had been of
her mother. This was made easier by the fact that she was not in love
with me, nor I with her. I was happy when with Lucrezia, but she
was a luxury that I was not sure I deserved. Nothing really interested
me as much as my presumptuous dreams. And I felt a certain reluctance, perhaps it was selfishness, to initiate Lucrezia into my secrets.

However, the waning pleasures of friendship, as well as thinking
and writing about my dreams, were not at that time all of which I
was capable. I was a young man still, and it was natural for me to
translate part of my restlessness into activity. Amid all my inner perplexities, I also wanted to live more actively—with the proviso that I
not bind myself to any useful, remunerative, or self-advancing occupation. It was thus that, in place of a life of action, I settled for a brief
career as an actor. Through the group of people formerly collected by
Frau Anders and now presided over by her daughter Lucrezia, I met
a number of independent filmmakers and began to work with them.
My first job was rewriting scripts for a young photographer who was
doing some short films on night life in the capital. Four were made:
one about the barges that ply up and down the river, one about two
lovers on the Metro at midnight, one on the prefecture of police, and
one on the Arab quarter near the university. Then I wrote a screen-
play of my own, about a nun. It was filmed, though the changes and
excisions did not have my approval. Work on this script took over a
year; I write very slowly. During this time I also had several small
acting parts.

Eventually, as an actor rather than a writer, I graduated to the
commercial cinema. This was the first decade of sound films, and
although foreign directors can claim preeminence during the silent
period, at this time my country's cinema was, I think, the best. I
never had or aspired to leading parts, but I at least avoided being
typecast. I played the butler and the jilted suitor in two romantic
comedies, the older brother in a family melodrama, and the patriotic
schoolteacher in a film about the conscription of schoolboys at the
close of the First World War.

In performing a role, I liked to imagine myself inserting a surrep-
titious footnote to the audience. When I was supposed to play a good-
hearted lover, I tried to insert a promise of cruelty in my embrace.
When I played the villain, I hinted at tenderness. When I crawled, I
imagined I was flying. When I danced, I was a cripple.

The need to contradict, at least in my private thoughts, seems to
have grown on me during that period. While in my daily comport-

ment I rarely contradicted the wishes of others, except when I was entirely convinced that I was in the right, every word I heard made me think of its opposite. This was why acting was so felicitous an occupation for me. Acting was a happy compromise between word and deed. A role could be condensed into a single word or phrase; a word or phrase could be expanded into a role. "Butler!" "I do not love you." "Liberty, equality, fraternity"—to give but a few examples. And while I played the role, enunciated the word or phrase, I could think of its opposite with impunity.

Eventually, of course, I could not help but wish for roles which would themselves exemplify these contradictions. I wanted to play a fat African, whose flat cavernous nostrils twitch in disgust at the floral scent of a white woman. I wanted to play a painter, blind from birth, who hears the murmur of colors in his paint tubes and considers himself a musician. I wanted to play a rotund and genial politician who, when his prosperous country's farmlands are afflicted with drought, sends the nation's grain reserves as a gift to the starving millions of India. Such roles, unfortunately, are not often available. There is a need for more writers to create them. Jean-Jacques could have written parts like these, if he had wanted to; but his art was in the service of other ideals—an idea of comedy, both measured and extravagant, which I have always been either too solemn or not finely tuned enough to appreciate.

Why did I not write such roles myself? you may ask. And why did I give myself to acting? Though I was approaching my thirtieth birthday, it was not that I suddenly felt the lack of a profession. No, the truth was that I was enjoying myself (I am capable of enjoying myself in many ways). I must not omit, however, that the enjoyment was somewhat tainted by vanity. Vanity surely played a part in my preferring acting in films to the theater. But I enjoyed the fact that in a film the role and my performance were indissoluble, one and the same; while, in the theater, the same role has been and will be performed by many actors. (Are the films in this respect more like life than is the stage?) Also—another incentive to vanity—what one does in a film is recorded and as imperishable as celluloid; while performances in the theater are without record.

I also preferred the cinema to the theater because there is no audience present except one's working colleagues, and no applause. In fact, not only is there no audience, there is really no acting either. Acting in films is not like acting in a play, which is, whatever the interruptions of rehearsal, in performance continuous, cumulative, and replete with consummated movement and emotion. What is called acting in the films is, on the contrary, much closer to stillness, to posing for a sequence of still photographs like those in monthly *roman-photos* read by shop girls and housewives. In a film every scene is subdivided into dozens of separate shots, each of which entails no more than a line or two of dialogue, a single expression on the actor's face. The camera creates motion, animates these brief frozen moments—like the eye of the dreamer inhabiting and at the same time being a spectator to his own dreams.

I find the cinema a much more rigorous art than the theater; and one which gave me a profound analogue to the way of behaving whose initial model came from my dreams. I don't mean that watching a film, in a darkened theater which one can enter on the spur of the moment without prior appointment, is like entering a dream. I am not talking about the dream-like freedom which the camera has with time and space. I speak here not of the spectator's experience but of the actor's: in acting in the films, one must forget passion, and replace it by a sort of extreme coldness. This is easy, even necessary, because the scenes are not filmed consecutively; the actor before the camera is not propelled by the quasi-natural emotions which accumulate in the course of any single performance of a play.

The only advantage I could see which the theater has over the cinema is that one can repeat the same role night after night—more times than the number of takes a director requires before he is satisfied that he has a shot he can print. And while in each take the actor tries to improve his performance (a period corresponding to rehearsals in the theater), once the actor has done it correctly the shot is concluded. In the theater, once the actor has learned to do it correctly, he is ready to begin to do it over and over as long as there is an audience for the play. This is the final analogue between acting and my dreams. Those things we do well are those we do over and over, and best are those which have themselves an essentially monotonous form: dancing, making love, playing a musical instrument. I was fortunate in that the activity of dreaming had for me this character. There was enough time and repetitiveness for me to become good at it. I became a good dreamer, while I never became an outstanding actor.

Through my cinemaphile friends, I made the acquaintance of Larsen, the well-known Scandinavian director, who was casting a film based on the life of a fascinating personage in my country's history. This person, whom no doubt most of my readers can identify, was a nobleman, of ample fortune and aristocratic title, who as a young man fought alongside the devout peasant girl who freed the nation from a hated invader, and somewhat later in life was denounced as an apostate, heretic, and criminal. For his apostasy, for heresy, and for crimes which included having lured to his castle, violated, and murdered hundreds of children, he was tried and sent to the scaffold. Before his execution he repented fully and most movingly of his crimes, and was forgiven by the Church and mourned by the populace.

I read the script, and expressed strong interest in the project. Larsen had me audition for the role of the confessor who is assigned to the nobleman after his arrest. He liked my performance and engaged me. I would have preferred a smaller part—say, one of the judges—which would have taken less of my time, but Larsen insisted that my face was exactly as he imagined the face of the zealous priest who procures the nobleman's repentance.

Work on this film occupied me for the next half year. We went on location to the south, and most of the film was made in a small farming village in the neighborhood of the nobleman's castle, the very castle, now in ruins and visited only by truant schoolboys and adolescent lovers, to which he had brought his victims many centuries ago. Social life in this town was dull. I had a tender affair with the mayor's daughter, whom I used to meet clandestinely in an abandoned barn on the edge of the town. I also passed time with the village priest, arguing about religion and politics. But it was difficult to escape the company of my colleagues. There was only one small hotel in the town, and the actors and entire production staff lived there. It became virtually a dormitory. The director, cameraman, script girl, and cast would meet each morning for breakfast to discuss the day's shooting, and in the evening sit together in the parlor to listen to the hotel's radio, one of the few in the entire town, for news of the civil war which was raging at the time in the country to the south.

I got along with the other members of the company, in particular with Larsen and his pleasant young wife. The one exception was the makeup man, who on the first day of the shooting schedule took a dislike to me. We were to begin with a scene in which the nobleman is led through the village to the place of execution; the cameraman wanted morning light, so the cast had to arrive at six o'clock to be made up in order to get the first take no later than nine. I arrived promptly, but the moment I sat down in the chair in the basement room of the grain warehouse where our props and costumes were stored, and the man in charge of makeup examined my face, he grimaced and began complaining under his breath. For an hour he labored over me to apply a small amount of rouge and powder, for, he told me, I was a hopeless case: I had a type of skin, not too rare but thankfully uncommon in the acting profession, which resisted the application of makeup. "Your skin is matte," he said.

"This is my only face," I replied sarcastically.

"The director won't like it. But he can't blame me."

"Nobody will blame you," I told him.

I had been told something of the sort by makeup men in other films in which I had worked, but never in so surly a manner. Needless to say, my non-absorbent face caused no difficulty that morning.

The actual making of the film went smoothly, though it is difficult to see progress when one proceeds so piecemeal. We worked in a jungle of ladders, scaffolding, cables on the floor, lights and gauze shades for the lights, mimeographed copies of the script, stacks of free cigarettes, and bottles of wine for the crew. We seemed, as befitted a historical spectacle, a multitude. Besides over twoscore of staff, film crew, and principal actors, extras were recruited from the town, as well as tanned, bare-chested men and boys in khaki shorts and sneakers to haul the camera, lights, and props about, and to bring lunch to us while we were shooting. The only still point in all this activity was Mme Larsen, the director's wife, who spent most of each day in a corner of the set knitting first a beige sweater and then a blanket.

There was some trouble with the investors in the capital, who had chronic doubts about the film's commercial soundness. Everyone on the set learned to respect Larsen's scowl when he was brought his mail at four o'clock each afternoon, sat apart to read it, then stuffed it in the back pocket of his knickers. He also was frequently called to the hotel for long-distance telephone calls. Whatever pressures were being put on him, though, I felt it was principally due to his own indecision that it took as long as it did (seventy-three days of shooting spread over a period of four and a half months) to finish the film. We arrived with a complete shooting script, but he was continually making changes, and much of the breakfast conferences were wasted in debate over sexual motives and theological ideas. I played a modest role in these discussions, and can take some credit for keeping the film from turning into an anti-clerical tract. For Larsen, who had written the script, could not decide how to represent the nobleman. Some mornings he would threaten to halt production so he could rewrite the whole middle of the script, to show that the nobleman was entirely innocent of the extraordinary crimes of which he was accused. At least, he wanted to exonerate the offending nobleman—

as a man broken by the torments which an overscrupulous conscience imposes upon an unconventional sexual temperament.

"He must have been a very passionate man," mused the director. "Antoine," he said, turning to the actor who was playing the nobleman, "you must get more of that into your performance."

I demurred. "I imagine him as very serene," I said. "Such a great quantity of victims testifies to an immensity of appetite which amounts to indifference."

Everyone at the table disagreed with me. "How could anyone be so cruel!" exclaimed the short-haired young woman who was playing the patriot. "Think of all those little children."

I tried to explain. "I don't think the nobleman illustrates the extreme of cruelty of which human nature is capable. He illustrates the problem of satiety. Don't you see? All acts are undertaken in the hope of their consequences. What passes for being satiated is simply the arrival at the consequences—the fulfillment—of one's act. But sometimes the moral atmosphere becomes clogged. There is a backlog of consequences. It takes a long time for the consequences to catch up with the act. Then one must go on repeating oneself, and boring others, in the interval between act and consequences. This is when people say he is insatiable. And sometimes—very rarely to be sure— there are no consequences, and one has the impression of not being alive at all."

"You're trying to exonerate him, too," said the script girl.

"No, not at all," I replied. "I would be the first to agree that he should have been executed. For who would act as he did except for the purpose of incurring punishment? It's just that he was very literal-minded. He repeated himself—that is, his crimes—extravagantly. He became a machine. The only questions for me"—I turned to address Larsen—"are these. With each repetition, with each revolution of the machine, did he become less oppressed, until it was as nothing for him eventually to confess and to be sent to his death? Or would he have been satisfied with one murder, if he had been caught?"

"Go on," said Larsen. "I see you have given the matter much thought."

"What does it mean for someone to murder three hundred children, when one murder more than suffices most people?" I said. "Did this man have three hundred times the capacity for murder that you and I have? Or does it not rather suggest that for him one murder could only weigh one three-hundredth of what it does for an ordinary person?"

I do not remember the rest of the discussion, except that I was overruled when I made some specific suggestions for changing the script. My colleagues, understandably, did not share my desire to re-shape this fascinating subject in the languorous style of my dreams. But I would still argue that Larsen's interpretation was lacking in imaginativeness. To my taste, he devoted too much of the film to the nobleman's association with the adolescent patriot; and in the final scenes he failed to do justice to the astonishing procession in which the sodomist and mass murderer was followed to the scaffold by hundreds of weeping citizens, many of them the parents of his tiny victims.

Why did they weep? Could it be because his crimes had somehow the odor of sanctity? More exactly, that the nobleman was a convert to certain heretical religious ideas, which prompted and even sancti-fied his abominable crimes? And that peasant girl, the national her-oine of my country—I argued that his association with her did not partly redeem him, as Larsen would have it. On the contrary. Was not the girl herself brought to trial and burned at the stake? The virgin and the child-murderer, these two persons so opposite in the judgment of history and apparently connected only by the exploits of battle, did have something in common; namely, heresy, the principal charge (be it remembered) in both trials. Both were accused of her-esy first, of insurrection and crime only secondarily. Is it possible that both were punished for something never disclosed in either trial? Ac-cording to Professor Bulgaraux, who sent me several convincing let-ters on the subject, both were volunteer scapegoats of an under-ground cult whose doctrines bear some resemblance to the ideas of the Autogenists.

But if this is so, then one must say that of the two it was the no-bleman who better fulfilled the sacred mission of defiling himself in the eyes of the world. The peasant girl, though she wore men's cloth-ing and heard voices and went into battle, could not avoid being made into a saint by the church which condemned her. But no church, however imaginative, could canonize the nobleman. Thus, to make his crimes issue from sexual distress, as Larsen would have it, showed the greatest lack of moral tact. His crimes were monstrous because they were real, whatever the motive. Don't exonerate him, I urged Larsen. Respect his choice and don't try to turn evil into good. Let nothing be interpreted. No part of the modern sensibility is more tire-some than its eagerness to excuse and to have one thing always mean something else!

By these reflections, I was moved to adopt a new attitude while before the camera. For once in my brief acting career, I played a role without duplicity. I played the priest as though I had nothing but his words in my head, his compassion and horror inscribed on my face. When I pleaded with the nobleman to repent, I truly prayed that his crimes could be undone and all the little children be restored to their mothers. I hoped that the actor who played the nobleman thought of those crimes as real. How else could he pretend to commit them, repent of them, or die for them?

My performance in this film was my last work as an actor. It is not for me to say whether it was my best, though the reader may perhaps have an opportunity to judge for himself, since the film is still often shown by film societies. All that is important to mention now is that my new attitude toward acting, in which I wanted to be without reservation or inner distraction the character I was playing, had abolished the value of acting for me. There was no point in being someone else, if I were really to be someone else. For then I might just as well be myself. Besides, the work was demanding and left me less time than I wished for the occupations of solitude.

I returned to the capital after the conclusion of the film, and took a room near the great market in the center of the city. This was furnished, or rather unfurnished, in the same way as my old place. Lucrezia became again my constant companion, and I shared with her the ideas about good and evil which arose from my audiences with Professor Bulgaraux and my part in the film about the nobleman. She had a quiet, independent intelligence and could never have needed any liberating counsel from her mother. One day, however, something happened which changed our friendship, or rather, prevented our friendship from changing. She had come to my room directly from the hairdresser, and after admiring her coiffure and thinking of taking her into my arms, I had offered her a drink and we had begun to talk.

"Hippolyte," she said, breaking into our conversation which was about the Offending Nobleman, as Lucrezia and I called him, "do you ever think of Mother?"

"Yes," I replied truthfully, "I do."

"I know Mother liked you very much." I reached for her hand, sympathetically. "Do you think it's very wicked of me not to miss her?"

"I'm sure she is happy, wherever she is," I said.

"I do hope so," said Lucrezia. "Because I have received a letter which purports to be from her—although Mother had always a rather elegant script and this letter is unevenly written, on soiled brown paper. This letter, Hippolyte"—she grasped my hand warmly—"contains many curious reproaches, directed to you as well as to me."

"Tell me about them," I said.

"Oh, Hippolyte, I didn't think Mother loved you." She brushed some moisture from one eye.

"But surely you knew . . ."

"Yes, yes," she said hurriedly. "But I didn't know you went away with her. She says she is so angry with you she will not come back. She says that she imagines I, too, am happier without her. And that she is very happy where she is. Oh, my dear, she does not sound at all happy, does she?"

"I think she has every reason to be happy," I said, "if the fulfillment of a powerful fantasy ever brings happiness."

"Only it would be most unlike Mother to be happy, Hippolyte. She is not that sort of person. Perhaps it isn't Mother, after all. The person who wrote the letter signs herself Scheherazade."

"It is your mother, I am sure."

"But do you know how she is living now? The letter doesn't give any details."

"When last I saw her," I explained, "she had entered the household of an Arab merchant who greatly desired her. This seemed to be the perfect solution to her perennial dissatisfactions. You remember, do you not, the letters she wrote you?"

"Yes! Were you with her when she wrote those embarrassing letters, Hippolyte? Did you read them? Oh, but I'm becoming jealous again! The letters were very touching, weren't they?"

"Your mother wanted to try a way of life entirely different from the one she led here, Lucrezia, but she didn't have the courage to discard this life by herself. She had to be helped."

"Pushed."

"She wanted to be pushed."

"Oh, Hippolyte, sometimes I wish you would push me!"

"You are not at all like your mother," I reminded her.

"Yes," she said, "that's true. I don't long for the primitive, as Mother did. Life in this careful city is already too primitive for me."

"Does your mother ask for money?"

"She hints at ransom. She says she's a prisoner of love. That sounds as if we could coax her to come back."

"Would you allow me to donate the sum of thirteen thousand francs toward her return?"

"Hippolyte, that will pay for ten returns! Why so much?"

"Because that was the amount for which I sold her. I did not dare take less, for fear the merchant would not value her properly."

And for a while the conversation turned to the question of how money may operate to create value as well as to measure it.

"I am very fond of money," Lucrezia said in a self-congratulatory tone. "While Mother, who is more generous than I, will only give the money to her lover. Perhaps she will buy him a herd of camels with it."

Frowning at her snobbery, I said, "I give you the money in her name." I went to a drawer, and handed the sum to her, still in the merchant's envelope, with a feeling of relief. I should never have liked it to appear that money played anything but an aesthetic role in that curious incident.

"I begin to think you were very fond of my mother," Lucrezia said, taking off her gloves to count the bills, and then putting them in her bag.

I became annoyed. "She was most generous with herself to me," I said.

"Nonsense!"

I was astonished at the way Lucrezia persisted in this scene of jealousy which I could not believe was sincere.

"What do you want from me, Lucrezia?"

"Nothing," she said, reddening. It embarrassed her to discover herself seeking intimacy instead of conferring it.

When she said she wanted nothing from me, I resolved to give nothing more than I had thus far. For some time I had been in doubt about my friendship with Lucrezia. My restrained conduct with her testifies to that. I was not unaware that there was something unseemly in my inheriting the daughter after enjoying the mother; and considerations of good taste, although not in the way they did with my friend Jean-Jacques, have always weighed strongly with me. Now I saw that there was no reason for us to be more to each other than we already were. Who knows what perverse impulses lay behind Lucrezia's feeling for me, which I had up to that point taken for granted, being accustomed at that age and state of good looks to the attention of women.

Lucrezia and I continued talking until dark, and then went out to stroll by the river. We were speaking then, as I recall, of how coarsely praise and blame are distributed in the world. We agreed that many bad things are commonly praised, and many good things are censured.

"Do you admire effort?" I asked. "Do you esteem feelings which correct themselves, and behavior which does not rest until it is different?"

"No," she replied, "I don't admire effort. I admire excellence, which is less accomplished when it results from effort. And less graceful, too."

For a moment, I wondered why I was set on rejecting the affection of this intelligent woman with whom I shared so many ideas. Whenever we disagreed, as now, I enjoyed her even more.

"And beauty?" I asked. Lucrezia had blond hair, china-blue eyes, and very fine features.

"Oh, yes. I forgive anything that is beautiful."

"I don't see why we should praise beauty," I replied thoughtfully. "It's too easy to learn from the world what is beautiful and what is not. We should allow ourselves to find beautiful anything which holds our complete interest—those things, and only those things, no matter how disfigured and terrifying."

"In short," she said quizzically, "the only thing you admire is what preoccupies you."

"I admire the preoccupying. I respect the preoccupied."

"Nothing else! Where is love? Fear? Remorse?"

"Nothing else."

After this conversation adjourned, I dismissed Lucrezia from my thoughts as anything other than a graceful and urbane friend. The specter of her mother had risen between us, and I could not bear the thought of any rivalry between the two women, either in Lucrezia's mind or in mine. Although we continued to meet, often to go to the films together, Lucrezia accepted the stasis in our friendship and turned her amorous interest to more promising candidates.

For the months that followed, I find more dreams in my notebooks and a greater serenity in their interpretation. My effort was less, my attention greater. I still pursued the same preoccupations, but I learned from the dreams how to pursue them better. The dreams taught me the secret of perpetual presentness, and freed me from the desire to adorn my life and my conversation.

Let me explain. Imagine that something happens—say, an act of assault—and someone comes in immediately afterwards.

"What happened?" asks the visitor.

"Help!" Moans, cries, and so forth.

"What happened?"

"They . . . came . . . through the window." More moans.

"And then?" says the visitor.

"They . . . hit me . . . with an ax."

In these first moments, the bleeding victim is not interested in persuading anyone of the reality of the event. It has just occurred, and he cannot imagine how anyone could doubt it. Should anyone doubt the story, he has his wounds to show. No, even this would not occur to him. Should anyone doubt the story, he would not care, as long as a doctor is sent for. His wounds would be companions enough.

It is not until later, when the wounds have begun to heal, that the victim wants to talk. And as the event becomes more distant in time, the victim—healed and restored to the bosom of his family—gives it dramatic form. He embellishes his narrative and sets it to music. He puts drums in the background. The ax gleams. He sees the whites of the man's eyes. He tells his children that the attacker wore a blue scarf. "And he sprang through the window with a great noise," says the aging and healthy victim to his children. "He raised his arm and I was terrified and . . ."

Why has he become so verbose? Because he no longer has the companionship of his pain. He has only an audience, whose attentiveness he doubts. In telling the story he is attempting to convince his audience that "it" really happened, that it was like this, that he felt violent emotions and was in great danger. He craves reassurance. He also learns he can collect from the telling—money, respect, sympathy. With time, the event is not quite real to him, to whom it happened. He believes less in the reality of the assault; more real to him are all the ways he has found to describe it. His narrative becomes persuasive.

But in the beginning, when the assault was real, when it did not occur to him to persuade anyone, his narration was laconic and honorable.

This is what I learned from dreams. Dreams always have the quality of being present—even when, as I am doing, one related them ten, twenty, thirty years after. They do not age, or become less credible; they are what they are. The loyal dreamer does not seek his hearer's credence, he does not need to convince his hearer that such and such amazing thing happened in the dream. Since all events in the dream are equally fantastic, they are independent of the assent of other people. This reveals, by the way, the falsity of that line which people of taste insist on drawing and redrawing between the banal and the extraordinary. All events in dreams are extraordinary, and banal, at the same time.

In dreams, assaults happen. We kill, we fall, we fly, we rape. But things are as they are. We accept them in the dream; they are irrevocable, though often without consequences. When someone disappears from the stage of the dream, one does not in the dream wonder where he has gone. Anyone relating his dream who says "The clerk left me at the counter. I believe he went to consult his supervisor about my request" is telling the dream wrong. He is not being honest: he is trying to persuade. One says, "I was at the counter talking to a clerk. Then I was alone."

I should like to describe my life to you with the same evenness that one recounts one's dreams. Such a narration would be the only honest one. If I have not entirely succeeded in doing this, at least I continue to aim at this goal as I write. I have tried not to extract from my life any excitement which it does not yield of itself, or to overstimulate the reader with names and dates, with tiresome descriptions of my own person and appearance, of those whom I knew, with the furniture of rooms, the progress of wars, the swirl of cigarette smoke, and other matters which took place concurrently with the encounters and conversations I have reported. That only one passion, or one idea, be made clear is task enough to fill a hundred volumes— and beyond my powers to do more, in these pages, than to suggest.

• • • • •

(1963)

FROM

Against
Interpretation

Simone Weil

The culture heroes of our liberal bourgeois civilization are anti-liberal and anti-bourgeois; they are writers who are repetitive, obsessive, and impolite, who impress by force—not simply by their tone of personal authority and by their intellectual ardor, but by the sense of acute personal and intellectual extremity. The bigots, the hysterics, the destroyers of the self—these are the writers who bear witness to the fearful polite time in which we live. Mostly it is a matter of tone: it is hardly possible to give credence to ideas uttered in the impersonal tones of sanity. There are certain eras which are too complex, too deafened by contradictory historical and intellectual experiences, to hear the voice of sanity. Sanity becomes compromise, evasion, a lie. Ours is an age which consciously pursues health, and yet only believes in the reality of sickness. The truths we respect are those born of affliction. We measure truth in terms of the cost to the writers in suffering—rather than by the standard of an objective truth to which a writer's words correspond. Each of our truths must have a martyr.

What revolted the mature Goethe in the young Kleist, who submitted his works to the elder statesman of German letters "on the knees of his heart"—the morbid, the hysterical, the sense of the unhealthy, the enormous indulgence in suffering out of which Kleist's plays and tales were mined—is just what we value today. Today Kleist gives pleasure, most of Goethe is a classroom bore. In the same way, such writers as Kierkegaard, Nietzsche, Dostoevsky, Kafka, Baudelaire, Rimbaud, Genet—and Simone Weil—have their authority with us precisely because of their air of unhealthiness. Their unhealthiness is their soundness, and is what carries conviction.

Perhaps there are certain ages which do not need truth as much as they need a deepening of the sense of reality, a widening of the imagination. I, for one, do not doubt that the sane view of the world is the true one. But is that what is always wanted, truth? The need for truth is not constant; no more than is the need for repose. An idea which is a distortion may have a greater intellectual thrust than the truth; it may better serve the needs of the spirit, which vary. The truth is balance, but the opposite of truth, which is unbalance, may not be a lie.

Thus I do not mean to decry a fashion, but to underscore the motive behind the contemporary taste for the extreme in art and thought. All that is necessary is that we not be hypocritical, that we recognize why we read and admire writers like Simone Weil. I cannot believe that more than a handful of the tens of thousands of readers she has won since the posthumous publication of her books and essays really share her ideas. Nor is it necessary—necessary to share Simone Weil's anguished and unconsummated love affair with the Catholic Church, or accept her gnostic theology of divine absence, or espouse her ideals of body denial, or concur in her violently unfair hatred of Roman civilization and the Jews. Similarly, with Kierkegaard and Nietzsche; most of their modern admirers could not, and do not, embrace their ideas. We read writers of such scathing originality for their personal authority, for the example of their seriousness, for their manifest willingness to sacrifice themselves for their truths, and—only piecemeal—for their "views." As the corrupt Alcibiades followed Socrates, unable and unwilling to change his own life, but moved, enriched, and full of love, so the sensitive modern reader pays his respect to a level of spiritual reality which is not, could not, be his own.

Some lives are exemplary, others not; and of exemplary lives, there are those which invite us to imitate them, and those which we regard from a distance with a mixture of revulsion, pity, and reverence. It is, roughly, the difference between the hero and the saint (if one may use the latter term in an aesthetic rather than a religious sense). Such a life, absurd in its exaggerations and degree of self-mutilation— like Kleist's, like Kierkegaard's—was Simone Weil's. I am thinking of the fanatical asceticism of Simone Weil's life, her contempt for pleasure and for happiness, her noble and ridiculous political gestures, her elaborate self-denials, her tireless courting of affliction; and I do not exclude her homeliness, her physical clumsiness, her migraines, her tuberculosis. No one who loves life would wish to imitate her dedication to martyrdom, or would wish it for his children or for anyone else whom he loves. Yet so far as we love seriousness, as well as life, we are moved by it, nourished by it. In the respect we pay to such lives, we acknowledge the presence of mystery in the world— and mystery is just what the secure possession of the truth, an objective truth, denies. In this sense, all truth is superficial; and some (but not all) distortions of the truth, some (but not all) insanity, some (but not all) unhealthiness, some (but not all) denials of life are truth-giving, sanity-producing, health-creating, and life-enhancing.

(1963)

Against Interpretation

Content is a glimpse of something, an encounter like a flash. It's very tiny—very tiny, content.

WILLEM DE KOONING,
in an interview

It is only shallow people who do not judge by appearances. The mystery of the world is the visible, not the invisible.

OSCAR WILDE,
in a letter

I

The earliest experience of art must have been that it was incantatory, magical; art was an instrument of ritual. (Cf. the paintings in the caves at Lascaux, Altamira, Niaux, La Pasiega, etc.) The earliest *theory* of art, that of the Greek philosophers, proposed that art was mimesis, imitation of reality.

It is at this point that the peculiar question of the value of art arose. For the mimetic theory, by its very terms, challenges art to justify itself.

Plato, who proposed the theory, seems to have done so in order to rule that the value of art is dubious. Since he considered ordinary material things as themselves mimetic objects, imitations of transcendent forms or structures, even the best painting of a bed would be only an "imitation of an imitation." For Plato, art is neither particularly useful (the painting of a bed is no good to sleep on) nor, in the strict sense, true. And Aristotle's arguments in defense of art do not really challenge Plato's view that all art is an elaborate *trompe l'oeil*, and therefore a lie. But he does dispute Plato's idea that art is useless. Lie or no, art has a certain value according to Aristotle because it is a form of therapy. Art is useful, after all, Aristotle counters, medicinally useful in that it arouses and purges dangerous emotions.

In Plato and Aristotle, the mimetic theory of art goes hand in hand with the assumption that art is always figurative. But advocates of the mimetic theory need not close their eyes to decorative and abstract art. The fallacy that art is necessarily a "realism" can be modified or scrapped without ever moving outside the problems delimited by the mimetic theory.

The fact is, all Western consciousness of and reflection upon art have remained within the confines staked out by the Greek theory of art as mimesis or representation. It is through this theory that art as such—above and beyond given works of art—becomes problematic, in need of defense. And it is the defense of art which gives birth to the odd vision by which something we have learned to call "form" is separated off from something we have learned to call "content," and to the well-intentioned move which makes content essential and form accessory.

Even in modern times, when most artists and critics have discarded the theory of art as representation of an outer reality in favor of the theory of art as subjective expression, the main feature of the mimetic theory persists. Whether we conceive of the work of art on the model of a picture (art as a picture of reality) or on the model of a statement (art as the statement of the artist), content still comes first. The content may have changed. It may now be less figurative, less lucidly realistic. But it is still assumed that a work of art *is* its content. Or, as it's usually put today, that a work of art by definition says something. ("What X is saying is . . ." "What X is trying to say is . . ." "What X said is . . ." etc., etc.)

II

None of us can ever retrieve that innocence before all theory when art knew no need to justify itself, when one did not ask of a work of art what it said because one knew (or thought one knew) what it did. From now to the end of consciousness, we are stuck with the task of defending art. We can only quarrel with one or another means of defense. Indeed, we have an obligation to overthrow any means of defending and justifying art which becomes particularly obtuse or onerous or insensitive to contemporary needs and practice.

This is the case, today, with the very idea of content itself. Whatever it may have been in the past, the idea of content is today mainly a hindrance, a nuisance, a subtle or not so subtle philistinism.

Though the actual developments in many arts may seem to be leading us away from the idea that a work of art is primarily its content, the idea still exerts an extraordinary hegemony. I want to suggest that this is because the idea is now perpetuated in the guise of a certain way of encountering works of art thoroughly ingrained among most people who take any of the arts seriously. What the overemphasis on the idea of content entails is the perennial, never-consummated project of *interpretation*. And, conversely, it is the habit of approaching works of art in order to *interpret* them that sustains the fancy that there really is such a thing as the content of a work of art.

III

Of course, I don't mean interpretation in the broadest sense, the sense in which Nietzsche (rightly) says, "There are no facts, only interpretations." By interpretation, I mean here a conscious act of the mind which illustrates a certain code, certain "rules" of interpretation.

Directed to art, interpretation means plucking a set of elements (the X, the Y, the Z, and so forth) from the whole work. The task of interpretation is virtually one of translation. The interpreter says, Look, don't you see that X is really—or, really means—A? That Y is really B? That Z is really C?

What situation could prompt this curious project for transforming a text? History gives us the materials for an answer. Interpretation first appears in the culture of late classical antiquity, when the power and credibility of myth had been broken by the "realistic" view of the world introduced by scientific enlightenment. Once the question that haunts post-mythic consciousness—that of the *seemliness* of religious symbols—had been asked, the ancient texts were, in their pristine form, no longer acceptable. Then interpretation was summoned, to reconcile the ancient texts to "modern" demands. Thus, the Stoics, to accord with their view that the gods had to be moral, allegorized away the rude features of Zeus and his boisterous clan in Homer's epics. What Homer really designated by the adultery of Zeus with Leto, they explained, was the union between power and wisdom. In the same vein, Philo of Alexandria interpreted the literal historical narratives of the Hebrew Bible as spiritual paradigms. The story of the exodus from Egypt, the wandering in the desert for forty years, and the entry into the promised land, said Philo, was really an allegory of the individual soul's emancipation, tribulations, and final deliverance. Interpretation thus presupposes a discrepancy between the clear meaning of the text and the demands of (later) readers. It seeks to resolve that discrepancy. The situation is that for some reason a text has become unacceptable; yet it cannot be discarded. Interpretation is a radical strategy for conserving an old text, which is thought too precious to repudiate, by revamping it. The interpreter, without actually erasing or rewriting the text, *is* altering it. But he can't admit to doing this. He claims to be only making it intelligible, by disclosing its true meaning. However far the interpreters alter the text (another notorious example is the rabbinic and Christian "spiritual" interpretations of the clearly erotic Song of Songs), they must claim to be reading off a sense that is already there.

Interpretation in our own time, however, is even more complex. For the contemporary zeal for the project of interpretation is often prompted not by piety toward the troublesome text (which may conceal an aggression) but by an open aggressiveness, an overt contempt for appearances. The old style of interpretation was insistent, but respectful; it erected another meaning on top of the literal one. The modern style of interpretation excavates, and as it excavates, destroys; it digs "behind" the text, to find a sub-text which is the true one. The most celebrated and influential modern doctrines, those of Marx and Freud, actually amount to elaborate systems of hermeneutics, aggressive and impious theories of interpretation. All observable phenomena are bracketed, in Freud's phrase, as *manifest content*. This manifest content must be probed and pushed aside to find the true meaning—the *latent content*—beneath. For Marx, social events like revolutions and wars; for Freud, the events of individual lives (like neurotic symptoms and slips of the tongue) as well as texts (like a dream or a work of art)—all are treated as occasions for interpretation. According to Marx and Freud, these events only *seem* to be intelligible. Actually, they have no meaning without interpretation. To understand *is* to interpret. And to interpret is to restate the phenomenon, in effect to find an equivalent for it.

Thus, interpretation is not (as most people assume) an absolute value, a gesture of mind situated in some timeless realm of capabilities. Interpretation must itself be evaluated, within a historical view of human consciousness. In some cultural contexts, interpretation is a liberating act. It is a means of revising, of transvaluing, of escaping the dead past. In other cultural contexts, it is reactionary, impertinent, cowardly, stifling.

IV

Today is such a time, when the project of interpretation is largely reactionary, stifling. Like the fumes of the automobile and of heavy industry which befoul the urban atmosphere, the effusion of interpretations of art today poisons our sensibilities. In a culture whose already classical dilemma is the hypertrophy of the intellect at the expense of energy and sensual capability, interpretation is the revenge of the intellect upon art.

Even more. It is the revenge of the intellect upon the world. To interpret is to impoverish, to deplete the world—in order to set up a shadow world of "meanings." It is to turn *the* world into *this* world. ("This world"! As if there were any other.)

The world, our world, is depleted, impoverished enough. Away with all duplicates of it, until we again experience more immediately what we have.

V

In most modern instances, interpretation amounts to the philistine refusal to leave the work of art alone. Real art has the capacity to make us nervous. By reducing the work of art to its content and then interpreting *that,* one tames the work of art. Interpretation makes art manageable, comfortable.

This philistinism of interpretation is more rife in literature than in any other art. For decades now, literary critics have understood it to be their task to translate the elements of the poem or play or novel or story into something else. Sometimes a writer will be so uneasy before the naked power of his art that he will install within the work itself—albeit with a little shyness, a touch of the good taste of irony— the clear and explicit interpretation of it. Thomas Mann is an example of such an overcooperative author. In the case of more stubborn authors, the critic is only too happy to perform the job.

The work of Kafka, for example, has been subjected to a mass ravishment by no less than three armies of interpreters. Those who read Kafka as a social allegory see case studies of the frustrations and insanity of modern bureaucracy and its ultimate issuance in the totalitarian state. Those who read Kafka as a psychoanalytic allegory see desperate revelations of Kafka's fear of his father, his castration anxieties, his sense of his own impotence, his thralldom to his dreams. Those who read Kafka as a religious allegory explain that K. in *The Castle* is trying to gain access to heaven, that Joseph K. in *The Trial* is being judged by the inexorable and mysterious justice of God . . . Another body of work that has attracted interpreters like leeches is that of Samuel Beckett. Beckett's delicate dramas of the withdrawn consciousness—pared down to essentials, cut off, often represented as physically immobilized—are read as a statement about modern man's alienation from meaning or from God, or as an allegory of psychopathology.

Proust, Joyce, Faulkner, Rilke, Lawrence, Gide . . . one could go on citing author after author; the list is endless of those around whom thick encrustations of interpretation have taken hold. But it should be noted that interpretation is not simply the compliment that mediocrity pays to genius. It is, indeed, the modern way of understanding something, and is applied to works of every quality. Thus, in the notes that Elia Kazan published on his production of *A Streetcar Named Desire,* it becomes clear that, in order to direct the play, Kazan had to discover that Stanley Kowalski represented the sensual and vengeful barbarism that was engulfing our culture, while Blanche DuBois was Western civilization, poetry, delicate apparel, dim lighting, refined feelings and all, though a little the worse for wear, to be sure. Tennessee Williams's forceful psychological melodrama now became intelligible: it was about something, about the decline of Western civilization. Apparently, were it to go on being a play about a handsome brute named Stanley Kowalski and a faded mangy belle named Blanche DuBois, it would not be manageable.

VI

It doesn't matter whether artists intend, or don't intend, for their works to be interpreted. Perhaps Tennessee Williams thinks *Streetcar* is about what Kazan thinks it to be about. It may be that Cocteau in *The Blood of a Poet* and in *Orpheus* wanted the elaborate readings which have been given these films, in terms of Freudian symbolism and social critique. But the merit of these works certainly lies elsewhere than in their "meanings." Indeed, it is precisely to the extent that Williams's plays and Cocteau's films do suggest these portentous meanings that they are defective, false, contrived, lacking in conviction.

From interviews, it appears that Resnais and Robbe-Grillet consciously designed *Last Year at Marienbad* to accommodate a multiplicity of equally plausible interpretations. But the temptation to interpret *Marienbad* should be resisted. What matters in *Marienbad* is the pure, untranslatable, sensuous immediacy of some of its images, and its rigorous if narrow solutions to certain problems of cinematic form.

Again, Ingmar Bergman may have meant the tank rumbling down the empty night street in *The Silence* as a phallic symbol. But if he did, it was a foolish thought. ("Never trust the teller, trust the tale," said Lawrence.) Taken as a brute object, as an immediate sensory equivalent for the mysterious abrupt armored happenings going on inside the hotel, that sequence with the tank is the most striking moment in the film. Those who reach for a Freudian interpretation of the tank are only expressing their lack of response to what is there on the screen.

It is always the case that interpretation of this type indicates a dissatisfaction (conscious or unconscious) with the work, a wish to replace it by something else.

Interpretation, based on the highly dubious theory that a work of art is composed of items of content, violates art. It makes art into an article for use, for arrangement into a mental scheme of categories.

VII

Interpretation does not, of course, always prevail. In fact, a great deal of today's art may be understood as motivated by a flight from interpretation. To avoid interpretation, art may become parody. Or it may become abstract. Or it may become ("merely") decorative. Or it may become non-art.

The flight from interpretation seems particularly a feature of modern painting. Abstract painting is the attempt to have, in the ordinary sense, no content; since there is no content, there can be no interpretation. Pop Art works by the opposite means to the same result; using a content so blatant, so "what it is," it, too, ends by being uninterpretable.

A great deal of modern poetry as well, starting from the great experiments of French poetry (including the movement that is misleadingly called Symbolism) to put silence into poems and to reinstate the *magic* of the word, has escaped from the rough grip of interpretation. The most recent revolution in contemporary taste in poetry— the revolution that has deposed Eliot and elevated Pound—represents a turning away from content in poetry in the old sense, an impatience with what made modern poetry prey to the zeal of interpreters.

I am speaking mainly of the situation in America, of course. Interpretation runs rampant here in those arts with a feeble and negligible avant-garde: fiction and the drama. Most American novelists and playwrights are really either journalists or gentlemen sociologists and psychologists. They are writing the literary equivalent of program music. And so rudimentary, uninspired, and stagnant has been the sense of what might be done with form in fiction and drama that even when the content isn't simply information, news, it is still peculiarly visible, handier, more exposed. To the extent that novels and plays (in America), unlike poetry and painting and music, don't reflect any interesting concern with changes in their form, these arts remain prone to assault by interpretation.

But programmatic avant-gardism—which has meant, mostly, experiments with form at the expense of content—is not the only defense against the infestation of art by interpretations. At least, I hope not. For this would be to commit art to being perpetually on the run.

(It also perpetuates the very distinction between form and content which is, ultimately, an illusion.) Ideally, it is possible to elude the interpreters in another way, by making works of art whose surface is so unified and clean, whose momentum is so rapid, whose address is so direct that the work can be . . . just what it is. Is this possible now? It does happen in films, I believe. This is why cinema is the most alive, the most exciting, the most important of all art forms right now. Perhaps the way one tells how alive a particular art form is is by the latitude it gives for making mistakes in it and still being good. For example, a few of the films of Bergman—though crammed with lame messages about the modern spirit, thereby inviting interpretations—still triumph over the pretentious intentions of their director. In *Winter Light* and *The Silence,* the beauty and visual sophistication of the images subvert before our eyes the callow pseudo-intellectuality of the story and some of the dialogue. (The most remarkable instance of this sort of discrepancy is the work of D. W. Griffith.) In good films, there is always a directness that entirely frees us from the itch to interpret. Many old Hollywood films, like those of Cukor, Walsh, Hawks, and countless other directors, have this liberating anti-symbolic quality, no less than the best work of the new European directors, like Truffaut's *Shoot the Piano Player* and *Jules and Jim,* Godard's *Breathless* and *Vivre sa Vie,* Antonioni's *L'Avventura,* and Olmi's *The Fiancés.*

The fact that films have not been overrun by interpreters is in part due simply to the newness of cinema as an art. It also owes to the happy accident that films for such a long time were just movies; in other words, that they were understood to be part of mass, as opposed to high, culture, and were left alone by most people with minds. Then, too, there is always something other than content in the cinema to grab hold of, for those who want to analyze. For the cinema, unlike the novel, possesses a vocabulary of forms—the explicit, complex, and discussable technology of camera movements, cutting, and composition of the frame that goes into the making of a film.

VIII

What kind of criticism, of commentary on the arts, is desirable today? For I am not saying that works of art are ineffable, that they cannot be described or paraphrased. They can be. The question is how. What would criticism look like that would serve the work of art, not usurp its place?

What is needed, first, is more attention to form in art. If excessive stress on *content* provokes the arrogance of interpretation, more extended and more thorough descriptions of *form* would silence. What is needed is a vocabulary—a descriptive, rather than prescriptive, vocabulary—for forms.* The best criticism, and it is uncommon, is of this sort that dissolves considerations of content into those of form. On film, drama, and painting respectively, I can think of Erwin Panofsky's essay "Style and Medium in the Motion Pictures," Northrop Frye's essay "A Conspectus of Dramatic Genres," Pierre Francastel's essay "The Destruction of a Plastic Space." Roland Barthes's book *On Racine* and his two essays on Robbe-Grillet are examples of formal analysis applied to the work of a single author. (The best essays in Erich Auerbach's *Mimesis,* like "The Scar of Odysseus," are also of this type.) An example of formal analysis applied simultaneously to genre and author is Walter Benjamin's essay "The Storyteller: Reflections on the Works of Nicolai Leskov."

Equally valuable would be acts of criticism which would supply a really accurate, sharp, loving description of the appearance of a work of art. This seems even harder to do than formal analysis. Some of Manny Farber's film criticism, Dorothy Van Ghent's essay "The Dickens World: A View from Todgers'," Randall Jarrell's essay on Walt Whitman are among the rare examples of what I mean. These are essays which reveal the sensuous surface of art without mucking about in it.

IX

Transparence is the highest, most liberating value in art—and in criticism—today. Transparence means experiencing the luminousness of the thing in itself, of things being what they are. This is the greatness of, for example, the films of Bresson and Ozu and Renoir's *The Rules of the Game.*

Once upon a time (say, for Dante), it must have been a revolutionary and creative move to design works of art so that they might be experienced on several levels. Now it is not. It reinforces the principle of redundancy that is the principal affliction of modern life.

Once upon a time (a time when high art was scarce), it must have

---

*One of the difficulties is that our idea of form is spatial (the Greek metaphors for form are all derived from notions of space). This is why we have a more ready vocabulary of forms for the spatial than for the temporal arts. The exception among the temporal arts, of course, is the drama; perhaps this is because the drama is a narrative (i.e., temporal) form that extends itself visually and pictorially, upon a stage. What we don't have yet is a poetics of the novel, any clear notion of the forms of narration. Perhaps film criticism will be the occasion of a breakthrough here, since films are primarily a visual form, yet they are also a subdivision of literature.

been a revolutionary and creative move to interpret works of art. Now it is not. What we decidedly do not need now is further to assimilate Art into Thought, or (worse yet) Art into Culture.

Interpretation takes the sensory experience of the work of art for granted, and proceeds from there. This cannot be taken for granted now. Think of the sheer multiplication of works of art available to every one of us, super-added to the conflicting tastes and odors and sights of the urban environment that bombard our senses. Ours is a culture based on excess, on overproduction; the result is a steady loss of sharpness in our sensory experience. All the conditions of modern life—its material plenitude, its sheer crowdedness—conjoin to dull our sensory faculties. And it is in the light of the condition of our senses, our capacities (rather than those of another age), that the task of the critic must be assessed.

What is important now is to recover our senses. We must learn to *see* more, to *hear* more, to *feel* more.

Our task is not to find the maximum amount of content in a work of art, much less to squeeze more content out of the work than is already there. Our task is to cut back content so that we can see the thing at all.

The aim of all commentary on art now should be to make works of art—and, by analogy, our own experience—more, rather than less, real to us. The function of criticism should be to show *how it is what it is,* even *that it is what it is,* rather than to show *what it means.*

X

In place of a hermeneutics we need an erotics of art.

(1964)

Notes on "Camp"

$\mathbf{M}$any things in the world have not been named; and many
things, even if they have been named, have never been described.
One of these is the sensibility—unmistakably modern, a variant of
sophistication but hardly identical with it—that goes by the cult name
of "Camp."

A sensibility (as distinct from an idea) is one of the hardest things
to talk about; but there are special reasons why Camp, in particular,
has never been discussed. It is not a natural mode of sensibility, if
there be any such. Indeed, the essence of Camp is its love of the
unnatural: of artifice and exaggeration. And Camp is esoteric—something of a private code, a badge of identity even, among small urban
cliques. Apart from a lazy two-page sketch in Christopher Isher-
wood's novel *The World in the Evening* (1954), it has hardly broken
into print. To talk about Camp is therefore to betray it. If the betrayal
can be defended, it will be for the edification it provides, or the dignity of the conflict it resolves. For myself, I plead the goal of self-
edification, and the goad of a sharp conflict in my own sensibility. I
am strongly drawn to Camp, and almost as strongly offended by it.
That is why I want to talk about it, and why I can. For no one who
wholeheartedly shares in a given sensibility can analyze it; he can
only, whatever his intention, exhibit it. To name a sensibility, to draw
its contours and to recount its history, requires a deep sympathy
modified by revulsion.

Though I am speaking about sensibility only—and about a sensibility that, among other things, converts the serious into the frivo-

lous—these are grave matters. Most people think of sensibility or taste as the realm of purely subjective preferences, those mysterious attractions, mainly sensual, that have not been brought under the sovereignty of reason. They *allow* that considerations of taste play a part in their reactions to people and to works of art. But this attitude is naïve. And even worse. To patronize the faculty of taste is to patronize oneself. For taste governs every free—as opposed to rote—human response. Nothing is more decisive. There is taste in people, visual taste, taste in emotion—and there is taste in acts, taste in morality. Intelligence, as well, is really a kind of taste: taste in ideas. (One of the facts to be reckoned with is that taste tends to develop very unevenly. It's rare that the same person has good visual taste *and* good taste in people *and* taste in ideas.)

Taste has no system and no proofs. But there is something like a logic of taste: the consistent sensibility which underlies and gives rise to a certain taste. A sensibility is almost, but not quite, ineffable. Any sensibility which can be crammed into the mold of a system, or handled with the rough tools of proof, is no longer a sensibility at all. It has hardened into an idea . . .

To snare a sensibility in words, especially one that is alive and powerful,* one must be tentative and nimble. The form of jottings, rather than an essay (with its claim to a linear, consecutive argument), seemed more appropriate for getting down something of this particular fugitive sensibility. It's embarrassing to be solemn and treatise-like about Camp. One runs the risk of having, oneself, produced a very inferior piece of Camp.

These notes are for Oscar Wilde.

> *One should either be a work of art, or wear a work of art.*
> —PHRASES & PHILOSOPHIES
> FOR THE USE OF THE YOUNG

1. To start very generally: Camp is a certain mode of aestheticism. It is one way of seeing the world as an aesthetic phenomenon. That way, the way of Camp, is not in terms of beauty but in terms of the degree of artifice, of stylization.

---

*The sensibility of an era is not only its most decisive but also its most perishable aspect. One may capture the ideas (intellectual history) and the behavior (social history) of an epoch without ever touching upon the sensibility or taste which informed those ideas, that behavior. Rare are those historical studies—like Huizinga on the late Middle Ages, Febvre on sixteenth-century France—which do tell us something about the sensibility of the period.

2. To emphasize style is to slight content, or to introduce an attitude which is neutral with respect to content. It goes without saying that the Camp sensibility is disengaged, depoliticized—or at least apolitical.

3. Not only is there a Camp vision, a Camp way of looking at things. Camp is as well a quality discoverable in objects and the behavior of persons. There are "campy" movies, clothes, furniture, popular songs, novels, people, buildings . . . This distinction is important. True, the Camp eye has the power to transform experience. But not everything can be seen as Camp. It's not *all* in the eye of the beholder.

4. Random examples of items which are part of the canon of Camp:

Zuleika Dobson
Tiffany lamps
Scopitone films
The Brown Derby restaurant on Sunset Boulevard in L.A.
The Enquirer, headlines and stories
Aubrey Beardsley drawings
Swan Lake
Bellini's operas
Visconti's direction of *Salome* and *'Tis Pity She's a Whore*
certain turn-of-the-century picture postcards
Schoedsack's *King Kong*
the Cuban pop singer La Lupe
Lynn Ward's novel in woodcuts, *God's Man*
the old Flash Gordon comics
women's clothes of the twenties (feather boas, fringed and beaded
    dresses, etc.)
the novels of Ronald Firbank and Ivy Compton-Burnett
stag movies seen without lust

5. Camp taste has an affinity for certain arts rather than others. Clothes, furniture, all the elements of visual décor, for instance, make up a large part of Camp. For Camp art is often decorative art, emphasizing texture, sensuous surface, and style at the expense of content. Concert music, though, because it is contentless, is rarely Camp. It offers no opportunity, say, for a contrast between silly or extravagant content and rich form . . . Sometimes whole art forms become saturated with Camp. Classical ballet, opera, movies have seemed so for a long time. In the last two years, popular music (post rock-'n'-roll, what the French call yé-yé) has been annexed. And movie criticism (like lists of "The 10 Best Bad Movies I Have Seen") is probably the

greatest popularizer of Camp taste today, because most people still go to the movies in a high-spirited and unpretentious way.

6. There is a sense in which it is correct to say "It's too good to be Camp." Or "too important," not marginal enough. (More on this later.) Thus, the personality and many of the works of Jean Cocteau are Camp, but not those of André Gide; the operas of Richard Strauss, but not those of Wagner; concoctions of Tin Pan Alley and Liverpool, but not jazz. Many examples of Camp are things which, from a "serious" point of view, are either bad art or kitsch. Not all, though. Not only is Camp not necessarily bad art, but some art which can be approached as Camp (example: the major films of Louis Feuillade) merits the most serious admiration and study.

> *The more we study Art, the less we care for Nature.*
> —THE DECAY OF LYING

7. All Camp objects, and persons, contain a large element of artifice. Nothing in nature can be campy . . . Rural Camp is still man-made, and most campy objects are urban. (Yet they often have a serenity—or a naïveté—which is the equivalent of pastoral. A great deal of Camp suggests Empson's phrase, "urban pastoral.")

8. Camp is a vision of the world in terms of style—but a particular kind of style. It is the love of the exaggerated, the "off," of things-being-what-they-are-not. The best example is in Art Nouveau, the most typical and fully developed Camp style. Art Nouveau objects, typically, convert one thing into something else: the lighting fixtures in the form of flowering plants, the living room which is really a grotto. A remarkable example: the Paris Metro entrances designed by Hector Guimard in the late 1890s in the shape of cast-iron orchid stalks.

9. As a taste in persons, Camp responds particularly to the markedly attenuated and to the strongly exaggerated. The androgyne is certainly one of the great images of Camp sensibility. Examples: the swooning, slim, sinuous figures of pre-Raphaelite painting and poetry; the thin, flowing, sexless bodies in Art Nouveau prints and posters, presented in relief on lamps and ashtrays; the haunting androgynous vacancy behind the perfect beauty of Greta Garbo. Here Camp taste draws on a mostly unacknowledged truth of taste: the most refined form of sexual attractiveness (as well as the most refined form of sexual pleasure) consists in going against the grain of one's sex. What is most beautiful in virile men is something feminine; what is most beautiful in feminine women is something masculine . . . Allied to the Camp taste for the androgynous is some-

thing that seems quite different but isn't: a relish for the exaggeration of sexual characteristics and personality mannerisms. For obvious reasons, the best examples that can be cited are movie stars. The corny flamboyant femaleness of Jayne Mansfield, Gina Lollobrigida, Jane Russell, Virginia Mayo; the exaggerated he-manness of Steve Reeves, Victor Mature. The great stylists of temperament and mannerism, like Bette Davis, Barbara Stanwyck, Tallulah Bankhead, Edwige Feuillère.

10. Camp sees everything in quotation marks. It's not a lamp, but a "lamp"; not a woman, but a "woman." To perceive Camp in objects and persons is to understand Being-as-Playing-a-Role. It is the farthest extension, in sensibility, of the metaphor of life as theater.

11. Camp is the triumph of the epicene style. (The convertibility of "man" and "woman," "person" and "thing.") But all style, that is, artifice, is, ultimately, epicene. Life is not stylish. Neither is nature.

12. The question isn't "Why travesty, impersonation, theatricality?" The question is, rather, "When does travesty, impersonation, theatricality acquire the special flavor of Camp?" Why is the atmosphere of Shakespeare's comedies (*As You Like It,* etc.) not epicene, while that of *Der Rosenkavalier* is?

13. The dividing line seems to fall in the eighteenth century; there the origins of Camp taste are to be found (Gothic novels, Chinoiserie, caricature, artificial ruins, and so forth). But the relation to nature was quite different then. In the eighteenth century, people of taste either patronized nature (Strawberry Hill) or attempted to remake it into something artificial (Versailles). They also indefatigably patronized the past. Today's Camp taste effaces nature, or else contradicts it outright. And the relation of Camp taste to the past is extremely sentimental.

14. A pocket history of Camp might, of course, begin farther back— with the mannerist artists like Pontormo, Rosso, and Caravaggio, or the extraordinarily theatrical painting of Georges de La Tour, or euphuism (Lyly, etc.) in literature. Still, the soundest starting point seems to be the late seventeenth and early eighteenth century, because of that period's extraordinary feeling for artifice, for surface, for symmetry; its taste for the picturesque and the thrilling, its elegant conventions for representing instant feeling and the total presence of character—the epigram and the rhymed couplet (in words), the flourish (in gesture and in music). The late seventeenth and early eighteenth century is the great period of Camp: Pope, Congreve, Walpole, but not Swift; *les précieux* in France; the rococo churches of Munich; Pergolesi. Somewhat later: much of Mozart. But in the nine-

teenth century, what had been distributed throughout all of high culture now becomes a special taste; it takes on overtones of the acute,
the esoteric, the perverse. Confining the story to England alone, we
see Camp continuing wanly through nineteenth-century aestheticism
(Burne-Jones, Pater, Ruskin, Tennyson), emerging full-blown with
the Art Nouveau movement in the visual and decorative arts, and
finding its conscious ideologists in such "wits" as Wilde and Firbank.

15. Of course, to say all these things are Camp is not to argue they
are simply that. A full analysis of Art Nouveau, for instance, would
scarcely equate it with Camp. But such an analysis cannot ignore
what in Art Nouveau allows it to be experienced as Camp. Art Nouveau is full of "content," even of a political-moral sort; it was a revolutionary movement in the arts, spurred on by a utopian vision
(somewhere between William Morris and the Bauhaus group) of an
organic politics and taste. Yet there is also a feature of the Art Nouveau objects which suggests a disengaged, unserious, "aesthete's"
vision. This tells us something important about Art Nouveau—and
about what the lens of Camp, which blocks out content, is.

16. Thus, the Camp sensibility is one that is alive to a double sense
in which some things can be taken. But this is not the familiar split-
level construction of a literal meaning, on the one hand, and a symbolic meaning, on the other. It is the difference, rather, between the
thing as meaning something, anything, and the thing as pure artifice.

17. This comes out clearly in the vulgar use of the word Camp as
a verb, "to camp," something that people do. To camp is a mode of
seduction—one which employs flamboyant mannerisms susceptible
of a double interpretation; gestures full of duplicity, with a witty
meaning for cognoscenti and another, more impersonal, for outsiders.
Equally and by extension, when the word becomes a noun, when a
person or a thing is "a camp," a duplicity is involved. Behind the
"straight" public sense in which something can be taken, one has
found a private zany experience of the thing.

> To be natural is such a very difficult pose to keep up.
>
> —AN IDEAL HUSBAND

18. One must distinguish between naïve and deliberate Camp. Pure
Camp is always naïve. Camp which knows itself to be Camp ("camping") is usually less satisfying.

19. The pure examples of Camp are unintentional; they are dead-
serious. The Art Nouveau craftsman who makes a lamp with a snake
coiled around it is not kidding, nor is he trying to be charming. He is

saying, in all earnestness: Voilà! the Orient! Genuine Camp—for instance, the numbers devised for the Warner Brothers musicals of the early thirties (*42nd Street; The Golddiggers of 1933; . . . of 1935; . . . of 1937;* etc.) by Busby Berkeley—does not *mean* to be funny. Camping—say, the plays of Noël Coward—does. It seems unlikely that much of the traditional opera repertoire could be such satisfying Camp if the melodramatic absurdities of most opera plots had not been taken seriously by their composers. One doesn't need to know the artist's private intentions. The work tells all. (Compare a typical nineteenth-century opera with Samuel Barber's *Vanessa,* a piece of manufactured, calculated Camp, and the difference is clear.)

20. Probably, intending to be campy is always harmful. The perfection of *Trouble in Paradise* and *The Maltese Falcon,* among the greatest Camp movies ever made, comes from the effortless smooth way in which tone is maintained. This is not so with such famous would-be Camp films of the fifties as *All About Eve* and *Beat the Devil.* These more recent movies have their fine moments, but the first is so slick and the second so hysterical; they want so badly to be campy that they're continually losing the beat . . . Perhaps, though, it is not so much a question of the unintended effect versus the conscious intention, as of the delicate relation between parody and self-parody in Camp. The films of Hitchcock are a showcase for this problem. When self-parody lacks ebullience but instead reveals (even sporadically) a contempt for one's themes and one's materials—as in *To Catch a Thief, Rear Window, North by Northwest*—the results are forced and heavy-handed, rarely Camp. Successful Camp—a movie like Carné's *Drôle de Drame;* the film performances of Mae West and Edward Everett Horton; portions of the Goon Show—even when it reveals self-parody, reeks of self-love.

21. So, again, Camp rests on innocence. That means Camp discloses innocence, but also, when it can, corrupts it. Objects, being objects, don't change when they are singled out by the Camp vision. Persons, however, respond to their audiences. Persons begin "camping": Mae West, Bea Lillie, La Lupe, Tallulah Bankhead in *Lifeboat,* Bette Davis in *All About Eve.* (Persons can even be induced to camp without their knowing it. Consider the way Fellini got Anita Ekberg to parody herself in *La Dolce Vita.*)

22. Considered a little less strictly, Camp is either completely naïve or else wholly conscious (when one plays at being campy). An example of the latter: Wilde's epigrams themselves.

It's absurd to divide people into good and bad. People are either charming or tedious.

—LADY WINDEMERE'S FAN

23. In naïve, or pure, Camp, the essential element is seriousness, a seriousness that fails. Of course, not all seriousness that fails can be redeemed as Camp. Only that which has the proper mixture of the exaggerated, the fantastic, the passionate, and the naïve.

24. When something is just bad (rather than Camp), it's often because it is too mediocre in its ambition. The artist hasn't attempted to do anything really outlandish. ("It's too much," "It's too fantastic," "It's not to be believed," are standard phrases of Camp enthusiasm.)

25. The hallmark of Camp is the spirit of extravagance. Camp is a woman walking around in a dress made of three million feathers. Camp is the paintings of Carlo Crivelli, with their real jewels and *trompe-l'oeil* insects and cracks in the masonry. Camp is the outrageous aestheticism of Sternberg's six American movies with Dietrich, all six, but especially the last, *The Devil Is a Woman* . . . In Camp there is often something *démesuré* in the quality of the ambition, not only in the style of the work itself. Gaudí's lurid and beautiful buildings in Barcelona are Camp not only because of their style but because they reveal—most notably in the Cathedral of the Sagrada Familia—the ambition on the part of one man to do what it takes a generation, a whole culture to accomplish.

26. Camp is art that proposes itself seriously, but cannot be taken altogether seriously because it is "too much." *Titus Andronicus* and *Strange Interlude* are almost Camp, or could be played as Camp. The public manner and rhetoric of de Gaulle, often, are pure Camp.

27. A work can come close to Camp but not make it because it succeeds. Eisenstein's films are seldom Camp because, despite all exaggeration, they do succeed (dramatically) without surplus. If they were a little more "off," they could be great Camp—particularly *Ivan the Terrible I & II.* The same for Blake's drawings and paintings, weird and mannered as they are. They aren't Camp; though Art Nouveau, influenced by Blake, is.

What is extravagant in an inconsistent or an unpassionate way is not Camp. Neither can anything be Camp that does not seem to spring from an irrepressible, a virtually uncontrolled sensibility. Without passion, one gets pseudo-Camp—what is merely decorative, safe, in a word, chic. On the barren edge of Camp lie a number of attractive things: the sleek fantasies of Dali, the haute-couture preciosity of Albicocco's *The Girl with the Golden Eyes*. But the two things—Camp and preciosity—must not be confused.

28. Again, Camp is the attempt to do something extraordinary. But extraordinary in the sense, often, of being special, glamorous. (The curved line, the extravagant gesture.) Not extraordinary merely in the sense of effort. Ripley's Believe-It-Or-Not items are rarely campy. These items, either natural oddities (the two-headed rooster, the eggplant in the shape of a cross) or else the products of immense labor (the man who walked from here to China on his hands, the woman who engraved the New Testament on the head of a pin), lack the visual reward—the glamour, the theatricality—that marks off certain extravagances as Camp.

29. The reason a movie like *On the Beach,* books like *Winesburg, Ohio* and *For Whom the Bell Tolls* are bad to the point of being laughable, but not bad to the point of being enjoyable, is that they are too dogged and pretentious. They lack fantasy. There is Camp in such bad movies as *The Prodigal* and *Samson and Delilah,* the series of Italian color spectacles featuring the super-hero Maciste, numerous Japanese science-fiction films (*Rodan, The Mysterians, The H-Man*), because, in their relative unpretentiousness and vulgarity, they are more extreme and irresponsible in their fantasy—and therefore touching and quite enjoyable.

30. Of course, the canon of Camp can change. Time has a great deal to do with it. Time may enhance what seems simply dogged or lacking in fantasy now because we are too close to it, because it resembles too closely our own everyday fantasies, the fantastic nature of which we don't perceive. We are better able to enjoy a fantasy as fantasy when it is not our own.

31. This is why so many of the objects prized by Camp taste are old-fashioned, out-of-date, *démodé.* It's not a love of the old as such. It's simply that the process of aging or deterioration provides the necessary detachment—or arouses a necessary sympathy. When the theme is important, and contemporary, the failure of a work of art may make us indignant. Time can change that. Time liberates the work of art from moral relevance, delivering it over to the Camp sensibility . . . Another effect: time contracts the sphere of banality. (Banality is, strictly speaking, always a category of the contemporary.) What was banal can, with the passage of time, become fantastic. Many people who listen with delight to the style of Rudy Vallee revived by the English pop group The Temperance Seven would have been driven up the wall by Rudy Vallee in his heyday.

Thus, things are campy, not when they become old—but when we become less involved in them, and can enjoy, instead of be frustrated by, the failure of the attempt. But the effect of time is unpredictable. Maybe Method Acting (James Dean, Rod Steiger, Warren Beatty) will seem as Camp someday as Ruby Keeler's does now—or as Sarah Bernhardt's does, in the films she made at the end of her career. And maybe not.

32. Camp is the glorification of "character." The statement is of no importance—except, of course, to the person (Loie Fuller, Gaudí, Cecil B. De Mille, Crivelli, de Gaulle, etc.) who makes it. What the Camp eye appreciates is the unity, the force of the person. In every move the aging Martha Graham makes she's being Martha Graham, etc., etc. . . . This is clear in the case of the great serious idol of Camp taste, Greta Garbo. Garbo's incompetence (at the least, lack of depth) as an *actress* enhances her beauty. She's always herself.

33. What Camp taste responds to is "instant character" (this is, of course, very eighteenth century); and, conversely, what it is not stirred by is the sense of the development of character. Character is understood as a state of continual incandescence—a person being one, very intense thing. This attitude toward character is a key element of the theatricalization of experience embodied in the Camp sensibility. And it helps account for the fact that opera and ballet are experienced as such rich treasures of Camp, for neither of these forms can easily do justice to the complexity of human nature. Wherever there is development of character, Camp is reduced. Among operas, for example, *La Traviata* (which has some small development of character) is less campy than *Il Trovatore* (which has none).

> *Life is too important a thing ever to talk seriously about it.*
>
> —VERA, OR THE NIHILISTS

34. Camp taste turns its back on the good-bad axis of ordinary aesthetic judgment. Camp doesn't reverse things. It doesn't argue that the good is bad, or the bad is good. What it does is to offer for art (and life) a different—a supplementary—set of standards.

35. Ordinarily we value a work of art because of the seriousness and dignity of what it achieves. We value it because it succeeds—in being what it is and, presumably, in fulfilling the intention that lies behind it. We assume a proper, that is to say, straightforward relation between intention and performance. By such standards, we appraise *The Iliad*, Aristophanes's plays, The Art of the Fugue, *Middlemarch*, the paintings of Rembrandt, Chartres, the poetry of Donne, *The Divine Comedy*, Beethoven's quartets, and—among people—Socrates, Jesus, St. Francis, Napoleon, Savonarola. In short, the pantheon of high culture: truth, beauty, and seriousness.

36. But there are other creative sensibilities besides the seriousness (both tragic and comic) of high culture and of the high style of

evaluating people. And one cheats oneself, as a human being, if one has *respect* only for the style of high culture, whatever else one may do or feel on the sly.

For instance, there is the kind of seriousness whose trademark is anguish, cruelty, derangement. Here we do accept a disparity between intention and result. I am speaking, obviously, of style of personal existence as well as of a style in art; but the examples had best come from art. Think of Bosch, Sade, Rimbaud, Jarry, Kafka, Artaud, think of most of the important works of art of the twentieth century, that is, art whose goal is not that of creating harmonies but of overstraining the medium and introducing more and more violent, and unresolvable, subject matter. This sensibility also insists on the principle that an *oeuvre* in the old sense (again, in art, but also in life) is not possible. Only "fragments" are possible . . . Clearly, different standards apply here than to traditional high culture. Something is good not because it is achieved but because another kind of truth about the human situation, another experience of what it is to be human—in short, another valid sensibility—is being revealed.

And third among the great creative sensibilities is Camp: the sensibility of failed seriousness, of the theatricalization of experience. Camp refuses both the harmonies of traditional seriousness and the risks of fully identifying with extreme states of feeling.

37. The first sensibility, that of high culture, is basically moralistic. The second sensibility, that of extreme states of feeling, represented in much contemporary "avant-garde" art, gains power by a tension between moral and aesthetic passion. The third, Camp, is wholly aesthetic.

38. Camp is the consistently aesthetic experience of the world. It incarnates a victory of "style" over "content," "aesthetics" over "morality," of irony over tragedy.

39. Camp and tragedy are antitheses. There is seriousness in Camp (seriousness in the degree of the artist's involvement) and, often, pathos. The excruciating is also one of the tonalities of Camp; it is the quality of excruciation in much of Henry James (for instance, *The Europeans, The Awkward Age, The Wings of the Dove*) that is responsible for the large element of Camp in his writings. But there is never, never tragedy.

40. Style is everything. Genet's ideas, for instance, are very Camp. Genet's statement that "the only criterion of an act is its elegance"* is virtually interchangeable, as a statement, with Wilde's "in matters

---

* Sartre's gloss on this in *Saint Genet* is: "Elegance is the quality of conduct which transforms the greatest amount of being into appearing."

of great importance, the vital element is not sincerity, but style." But what counts, finally, is the style in which ideas are held. The ideas about morality and politics in, say, *Lady Windemere's Fan* and *Major Barbara* are Camp, but not just because of the nature of the ideas themselves. It is those ideas, held in a special playful way. The Camp ideas in *Our Lady of the Flowers* are maintained too grimly, and the writing itself is too successfully elevated and serious, for Genet's books to be Camp.

41. The whole point of Camp is to dethrone the serious. Camp is playful, anti-serious. More precisely, Camp involves a new, more complex relation to "the serious." One can be serious about the frivolous, frivolous about the serious.

42. One is drawn to Camp when one realizes that "sincerity" is not enough. Sincerity can be simple philistinism, intellectual narrowness.

43. The traditional means for going beyond straight seriousness—irony, satire—seem feeble today, inadequate to the culturally oversaturated medium in which contemporary sensibility is schooled. Camp introduces a new standard: artifice as an ideal, theatricality.

44. Camp proposes a comic vision of the world. But not a bitter or polemical comedy. If tragedy is an experience of hyper-involvement, comedy is an experience of under-involvement, of detachment.

I adore simple pleasures, they are the last refuge of the complex.
—A WOMAN OF NO IMPORTANCE

45. Detachment is the prerogative of an elite; and as the dandy is the nineteenth century's surrogate for the aristocrat in matters of culture, so Camp is the modern dandyism. Camp is the answer to the problem: how to be a dandy in the age of mass culture.

46. The dandy was overbred. His posture was disdain, or else ennui. He sought rare sensations, undefiled by mass appreciation. (Models: Des Esseintes in Huysmans's *A Rebours, Marius the Epicurean,* Valéry's *Monsieur Teste.*) He was dedicated to "good taste."

The connoisseur of Camp has found more ingenious pleasures. Not in Latin poetry and rare wines and velvet jackets, but in the coarsest, commonest pleasures, in the arts of the masses. Mere use does not defile the objects of his pleasure, since he learns to possess them in a rare way. Camp—Dandyism in the age of mass culture—makes no distinction between the unique object and the mass-produced object. Camp taste transcends the nausea of the replica.

47. Wilde himself is a transitional figure. The man who, when he

first came to London, sported a velvet beret, lace shirts, velveteen knee breeches and black silk stockings could never depart too far in his life from the pleasures of the old-style dandy; this conservatism is reflected in *The Picture of Dorian Gray*. But many of his attitudes suggest something more modern. It was Wilde who formulated an important element of the Camp sensibility—the equivalence of all objects—when he announced his intention of "living up" to his blue-and-white china, or declared that a doorknob could be as admirable as a painting. When he proclaimed the importance of the necktie, the boutonniere, the chair, Wilde was anticipating the democratic *esprit* of Camp.

48. The old-style dandy hated vulgarity. The new-style dandy, the lover of Camp, appreciates vulgarity. Where the dandy would be continually offended or bored, the connoisseur of Camp is continually amused, delighted. The dandy held a perfumed handkerchief to his nostrils and was liable to swoon; the connoisseur of Camp sniffs the stink and prides himself on his strong nerves.

49. It is a feat, of course. A feat goaded on, in the last analysis, by the threat of boredom. The relation between boredom and Camp taste cannot be overestimated. Camp taste is by its nature possible only in affluent societies, in societies or circles capable of experiencing the psychopathology of affluence.

> *What is abnormal in Life stands in normal relations to Art. It is the only thing in Life that stands in normal relations to Art.*
> —A FEW MAXIMS FOR THE INSTRUCTION
> OF THE OVER-EDUCATED

50. Aristocracy is a position vis-à-vis culture (as well as vis-à-vis power), and the history of Camp taste is part of the history of snob taste. But since no authentic aristocrats in the old sense exist today to sponsor special tastes, who is the bearer of this taste? Answer: an improvised self-elected class, mainly homosexuals, who constitute themselves as aristocrats of taste.

51. The peculiar relation between Camp taste and homosexuality has to be explained. While it's not true that Camp taste *is* homosexual taste, there is no doubt a peculiar affinity and overlap. Not all liberals are Jews, but Jews have shown a peculiar affinity for liberal and reformist causes. So, not all homosexuals have Camp taste. But homosexuals, by and large, constitute the vanguard—and the most articulate audience—of Camp. (The analogy is not frivolously chosen. Jews and homosexuals are the outstanding creative minorities in con-

temporary urban culture. Creative, that is, in the truest sense: they are creators of sensibilities. The two pioneering forces of modern sensibility are Jewish moral seriousness and homosexual aestheticism and irony.)

52. The reason for the flourishing of the aristocratic posture among homosexuals also seems to parallel the Jewish case. For every sensibility is self-serving to the group that promotes it. Jewish liberalism is a gesture of self-legitimization. So is Camp taste, which definitely has something propagandistic about it. Needless to say, the propaganda operates in exactly the opposite direction. The Jews pinned their hopes for integrating into modern society on promoting the moral sense. Homosexuals have pinned their integration into society on promoting the aesthetic sense. Camp is a solvent of morality. It neutralizes moral indignation, sponsors playfulness.

53. Nevertheless, even though homosexuals have been its vanguard, Camp taste is much more than homosexual taste. Obviously, its metaphor of life as theater is peculiarly suited as a justification and projection of a certain aspect of the situation of homosexuals. (The Camp insistence on not being "serious," on playing, also connects with the homosexual's desire to remain youthful.) Yet one feels that if homosexuals hadn't more or less invented Camp, someone else would. For the aristocratic posture with relation to culture cannot die, though it may persist only in increasingly arbitrary and ingenious ways. Camp is (to repeat) the relation to style in a time in which the adoption of style—as such—has become altogether questionable. (In the modern era, each new style, unless frankly anachronistic, has come on the scene as an anti-style.)

> *One must have a heart of stone to read the death of Little Nell*
> *without laughing.*
>
> —IN CONVERSATION

54. The experiences of Camp are based on the great discovery that the sensibility of high culture has no monopoly upon refinement. Camp asserts that good taste is not simply good taste; that there exists, indeed, a good taste of bad taste. (Genet talks about this in *Our Lady of the Flowers*.) The discovery of the good taste of bad taste can be very liberating. The man who insists on high and serious pleasures is depriving himself of pleasure; he continually restricts what he can enjoy; in the constant exercise of his good taste he will eventually price himself out of the market, so to speak. Here Camp taste supervenes upon good taste as a daring and witty hedonism. It makes

the man of good taste cheerful, where before he ran the risk of being chronically frustrated. It is good for the digestion.

55. Camp taste is, above all, a mode of enjoyment, of appreciation—not judgment. Camp is generous. It wants to enjoy. It only seems like malice, cynicism. (Or, if it is cynicism, it's not a ruthless but a sweet cynicism.) Camp taste doesn't propose that it is in bad taste to be serious; it doesn't sneer at someone who succeeds in being seriously dramatic. What it does is to find the success in certain passionate failures.

56. Camp taste is a kind of love, love for human nature. It relishes, rather than judges, the little triumphs and awkward intensities of "character" . . . Camp taste identifies with what it is enjoying. People who share this sensibility are not laughing at the thing they label as "a camp," they're enjoying it. Camp is a tender feeling.

(Here one may compare Camp with much of Pop Art, which—when it is not just Camp—embodies an attitude that is related, but still very different. Pop Art is more flat and more dry, more serious, more detached, ultimately nihilistic.)

57. Camp taste nourishes itself on the love that has gone into certain objects and personal styles. The absence of this love is the reason why such kitsch items as *Peyton Place* (the book) and the Tishman Building aren't Camp.

58. The ultimate Camp statement: it's good because it's awful . . . Of course, one can't always say that. Only under certain conditions, those which I've tried to sketch in these notes.

(1964)

Spiritual Style in the Films of Robert Bresson

I

Some art aims directly at arousing the feelings; some art appeals to the feelings through the route of the intelligence. There is art that involves, that creates empathy. There is art that detaches, that provokes reflection.

Great reflective art is not frigid. It can exalt the spectator, it can present images that appall, it can make him weep. But its emotional power is mediated. The pull toward emotional involvement is counterbalanced by elements in the work that promote distance, disinterestedness, impartiality. Emotional involvement is always, to a greater or lesser degree, postponed.

The contrast can be accounted for in terms of techniques or means—even of ideas. No doubt, though, the sensibility of the artist is, in the end, decisive. It is a reflective art, a detached art that Brecht is advocating when he talks about the "Alienation Effect." The didactic aims which Brecht claimed for his theater are really a vehicle for the cool temperament that conceived those plays.

II

In the film, the master of the reflective mode is Robert Bresson.

Though Bresson was born in 1911, his extant work in the cinema has all been done in the last twenty years, and consists of six feature films. (He made a short film in 1934 called *Les Affaires Publiques*, reportedly a comedy in the manner of René Clair, all copies of which have been lost; did some work on the scripts of two obscure commercial films in the mid-thirties; and in 1940 was assistant director to

Clair on a film that was never finished.) Bresson's first full-length film was begun when he returned to Paris in 1941 after spending eighteen months in a German prison camp. He met a Dominican priest and writer, Father Bruckberger, who suggested that they collaborate on a film about Bethany, the French Dominican order devoted to the care and rehabilitation of women ex-convicts. A scenario was written, Jean Giraudoux was enlisted to write the dialogue, and the film—at first called *Béthanie,* and finally, at the producers' insistence, *Les Anges du Peché (The Angels of Sin)*—was released in 1943. It was enthusiastically acclaimed by the critics and had a success with the public as well.

The plot of his second film, begun in 1944 and released in 1945, was a modern version of one of the interpolated stories in Diderot's great anti-novel *Jacques le Fataliste;* Bresson wrote the scenario and Jean Cocteau the dialogue. Bresson's first success was not repeated, however. *Les Dames du Bois de Boulogne* was panned by the critics and failed at the box office, too.

Bresson's third film, *Le Journal d'un Curé de Campagne (The Diary of a Country Priest)*, did not appear until 1951; his fourth film, *Un Condamné à Mort s'est Échappé* (called, here, *A Man Escaped*) in 1956; his fifth film, *Pickpocket,* in 1959; and his sixth film, *Procès de Jeanne d'Arc (The Trial of Joan of Arc)*, in 1962. All have had a certain success with critics but scarcely any with the public—with the exception of the last film, which most critics disliked, too. Once hailed as the new hope of the French cinema, Bresson is now firmly labeled as an esoteric director. He has never had the attention of the art-house audience that flocks to Buñuel, Bergman, Fellini—though he is a far greater director than these; even Antonioni has almost a mass audience compared with Bresson's. And, except among a small coterie, he has had only the scantest critical attention.

The reason that Bresson is not generally ranked according to his merits is that the tradition to which his art belongs, the reflective or contemplative, is not well understood. Particularly in England and America, Bresson's films are often described as cold, remote, overintellectualized, geometrical. But to call a work of art "cold" means nothing more or less than to compare it (often unconsciously) to a work that is "hot." And not all art is—or could be—hot, any more than all persons have the same temperament. The generally accepted notions of the range of temperament in art are provincial. Certainly, Bresson is cold next to Pabst or Fellini. (So is Vivaldi cold next to Brahms, and Keaton cold next to Chaplin.) One has to understand the aesthetics—that is, find the beauty—of such coldness. And Bresson offers a particularly good case for sketching such an aesthetic, because of his range. Exploring the possibilities of a reflective, as opposed to an emotionally immediate, art, Bresson moves from the diagrammatic perfection of *Les Dames du Bois de Boulogne* to the almost lyrical, almost "humanistic" warmth of *Un Condamné à Mort s'est Échappé*. He also shows—and this is instructive, too—how such art can become too rarefied, in his latest film, *Procès de Jeanne d'Arc*.

III

In reflective art, the *form* of the work of art is present in an emphatic way.

The effect of the spectator's being aware of the form is to elongate or to retard the emotions. For, to the extent that we are conscious of form in a work of art, we become somewhat detached; our emotions do not respond in the same way as they do in real life. Awareness of form does two things simultaneously: it gives a sensuous pleasure independent of the "content," and it invites the use of intelligence. It may be a very low order of reflection which is invited, as, for instance, by the narrative form (the interweaving of the four separate stories) of Griffith's *Intolerance*. But it is reflection, nonetheless.

The typical way in which "form" shapes "content" in art is by doubling, duplicating. Symmetry and the repetition of motifs in painting, the double plot in Elizabethan drama, and rhyme schemes in poetry are a few obvious examples.

The evolution of forms in art is partly independent of the evolution of subject matters. (The history of forms is dialectical. As types of sensibility become banal, boring, and are overthrown by their opposites, so forms in art are, periodically, exhausted. They become banal, unstimulating, and are replaced by new forms which are at the same time anti-forms.) Sometimes the most beautiful effects are gained when the material and the form are at cross-purposes. Brecht does this often: placing a hot subject in a cold frame. Other times, what satisfies is that the form is perfectly appropriate to the theme. This is the case with Bresson.

Why Bresson is not only a much greater but also a more interesting director than, say, Buñuel is that he has worked out a form that perfectly expresses and accompanies what he wants to say. In fact, it *is* what he wants to say.

Here one must carefully distinguish between form and manner. Welles, the early René Clair, Sternberg, Ophuls are examples of directors with unmistakable stylistic inventions. But they never created a rigorous narrative form. Bresson, like Ozu, has. And the form of

Bresson's films is designed (like Ozu's) to discipline the emotions at the same time that it arouses them: to induce a certain tranquillity in the spectator, a state of spiritual balance that is itself the subject of the film.

Reflective art is art which, in effect, imposes a certain discipline on the audience—postponing easy gratification. Even boredom can be a permissible means of such discipline. Giving prominence to what is artifice in the work of art is another means. One thinks here of Brecht's idea of theater. Brecht advocated strategies of staging—like having a narrator, putting musicians on stage, interposing filmed scenes—and a technique of acting so that the audience could distance itself, and not become uncritically "involved" in the plot and the fate of the characters. Bresson wishes distance, too. But his aim, I would imagine, is not to keep hot emotions cool so that intelligence can prevail. The emotional distance typical of Bresson's films seems to exist for a different reason altogether: because all identification with characters, deeply conceived, is an impertinence—an affront to the mystery that is human action and the human heart.

But—all claims for intellectual coolness or respect for the mystery of action laid aside—surely Brecht knew, as must Bresson, that such distancing is a source of great emotional power. It is precisely the defect of the naturalistic theater and cinema that, giving itself too readily, it easily consumes and exhausts its effects. Ultimately, the greatest source of emotional power in art lies not in any particular subject matter, however passionate, however universal. It lies in form. The detachment and retarding of the emotions, through the consciousness of form, makes them far stronger and more intense in the end.

IV

Despite the venerable critical slogan that film is primarily a visual medium, and despite the fact that Bresson was a painter before he turned to making films, form for Bresson is not mainly visual. It is, above all, a distinctive form of narration. For Bresson film is not a plastic but a narrative experience.

Bresson's form fulfills beautifully the prescription of Alexandre Astruc, in his famous essay "Le Camera-Stylo," written in the late forties. According to Astruc, the cinema will, ideally, become a language.

By a language I mean the form in which and through which an artist can express his thoughts, however abstract they may be, or translate his obsessions, just as in an essay or a novel. . . . The film will gradually free itself from the tyranny of the visual, of the image for its own sake, of the immediate and concrete anecdote, to become a means of writing as supple and subtle as the written word. . . . What interests us in the cinema today is the creation of this language.

Cinema-as-language means a break with the traditional dramatic and visual way of telling a story in film. In Bresson's work, this creation of a language for films entails a heavy emphasis on the word. In the first two films, where the action is still relatively dramatic, and the plot employs a group of characters,* language (in the literal sense) appears in the form of dialogue. This dialogue definitely calls attention to itself. It is very theatrical dialogue, concise, aphoristic, deliberate, literary. It is the opposite of the improvised-sounding dialogue favored by the new French directors—including Godard in *Vivre sa Vie* and *Une Femme Mariée,* the most Bressonian of the New Wave films.

But in the next four films, in which the action has contracted from that which befalls a group to the fortunes of the lonely self, dialogue is often displaced by first-person narration. Sometimes the narration can be justified as providing links between scenes. But, more interestingly, it often doesn't tell us anything we don't know or are about to learn. It "doubles" the action. In this case, we usually get the word first, then the scene. For example, in *Pickpocket:* we see the hero writing (and hear his voice reading) his memoirs. Then we see the event which he has already curtly described.

But sometimes we get the scene first, then the explanation, the description of what has just happened. For example, in *Le Journal d'un Curé de Campagne,* there is a scene in which the priest calls anxiously on the Vicar of Torcy. We see the priest wheeling his bicycle up to the vicar's door, then the housekeeper answering (the vicar is obviously not at home, but we don't hear the housekeeper's voice), then the door shutting, and the priest leaning against it. Then, we hear: "I was so disappointed, I had to lean against the door." Another example: in *Un Condamné à Mort s'est Échappé,* we see Fon-

---

*Even here, though, there is a development. In *Les Anges du Peché,* there are five main characters—the young novice Anne-Marie; another novice, Madeleine; the Prioress; the Prioress's assistant, Mother Saint-Jean; and the murderess, Thérèse—as well as a great deal of background: the daily life of the convent, and so forth. In *Les Dames du Bois de Boulogne,* there is already a simplification, less background. Four characters are clearly outlined—Hélène, her former lover Jean, Agnès, and Agnès's mother. Everyone else is virtually invisible. We never see the servants' faces, for instance.

taine tearing up the cloth of his pillow, then twisting the cloth around wire which he has stripped off the bed frame. Then, the voice: "I twisted it strongly."

The effect of this "superfluous" narration is to punctuate the scene with intervals. It puts a brake on the spectator's direct imaginative participation in the action. Whether the order is from comment to scene or from scene to comment, the effect is the same: such doublings of the action both arrest and intensify the ordinary emotional sequence.

Notice, too, that in the first type of doubling—where we hear what's going to happen before we see it—there is a deliberate flouting of one of the traditional modes of narrative involvement: suspense. Again, one thinks of Brecht. To eliminate suspense, at the beginning of a scene Brecht announces, by means of placards or a narrator, what is to happen. (Godard adopts this technique in *Vivre sa Vie*.) Bresson does the same thing, by jumping the gun with narration. In many ways, the perfect story for Bresson is that of his *Procès de Jeanne d'Arc*—in that the plot is wholly known, foreordained; the words of the actors are not invented but those of the actual trial record. Ideally, there is no suspense in a Bresson film. Thus, in the one film where suspense should normally play a large role, *Un Condamné à Mort s'est Échappé*, the title deliberately—even awkwardly—gives the outcome away: we know Fontaine is going to make it.* In this respect, of course, Bresson's escape film differs from Jacques Becker's last work, *Le Trou*, though in other ways Becker's excellent film owes a great deal to *Un Condamné à Mort s'est Échappé*. (It is to Becker's credit that he was the only prominent person in the French film world who defended *Les Dames du Bois de Boulogne* when it came out.)

Thus, form in Bresson's films is anti-dramatic, though strongly linear. Scenes are cut short, and set end to end without obvious emphasis. In *Le Journal d'un Curé de Campagne*, there must be thirty such short scenes. This method of constructing the story is most rigorously observed in *Procès de Jeanne d'Arc*. The film is composed of static, medium shots of people talking; the scenes are the inexorable sequence of Jeanne's interrogations. The principle of eliding anecdotal material—in *Un Condamné à Mort s'est Échappé*, for instance, one knows little about why Fontaine is in prison in the first place—is here carried to its extreme. There are no interludes of any sort. An interrogation ends; the door slams behind Jeanne; the scene fades out.

---

* The film has a co-title, which expresses the theme of inexorability: *Le Vent Souffle où il veut.*

The key clatters in the lock; another interrogation; again the door clangs shut; fadeout. It is a very dead-pan construction, which puts a sharp brake on emotional involvement.

Bresson also came to reject the species of involvement created in films by the expressiveness of the acting. Again, one is reminded of Brecht by Bresson's particular way of handling actors, in the exercise of which he has found it preferable to use non-professionals in major roles. Brecht wanted the actor to "report" a role rather than "be" it. He sought to divorce the actor from identifying with the role, as he wanted to divorce the spectator from identifying with the events that he saw being "reported" on the stage. "The actor," Brecht insists, "must remain a demonstrator; he must present the person demonstrated as a stranger, he must not suppress the '*he* did that, *he* said that' element in his performance." Bresson, working with non-professional actors in his last four films (he used professionals in *Les Anges du Peché* and *Les Dames du Bois de Boulogne*), also seems to be striving for the same effect of strangeness. His idea is for the actors not to act out their lines but simply to say them with as little expression as possible. (To get this effect, Bresson rehearses his actors for several months before shooting begins.) Emotional climaxes are rendered very elliptically.

But the reason is really quite different in the two cases. The reason that Brecht rejected acting reflects his idea of the relation of dramatic art to critical intelligence. He thought that the emotional force of the acting would get in the way of the ideas represented in plays. (From what I saw of the work of the Berliner Ensemble six years ago, though, it didn't seem to me that the somewhat low-keyed acting really diminished emotional involvement; it was the highly stylized staging which did that.) The reason that Bresson rejects acting reflects his notion of the purity of the art itself. "Acting is for the theater, which is a bastard art," he has said. "The film can be a true art because in it the author takes fragments of reality and arranges them in such a way that their juxtaposition transforms them." Cinema, for Bresson, is a total art, in which acting corrodes. In a film,

> each shot is like a word, which means nothing by itself, or rather means so many things that in effect it is meaningless. But a word in a poem is transformed, its meaning made precise and unique, by its placing in relation to the words around it: in the same way a shot in a film is given its meaning by its context, and each shot modifies the meaning of the previous one until with the last shot a total, unparaphrasable meaning has been arrived at. Acting has nothing to do with that, it can only get in the

way. Films can only be made by bypassing the will of those who appear in them; using not what they do, but what they are.

In sum: there are spiritual resources beyond effort, which appear only when effort is stilled. One imagines that Bresson never treats his actors to an "interpretation" of their roles: Claude Laydu, who plays the priest in *Le Journal d'un Curé de Campagne,* has said that while he was making the film he was never told to try to represent sanctity, though that is exactly what he appears to do. In the end, everything depends on the actor, who either has a luminous presence or doesn't. Laydu has it. So does François Leterrier, who is Fontaine in *Un Condamné à Mort s'est Échappé.* But Martin Lassalle as Michel in *Pickpocket* conveys something wooden, at times evasive. With Florence Carrez in *Procès de Jeanne d'Arc,* Bresson has experimented with the limit of the unexpressive. There is no acting at all; she simply reads the lines. It could have worked. But it doesn't —because she is the least luminous of all the presences Bresson has "used" in his later films. The thinness of Bresson's latest film is, partly, a failure of communicated intensity on the part of the actress who plays Jeanne, upon whom the film depends.

V

All of Bresson's films have a common theme: the meaning of confinement and liberty. The imagery of the religious vocation and of crime are used jointly. Both lead to "the cell."

The plots all have to do with incarceration and its sequel. *Les Anges du Peché* takes place mostly inside a convent. Thérèse, an ex-convict who (unknown to the police) has just murdered the lover who betrayed her, is delivered into the hands of the Bethany nuns. One young novice, who tries to create a special relationship with Thérèse and, learning her secret, to get her to surrender herself voluntarily to the police, is expelled from the convent for insubordination. One morning, she is found dying in the convent garden. Thérèse is finally moved, and the last shot is of her extending her hands to the policeman's manacles . . . In *Les Dames du Bois de Boulogne,* the metaphor of confinement is repeated several times. Hélène and Jean have been confined in their love; he urges her to return to the world now that she is "free." But she doesn't, and instead devotes herself to setting a trap for him—a trap which requires that she find two pawns (Agnès and her mother), whom she virtually confines in an apartment while they await her orders. Like *Les Anges du Peché,* this is the story of the redemption of a lost girl. In *Les Anges du Peché,*

Thérèse is liberated by accepting imprisonment; in *Les Dames du Bois de Boulogne,* Agnès is imprisoned, and then, arbitrarily, as by a miracle, is forgiven, set free . . . In *Le Journal d'un Curé de Campagne,* the emphasis has shifted. The bad girl, Chantal, is kept in the background. The drama of confinement is in the priest's confinement in himself, his despair, his weakness, his mortal body. ("I was a prisoner of the Holy Agony.") He is liberated by accepting his senseless and agonizing death from stomach cancer . . . In *Un Condamné à Mort s'est Échappé,* which is set in a German-run prison in occupied France, confinement is most literally represented. So is liberation: the hero triumphs over himself (his despair, the temptation of inertia) and escapes. The obstacles are embodied both in material things and in the incalculability of the human beings in the vicinity of the solitary hero. But Fontaine risks trusting the two strangers in the courtyard at the beginning of his imprisonment, and his trust is not betrayed. And because he risks trusting the youthful collaborationist who is thrown into his cell with him on the eve of his escape (the alternative is to kill the boy), he is able to get out . . . In *Pickpocket,* the hero is a young recluse who lives in a closet of a room, a petty criminal who, in Dostoevskian fashion, appears to crave punishment. Only at the end, when he has been caught and is in jail, talking through the bars with the girl who has loved him, is he depicted as being, possibly, able to love . . . In *Procès de Jeanne d'Arc,* again the entire film is set in prison. As in *Le Journal d'un Curé de Campagne,* Jeanne's liberation comes through a hideous death; but Jeanne's martyrdom is much less affecting than the priest's, because she is so depersonalized (unlike Falconetti's Jeanne in Dreyer's great film) that she does not seem to mind dying.

The nature of drama being conflict, the real drama of Bresson's stories is interior conflict: the fight against oneself. And all the static and formal qualities of his films work to that end. Bresson has said, of his choice of the highly stylized and artificial plot of *Les Dames du Bois de Boulogne,* that it allowed him to "eliminate anything which might distract from the interior drama." Still, in that film and the one before it, interior drama is represented in an exterior form, however fastidious and stripped down. *Les Anges du Péché* and *Les Dames du Bois de Boulogne* depict conflicts of will among the various characters as much as or more than they concern a conflict within the self.

It is only in the films following *Les Dames du Bois de Boulogne* that Bresson's drama has been really interiorized. The theme of *Le Journal d'un Curé de Campagne* is the young priest's conflict with himself: only secondarily is this acted out in his relation with the

Vicar of Torcy, with Chantal, and with the Countess, Chantal's mother. This is even clearer in *Un Condamné à Mort s'est Échappé*—where the principal character is literally isolated in a cell, struggling against despair. Solitude and interior conflict pair off in another way in *Pickpocket,* where the solitary hero refuses despair only at the price of refusing love, and gives himself over to masturbatory acts of theft. But in the last film, where we know the drama should be taking place, there is scarcely any evidence of it. Conflict has been virtually suppressed; it must be inferred. Bresson's Jeanne is an automaton of grace. But, however interior the drama, there must be drama. This is what *Procès de Jeanne d'Arc* withholds.

Notice, though, that the "interior drama" which Bresson seeks to depict does not mean *psychology.* In realistic terms, the motives of Bresson's characters are often hidden, sometimes downright incredible. In *Pickpocket,* for instance, when Michel sums up his two years in London with "I lost all my money on gambling and women," one simply does not believe it. Nor is it any more convincing that during this time the good Jacques, Michel's friend, has made Jeanne pregnant and then deserted her and their child.

Psychological implausibility is scarcely a virtue; and the narrative passages I have just cited are flaws in *Pickpocket.* But what is central to Bresson and, I think, not to be caviled at, is his evident belief that psychological analysis is superficial. (Reason: it assigns to action a paraphrasable meaning that true art transcends.) He does not intend his characters to be implausible, I'm sure; but he does, I think, intend them to be opaque. Bresson is interested in the forms of spiritual action—in the physics, as it were, rather than in the psychology of souls. Why persons behave as they do is, ultimately, not to be understood. (Psychology, precisely, does claim to understand.) Above all, persuasion is inexplicable, unpredictable. That the priest *does* reach the proud and unyielding Countess (in *Le Journal d'un Curé de Campagne*), that Jeanne *doesn't* persuade Michel (in *Pickpocket*) are just facts—or mysteries, if you like.

Such a physics of the soul was the subject of Simone Weil's most remarkable book, *Gravity and Grace.* And the following sentences of Simone Weil's:

> All the natural movements of the soul are controlled by laws analogous to those of physical gravity. Grace is the only exception.
>
> Grace fills empty spaces, but it can only enter where there is a void to receive it, and it is grace itself which makes this void.
>
> The imagination is continually at work filling up all the fissures through which grace might pass.

supply the three basic theorems of Bresson's "anthropology." Some souls are heavy, others light; some are liberated or capable of being liberated, others not. All one can do is be patient, and as empty as possible. In such a regimen there is no place for the imagination, much less for ideas and opinions. The ideal is neutrality, transparence. This is what is meant when the Vicar of Torcy tells the young priest in *Le Journal d'un Curé de Campagne,* "A priest has no opinions."

Except in an ultimate unrepresentable sense, a priest has no attachments either. In the quest for spiritual lightness ("grace"), attachments are a spiritual encumbrance. Thus, the priest, in the climactic scene of *Le Journal d'un Curé de Campagne,* forces the Countess to relinquish her passionate mourning for her dead son. True contact between persons is possible, of course; but it comes not through will but unasked for, through grace. Hence in Bresson's films human solidarity is represented only at a distance—as it is between the priest and the Vicar of Torcy in *Le Journal d'un Curé de Campagne,* or between Fontaine and the other prisoners in *Un Condamné à Mort s'est Échappé.* The actual coming together of two people in a relation of love can be stated, ushered in, as it were, before our eyes: Jean crying out "Stay! I love you!" to the nearly dead Agnès in *Les Dames du Bois de Boulogne;* Fontaine putting his arm around Jost in *Un Condamné à Mort s'est Échappé;* Michel in *Pickpocket* saying to Jeanne through prison bars, "How long it has taken me to come to you." But we do not see love lived. The moment in which it is declared terminates the film.

In *Un Condamné à Mort s'est Échappé,* the elderly man in the adjoining cell asks the hero, querulously, "Why do you fight?" Fontaine answers, "To fight. To fight against myself." The true fight against oneself is against one's heaviness, one's gravity. And the instrument of this fight is the idea of work, a project, a task. In *Les Anges du Peché,* it is Anne-Marie's project of "saving" Thérèse. In *Les Dames du Bois de Boulogne,* it is the revenge plot of Hélène. These tasks are cast in traditional form—constantly referring back to the intention of the character who performs them, rather than decomposed into separately engrossing acts of behavior. In *Le Journal d'un Curé de Campagne* (which is transitional in this respect) the most affecting images are not those of the priest in his role, struggling for the souls of his parishioners, but of the priest in his homely moments: riding his bicycle, removing his vestments, eating bread, walking. In Bresson's next two films, work has dissolved into the idea of the infinite taking of pains. The project has become totally concrete, incarnate, and at the same time more impersonal. In *Un Con-*

damné à Mort s'est Échappé, the most powerful scenes are those which show the hero absorbed in his labors: Fontaine scraping at his door with the spoon, Fontaine sweeping the wood shavings which have fallen on the floor into a tiny pile with a single straw pulled from his broom. ("One month of patient work—my door opened.") In *Pickpocket,* the emotional center of the film is where Michel is wordlessly, disinterestedly, taken in hand by a professional pickpocket and initiated into the real art of what he has only practiced desultorily: difficult gestures are demonstrated, the necessity of repetition and routine is made clear. Large sections of *Un Condamné à Mort s'est Échappé* and *Pickpocket* are wordless; they are about the beauties of personality effaced by a project. The face is very quiet, while other parts of the body, represented as humble servants of projects, become expressive, transfigured. One remembers Thérèse kissing the white feet of the dead Anne-Marie at the end of *Les Anges du Peché,* the bare feet of the monks filing down the stone corridor in the opening sequence of *Procès de Jeanne d'Arc.* One remembers Fontaine's large graceful hands at their endless labors in *Un Condamné à Mort s'est Échappé,* the ballet of agile thieving hands in *Pickpocket.*

Through the "project"—exactly contrary to "imagination"—one overcomes the gravity that weighs down the spirit. Even *Les Dames du Bois de Boulogne,* whose story seems most un-Bressonian, rests on this contrast between a project and gravity (or, immobility). Hélène has a project—revenging herself on Jean. But she is immobile, too—from suffering and vengefulness. Only in *Procès de Jeanne d'Arc,* the most Bressonian of stories, is this contrast (to the detriment of the film) not exploited. Jeanne has no project. Or if she may be said to have a project, her martyrdom, we only know about it; we are not privy to its development and consummation. She appears to be passive. If only because Jeanne is not portrayed for us in her solitude, alone in her cell, Bresson's film seems, next to the others, so undialectical.

VI

Jean Cocteau has said (*Cocteau on the Film,* A Conversation Recorded by André Fraigneau, 1951) that minds and souls today "live without a syntax; that is to say, without a moral system. This moral system has nothing to do with morality proper, and should be built up by each one of us as an inner style, without which no outer style is possible." Cocteau's films may be understood as portraying this inwardness which is the true morality; so may Bresson's. Both are concerned, in their films, with depicting spiritual style. This similar-

ity is less than obvious because Cocteau conceives of spiritual style
aesthetically, while in at least three of his films (*Les Anges du Peché,
Le Journal d'un Curé de Campagne,* and *Procès de Jeanne d'Arc*)
Bresson seems committed to an explicit religious point of view. But
the difference is not as great as it appears. Bresson's Catholicism is a
language for rendering a certain vision of human action, rather than
a "position" that is stated. (For contrast, compare the direct piety of
Rossellini's *The Flowers of Saint Francis* and the complex debate on
faith expounded in Melville's *Léon Morin, Prêtre.*) The proof of this
is that Bresson is able to say the same thing without Catholicism—
in his three other films. In fact, the most entirely successful of all
Bresson's films—*Un Condamné à Mort s'est Échappé*—is one which,
while it has a sensitive and intelligent priest in the background (one
of the prisoners), bypasses the religious way of posing the problem.
The religious vocation supplies one setting for ideas about gravity,
lucidity, and martyrdom. But the drastically secular subjects of crime,
the revenge of betrayed love, and solitary imprisonment also yield the
same themes.

Bresson is really more like Cocteau than appears—an ascetic Cocteau, Cocteau divesting himself of sensuousness, Cocteau without
poetry. The aim is the same: to build up an image of spiritual style.
But the sensibility, needless to say, is altogether different. Cocteau's
is a clear example of the homosexual sensibility that is one of the
principal traditions of modern art: both romantic and witty, languor-
ously drawn to physical beauty and yet always decorating itself with
stylishness and artifice. Bresson's sensibility is anti-romantic and solemn, pledged to ward off the easy pleasures of physical beauty and
artifice for a pleasure which is more permanent, more edifying, more
sincere.

In the evolution of this sensibility, Bresson's cinematic means become more and more chaste. His first two films, which were photographed by Philippe Agostini, stress visual effects in a way that the
other four do not. Bresson's very first film, *Les Anges du Peché,* is
more conventionally beautiful than any which have followed. And in
Les Dames du Bois de Boulogne, whose beauty is more muted, there
are lyrical camera movements, like the shot which follows Hélène
running down the stairs to arrive at the same time as Jean, who is
descending in an elevator, and stunning cuts, like the one which
moves from Hélène alone in her bedroom, stretched out on the bed,
saying, "I will be revenged," to the first shot of Agnès, in a crowded
nightclub, wearing tights and net stockings and top hat, in the throes
of a sexy dance. Extremes of black and white succeed one another

with great deliberateness. In *Les Anges du Peché,* the darkness of the prison scene is set off by the whiteness of the convent wall and of the nuns' robes. In *Les Dames du Bois de Boulogne,* the contrasts are set by clothes even more than by interiors. Hélène always wears long black velvet dresses, whatever the occasion. Agnès has three costumes: the scant black dancing outfit in which she appears the first time, the light-colored trench coat she wears during most of the film, and the white wedding dress at the end . . . The last four films, which were photographed by L. H. Burel, are much less striking visually, less chic. The photography is almost self-effacing. Sharp contrasts, as between black and white, are avoided. (It is almost impossible to imagine a Bresson film in color.) In *Le Journal d'un Curé de Campagne,* for instance, one is not particularly aware of the blackness of the priest's habit. One barely notices the bloodstained shirt and dirty pants which Fontaine has on throughout *Un Condamné à Mort s'est Échappé,* or the drab suits which Michel wears in *Pickpocket.* Clothes and interiors are as neutral, inconspicuous, functional as possible.

Besides refusing the visual, Bresson's later films also renounce "the beautiful." None of his non-professional actors are handsome in an outward sense. One's first feeling, when seeing Claude Laydu (the priest in *Le Journal d'un Curé de Campagne*), François Leterrier (Fontaine in *Un Condamné à Mort s'est Échappé*), Martin Lassalle (Michel in *Pickpocket*), and Florence Carrez (Jeanne in *Procès de Jeanne d'Arc*), is how plain they are. Then, at some point or other, one begins to see the face as strikingly beautiful. The transformation is most profound, and satisfying, with François Leterrier as Fontaine. Here lies an important difference between the films of Cocteau and Bresson, a difference which indicates the special place of *Les Dames du Bois de Boulogne* in Bresson's work; for this film (for which Cocteau wrote the dialogue) is in this respect very Cocteauish. Maria Casarès's black-garbed demonic Hélène is, visually and emotionally, of a piece with her brilliant performance in Cocteau's *Orphée* (1950). Such a hard-edge character, a character with a "motive" that remains constant throughout the story, is very different from the treatment of character, typical of Bresson, in *Le Journal d'un Curé de Campagne, Un Condamné à Mort s'est Échappé,* and *Pickpocket.* In the course of each of these three films, there is a subliminal revelation: a face which at first seems plain reveals itself to be beautiful; a character which at first seems opaque becomes oddly and inexplicably transparent. But in Cocteau's films—and in *Les Dames du Bois de Boulogne*—neither character nor beauty is revealed. They are there to be assumed, to be transposed into drama.

While the spiritual style of Cocteau's heroes (who are played, usually, by Jean Marais) tends toward narcissism, the spiritual style of Bresson's heroes is one variety or other of unself-consciousness. (Hence the role of the project in Bresson's films: it absorbs the energies that would otherwise be spent on the self. It effaces personality, in the sense of personality as what is idiosyncratic in each human being, the limit inside which we are locked.) Consciousness of self is the "gravity" that burdens the spirit; the surpassing of the consciousness of self is "grace," or spiritual lightness. The climax of Cocteau's films is a voluptuous movement: a falling down, either in love (*Orphée*) or in death (*L'Aigle à Deux Têtes*, *L'Éternel Retour*); or a soaring up (*La Belle et la Bête*). With the exception of *Les Dames du Bois de Boulogne* (with its final glamorous image, shot from above, of Jean bending over Agnès, who lies on the floor like a great white bird), the end of Bresson's films is countervoluptuous, reserved.

While Cocteau's art is irresistibly drawn to the logic of dreams, and to the truth of invention over the truth of "real life," Bresson's art moves increasingly away from the story and toward documentary. *Le Journal d'un Curé de Campagne* is a fiction, drawn from the superb novel of the same name by Georges Bernanos. But the journal device allows Bresson to relate the fiction in a quasi-documentary fashion. The film opens with a shot of a notebook and a hand writing in it, followed by a voice on the sound track reading what has been written. Many scenes start with the priest writing in his journal. The film ends with a letter from a friend to the Vicar of Torcy relating the priest's death—we hear the words while the whole screen is occupied with the silhouette of a cross. Before *Un Condamné à Mort s'est Échappé* begins, we read the words on the screen: "This story actually happened. I have set it down without embellishment," and then: "Lyons, 1943." (Bresson had the original of Fontaine constantly present while the film was being made, to check on its accuracy.) *Pickpocket*, again a fiction, is told—partly—through journal form. Bresson returned to documentary in *Procès de Jeanne d'Arc*, this time with the greatest severity. Even music, which aided in setting tone in the earlier films, has been discarded. The use of the Mozart Mass in C minor in *Un Condamné à Mort s'est Échappé*, of Lully in *Pickpocket*, is particularly brilliant; but all that survives of music in *Procès de Jeanne d'Arc* is the drumbeat at the opening of the film.

Bresson's attempt is to insist on the irrefutability of what he is presenting. Nothing happens by chance; there are no alternatives, no fantasy; everything is inexorable. Whatever is not necessary, whatever is merely anecdotal or decorative, must be left out. Unlike Cocteau, Bresson wishes to pare down—rather than to enlarge—the dramatic and visual resources of the cinema. (In this, Bresson again reminds one of Ozu, who in the course of his thirty years of filmmaking renounced the moving camera, the dissolve, the fade.) True, in the latest, most ascetic of all his films, Bresson seems to have left out too much, to have overrefined his conception. But a conception as ambitious as this cannot help but have its extremism, and Bresson's "failures" are worth more than most directors' successes. For Bresson, art is the discovery of what is necessary—of that, and nothing more. The power of Bresson's six films lies in the fact that his purity and fastidiousness are not just an assertion about the resources of the cinema, as much of modern painting is mainly a comment in paint about painting. They are at the same time an idea about life, about what Cocteau called "inner style," about the most serious way of being human.

(1964)

On Style

It would be hard to find any reputable literary critic today who would care to be caught defending *as an idea* the old antithesis of style versus content. On this issue a pious consensus prevails. Everyone is quick to avow that style and content are indissoluble, that the strongly individual style of each important writer is an organic aspect of his work and never something merely "decorative."

In the *practice* of criticism, though, the old antithesis lives on, virtually unassailed. Most of the same critics who disclaim, in passing, the notion that style is an accessory to content maintain the duality whenever they apply themselves to particular works of literature. It is not so easy, after all, to get unstuck from a distinction that practically holds together the fabric of critical discourse, and serves to perpetuate certain intellectual aims and vested interests which themselves remain unchallenged and would be difficult to surrender without a fully articulated working replacement at hand.

In fact, to talk about the style of a particular novel or poem at all as a "style," without implying, whether one wishes to or not, that style is merely decorative, accessory, is extremely hard. Merely by employing the notion, one is almost bound to invoke, albeit implicitly, an antithesis between style and something else. Many critics appear not to realize this. They think themselves sufficiently protected by a theoretical disclaimer on the vulgar filtering-off of style from content, all the while their judgments continue to reinforce precisely what they are, in theory, eager to deny.

•

One way in which the old duality lives on in the practice of criticism, in concrete judgments, is the frequency with which quite admirable works of art are defended as good although what is miscalled their style is acknowledged to be crude or careless. Another is the frequency with which a very complex style is regarded with a barely concealed ambivalence. Contemporary writers and other artists with a style that is intricate, hermetic, demanding—not to speak of "beautiful"—get their ration of unstinting praise. Still, it is clear that such a style is often felt to be a form of insincerity: evidence of the artist's intrusion upon his materials, which should be allowed to deliver themselves in a pure state.

Whitman, in the preface to the 1855 edition of *Leaves of Grass,* expresses the disavowal of "style" which is, in most arts since the last century, a standard ploy for ushering in a new stylistic vocabulary. "The greatest poet has less a marked style and is more the free channel of himself," that great and very mannered poet contends. "He says to his art, I will not be meddlesome, I will not have in my writing any elegance or effect or originality to hang in the way between me and the rest like curtains. I will have nothing hang in the way, not the richest curtains. What I tell I tell for precisely what it is."

Of course, as everyone knows or claims to know, there is no neutral, absolutely transparent style. Sartre has shown, in his review of *The Stranger,* how the celebrated "white style" of Camus's novel—impersonal, expository, lucid, flat—is itself the vehicle of Meursault's image of the world (as made up of absurd, fortuitous moments). What Roland Barthes calls "the zero degree of writing" is, precisely by being anti-metaphorical and dehumanized, as selective and artificial as any traditional style of writing. Nevertheless, the notion of a style-less, transparent art is one of the most tenacious fantasies of modern culture. Artists and critics pretend to believe that it is no more possible to get the artifice out of art than it is for a person to lose his personality. Yet the aspiration lingers—a permanent dissent from modern art, with its dizzying velocity of style *changes*.

•

To speak of style is one way of speaking about the totality of a work of art. Like all discourse about totalities, talk of style must rely on metaphors. And metaphors mislead.

Take, for instance, Whitman's very material metaphor. By likening style to a curtain, he has of course confused style with decoration and for this would be speedily faulted by most critics. To conceive of style as a decorative encumbrance on the matter of the work suggests that the curtain could be parted and the matter revealed; or, to vary the metaphor slightly, that the curtain could be rendered transparent. But this is not the only erroneous implication of the metaphor. What the metaphor also suggests is that style is a matter of more or less (quantity), thick or thin (density). And, though less obviously so, this is just as wrong as the fancy that an artist possesses the genuine option to have or not to have a style. Style is not quantitative, any more than it is super-added. A more complex stylistic convention— say, one taking prose further away from the diction and cadences of ordinary speech—does not mean that the work has more style.

Indeed, practically all metaphors for style amount to placing matter on the inside, style on the outside. It would be more to the point to reverse the metaphor. The matter, the subject, is on the outside; the style is on the inside. As Cocteau writes: "Decorative style has never existed. Style is the soul, and unfortunately with us the soul assumes the form of the body." Even if one were to define style as the manner of our appearing, this by no means necessarily entails an opposition between a style that one assumes and one's true being. In fact, such a disjunction is extremely rare. In almost every case, our manner of appearing *is* our manner of being. The mask *is* the face.

I should make clear, however, that what I have been saying about dangerous metaphors doesn't rule out the use of limited and concrete metaphors to describe the impact of a particular style. It seems harmless to speak of a style, drawing from the crude terminology used to render physical sensations, as being "loud" or "heavy" or "dull" or "tasteless" or, employing the image of an argument, as "inconsistent."

•

The antipathy to style is always an antipathy to a given style. There are no style-less works of art, only works of art belonging to different, more or less complex stylistic traditions and conventions.

This means that the notion of style, generically considered, has a specific, historical meaning. It is not only that styles belong to a time and a place; and that our perception of the style of a given work of art is always charged with an awareness of the work's historicity, its place in a chronology. Further: the visibility of styles is itself a product of historical consciousness. Were it not for departures from, or experimentation with, previous artistic norms which are known to us, we could never recognize the profile of a new style. Still further: the very notion of style needs to be approached historically. Awareness of style as a problematic and isolable element in a work of art has emerged in the audience for art only at certain historical moments—as a front behind which other issues, ultimately ethical and political, are being debated. The notion of "having a style" is one of the solutions that has arisen, intermittently since the Renaissance, to the crises that have threatened old ideas of truth, of moral rectitude, and also of naturalness.

•

But suppose all this is admitted. That all representation is incarnated in a given style (easy to say). That there is, therefore, strictly speaking, no such thing as realism, except as, itself, a special stylistic convention (a little harder). Still, there are styles and styles. Everyone is acquainted with movements in art—two examples: Mannerist painting of the late sixteenth and early seventeenth centuries, Art Nouveau in painting, architecture, furniture, and domestic objects—which do more than simply have "a style." Artists such as Parmigianino, Pontormo, Rosso, Bronzino, such as Gaudí, Guimard, Beardsley, and Tiffany, in some obvious way cultivate style. They seem to be preoccupied with stylistic questions and indeed to place the accent less on what they are saying than on the manner of saying it.

To deal with art of this type, which seems to demand the distinction I have been urging be abandoned, a term such as "stylization" or its equivalent is needed. "Stylization" is what is present in a work of art precisely when an artist does make the by no means inevitable distinction between matter and manner, theme and form. When that happens, when style and subject are so distinguished, that is, played off against each other, one can legitimately speak of subjects being treated (or mistreated) in a certain style. Creative mistreatment is more the rule. For when the material of art is conceived of as "subject matter," it is also experienced as capable of being exhausted. And as subjects are understood to be fairly far along in this process of exhaustion, they become available to further and further stylization.

Compare, for example, certain silent movies of Sternberg (*Salvation Hunters, Underworld, The Docks of New York*) with the six American movies he made in the 1930s with Marlene Dietrich. The best of the early Sternberg films have pronounced stylistic features, a very sophisticated aesthetic surface. But we do not feel about the narrative of the sailor and the prostitute in *The Docks of New York* as we do about the adventures of the Dietrich character in *Blonde Venus* or *The Scarlet Empress,* that it is an exercise in style. What informs these later films of Sternberg's is an ironic attitude toward the subject matter (romantic love, the femme fatale), a judgment on the subject matter as interesting only so far as it is transformed by exaggeration; in a word, stylized . . . Cubist painting, or the sculpture of Giacometti, would not be an example of "stylization" as distinguished from "style" in art; however extensive the distortions of the human face and figure, these are not present to make the face and figure *interesting.* But the paintings of Crivelli and Georges de La Tour are examples of what I mean.

Stylization in a work of art, as distinct from style, reflects an ambivalence (affection contradicted by contempt, obsession contradicted by irony) toward the subject matter. This ambivalence is handled by maintaining, through the rhetorical overlay that is stylization, a special distance from the subject. But the common result is that either the work of art is excessively narrow and repetitive or else the different parts seem unhinged, dissociated. (A good example of the latter is the relation between the visually brilliant denouement of Orson Welles's *The Lady from Shanghai* and the rest of the film.) No doubt, in a culture pledged to the utility (particularly the moral utility) of art, burdened with a useless need to fence off solemn art from arts which provide amusement, the eccentricities of stylized art supply a valid and valuable satisfaction. I have described these satisfactions in another essay, under the name of camp taste. Yet it is evident that stylized art, palpably an art of excess, lacking harmoniousness, can never be of the very greatest kind.

•

What haunts all contemporary use of the notion of style is the putative opposition between form and content. How is one to exorcise the feeling that style, which functions like the notion of form, subverts content? One thing seems certain. No affirmation of the organic relation between style and content will really carry conviction—or guide critics who make this affirmation to the recasting of their specific discourse—until the notion of content is put in its place.

Most critics would agree that a work of art does not "contain" a certain amount of content (or function—as in the case of architecture) embellished by style. But few address themselves to the positive consequences of what they seem to have agreed to. What is "content"? Or, more precisely, what is left of the notion of content when we have transcended the antithesis of style (or form) and content? Part of the answer lies in the fact that for a work of art to have "content" is, in itself, a rather special stylistic convention. The great task which remains to critical theory is to examine in detail the *formal* function of subject matter.

•

Until this function is acknowledged and properly explored, it is inevitable that critics will go on treating works of art as "statements." (Less so, of course, in those arts which are abstract or have largely gone abstract, like music and painting and the dance. In these arts, the critics have not solved the problem; it has been taken from them.) Of course, a work of art can be considered as a statement; that is, as the answer to a question. On the most elementary level, Goya's portrait of the Duke of Wellington may be examined as the answer to the question: What did Wellington look like? *Anna Karenina* may be treated as an investigation of the problems of love, marriage, and adultery. Though the issue of the adequacy of artistic representation to life has pretty much been abandoned in, for example, painting, such adequacy continues to constitute a powerful standard of judgment in most appraisals of serious novels, plays, and films. In critical theory, the notion is quite old. At least since Diderot, the main tradition of criticism in all the arts, appealing to such apparently dissimilar criteria as verisimilitude and moral correctness, in effect treats the work of art as *a statement being made in the form of a work of art.*

To treat works of art in this fashion is not wholly irrelevant. But it is, obviously, putting art to use—for such purposes as inquiring into the history of ideas, diagnosing contemporary culture, or creating social solidarity. Such a treatment has little to do with what actually happens when a person possessing some training and aesthetic sensibility looks at a work of art appropriately. A work of art encountered as a work of art is an experience, not a statement or an answer to a question. Art is not only about something; it is something. A work of art is a thing *in* the world, not just a text or commentary *on* the world.

I am not saying that a work of art creates a world which is entirely self-referring. Of course, works of art (with the important exception of music) refer to the real world—to our knowledge, to our experience, to our values. They present information and evaluations. But their distinctive feature is that they give rise not to conceptual knowledge (which *is* the distinctive feature of discursive or scientific knowledge—e.g., philosophy, sociology, psychology, history) but to something like an excitation, a phenomenon of commitment, judgment in a state of thralldom or captivation. Which is to say that the knowledge we gain through art is an experience of the form or style of knowing something, rather than a knowledge of something (like a fact or a moral judgment) in itself.

This explains the preeminence of the value of *expressiveness* in works of art; and how the value of expressiveness—that is, of style—rightly takes precedence over content (when content is, falsely, isolated from style). The satisfactions of *Paradise Lost* for us do not lie in its views on God and man but in the superior kinds of energy, vitality, expressiveness which are incarnated in the poem.

Hence, too, the peculiar dependence of a work of art, however expressive, upon the cooperation of the person having the experience, for one may see what is "said" but remain unmoved, either through dullness or distraction. Art is seduction, not rape. A work of art proposes a type of experience designed to manifest the quality of imperiousness. But art cannot seduce without the complicity of the experiencing subject.

•

Inevitably, critics who regard works of art as statements will be wary of "style," even as they pay lip service to "imagination." All that imagination really means for them, anyway, is the supersensitive rendering of "reality." It is this "reality" snared by the work of art that they continue to focus on, rather than on the extent to which a work of art engages the mind in certain transformations.

But when the metaphor of the work of art as a statement loses its authority, the ambivalence toward "style" should dissolve; for this ambivalence mirrors the presumed tension between the statement and the manner in which it is stated.

•

In the end, however, attitudes toward style cannot be reformed merely by appealing to the "appropriate" (as opposed to utilitarian) way of looking at works of art. The ambivalence toward style is not rooted in simple error—it would then be quite easy to uproot—but in a passion, the passion of an entire culture. This passion is to protect and defend values traditionally conceived of as lying "outside" art, namely truth and morality, but which remain in perpetual danger of being compromised by art. Behind the ambivalence toward style is, ultimately, the historic Western confusion about the relation between art and morality, the aesthetic and the ethical.

For the problem of art versus morality is a pseudo-problem. The distinction itself is a trap; its continued plausibility rests on not putting the ethical into question, but only the aesthetic. To argue on these grounds at all, seeking to defend the autonomy of the aesthetic

(and I have, rather uneasily, done so myself), is already to grant
something that should not be granted—namely, that there exist two
independent sorts of response, the aesthetic and the ethical, which
vie for our loyalty when we experience a work of art. As if during the
experience one really had to choose between responsible and humane conduct, on the one hand, and the pleasurable stimulation of
consciousness, on the other!

Of course, we never have a purely aesthetic response to works of
art—neither to a play or a novel, with its depicting of human beings
choosing and acting, nor, though it is less obvious, to a painting by
Jackson Pollock or a Greek vase. (Ruskin has written acutely about
the moral aspects of the formal properties of painting.) But neither
would it be appropriate for us to make a moral response to something
in a work of art in the same sense that we do to an act in real life. I
would undoubtedly be indignant if someone I knew murdered his
wife and got away with it (psychologically, legally), but I can hardly
become indignant, as many critics seem to be, when the hero of Norman Mailer's *An American Dream* murders his wife and goes unpun-
ished. Divine, Darling, and the others in Genet's *Our Lady of the
Flowers* are not real people whom we are being asked to decide
whether to invite into our living rooms; they are figures in an imaginary landscape. The point may seem obvious, but the prevalence of
genteel-moralistic judgments in contemporary literary (and film) criticism makes it worth repeating a number of times.

For most people, as Ortega y Gasset has pointed out in *The Dehumanization of Art,* aesthetic pleasure is a state of mind essentially
indistinguishable from their ordinary responses. By art, they understand a means through which they are brought in contact with interesting human affairs. When they grieve and rejoice at human destinies in a play or film or novel, it is not really different from grieving
and rejoicing over such events in real life—except that the experience of human destinies in art contains less ambivalence, it is relatively disinterested, and it is free from painful consequences. The
experience is also, in a certain measure, more intense; for when suffering and pleasure are experienced vicariously, people can afford to
be avid. But, as Ortega argues, "a preoccupation with the human
content of the work [of art] is in principle incompatible with aesthetic
judgment."*

---

* Ortega continues: "A work of art vanishes from sight for a beholder who seeks in it
nothing but the moving fate of John and Mary or Tristan and Isolde and adjusts his
vision to this. Tristan's sorrows are sorrows and can evoke compassion only insofar as
they are taken as real. But an object of art is artistic only insofar as it is not real. . . .

Ortega is entirely correct, in my opinion. But I would not care to leave the matter where he does, which tacitly isolates aesthetic from moral response. Art is connected with morality, I should argue. One way that it is so connected is that art may yield moral *pleasure;* but the moral pleasure peculiar to art is not the pleasure of approving of acts or disapproving of them. The moral pleasure in art, as well as the moral service that art performs, consists in the intelligent gratification of consciousness.

●

What "morality" means is a habitual or chronic type of behavior (including feelings and acts). Morality is a code of acts, and of judgments and sentiments by which we reinforce our habits of acting in a certain way, which prescribe a standard for behaving or trying to behave toward other human beings *generally* (that is, to all who are acknowledged to be human) as if we were inspired by love. Needless to say, love is something we feel in truth for just a few individual human beings, among those who are known to us in reality and in our imagination . . . Morality is a *form* of acting and not a particular repertoire of choices.

If morality is so understood—as one of the achievements of human will, dictating to itself a mode of acting and being in the world—it becomes clear that no generic antagonism exists between the form of consciousness, aimed at action, which is morality, and the nourishment of consciousness, which is aesthetic experience. Only when works of art are reduced to statements which propose a specific content, and when morality is identified with a particular morality (and any particular morality has its dross, those elements which are no more than a defense of limited social interests and class values)— only then can a work of art be thought to undermine morality. Indeed, only then can the full distinction between the aesthetic and the ethical be made.

But if we understand morality in the singular, as a generic decision on the part of consciousness, then it appears that our response to art is "moral" insofar as it is, precisely, the enlivening of our sensibility

But not many people are capable of adjusting their perceptive apparatus to the pane and the transparency that is the work of art. Instead, they look right through it and revel in the human reality with which the work deals. . . . During the nineteenth century, artists proceeded in all too impure a fashion. They reduced the strictly aesthetic elements to a minimum and let the work consist almost entirely in a fiction of human realities. . . . Works of this kind [both Romanticism and Naturalism] are only partially works of art, or artistic objects . . . No wonder that nineteenth-century art has been so popular . . . it is not art but an extract from life."

and consciousness. For it is sensibility that nourishes our capacity for moral choice, and prompts our readiness to act, assuming that we do choose, which is a prerequisite for calling an act moral, and are not just blindly and unreflectively obeying. Art performs this "moral" task because the qualities which are intrinsic to the aesthetic experience (disinterestedness, contemplativeness, attentiveness, the awakening of the feelings) and to the aesthetic object (grace, intelligence, expressiveness, energy, sensuousness) are also fundamental constituents of a moral response to life.

•

In art, "content" is, as it were, the pretext, the goal, the lure which engages consciousness in essentially *formal* processes of transformation.

This is how we can, in good conscience, cherish works of art which, considered in terms of "content," are morally objectionable to us. (The difficulty is of the same order as that involved in appreciating works of art, such as *The Divine Comedy,* whose premises are intellectually alien.) To call Leni Riefenstahl's *Triumph of the Will* and *Olympia* masterpieces is not to gloss over Nazi propaganda with aesthetic lenience. The Nazi propaganda is there. But something else is there, too, which we reject at our loss. Because they project the complex movements of intelligence and grace and sensuousness, these two films of Riefenstahl (unique among works of Nazi artists) transcend the categories of propaganda or even reportage. And we find ourselves—to be sure, rather uncomfortably —seeing "Hitler" and not Hitler, the "1936 Olympics" and not the 1936 Olympics. Through Riefenstahl's genius as a filmmaker, the "content" has—let us even assume, against her intentions—come to play a purely formal role.

A work of art, so far as it is a work of art, cannot—whatever the artist's personal intentions—advocate anything at all. The greatest artists attain a sublime neutrality. Think of Homer and Shakespeare, from whom generations of scholars and critics have vainly labored to extract particular "views" about human nature, morality, and society.

Again, take the case of Genet—though, here, there is additional evidence for the point I am trying to make, because the artist's intentions are known. Genet, in his writings, may seem to be asking us to approve of cruelty, treacherousness, licentiousness, and murder. But so far as he is making a work of art, Genet is not advocating anything at all. He is recording, devouring, transfiguring his experience. In Genet's books, as it happens, this very process itself is his explicit subject; his books are not only works of art but works about art. However, even when (as is usually the case) this process is not in the foreground of the artist's demonstration, it is still this, the processing of experience, to which we owe our attention. It is immaterial that Genet's characters might repel us in real life. So would most of the characters in *King Lear*. The interest of Genet lies in the manner whereby his "subject" is annihilated by the serenity and intelligence of his imagination.

Approving or disapproving morally of what a work of art "says" is just as extraneous as becoming sexually excited by a work of art. (Both are, of course, very common.) And the reasons urged against the propriety and relevance of one apply as well to the other. Indeed, in this notion of the annihilation of the subject we have perhaps the only serious criterion for distinguishing between erotic literature or films or paintings which are art and those which (for want of a better word) one has to call pornography. Pornography has a "content" and is designed to make us connect (with disgust, desire) with that content. It is a substitute for life. But art does not excite; or, if it does, the excitation is appeased, within the terms of the aesthetic experience. All great art induces contemplation, a dynamic contemplation. However much the reader or listener or spectator is aroused by a provisional identification of what is in the work of art with real life, his ultimate reaction—so far as he is reacting to the work as a work of art—must be detached, restful, contemplative, emotionally free, beyond indignation and approval. It is interesting that Genet has recently said that he now thinks that if his books arouse readers sexually, "they're badly written, because the poetic emotion should be so strong that no reader is moved sexually. Insofar as my books are pornographic, I don't reject them. I simply say that I lacked grace."

A work of art may contain all sorts of information and offer instruction in new (and sometimes commendable) attitudes. We may learn about medieval theology and Florentine history from Dante; we may have our first experience of passionate melancholy from Chopin; we may become convinced of the barbarity of war by Goya and of the inhumanity of capital punishment by *An American Tragedy*. But so far as we deal with these works as works of art, the gratification they impart is of another order. It is an experience of the qualities or forms of human consciousness.

The objection that this approach reduces art to mere "formalism" must not be allowed to stand. (That word should be reserved for those works of art which mechanically perpetuate outmoded or depleted aesthetic formulas.) An approach which considers works of art as living, autonomous models of consciousness will seem objectionable only so long as we refuse to surrender the shallow distinction of form and content. For the sense in which a work of art has no content is no different from the sense in which the world has no content. Both are. Both need no justification; nor could they possibly have any.

•

The hyper-development of style in, for example, Mannerist painting and Art Nouveau, is an emphatic form of experiencing the world as an aesthetic phenomenon. But only a particularly emphatic form, which arises in reaction to an oppressively dogmatic style of realism. All style—that is, all art—proclaims this. And the world *is*, ultimately, an aesthetic phenomenon.

That is to say, the world (all there is) cannot, ultimately, be justified. Justification is an operation of the mind which can be performed only when we consider one part of the world in relation to another— not when we consider all there is.

•

The work of art, so far as we give ourselves to it, exercises a total or absolute claim on us. The purpose of art is not as an auxiliary to truth, either particular and historical or eternal. "If art is anything," as Robbe-Grillet has written, "it is everything; in which case it must be self-sufficient, and there can be nothing beyond it."

But this position is easily caricatured, for we live in the world, and it is in the world that objects of art are made and enjoyed. The claim that I have been making for the autonomy of the work of art—its freedom to "mean" nothing—does not rule out consideration of the effect or impact or function of art, once it be granted that in this functioning of the art object as art object the divorce between the aesthetic and the ethical is meaningless.

I have several times applied to the work of art the metaphor of a mode of nourishment. To become involved with a work of art entails, to be sure, the experience of detaching oneself from the world. But the work of art itself is also a vibrant, magical, and exemplary object which returns us to the world in some way more open and enriched.

•

Raymond Bayer has written: "What each and every aesthetic object imposes upon us, in appropriate rhythms, is a unique and singular formula for the flow of our energy. . . . Every work of art embodies a principle of proceeding, of stopping, of scanning; an image of energy or relaxation, the imprint of a caressing or destroying hand which is [the artist's] alone." We can call this the physiognomy of the work, or its rhythm, or, as I would rather do, its style. Of course, when we employ the notion of style historically, to group works of art into schools and periods, we tend to efface the individuality of styles. But this is not our experience when we encounter a work of art from an aesthetic (as opposed to a conceptual) point of view. Then, so far as the work is successful and still has the power to communicate with us, we experience only the individuality and contingency of the style.

It is the same with our own lives. If we see them from the outside, as the influence and popular dissemination of the social sciences and psychiatry has persuaded more and more people to do, we view ourselves as instances of generalities, and in so doing become profoundly and painfully alienated from our own experience and our humanity.

As William Earle has recently noted, if *Hamlet* is "about" anything, it is about Hamlet, his particular situation, not about the human condition. A work of art is a kind of showing or recording or witnessing which gives palpable form to consciousness; its object is to make something singular explicit. So far as it is true that we cannot judge (morally, conceptually) unless we generalize, then it is also true that the experience of works of art, and what is represented in works of art, transcends judgment—though the work itself may be judged as art. Isn't this just what we recognize as a feature of the greatest art, like the *Iliad* and the novels of Tolstoy and the plays of Shakespeare? That such art overrides our petty judgments, our facile labeling of persons and acts as good or bad? And that this can happen is all to the good. (There is even a gain for the cause of morality in it.)

For morality, unlike art, *is* ultimately justified by its utility: that it makes, or is supposed to make, life more humane and livable for us all. But consciousness—what used to be called, rather tendentiously, the faculty of contemplation—can be, and is, wider and more various than action. It has its nourishment, art and speculative thought, activities which can be described either as self-justifying or in no need of justification. What a work of art does is to make us see or comprehend something singular, not judge or generalize. This act of comprehension accompanied by voluptuousness is the only valid end, and sole sufficient justification, of a work of art.

•

Perhaps the best way of clarifying the nature of our experience of works of art, and the relation between art and the rest of human feeling and doing, is to invoke the notion of will. It is a useful notion because will is not just a particular posture of consciousness, energized consciousness. It is also an attitude toward the world, of a subject toward the world.

The complex kind of willing that is embodied, and communicated, in a work of art both abolishes the world and encounters it in an extraordinary intense and specialized way. This double aspect of the will in art is succinctly expressed by Bayer when he says: "Each work of art gives us the schematized and disengaged memory of a volition." Insofar as it is schematized, disengaged, a memory, the willing involved in art sets itself at a distance from the world.

All of which harks back to Nietzsche's famous statement in *The Birth of Tragedy:* "Art is not an imitation of nature but its metaphysical supplement, raised up beside it in order to overcome it."

•

All works of art are founded on a certain distance from the lived reality which is represented. This "distance" is, by definition, inhuman or impersonal to a certain degree; for in order to appear to us as art, the work must restrict sentimental intervention and emotional participation, which are functions of "closeness." It is the degree and manipulating of this distance, the conventions of distance, which constitute the style of the work. In the final analysis, "style" *is* art. And art is nothing more or less than various modes of stylized, dehumanized representation.

But this view—expounded by Ortega y Gasset, among others—can easily be misinterpreted, since it seems to suggest that art, so far as it approaches its own norm, is a kind of irrelevant, impotent toy. Ortega himself greatly contributes to such a misinterpretation by omitting the various dialectics between self and world involved in the experiencing of works of art. Ortega focuses too exclusively on the notion of the work of art as a certain kind of object, with its own, spiritually aristocratic, standards for being savored. A work of art *is* first of all an object, not an imitation; and it is true that all great art is founded on distance, on artificiality, on style, on what Ortega calls dehumanization. But the notion of distance (and of dehumanization, as well) is misleading, unless one adds that the movement is not just away from but toward the world. The overcoming or transcending of the world in art is also a way of encountering the world, and of training or educating the will to be in the world. It would seem that Ortega and even Robbe-Grillet, a more recent exponent of the same position, are still not wholly free of the spell of the notion of "content." For, in order to limit the human content of art, and to fend off tired ideologies like humanism or socialist realism which would put art in the service of some moral or social idea, they feel required to ignore or scant the function of art. But art does not become function-less when it is seen to be, in the last analysis, content-less. For all the persuasiveness of Ortega's and Robbe-Grillet's defense of the formal nature of art, the specter of banished "content" continues to lurk around the edges of their argument, giving to "form" a defiantly anemic, salutarily eviscerated look.

The argument will never be complete until "form" or "style" can be thought of without that banished specter, without a feeling of loss. Valéry's daring inversion—"Literature. What is 'form' for anyone else is 'content' for me"—scarcely does the trick. It is hard to think oneself out of a distinction so habitual and apparently self-evident. One can do so only by adopting a different, more organic, theoretical vantage point—such as the notion of will. What is wanted of such a vantage point is that it do justice to the twin aspects of art: as object and as function, as artifice and as living form of consciousness, as the overcoming or supplementing of reality and as the making explicit of forms of encountering reality, as autonomous individual creation and as dependent historical phenomenon.

•

Art is the objectifying of the will in a thing or performance, and the provoking or arousing of the will. From the point of view of the artist, it is the objectifying of a volition; from the point of view of the spectator, it is the creation of an imaginary décor for the will.

Indeed, the entire history of the various arts could be rewritten as the history of different attitudes toward the will. Nietzsche and Spengler wrote pioneer studies on this theme. A valuable recent attempt is to be found in a book by Jean Starobinski, *The Invention of Liberty,* mainly devoted to eighteenth-century painting and architecture. Starobinski examines the art of this period in terms of the new ideas of self-mastery and of mastery of the world, as embodying new relations between the self and the world. Art is seen as the naming of emotions. Emotions, longings, aspirations, by thus being named, are virtually invented and certainly promulgated by art: for example, the "sentimental solitude" provoked by the gardens that were laid out in the eighteenth century and by much-admired ruins.

Thus, it should be clear that the account of the autonomy of art I have been outlining, in which I have characterized art as an imaginary landscape or décor of the will, not only does not preclude but rather invites the examination of works of art as historically specifiable phenomena.

The intricate stylistic convolutions of modern art, for example, are clearly a function of the unprecedented *technical* extension of the human will by technology, and the devastating commitment of human will to a novel form of social and psychological order, one based on incessant change. But it also remains to be said that the very possibility of the explosion of technology, of the contemporary disruptions of self and society, depends on the attitudes toward the will which are partly invented and disseminated by works of art at a certain historical moment, and then come to appear as a "realistic" reading of a perennial human nature.

•

Style is the principle of decision in a work of art, the signature of the artist's will. And as the human will is capable of an indefinite number of stances, there are an indefinite number of possible styles for works of art.

Seen from the outside, that is, historically, stylistic decisions can always be correlated with some historical development—like the invention of writing or of movable type, the invention or transformation of musical instruments, the availability of new materials to the sculptor or architect. But this approach, however sound and valuable, of necessity sees matters grossly; it treats of "periods" and "traditions" and "schools."

Seen from the inside, that is, when one examines an individual work of art and tries to account for its value and effect, every stylistic decision contains an element of arbitrariness, however much it may seem justifiable *propter hoc*. If art is the supreme game which the will plays with itself, "style" consists of the set of rules by which this game is played. And the rules are always, finally, an artificial and arbitrary limit, whether they are rules of form (like *terza rima* or the twelve-tone row or frontality) or the presence of a certain "content." The role of the arbitrary and unjustifiable in art has never been sufficiently acknowledged. Ever since the enterprise of criticism began with Aristotle's *Poetics,* critics have been beguiled into emphasizing the necessary in art. (When Aristotle said that poetry was more philosophical than history, he was justified insofar as he wanted to rescue poetry, that is, the arts, from being conceived as a type of factual, particular, descriptive statement. But what he said was misleading insofar as it suggests that art supplies something like what philosophy gives us: an argument. The metaphor of the work of art as an "argument," with premises and entailments, has informed most criticism since.) Usually critics who want to praise a work of art feel compelled to demonstrate that each part is justified, that it could not be other than it is. And every artist, when it comes to his own work, remembering the role of chance, fatigue, external distractions, knows what the critic says to be a lie, knows that it could well have been otherwise. The sense of inevitability that a great work of art projects is made up not of the inevitability or necessity of its parts but of the whole.

•

In other words, what is inevitable in a work of art is the style. To the extent that a work seems right, just, unimaginable otherwise (without loss or damage), what we are responding to is a quality of its style. The most attractive works of art are those which give us the illusion that the artist had no alternatives, so wholly centered is he *in* his style. Compare that which is forced, labored, synthetic in the construction of *Madame Bovary* and of *Ulysses* with the ease and harmony of such equally ambitious works as *Les Liaisons Dangereuses* and Kafka's *Metamorphosis*. The first two books I have mentioned are great indeed. But the greatest art seems secreted, not constructed.

For an artist's style to have this quality of authority, assurance, seamlessness, inevitability does not, of course, alone put his work at the very highest level of achievement. Radiguet's two novels have it as well as Bach.

•

The difference that I have drawn between "style" and "stylization" might be analogous to the difference between will and willfulness.

•

An artist's style is, from a technical point of view, nothing other than the particular idiom in which he deploys the *forms* of his art. It is for this reason that the problems raised by the concept of "style" overlap with those raised by the concept of "form," and their solutions will have much in common.

For instance, one function of style is identical with, because it is simply a more individual specification of, that important function of form pointed out by Coleridge and Valéry: to preserve the works of the mind against oblivion. This function is easily demonstrated in the rhythmical, sometimes rhyming, character of all primitive, oral literatures. Rhythm and rhyme, and the more complex formal resources of poetry such as meter, symmetry of figures, antitheses, are the means that words afford for creating a memory of themselves before

material signs (writing) are invented; hence everything that an ar-
chaic culture wishes to commit to memory is put in poetic form. "The
form of a work," as Valéry puts it, "is the sum of its perceptible characteristics, whose physical action compels recognition and tends to
resist all those varying causes of dissolution which threaten the
expressions of thought, whether it be inattention, forgetfulness, or
even the objections that may arise against it in the mind."

Thus, form—in its specific idiom, style—is a plan of sensory im-
printing, the vehicle for the transaction between immediate sensuous
impression and memory (be it individual or cultural). This mnemonic
function explains why every style depends on, and can be analyzed
in terms of, some principle of repetition or redundancy.

It also explains the difficulties of the contemporary period of the
arts. Today styles do not develop slowly and succeed each other gradually, over long periods of time which allow the audience for art to
assimilate fully the principles of repetition on which the work of art
is built; but instead succeed one another so rapidly as to seem to give
their audiences no breathing space to prepare. For, if one does not
perceive how a work repeats itself, the work is, almost literally, not
perceptible and therefore, at the same time, not intelligible. It is the
perception of repetitions that makes a work of art intelligible. Until
one has grasped, not the "content," but the principles of (and balance
between) variety and redundancy in Merce Cunningham's "Winter-
branch" or a chamber concerto by Charles Wuorinen or Burroughs's
Naked Lunch or the "black" paintings of Ad Reinhardt, these works
are bound to appear boring or ugly or confusing, or all three.

•

Style has other functions besides that of being, in the extended
sense that I have just indicated, a mnemonic device.

For instance, every style embodies an epistemological decision, an
interpretation of how and what we perceive. This is easiest to see in
the contemporary, self-conscious period of the arts, though it is no
less true of all art. Thus, the style of Robbe-Grillet's novels expresses
a perfectly valid, if narrow, insight into relationships between persons
and things: namely, that persons are also things and that things are
not persons. Robbe-Grillet's behavioristic treatment of persons and
refusal to "anthropomorphize" things amount to a stylistic decision—
to give an exact account of the visual and topographic properties of
things; to exclude, virtually, sense modalities other than sight, perhaps because the language that exists to describe them is less exact
and less neutral. The circular repetitive style of Gertrude Stein's *Me-*

lanctha expresses her interest in the dilution of immediate awareness by memory and anticipation, what she calls "association," which is obscured in language by the system of the tenses. Stein's insistence on the presentness of experience is identical with her decision to keep to the present tense, to choose commonplace short words and repeat groups of them incessantly, to use an extremely loose syntax and abjure most punctuation. Every style is a means of insisting on something.

It will be seen that stylistic decisions, by focusing our attention on some things, are also a narrowing of our attention, a refusal to allow us to see others. But the greater interestingness of one work of art over another does not rest on the greater number of things the stylistic decisions in that work allow us to attend to, but rather on the intensity and authority and wisdom of that attention, however narrow its focus.

•

In the strictest sense, all the contents of consciousness are ineffable. Even the simplest sensation is, in its totality, indescribable. Every work of art, therefore, needs to be understood not only as something rendered but also as a certain handling of the ineffable. In the greatest art, one is always aware of things that cannot be said (rules of "decorum"), of the contradiction between expression and the presence of the inexpressible. Stylistic devices are also techniques of avoidance. The most potent elements in a work of art are, often, its silences.

•

What I have said about style has been directed mainly to clearing up certain misconceptions about works of art and how to talk about them. But it remains to be said that style is a notion that applies to any experience (whenever we talk about its form or qualities). And just as many works of art which have a potent claim on our interest are impure or mixed with respect to the standard I have been proposing, so many items in our experience which could not be classed as works of art possess some of the qualities of art objects. Whenever speech or movement or behavior or objects exhibit a certain deviation from the most direct, useful, insensible mode of expression or being in the world, we may look at them as having a "style," and being both autonomous and exemplary.

(1965)

Death Kit

•　•　•　•　•

After spreading his windbreaker and sweater on the strip of ground between the pair of tracks, a few feet from Incardona's body, and unlacing and taking off his boots, he makes Hester lie down with him. Takes her in his arms—quite inert at first, not responding at all. But Diddy feels so elated, so confident in his desire, that he didn't doubt he can arouse Hester and make her join him. Begins to caress her breasts; then puts one hand between her legs while, with the other, lifting up her dress to her waist. Diddy lost in the sweet, wet flesh. Yes, she is beginning to love him again, in spite of herself. After slipping down his trousers and shorts as far as his knees, Diddy moves his body on top of hers. She is beginning to move, too; though her head is turned curiously far to one side, so Diddy has trouble kissing her face. Their movements begin to braid together. Without ever breaking their rhythm, Diddy unfastens her brassière from behind and lifts her dress even higher; kicks his pants completely off, and puts himself deep inside her. It is only the beginning, and already Diddy's pleasure is more acute and imperious than at any time they have made love, including the first. It must be true for Hester, too. For (now) she's with him in everything, though still with her face, guarded by the sunglasses, turned sharply away. They come once, but it's not enough. Each must offer every part of his body to the other—to genitals, mouth, hands, knees, hair, feet. Both crying, crooning, groaning, laughing, hissing, chanting obscenities—an arrangement of urgent sounds that Diddy has never heard from either of them. Diddy and Hester, like two wild creatures who have never coupled before. Trying to stay on top of Diddy's sweater and wind-breaker, but eventually rolling off, tearing any clothes they've still kept on, smearing themselves with filth, scraping their skin. All part of the same magma of sensation, in which pleasure and pain are one. They come together again. (Now) truly, Diddy feels forgiven. He is rising out of his lean weak body, like a sea creature out of its shell.

Hester fell back from his arms. Can she have fainted? Anxiously, he puts his cheek to her breast and listens to her breathing: the slow, regular inhalation and exhalation of someone deeply exhausted, who's mercifully fallen into a vast, much needed sleep. Asleep, then. Let her rest. Diddy draws Hester's nylon underpants back up her legs and around her hips, pulls her torn dress down to her knees; stuffs her cotton bra into her coat pocket; pushes her limp arms through the sleeves of her coat, and buttons it. Then, grasping Hester in his arms, he carries her several feet to the nearby shelter. Just inside; at the very mouth of the shelter, sets her down in a sitting position. Propped against the wall, near the heap of stone blocks that had once been part of the barrier.

Occurred to Diddy that it could be dangerous to leave Hester here. Safer, surely, to carry her out of the tunnel altogether, and lay her on the slope by the track. After depositing her there, Diddy could return to the tunnel again.

But he was afraid to leave the tunnel, even for a few minutes. He might not want, or not be able, to return. And it's only for a little while that Hester must lie here. A little farther that he must explore; while curiosity, the sensations of physical well-being, and the mood of orgiastic fulfillment still run at high tide in him.

Should he move Incardona, too? Hell, no. Let the bastard lie there in his filth.

Diddy should dress himself (now) before proceeding any further. But feels an aversion to putting back on those creased and ripped garments; like Hester's, spattered with Incardona's brain juices and blood; further stained with mud, grease, dirt, sweat, and sex. Of course, he would have put them on if he'd felt cold. But he's not, as it happens. Not only not cold, but feeling somewhat flushed and overheated. Perhaps Diddy has a fever. No matter. All that matters is that, for the present, he lacks all desire to dress.

Then thinks of a better use for his clothes. Hester's head, which he'd set against the shelter wall, has already slumped down in an awkward-looking position that must be uncomfortable. And the hard wall must hurt her spine. She'll ache when she wakes up. Folding his boots, trousers, shirt, and sweater into one bundle, Diddy pulls the unconscious girl forward for a moment, then arranges the bundle pillow-fashion behind her; after leaning her back again, drapes his windbreaker over her torso as a blanket. Much better (now).

Why keep anything on? Diddy stoops down, removes his socks and then his T shirt. Placing these just beside Hester.

(Now) he's free to go.

Diddy lifts one naked leg, then the other, over the incompletely dismantled barrier. Of course. Just as he'd secretly suspected all along. What lies beyond it isn't just a tame continuation of the tunnel and its two tracks. The tracks end only a little farther ahead, some twenty yards beyond the barricade. After that, the walls widened. (Now) widening still farther.

Why not? "There is another world but it is inside this one." Diddy no longer walking in a tunnel but, rather, through a long, wide, damp gallery. Once again, reminded of a mine. Except that this chamber is powerfully lit. By naked bulbs, set in fixtures on windowless walls at fairly close intervals. The lighting even powerful enough, perhaps, to produce a perceptible increase in the temperature. How else can one explain why Diddy, walking about naked in late January, isn't chilled? Can't be simply the odd climate of the gallery, the curious heat-producing dampness, can it? But whatever the cause, Diddy is (now) never less than warm. And occasionally close to sweltering; he could wish it a good deal colder.

Diddy, naked, with his seamless sense of well-being. The narrow toes of his highly arched feet grip the dirty stone flooring as he walks. His testicles, drooping in the warm air, fall pleasantly against the inside of his thighs. His arms swing freely at his sides. His shoulders are relaxed, not tensed; his head held erect. And the entire surface of his skin seems coated with an effulgent smoothness, as if rinsed in sleep.

The harsh, almost brutal lighting leaves Diddy in no doubt about the details of the enclosed space through which he's walking. And about its marked difference from the space of the tunnel. In contrast with the hard-packed earthen bed of the tunnel, here was a genuine floor. Paved with dark-gray stone; perforated at intervals of thirty feet or so by square drains, covered by heavy iron grilles. The walls were of the same dark-gray stone.

Diddy half expected, at any moment, to come upon an elderly guard dozing on a cane chair, from whom he could ask directions and thereby begin to orient himself. Imagined this functionary so clearly. An unkempt man about sixty, with sagging cheeks and a wen on his forehead, who hadn't shaved for at least two days. Who wore a shiny blue-serge uniform with frayed cuffs peeping out of the sleeves of his jacket; whose pockets were littered with old gum wrappers, canceled stamps, torn ticket stubs, and dirty Kleenexes. Who had a paunch, and suffered from bursitis. Who went home each night to a furnished room where he slept on a horsehair mattress with a picture of his dead wife above his bed . . . Diddy wanted to ask this old guard, tilted back against the wall on his chair: Where am I? The man would make some lazy reply. It would suffice. For Diddy doesn't expect much information. Grateful for what he can get. But, despite the modesty of his projected demands, doesn't find even a decrepit custodian—either at the start of the long gallery or stationed any-where throughout. Only finds on the floor, washed to the edge of one of the drains, a straw hat, size 7¾, which might have belonged to such a man.

The long gallery through which Diddy is walking, naked, is vir-tually empty. Except for numerous odd, nearly valueless items, which Diddy discovers at widely spaced intervals and which seem lost in the grandiose dimensions of this space. Objects that are abandoned? Lost? Hidden? Arranged here in sequence to convey some cryptic message?

First, the straw hat already mentioned.

Some yards farther down the gallery, along the wall, a Zenith radio circa 1930. All of whose tubes proved, upon examination, to be burnt out.

Still farther down, a large stack of 78 rpm records. Diddy stooped down for a moment, with the thought of rapidly sifting through them. But the records, all opera arias, were so dusty; and after looking at ten records, and dirtying the tips of his fingers, he had still to recognize the name of a single singer.

Farther, a crate of coconuts. Diddy picked one up, and shook it to listen for the sloshing sound of the milk. Felt thirsty. If only he had a small screwdriver, he could open one and take a drink. Such a small screwdriver—on his Swiss army knife—lies in the pocket of the pants he left back in the tunnel.

Farther yet, a box of cigars. The Cuban kind that Reager liked. It might be fun to smoke one (now), if they aren't too dried out. Unfortunately, the box doesn't contain any matches.

Still farther, along the spigotless wall, a long length

of orange plastic garden hose plus three different kinds of nozzles.

And still farther: a pair of rusted garden shears; a chamber pot decorated with a green, brown, and white curvilinear pattern and with the words "Minton" and "Nº 12" stamped on the underside; a bale of magazines, mainly *Popular Mechanics* and *Science & Mechanics;* a legal-size envelope containing a dozen stills from Mexican movies of the 1950s featuring Dolores del Rio; a worn-out automobile tire; a tattered Barbie doll, with no Ken in sight; a spool of brown thread; a neat small pile of autumn-colored leaves; a wooden hanger labeled "Hotel Luna"; an empty fifth of Smirnoff's vodka; a tube of dentifrice used for cleaning false teeth; and an incomplete deck of plastic playing cards. Diddy counts forty-nine.

Diddy appears to have stumbled into a world of things. A few, maybe, can count as collector's items; if somewhere there exists a taste odd enough to want to collect things like these. But granted that things are all that's native to this world, and even restricting things to objects of such a marginal or out-of-date character, what's also remarkable is how widely distributed the things are. An uncommon problem for Diddy: that of too much space. What would be clutter if dumped into most rooms, apartments, or houses is barely visible when spread about in a space as lavish as this.

Therefore, also a world of the absence of things. Apart from the aforementioned items, of a nature less plausibly described as "contents" than as "litter" or "debris," the gallery is devoid of furnishings. Bare.

Excepting, of course, what's on the walls. For what this extremely long, relatively narrow space lacked in the way of objects to fill it was partly made up for by the quantity of messages posted on both walls. A lengthy, unremitting pageant of quotations and mottoes.

For the first several hundred feet of the gallery, these were posted at irregular intervals and heights, rather casually. Sometimes simply painted or chalked on the stone wall. Or crudely lettered on cardboard, acoustic board, or plyboard; and then taped up or nailed on the wall. But the farther Diddy walks, the more densely they proliferate; and the more costly the means of mounting them. Some were printed on placards; and, of these, many had elaborate multi-colored initial letters and border designs. Some were incised on metal plates.

Still, one couldn't discern among the styles of typography, printing, and metalwork represented—whether primitive or naïve—any unifying or even dominant tendency or period. A wholly eclectic assortment of graphic styles and plastic standards.

Something similar might be said of the texts themselves, all relating loosely to the theme of death. A hodgepodge of lines from poems, of homiletic quotations, a few intact but most of them a truncated sentence or phrase, and of popular wisdom. There seemed to be no ethical, temperamental, or cultural consistency in these messages and mottoes. As if many randomly chosen people had been invited to contribute their favorite bit of wisdom, and done so. With no thought to the harmony of the whole.

"It is better never to have been born at all" was set alongside "The wages of sin are death." Which follows "Order, calm, and silence." Which was followed by "Gather ye rosebuds."

Others that Diddy noticed, among which are a few he might even have jotted down, if he'd carried a pad and pencil:

"I despise the dust of which I am composed and which speaks to you. I give it to you."

" 'The world has not promised anything to anyone.' Moroccan proverb."

"Easy come, easy go."

"O grave where is thy victory?"

"E dietro le venìa sì lunga tratta/ di gente ch'io non averei creduto/ che morte tanta n'avesse disfatta."

"Out of sight, out of mind."

"Et in Arcadia ego."

" 'The question is, is there a life before death?' Hungarian saying."

"That tossed the dog/ That worried the cat/ That killed the rat."

"Death and taxes."

"Enkidu, my friend, whom I loved so dearly/ Who underwent with me all hardships/ Him has overtaken the fate of mankind!/ Six days and seven nights I wept over him/ Until the worm fell out of his nose."

"When you gotta go, you gotta go."

"Because I could not stop for Death — He kindly stopped for me—"

"Ashes to ashes, dust to dust."

"My only regret is that I have but one life to give for my country."

"Wir Geretteten/ Aus deren hohlem Gebein der Tod schon seine Flöten schnitt/ An deren Sehnen der Tod schon seinen Bogen strich."

"What doesn't kill me makes me stronger."

"I am that which was, which is, and which shall be. And no man hath lifted my veil."

"Better Red than dead."

"And death shall have no dominion."

"Où sont les neiges d'antan?"

"Dead men tell no tales."

"This thought is as a death which cannot choose/ But weep to have that which it fears to lose."

"I went down to the Saint James Infirmary."

"Or discendiamo omai a maggior pièta;/ già ogni stella cade che saliva/ quand' io mi mossi, e 'l troppo star si vieta."

"And death comes as the end."

"In the palace of the troll king."

Passing from inscription to inscription. A surfeit of wisdom: harmless or blunt or antiquated or tactless. Interchangeable wisdom. Carrion wisdom. The plaques on the wall are thinning out (now). Before one of the last, two lines from a Donne sermon, Diddy pauses; almost tired. Lays his flushed cheek against the cold stone for a moment. His strength quickly returning, continued on his way. Diddy's nostrils suffused with the odor of lava, the stench of the sea. And just one layer beneath these, something unpleasant that smelled like vomit. His fingertips brushing the grimy granite walls, as Diddy walked slowly. The slurred sounds of his steps echoed in his lonely skull.

Then Diddy saw a spacious vaulted archway. Beyond which a room, four times as wide though less long than the gallery in which he'd been walking. Antechamber, rather. Of the room he (now) approaches. And at the end of this room, was there still another doorway? Perhaps. Diddy's view, from here, too obstructed to permit him to see. Nevertheless, has already occurred to him that both the long gallery and the room he's about to enter are only the start of a series of connecting, underground chambers.

Through the doorway, Diddy passing into a vast squarish basement-like space with a high vaulted ceiling. A room, except that it was windowless, eminently suitable as the interior of a church. A church in some poor, pious Balkan country.

But worship wasn't the use to which this space had been put. Diddy has entered something like a huge burial crypt. One which is extravagantly ill-kept. Although the central aisle in which Diddy walked was fairly clear, everywhere else coffins are lying about in the most careless profusion. Hundreds, perhaps more than a thousand of them. Aslant; or tilted on one end; or turned over on their sides; or precariously piled up, six or seven high, like logs for a fire. Looking as if they'd been heaped, tossed, thrown by someone in a state of exasperation and rage; or, maybe, fallen into the room. Rather than having been placed or even stacked. Nowhere giving the impression of any care or forethought. Too many of them, surely, even for this large space. But thus haphazardly disposed, disregarding every rule for the economical use of a limited space, the room appears far more crowded than it need have.

Maybe this wasn't a burial crypt in the ordinary sense, a place in which the dead were reverently placed, and periodically visited by grieving relatives and friends. Rather, a storage place for surplus bodies. Which would explain the shameless flouting of minimal standards of upkeep; as well as the absence of flowers, fresh or wax, and any of the other tributes that customarily decorate the resting places of the dead. Most of the coffins lack even a small plaque giving the name and birth and death dates of the deceased. Impossible to imagine this place being visited by anyone. How distressed any memory-burdened survivor would be to see the remains of someone he loved so ill-used, so negligently housed.

For it wasn't only the manner in which the coffins had been disposed. The coffins themselves in great disrepair. Diddy could see that fairly good wood had been used for some of them. But, whether mahogany or oak or cheap pine, the wood was usually scratched, scarred, chipped. Even gouged—a peculiar, fairly uniform chunk about the size of a half dollar taken out. On the side of some coffins, the scratches were deeply incised and continuous, suggesting cursive writing. Nothing that Diddy could read, though. Illegible graffiti. And where wood had been painted rather than left in its natural state or simply varnished, the paint was peeling and discolored. In some cases, the very frame of the casket was coming apart; boards separating off from each other. Diddy, walking about in nothing but his tender flesh, has to keep an eye out for protruding rusty nails. Also, stay alert for the occasional warped board or partly loose lid jutting into the aisle that could scrape his ankle or shin or thigh. And since the lids of many coffins had been completely pried off, and then, sometimes, laid diagonally across the open coffins, Diddy had to be careful not to bump into one of these. Especially when he left the aisle, as he did several times, to clamber among the dense forest of death chests on either side. If he didn't watch his step, he'd quickly be spotted with blue and yellow bruises. Must also watch out for his bare feet. The danger of nails on the floor. And of wooden splinters from some of the coffin lids that had been ripped off and, neither placed diagonally across the coffin itself nor simply carried away, had fallen on the floor.

One selfish advantage in the deplorable condition of the coffins, though. Diddy could see inside. The entire contents of those without lids, just by looking down. And many of those coffins whose lids remained in place, firmly nailed down or fastened with bronze hasps, featured a small square window in the lid. Just by bending over and, when necessary, pushing some debris off the top. Diddy could see inside these coffins as well. Faces, at least.

The corpses he examined were of both sexes and all ages. Fully and rather formally dressed. And remarkably well preserved. Often, the face and hands—all that was visible of flesh itself—had a full sheath of dry parchment-like skin. These faces were clearly human, mostly belonging to the white race, and, in many cases, recognizably American. Though overexpressive. Often badly distorted. Shrinkage of the skin, as it dried out under what was evidently a very superior embalming process, produced some painful grimaces and smiles. And not only was the skin mostly intact. Frequently, a full head of hair as well—in a color recognizably analogous to the original brown, blond, black, gray, or white as the case had been. And on about half of the men, beards and mustaches.

At first, this frequency of beards and mustaches puzzles Diddy, who recalls how few American men, either in his generation or in his father's, grew them. Until he realized that most of the bodies were much older than he'd assumed. All were decades, some even centuries, old. Diddy wouldn't have been able to guess their age simply from the color of the preserved skin, a strong sallow brown. But there were other clues.

Often, dress identified the period in which the dead person had lived. The woman in a coffin at the top of an unstable heap on the left, for instance, clad in a long, high-necked dress of the 1890s, with padded bosom. The man in the powdered wig and colonial shirt and breeches. But it was one particular coffin that gave Diddy what he considered virtually conclusive evidence for the considerable age of most of the bodies. This was a coffin in much better state than most, of highly polished oak, barely scratched, whose firmly secured lid had an almost full-length window. Diddy looking. The body of a little girl wearing a pink frock, white socks, and pink ankle-strap shoes of patent leather; according to the plaque on one side of the coffin, Martha Elizabeth Templeton, 1922–1933. But the child doesn't show any signs of decay that Diddy can detect through the glass. She looks alive. Just sleeping. Perhaps a little jaundiced, that's all. (Now) add to this striking sight the fact that, among the other coffins bearing names and dates, Diddy found, in an admittedly rapid, cursory search, no date as recent as 1933. And no body in as fresh and wholesome-looking a condition. So concludes that the others must go back in time, much further back.

Martha Elizabeth Templeton's coffin was sealed. But the temptation to touch was irresistible. Where touch was possible. Diddy reached out gingerly to several of the open coffins and stroked the withered, dusty faces. Most of the coffins containing, of course, only a single body. Sometimes accompanied by an object. Beloved or merely necessary, totem or tool. Beside one man in a full dress suit, a bassoon. A pair of crutches lay alongside a man in a brown tweed overcoat and cream-colored scarf; a man not visibly crippled; but perhaps the deformity would be visible if one rolled up his trouser legs, which Diddy started to do, but then stopped. He had glimpsed a piece of the white shinbone. What's rather touching, though, is the neat-looking old woman with gray hair who is still wearing her large pink plastic hearing aid.

In just a few of the coffins, Diddy found two people together. Because, having loved each other so much, they couldn't bear to rot separately; had rejected the idea of decaying anywhere except in each other's arms. Or because their families saw how much money they could save if they bought a single coffin? Peering through the pane of glass set in the top of one coffin, Diddy sees a withered youthful couple, the man on his left side and the woman on her right, embracing. Stretched out on her back in one of the lidless coffins, a woman in a long white lace dress has clamped an infant—also wearing a white dress, a tiny replica of hers—to her breast. Diddy reached down and stroked the baby's cheek. Its skin looks fairly fresh to the eye. But feels soft like newspaper, not skin, to the fingers; as dried out as that of the oldest person he's touched here.

On the far side of some coffins which had tumbled into the long aisle and which he has to shove aside with his bare feet, then grapple and haul with his hands, Diddy has sighted an impressive doorway.

He paused for a moment, indecisively. Wipes the sweat off his face with his forearm. Another moment of reflection. Chews at his lips with his teeth.

The answer to the unvoiced question is no. Not yet. Necessary for Diddy the Disciplined to proceed systematically, or he'll get lost. There's a system of priorities here, as anywhere else, that Diddy might be wise to observe. One thing at a time. (Now) the time to restrain mere curiosity. Diddy isn't ready for something new, since he has yet to explore with thoroughness the area in this room on both sides of the long aisle. That's why he turns back into the aisle, continuing for a distance of some fifty feet.

Diddy has ventured again into the intricate crowded space. Finding miniature pathways for his naked body between the heaped-up coffins when possible; more agile climbing over the coffins when necessary. Diddy's score: only one near-fall, plus a scrape on his right knee. And, as he expected, his efforts have yielded results. Diddy does uncover an exit in each of the walls parallel to the aisle. So, besides the room straight ahead, there's another room branching off to the left, still another to the right. Diddy has much to see.

These rooms, also crammed with coffins, are far smaller than the main crypt; with flat ceilings about ten feet high. And warmer, Diddy sweating. Making him feel even dustier and dirtier. Wipes away moisture from his palms, forehead, upper lip, the back of his neck. Anything to be done for him? One could hardly hope to find a thermostat in rooms as unsentimental, bare, and purely functional as these; Diddy is already fortunate to have this much good light, furnished by the naked bulbs jutting out of iron wall fixtures in all the rooms. Still wishes it weren't so warm. Perhaps the temperature of the place has to be kept high; part of the method by which the dead bodies are preserved. For them it may be just the right temperature. But not, altogether, for Diddy: lone subject in a world of objects. Think, though, that he could be worse off than he is. What a lucky whim that was long ago, when he decided to discard all his clothes.

Nakedness may mitigate heat, but it doesn't redeem the squalor of these rooms. Which continues to dishearten Diddy. None of the rooms are infested with either vermin or rats—as far as he's noticed, anyway. Still, everything is appallingly dirty. Not grime and soot. Nor blood, excrement, grease, semen. Not the dirt of animal secretions and excretions. Not industrial wastes, either. The dirt of time. Immortal dirt. Thick, thick dust.

Which Diddy is getting used to (now). Being naked may not render his surroundings less squalid, but at least it minimizes some of the penalties for being here rather than somewhere else. Diddy may dislike the contact of his own flesh with what's dirty or soiled or rotten or slimy. But doesn't, in addition, have to endure the indignity of getting his clothes dirty as well.

Becoming more accustomed to this new space and its stringent topography. Learning how to manage obstacles. The common case of new skills arriving just when they're needed, no sooner. Diddy the Vulnerable stands in acute need of being transformed into Diddy the Intrepid. Precisely at this moment. For Diddy had never suspected the tunnel to be this vast, so complex. And (now) he's eager to explore all of it.

Trying, in turn, each of the new rooms.

Finds, in every one of these smaller rooms, more coffins. Lying about in a foul disarray—that resembles, on a smaller scale, that of the large vaulted chamber. And the coffins themselves as poorly cared for. Individual caskets are coming apart; and some of them, perhaps once neatly stacked, have toppled over, broken open, and spilled out an arm or leg. Watch out! Don't trip over one of those. Several skulls that have gotten separated from their families, the bones below. Skulls like shells.

These rooms give on to still more rooms. Diddy the Naked passes through them very rapidly (now), his brisk walk sometimes breaking into a loose-limbed run. No need to gaze at everything closely, when everything looks more or less alike. Diddy the Surveyor just checking, to see if the general idea remains the same. But to do this, he must at least glance in every room. Usually possible. But not always. Diddy exasperated when, as happens several times, disorder mounts and clutter becomes so dense that there's not space enough to enable even a single person to pass through. To keep moving. One solution would be for Diddy to set to work and clear a narrow passageway for himself. But he doesn't. Not that he lacks the physical strength. It's a question of prudence and the best use of his time. At the entrance to one room, a rickety wall of coffins rises almost to the ceiling; ignorant of what lay on the far side of the doorway, Diddy thought it hardly prudent to undertake the strenuous labor of dismantling the improvised wall and hauling the coffins away, one by one. Similar decisions made on two other occasions when, exploring a new corridor, his route was halted by what looks like the aftermath of an avalanche of coffins.

Then what happens when the massive wooden casket boxes are piled so thickly as to obstruct Diddy's passage, preventing him altogether from getting by? Only one alternative. Diddy is reluctantly forced, several times, to retrace his steps. To regain the big chamber.

Then to move forward again in a straight line. Keeping to the central sequence.

Diddy is reconnoitering the future. Diddy is exploring his death. Cautiously, thoughtfully, diligently. He wills to know, he will know all the rooms in this place; even if it's the house of death.

Thought a moment ago he hears the throbbing of a fast train charging along the tracks. Coming closer (now). If that's what the sound is, he's safe. Diddy could hardly be in a safer place. No train can follow him here; no tracks have been laid on these stone floors, or possibly would be. Then let it come on as fast as it likes. Aren't there speeds so great they obtain immobility?

(Now) Diddy has entered another large chamber, fully as wide as the first and even longer. Only the ceiling isn't as high; and not vaulted. Still, it's more than twice the height of the ceilings in the small rooms. As before, the room is harshly lit by a plentiful number of naked bulbs. But for all the light, it's definitely cooler; for which Diddy, gleaming with sweat, was grateful.

Diddy in what could be called the second grand crypt. A room whose contents or furniture differ from those in the room he's already explored—the first large chamber and its dependencies. Here, not even a halfhearted sloppy attempt is made to enclose the dead in coffins. The dead (now) are simply in an upright posture, side by side. In three rows, using up all the space on all four walls from floor to ceiling. Each body is secured in place by two long heavy ropes: one wound once around the chest, passing out on either side under the armpits; and the other wound once tightly around each pair of knees. Both upper and lower ropes run from body to body; continuing unbroken, not even knotted once, the entire length of each wall.

If these three rows of bodies had been all, the second chamber would have had a remarkably uncluttered, spacious look. But, as before, the genius of disorder and overpopulation that governed this place had been at work here, too. Though every foot of the long walls was taken up with bodies, there were apparently more candidates for these spaces than could possibly have been accommodated. These surplus bodies lie, three and four high, at the base of the gray stone walls. And while the bodies suspended on the walls are arranged quite neatly—initially, at least, a good deal of care must have gone into their installation—those stacked on the floor lie in all sorts of awkward positions. About the only idea of order that appears to have been acknowledged at all is one concerning direction. Keep their heads to the wall, their feet pointing toward the center of the room. Needless to say, that rule had been violated or ignored a good many times.

In short: Diddy notices here the same lack of careful maintenance as in the rooms with the broken and heaped-up coffins. And, with better care, who knows how much more intact and lifelike these nonetheless remarkably preserved bodies might have been? A wider range on that matter, here. Some of these bodies seem better preserved than any he saw in the rooms with the coffins. Some are in far worse condition. So far as Diddy can determine—given that, as before, all the bodies are clothed—fewer here have an envelope of skin that is relatively intact. But the skin itself seems tougher, more durable. A very dark leathery skin, rather than the frailer parchment on the bodies laid out in the coffins. All too frequently, though, the leathery skin is falling away, and the bones sticking through. And some figures on the walls are virtually without any of this metamorphosed flesh. But even those that are merely skeletons are never bare skeletons. Always at least some patch of leathery skin adhering to the bones. As was the case with the coffined bodies, most of the faces here are very distorted. Because the shrinkage of the flesh has twisted the leather mask into grotesque expressions. Or—this additional reason, a penalty, no doubt, of upright posture—because the jawbone has fallen off. Producing the effect of a grotesque scream. But almost all the toothless skulls with their empty eye sockets retain some of their hair, if nothing else. A full head of perfectly preserved hair, like a wig, may lie above a face whose flesh has entirely dropped away. Some with only shreds of flesh sport thick chunks of scalp hair. Diddy noticed one skull with no flesh at all, except what could be presumed to lie under its flourishing beard and mustache.

Again, it's by the clothing that Diddy could always tell the sex of the body, usually the period in which the person lived, and often his or her occupation. The condition and color of the hair also give some evidence, though hardly conclusive, of the person's age at the time of death. Some of the guesses Diddy makes may be farfetched, but they are better than nothing. For, in this new chamber or zone of the space he's exploring, none of the bodies is labeled with name and dates of birth and death. Perhaps there is a book, somewhere. A huge, moldy, fascinating catalogue in which everyone is identified.

As if he were wandering through a warehouse, Diddy began taking stock. What are the contents, in more detail? This large chamber seemed to contain a random collection of bodies. Of both sexes, all ages, who lived in widely different periods. The earliest specimen Diddy could find belonged to the seventeenth century: a Pilgrim with a broad-brimmed hat, round stiff collar, breeches, and buckled shoes. But nearby, many modern types. A banker in a top hat and striped pants and cutaway coat. A boy in his Cub Scout uniform. A registered nurse. A policeman, one of New York's Finest. For this room, bodies seem to have been supplied right up to the present day. Many figures on the walls who postdate the unhappily brief span of Martha Elizabeth Templeton, *d.* 1933. For instance, a GI in the battle dress of the 1960s with a Silver Star pinned to his left breast pocket. But not one body, however recent, was as fresh, as nearly well preserved as that of Martha Elizabeth Templeton. Maybe she was just an exception to all the rules.

Passing on to some of the succeeding, small rooms, Diddy has to admit that a good deal of care has been taken here. At least, at the time the bodies were installed. For most of these small rooms were specialized. Bodies had had to be sorted out, and then the sub-groupings of bodies assembled.

A whole room, for instance, given over to young children. Just as many rows, three, of bodies less than five feet tall could be mounted on all the walls; even though the ceiling here is considerably lower than that of the large chamber. This room is the first on his tour to make Diddy feel sad. At least if the children had been put in coffins, they could lie hugging a favorite doll or some other toy. But hanging here, they look so abandoned and unloved. Each completely unrelated to all the others, as if they'd been captured and strung up while still alive; dying, not of starvation or physical mistreatment, but of loneliness. Look at that little girl in the second row near the corner, the one wearing her white communion dress. The splendor of children is never, really, more than pathos.

In another room, only firemen. Decked out in their uniforms, with rubber boots to the tops of their thighs. Many with the huge, red, oval-brimmed hat that's their trademark. Cocked on their skull; not so much rakishly as awkwardly, since the head, with or without meat and hair on it, tends to slump forward. (Now) the mood is quite different. Adult splendors are either satisfying or comic. Diddy feels these men are quite pleased with themselves. And that they know why they're here.

In another room, nothing but priests. Diddy looks about the walls for "his" priest, the plump smooth-voiced man with the breviary. But how can he tell any more? Any one of these grinning black-suited bodies might be that man. No point in not looking, though. Diddy came closer. Until he realized that these priests, especially those in purple and white ceremonial robes, have a bulk that cannot be genuine. Faking? Alas, yes. Even here. As Diddy discovers, most of the bodies—or rather, skeletons—have been stuffed with straw to give shape to their imposing clothes. Sometimes, when the trick fails, the effect is almost funny. As it must fail, of course, when the body has no skin left. For instance, with that very rotund priest wearing the black vestment for a Solemn High Requiem Mass. With bits of straw peeping out of his wide sleeve, above the few skinny bones which are all that remain of his wrist and hand.

And an entire room of figures wearing Civil War uniforms, both blue and gray. This room, on closer inspection, seems to be even more specialized than that description would indicate. Reserved not simply for men who had fought in the Civil War but, judging from their white hair and generally small stature, for aged veterans only. Many, perhaps, who hadn't died until quite recently. At a hundred years or more. A funerary parade for the Republic.

In another room, men and boys in the uniforms of various sports. After the experience of the roomful of stuffed priests, Diddy more suspicious (now). Could one be buried or interred—or whatever this is—in a uniform to which one has, properly, no title? After all, not everyone can be glamorous. But so many people want to be, or at least think they do. Is he genuine, that football player by the doorway whose massive shoulder pads come up, on either side, almost to the top of his bare, small skull? Even when fleshed and alive and running, must have had a small head. Over there, a catcher for the San Francisco Giants—if one can trust the evidence of the uniform and the mask whose metal bars cover the dead man's lean, contorted, well-preserved face. Diddy in a mood to be pigheaded, to take nothing on faith. But why should the dead pretend to be other than they are? And even if such was their dying wish, why should the survivors indulge it? Are there many among the living who would go to the trouble of masquerading these bodies to satisfy a vulgar vain fantasy that expired with the deceased's last heartbeat? Diddy scraps his policy of suspiciousness. Resolving to meet the evidence halfway or more; to give the corpses the benefit of the doubt. For instance, it's hardly likely that any of the figures dressed as basketball players are phonies, impersonators. Because of their height. The tallest of those assembled here being a seven-foot-seven skeleton in the uniform of the Cincinnati Royals, an impressive figure with his knee guards still clinging to his bare patellae.

In another room, figures in denim overalls and work shirts or similar tough, shapeless clothing. No pretensions here. Farmers and farmhands, Diddy supposed. Many types of blue-collar workers are probably represented, too: riveters and welders from automobile factories, sewing-machine operators, ditchdiggers, telephone-line repairmen, janitors, bricklayers, longshoremen, garage mechanics, and so forth. Is this where Incardona would be assigned a place? Here?

Strung on one of the walls of this very low-ceilinged airless room? As if he were in fact the admissions officer charged with making the decision, Diddy hesitates. Diddy behaving as if he has found some fault in the way Incardona's application has been filled out, as if he seeks some bureaucratic technicality that would bar the workman. Why? Because he thinks that Incardona deserves better accommodations than these, or because he wants to bar Incardona from the kingdom he has already come to regard as his own? Diddy is being tiresome. Whether it's the first, a misplaced solicitude, or the second, a burst of spite, he should stop. Stop stalling. Why not Incardona? Why not here, for God's sake? Or anywhere else. Surely Diddy can't take very seriously this ad hoc, amateurish system of filing the bodies? And if what moves him is not a habit of inane deliberateness when confronted with any organized system, then Diddy is being not only vindictive but snobbish. Where does he think he is? It's hardly an exclusive club. A candidate doesn't need to have a good character, or meet any other standards that might be applied to his life. The only prerequisite is being dead. Diddy the Reluctant Democrat. Well then, let's bury him. Diddy takes a step backwards, glancing over his shoulder at the doorway through which he has just come. But Diddy doesn't want to retrace his steps; would rather do almost anything than go back out into the tunnel. Someone else is there besides Incardona. But a stranger might go in Diddy's place. Voluntarily perform the arduous errand. As a favor. Or an act of charity.

Isn't there anyone else around to drag that heavy body in here, and hoist it on the wall and secure it with the ropes? Assuming, of course, that there's room. That a place can be made for him.

Indeed, space seemed to be rapidly becoming more of a problem. As Diddy ventured farther, quitting the room that was Incardona's prospective resting place for new rooms, noticed how much more crowded they are getting. Also that most of the bodies he saw (now) had scarcely begun to decay, which suggested that it was the population of the recently dead rising to unmanageable numbers? Strange. Doesn't the casualty rate remain fairly constant? Maybe not. Whatever the explanation, the density of the bodies is definitely increasing. The ones hanging on the walls more closely packed together, and sometimes in double rows; those on the floor, stacked higher and higher and also farther toward the center. One room succeeds another. The unachievable goal being, eventually, to leave no empty space at all. Let the vacuum be filled. The house properly ordered. A plenum of death.

What does Diddy feel as he reconnoiters the future, taking note of the inexhaustible contents of this charnel house? Except for being too warm, he's not physically uncomfortable; and dusty old-fashioned blade fans suspended from the ceiling in some of the rooms are slowly turning, circulating the musty air a little. His state of mind and heart not too uncomfortable, either. You might imagine he's overcome, some or all of the time, by disgust. But that's not so. Then is he at least depressed by what he sees? Not that either. Frightened? Which would seem to be natural. Again, no. As it happens, none of these emotions are the ones appropriate to this labyrinthine interior and its displays. Which, however somber, generate in Diddy a mood that's somehow light. Despite the squalor and overcrowding that had at first so upset Diddy, the effect of this place upon him is curiously soothing. Inducing a state that's almost emotionless.

Bathed in this dull iridescent state of feeling, Diddy continues walking. But gradually slowing down. Such his compromise between the urge to run and the insidious desire to dally along the way. Another barely perceptible conflict headed off.

Sometimes he visits the same room twice. Which isn't particularly his intention.

Yet Diddy is not just wandering, trying to pretend he isn't lost. Rather than feeling like a tourist bravely attempting to master an exotic town who lacks both guide and an adequate itinerary or agenda, he feels like a pilgrim who has been briefed thoroughly by his predecessors. If becalmed, then with the concentration of devoutness. What remains to be done has been done before many times, by many others. Diddy not in possession of all the details. Yet how could he feel so confident, so at home; why should everything novel he sees also look familiar? The explanation is easy. What has been happening thus far has constituted an order. Why shouldn't it so continue? Diddy can't be lost. Even though, at this point, in this place, has stumbled into a new medium. Entering a new phase. What phase? From one point of view, this space is a panoramic stage set, a kind of theatrical display. And Diddy may be invited to give his opinion of it. Unless he's got matters wrong, and he's not the judge at all. Maybe, if this space is a theater of judgment, Diddy's task is to find another person, a judge. Who will examine and render a verdict on him.

From another view, of course, nothing could be less relevant here than judgment. That's what death is about. They're all collected here, the guilty and the innocent, those who tried and those who didn't. Which thought makes Diddy laugh aloud. Absolved from the duty of classifying himself or appraising his surroundings.

What Diddy sees is, at the very least, never less than interesting. Death = an encyclopedia of life.

Is this place Diddy's nightmare? Or the resolution of his nightmare?

A false question, since there are in fact two nightmares. Distinct, if not contradictory. The nightmare that there are *two* worlds. The nightmare that there is only *one* world. This one.

Wait. Perhaps he has the answer to that desperate thought about the world. Life = the world. Death = being completely inside one's own head. Do those new equations refute the puzzle of the two nightmares?

Diddy pondering so intently about these matters that for long intervals he completely forgets where he is. Where and in what state is his body. Even (now), his thoughts bully him. Wouldn't you think he would have discarded them, along with his clothes, when he entered this place? But they're still with him, preserved in their own amber.

As though Diddy were living at last in his eyes, only in his eyes. The outward eye that names and itemizes, the inward eye that throbs with thought.

But he's not always so solemn. Sometimes almost gay. "Gather ye rosebuds." This is when, while perfectly able to see, he is not just a pair of wet vulnerable eyes lying in their sockets like molluscs in their shells. Swarms with the happiness of being in his body, and feels his nakedness as a delicious blessing. His alert head; the strength of his supple feet traversing the cool stone flooring; the easy hang of his shoulders and the bunched muscles of his calves; his sensitive capacious chest; the hard wall of his lean belly; the tender sex brushing the top of his thighs. Astonishing, isn't it, that any infant human being ever surrenders such pleasures. And consents to put on clothes.

Other moments, though, he can't help tensing his shoulders, raising them; his breathing becomes shallower and his step sags. Feels a sickening edge of something that resembles fear. A particular hush. A rancid smell. He may be about to ask himself what he has done. Whether all this is a dishonorable isolation, a useless ordeal. But Diddy knows how to cope with such vexing moments that threaten to subvert his courage. He dreams that he will find Hester at the end of his tour. That at this moment she is in some distant room or gallery, placidly awaiting him. Her role a perfectly clear one, and well within her powers. To save him, like the princess in some fairy tale. Love's power sweeping him up from the kingdom of death. "Death and the maiden."

All he has to do is keep walking. Put one foot in front of the other. Whether Hester is waiting or not.

More rooms. More deaths.

Has Diddy reached his destination?

Dying is overwork.

Again Diddy hears the sound of a train, and faint shouts. A dog barking.

A trim, youngish Negro wearing white jacket and pants wheels a cart to his bed. Recking of vomit. Who is? Diddy. Diddy the Soiled.

More rooms. Diddy walks on, looking for his death. Diddy has made his final chart; drawn up his last map. Diddy has perceived the inventory of the world.

(1967)

FROM

Styles of
Radical Will

The Aesthetics
of Silence

I

Every era has to reinvent the project of "spirituality" for itself. (Spirituality = plans, terminologies, ideas of deportment aimed at resolving the painful structural contradictions inherent in the human situation, at the completion of human consciousness, at transcendence.)

In the modern era, one of the most active metaphors for the spiritual project is "art." The activities of the painter, the musician, the poet, the dancer, once they were grouped together under that generic name (a relatively recent move), have proved a particularly adaptable site on which to stage the formal dramas besetting consciousness, each individual work of art being a more or less astute paradigm for regulating or reconciling these contradictions. Of course, the site needs continual refurbishing. Whatever goal is set for art eventually proves restrictive, matched against the widest goals of consciousness. Art, itself a form of mystification, endures a succession of crises of demystification; older artistic goals are assailed and, ostensibly, replaced; outworn maps of consciousness are redrawn. But what supplies all these crises with their energy—an energy held in common, so to speak—is the very unification of numerous, quite disparate activities into a single genus. At the moment when "art" comes into being, the modern period of art begins. From then on, any of the activities therein subsumed becomes a profoundly *problematic* activity, all of whose procedures and, ultimately, whose very right to exist can be called into question.

From the promotion of the arts into "art" comes the leading myth about art, that of the absoluteness of the artist's activity. In its first, more unreflective version, the myth treated art as an *expression* of human consciousness, consciousness seeking to know itself. (The evaluative standards generated by this version of the myth were fairly easily arrived at: some expressions were more complete, more ennobling, more informative, richer than others.) The later version of the myth posits a more complex, tragic relation of art to consciousness. Denying that art is mere expression, the later myth rather relates art to the mind's need or capacity for self-estrangement. Art is no longer understood as consciousness expressing and therefore, implicitly, affirming itself. Art is not consciousness per se, but rather its antidote—evolved from within consciousness itself. (The evaluative standards generated by this version of the myth proved much harder to get at.)

The newer myth, derived from a post-psychological conception of consciousness, installs within the activity of art many of the paradoxes involved in attaining an absolute state of being described by the great religious mystics. As the activity of the mystic must end in a *via negativa,* a theology of God's absence, a craving for the cloud of unknowing beyond knowledge and for the silence beyond speech, so art must tend toward anti-art, the elimination of the "subject" (the "object," the "image"), the substitution of chance for intention, and the pursuit of silence.

In the early, linear version of art's relation to consciousness, a struggle was discerned between the "spiritual" integrity of the creative impulses and the distracting "materiality" of ordinary life, which throws up so many obstacles in the path of authentic sublimation. But the newer version, in which art is part of a dialectical transaction with consciousness, poses a deeper, more frustrating conflict. The "spirit" seeking embodiment in art clashes with the "material" character of art itself. Art is unmasked as gratuitous, and the very concreteness of the artist's tools (and, particularly in the case of language, their historicity) appears as a trap. Practiced in a world furnished with secondhand perceptions, and specifically confounded by the treachery of words, the artist's activity is cursed with mediacy. Art becomes the enemy of the artist, for it denies him the realization—the transcendence—he desires.

Therefore, art comes to be considered something to be overthrown. A new element enters the individual artwork and becomes constitutive of it: the appeal (tacit or overt) for its own abolition—and, ultimately, for the abolition of art itself.

II

The scene changes to an empty room.

Rimbaud has gone to Abyssinia to make his fortune in the slave trade. Wittgenstein, after a period as a village schoolteacher, has chosen menial work as a hospital orderly. Duchamp has turned to chess. Accompanying these exemplary renunciations of a vocation, each man has declared that he regards his previous achievements in poetry, philosophy, or art as trifling, of no importance.

But the choice of permanent silence doesn't negate their work. On the contrary, it imparts retroactively an added power and authority to what was broken off—disavowal of the work becoming a new source of its validity, a certificate of unchallengeable seriousness. That seriousness consists in not regarding art (or philosophy practiced as an art form: Wittgenstein) as something whose seriousness lasts forever, an "end," a permanent vehicle for spiritual ambition. The truly serious attitude is one that regards art as a "means" to something that can perhaps be achieved only by abandoning art; judged more impatiently, art is a false way or (the word of the Dada artist Jacques Vaché) a stupidity.

Though no longer a confession, art is more than ever a deliverance, an exercise in asceticism. Through it, the artist becomes purified—of himself and, eventually, of his art. The artist (if not art itself) is still engaged in a progress toward "the good." But whereas formerly the artist's good was mastery of and fulfillment in his art, now the highest good for the artist is to reach the point where those goals of excellence become insignificant to him, emotionally and ethically, and he is more satisfied by being silent than by finding a voice in art. Silence in this sense, as termination, proposes a mood of ultimacy antithetical to the mood informing the self-conscious artist's traditional serious use of silence (beautifully described by Valéry and Rilke): as a zone of meditation, preparation for spiritual ripening, an ordeal that ends in gaining the right to speak.

So far as he is serious, the artist is continually tempted to sever the dialogue he has with an audience. Silence is the furthest extension of that reluctance to communicate, that ambivalence about making contact with the audience which is a leading motif of modern art, with its tireless commitment to the "new" and/or the "esoteric." Silence is the artist's ultimate otherworldly gesture: by silence, he frees himself from servile bondage to the world, which appears as patron, client, consumer, antagonist, arbiter, and distorter of his work.

Still, one cannot fail to perceive in this renunciation of "society" a highly social gesture. The cues for the artist's eventual liberation from the need to practice his vocation come from observing his fellow artists and measuring himself against them. An exemplary decision of this sort can be made only after the artist has demonstrated that he possesses genius and exercised that genius authoritatively. Once he has surpassed his peers by the standards which he acknowledges, his pride has only one place left to go. For, to be a victim of the craving for silence is to be, in still a further sense, superior to everyone else. It suggests that the artist has had the wit to ask more questions than other people, and that he possesses stronger nerves and higher standards of excellence. (That the artist *can* persevere in the interrogation of his art until he or it is exhausted scarcely needs proving. As René Char has written, "No bird has the heart to sing in a thicket of questions.")

III

The exemplary modern artist's choice of silence is rarely carried to this point of final simplification, so that he becomes literally silent. More typically, he continues speaking, but in a manner that his audience can't hear. Most valuable art in our time has been experienced by audiences as a move into silence (or unintelligibility or invisibility or inaudibility); a dismantling of the artist's competence, his responsible sense of vocation—and therefore as an aggression against them.

Modern art's chronic habit of displeasing, provoking, or frustrating its audience can be regarded as a limited, vicarious participation in the ideal of silence which has been elevated as a major standard of "seriousness" in contemporary aesthetics.

But it is also a contradictory form of participation in the ideal of silence. It is contradictory not only because the artist continues making works of art but also because the isolation of the work from its audience never lasts. With the passage of time and the intervention of newer, more difficult works, the artist's transgression becomes ingratiating, eventually legitimate. Goethe accused Kleist of having written his plays for an "invisible theater." But eventually the invisible theater becomes "visible." The ugly and discordant and senseless become "beautiful." The history of art is a sequence of successful transgressions.

The characteristic aim of modern art, to be *unacceptable* to its audience, inversely states the unacceptability to the artist of the very presence of an audience—audience in the modern sense, an assembly of voyeuristic spectators. At least since Nietzsche observed in *The Birth of Tragedy* that an audience of spectators as we know it, those present whom the actors ignore, was unknown to the Greeks, a good deal of contemporary art seems moved by the desire to eliminate the audience from art, an enterprise that often presents itself as an attempt to eliminate "art" altogether. (In favor of "life"?)

If the power of art is located in its power to *negate,* the ultimate weapon in the artist's inconsistent war with his audience is to verge closer and closer to silence. The sensory or conceptual gap between the artist and his audience, the space of the missing or ruptured dialogue, can also constitute the grounds for an ascetic affirmation. Beckett speaks of "my dream of an art unresentful of its insuperable indigence and too proud for the farce of giving and receiving." But there is no abolishing a minimal transaction, a minimal exchange of gifts—just as there is no talented and rigorous asceticism that, whatever its intention, doesn't produce a gain (rather than a loss) in the capacity for pleasure.

And none of the aggressions committed intentionally or inadvertently by modern artists has succeeded in either abolishing the audience or transforming it into something else, a community engaged in a common activity. They cannot. As long as art is understood and valued as an "absolute" activity, it will be a separate, elitist one. Elites presuppose masses. So far as the best art defines itself by essentially "priestly" aims, it presupposes and confirms the existence of a relatively passive, never fully initiated, voyeuristic laity that is regularly convoked to watch, listen, read, or hear—and then sent away.

The most the artist can do is to modify the different terms in this situation vis-à-vis the audience and himself. To discuss the idea of silence in art is to discuss the various alternatives within this essentially unalterable situation.

IV

How literally does silence figure in art?

Silence exists as a *decision*—in the exemplary suicide of the artist (Kleist, Lautréamont), who thereby testifies that he has gone "too far," and in the already cited model renunciations by the artist of his vocation.

Silence also exists as a *punishment*—self-punishment, in the exemplary madness of artists (Hölderlin, Artaud) who demonstrate that sanity itself may be the price of trespassing the accepted frontiers of consciousness; and, of course, in penalties (ranging from censorship and physical destruction of artworks to fines, exile, prison for the artist) meted out by "society" for the artist's spiritual nonconformity or subversion of the group sensibility.

Silence doesn't exist in a literal sense, however, as the *experience* of an audience. It would mean that the spectator was aware of no stimulus or that he was unable to make a response. But this can't happen; nor can it even be induced programmatically. The non-awareness of any stimulus, the inability to make a response, can result only from a defective presence on the part of the spectator, or a misunderstanding of his own reactions (misled by restrictive ideas about what would be a "relevant" response). As long as audiences, by definition, consist of sentient beings in a "situation," it is impossible for them to have no response at all.

Nor can silence, in its literal state, exist as the *property* of an artwork—even of works like Duchamp's readymades or Cage's *4'33"*, in which the artist has ostentatiously done no more to satisfy any established criteria of art than set the object in a gallery or situate the performance on a concert stage. There is no neutral surface, no neutral discourse, no neutral theme, no neutral form. Something is neutral only with respect to something else—like an intention or an expectation. As a property of the work of art itself, silence can exist only in a cooked or non-literal sense. (Put otherwise: if a work exists at all, its silence is only one element in it.) Instead of raw or achieved silence, one finds various moves in the direction of an ever-receding horizon of silence—moves which, by definition, can never be fully consummated. One result is a type of art that many people characterize pejoratively as dumb, depressed, acquiescent, cold. But these privative qualities exist in a context of the artist's objective intention, which is always discernible. Cultivating the metaphoric silence suggested by conventionally lifeless subjects (as in much of Pop Art) and constructing "minimal" forms that seem to lack emotional resonance are in themselves vigorous, often tonic choices.

And, finally, even without imputing objective intentions to the artwork, there remains the inescapable truth about perception: the positivity of all experience at every moment of it. As Cage has insisted, "There is no such thing as silence. Something is always happening that makes a sound." (Cage has described how, even in a soundless chamber, he still heard two things: his heartbeat and the coursing of the blood in his head.) Similarly, there is no such thing as empty space. As long as a human eye is looking, there is always something to see. To look at something which is "empty" is still to be looking, still to be seeing something—if only the ghosts of one's own expectations. In order to perceive fullness, one must retain an acute sense of the emptiness which marks it off; conversely, in order to perceive emptiness, one must apprehend other zones of the world as full. (In

Through the Looking Glass, Alice comes upon a shop "that seemed to be full of all manner of curious things—but the oddest part of it all was that whenever she looked hard at any shelf, to make out exactly what it had on it, that particular shelf was always quite empty, though the others round it were crowded full as they could hold.")

"Silence" never ceases to imply its opposite and to depend on its presence; just as there can't be "up" without "down" or "left" without "right," so one must acknowledge a surrounding environment of sound or language in order to recognize silence. Not only does silence exist in a world full of speech and other sounds, but any given silence has its identity as a stretch of time being perforated by sound. (Thus, much of the beauty of Harpo Marx's muteness derives from his being surrounded by manic talkers.)

A genuine emptiness, a pure silence are not feasible—either conceptually or in fact. If only because the artwork exists in a world furnished with many other things, the artist who creates silence or emptiness must produce something dialectical: a full void, an enriching emptiness, a resonating or eloquent silence. Silence remains, inescapably, a form of speech (in many instances, of complaint or indictment) and an element in a dialogue.

V

Programs for a radical reduction of means and effects in art—including the ultimate demand for the renunciation of art itself—can't be taken at face value, undialectically. Silence and allied ideas (like emptiness, reduction, the "zero degree") are boundary notions with a very complex set of uses, leading terms of a particular spiritual and cultural rhetoric. To describe silence as a rhetorical term is, of course, not to condemn this rhetoric as fraudulent or in bad faith. In my opinion, the myths of silence and emptiness are about as nourishing and viable as might be devised in an "unwholesome" time—which is, of necessity, a time in which "unwholesome" psychic states furnish the energies for most superior work in the arts. Yet one can't deny the pathos of these myths.

This pathos appears in the fact that the idea of silence allows, essentially, only two types of valuable development. Either it is taken to the point of utter self-negation (as art) or else it is practiced in a form that is heroically, ingeniously inconsistent.

VI

The art of our time is noisy with appeals for silence.

A coquettish, even cheerful nihilism. One recognizes the impera-

188 / SUSAN SONTAG

tive of silence, but goes on speaking anyway. Discovering that one has nothing to say, one seeks a way to say *that*.

Beckett has expressed the wish that art would renounce all further projects for disturbing matters on "the plane of the feasible," that art would retire, "weary of puny exploits, weary of pretending to be able, of being able, of doing a little better the same old thing, of going further along a dreary road." The alternative is an art consisting of "the expression that there is nothing to express, nothing from which to express, no power to express, no desire to express, together with the obligation to express." From where does this obligation derive? The very aesthetics of the death wish seems to make of that wish something incorrigibly lively.

Apollinaire says, "J'ai fait des gestes blancs parmi les solitudes." But he *is* making gestures.

Since the artist can't embrace silence literally and remain an artist, what the rhetoric of silence indicates is a determination to pursue his activity more deviously than before. One way is indicated by Breton's notion of the "full margin." The artist is enjoined to devote himself to filling up the periphery of the art space, leaving the central area of usage blank. Art becomes privative, anemic—as suggested by the title of Duchamp's only effort at filmmaking, *Anemic Cinema*, a work from 1924–26. Beckett projects the idea of an "impoverished painting," painting which is "authentically fruitless, incapable of any image whatsoever." Jerzy Grotowski's manifesto for his Theater Laboratory in Poland is called "Plea for a Poor Theater." These programs for art's impoverishment must not be understood simply as terroristic admonitions to audiences, but rather as strategies for improving the audience's experience. The notions of silence, emptiness, and reduction sketch out new prescriptions for looking, hearing, etc.—which either promote a more immediate, sensuous experience of art or confront the artwork in a more conscious, conceptual way.

VII

Consider the connection between the mandate for a reduction of means and effects in art, whose horizon is silence, and the faculty of attention. In one of its aspects, art is a technique for focusing attention, for teaching skills of attention. (While the whole of the human environment might be so described—as a pedagogic instrument—this description particularly applies to works of art.) The history of the arts is tantamount to the discovery and formulation of a repertory of objects on which to lavish attention. One could trace exactly and in order how the eye of art has panned over our environment, "naming," making its limited selection of things which people then become aware of as significant, pleasurable, complex entities. (Oscar Wilde pointed out that people didn't see fogs before certain nineteenth-century poets and painters taught them how to; and surely, no one saw as much of the variety and subtlety of the human face before the era of the movies.)

Once the artist's task seemed to be simply that of opening up new areas and objects of attention. That task is still acknowledged, but it has become problematic. The very faculty of attention has come into question, and been subjected to more rigorous standards. As Jasper Johns says: "Already it's a great deal to see anything *clearly*, for we don't see *anything* clearly."

Perhaps the quality of the attention one brings to bear on something will be better (less contaminated, less distracted), the less one is offered. Furnished with impoverished art, purged by silence, one might then be able to begin to transcend the frustrating selectivity of attention, with its inevitable distortions of experience. Ideally, one should be able to pay attention to everything.

The tendency is toward less and less. But never has "less" so ostentatiously advanced itself as "more."

In the light of the current myth, in which art aims to become a "total experience," soliciting total attention, the strategies of impoverishment and reduction indicate the most exalted ambition art could adopt. Underneath what looks like a strenuous modesty, if not actual debility, is to be discerned an energetic secular blasphemy: the wish to attain the unfettered, unselective, total consciousness of "God."

VIII

Language seems a privileged metaphor for expressing the mediated character of art-making and the artwork. On the one hand, speech is both an immaterial medium (compared with, say, images) and a human activity with an apparently essential stake in the project of transcendence, of moving beyond the singular and contingent (all words being abstractions, only roughly based on or making reference to concrete particulars). On the other hand, language is the most impure, the most contaminated, the most exhausted of all the materials out of which art is made.

This dual character of language—its abstractness, and its "fallenness" in history—serves as a microcosm of the unhappy character of the arts today. Art is so far along the labyrinthine pathways of the project of transcendence that one can hardly conceive of it turning back, short of the most drastic and punitive "cultural revolution." Yet at the same time art is foundering in the debilitating tide of what once seemed the crowning achievement of European thought: secular historical consciousness. In little more than two centuries, the consciousness of history has transformed itself from a liberation, an opening of doors, blessed enlightenment, into an almost insupportable burden of self-consciousness. It's scarcely possible for the artist to write a word (or render an image or make a gesture) that doesn't remind him of something already achieved.

As Nietzsche says: "Our preeminence: we live in the age of comparison, we can verify as has never been verified before." Therefore, "we enjoy differently, we suffer differently: our instinctive activity is to compare an unheard number of things."

Up to a point, the community and historicity of the artist's means are implicit in the very fact of intersubjectivity: each person is a being-in-a-world. But today, particularly in the arts using language, this normal state of affairs is felt as an extraordinary, wearying problem.

Language is experienced not merely as something shared but as something corrupted, weighed down by historical accumulation. Thus, for each conscious artist, the creation of a work means dealing with two potentially antagonistic domains of meaning and their relationships. One is his own meaning (or lack of it); the other is the set of second-order meanings that both extend his own language and encumber, compromise, and adulterate it. The artist ends by choosing between two inherently limiting alternatives, forced to take a position that is either servile or insolent. Either he flatters or appeases his audience, giving them what they already know, or he commits an aggression against his audience, giving them what they don't want.

Modern art thus transmits in full the alienation produced by historical consciousness. Whatever the artist does is in (usually conscious) alignment with something else already done, producing a compulsion to be continually checking his situation, his own stance against those of his predecessors and contemporaries. To compensate for this ignominious enslavement to history, the artist exalts himself with the dream of a wholly ahistorical, and therefore unalienated, art.

IX

Art that is "silent" constitutes one approach to this visionary, ahistorical condition.

Consider the difference between *looking* and *staring*. A look is voluntary; it is also mobile, rising and falling in intensity as its foci of interest are taken up and then exhausted. A stare has, essentially, the character of a compulsion; it is steady, unmodulated, "fixed."

Traditional art invites a look. Art that is silent engenders a stare. Silent art allows—at least in principle—no release from attention, because there has never, in principle, been any soliciting of it. A stare is perhaps as far from history, as close to eternity, as contemporary art can get.

X

Silence is a metaphor for a cleansed, non-interfering vision, appropriate to artworks that are unresponsive before being seen, unviolable in their essential integrity by human scrutiny. The spectator would approach art as he does a landscape. A landscape doesn't demand from the spectator his "understanding," his imputations of significance, his anxieties and sympathies; it demands, rather, his absence, it asks that he not add anything to *it*. Contemplation, strictly speaking, entails self-forgetfulness on the part of the spectator: an object worthy of contemplation is one which, in effect, annihilates the perceiving subject.

Toward such an ideal plenitude to which the audience can add nothing, analogous to the aesthetic relation to nature, a great deal of contemporary art aspires—through various strategies of blandness, of reduction, of deindividuation, of alogicality. In principle, the audience may not even add its thought. All objects, rightly perceived, are already full. This is what Cage must mean when, after explaining that there is no such thing as silence because something is always happening that makes a sound, he adds, "No one can have an idea once he starts really listening."

Plenitude—experiencing all the space as filled, so that ideas cannot enter—means impenetrability. A person who becomes silent becomes opaque for the other; somebody's silence opens up an array of possibilities for interpreting that silence, for imputing speech to it.

The way in which this opaqueness induces spiritual vertigo is the theme of Bergman's *Persona*. The actress's deliberate silence has two aspects: considered as a decision apparently relating to herself, the refusal to speak is apparently the form she has given to the wish for ethical purity; but it is also, as behavior, a means of power, a species of sadism, a virtually inviolable position of strength from which she manipulates and confounds her nurse-companion, who is charged with the burden of talking.

But the opaqueness of silence can be conceived more positively, as free from anxiety. For Keats, the silence of the Grecian urn is a locus of spiritual nourishment: "unheard" melodies endure, whereas those that pipe to "the sensual ear" decay. Silence is equated with arresting time ("slow time"). One can stare endlessly at the Grecian urn. Eternity, in the argument of Keats's poem, is the only interesting stimulus to thought and also the sole occasion for coming to the end of mental activity, which means interminable, unanswered questions ("Thou, silent form, dost tease us out of thought/ As doth eternity"), in order to arrive at a final equation of ideas ("Beauty is truth, truth beauty") which is both absolutely vacuous and completely full. Keats's poem quite logically ends in a statement that will seem, if the reader hasn't followed his argument, like empty wisdom, a banality. As time, or history, is the medium of definite, determinate thought, the silence of eternity prepares for a thought beyond thought, which must appear from the perspective of traditional thinking and the familiar uses of the mind as no thought at all—though it may rather be the emblem of new, "difficult" thinking.

XI

Behind the appeals for silence lies the wish for a perceptual and cultural clean slate. And, in its most hortatory and ambitious version, the advocacy of silence expresses a mythic project of total liberation. What's envisaged is nothing less than the liberation of the artist from himself, of art from the particular artwork, of art from history, of spirit from matter, of the mind from its perceptual and intellectual limitations.

As some people know now, there are ways of thinking that we don't yet know about. Nothing could be more important or precious than that knowledge, however unborn. The sense of urgency, the spiritual restlessness it engenders, cannot be appeased, and continues to fuel the radical art of this century. Through its advocacy of silence and reduction, art commits an act of violence upon itself, turning art into a species of auto-manipulation, of conjuring—trying to bring these new ways of thinking to birth.

Silence is a strategy for the transvaluation of art, art itself being the herald of an anticipated radical transvaluation of human values. But the success of this strategy must mean its eventual abandonment, or at least its significant modification.

Silence is a prophecy, one which the artist's actions can be understood as attempting both to fulfill and to reverse.

As language points to its own transcendence in silence, silence points to its own transcendence—to a speech beyond silence.

But can the whole enterprise become an act of bad faith if the artist knows *this*, too?

XII

A famous quotation: "Everything that can be thought at all can be thought clearly. Everything that can be said at all can be said clearly. But not everything that can be thought can be said."

Notice that Wittgenstein, with his scrupulous avoidance of the psychological issue, doesn't ask why, when, and in what circumstances someone would *want* to put into words "everything that can be thought" (even if he could), or even to utter (whether clearly or not) "everything that could be said."

XIII

Of everything that's said, one can ask: *why?* (Including: why should I say *that*? And: why should I say anything at all?)

Moreover, strictly speaking, nothing that's *said* is true. (Though a person can *be* the truth, one can't ever say it.)

Still, things that are said can sometimes be helpful—which is what people ordinarily mean when they regard something *said* as being true. Speech can enlighten, relieve, confuse, exalt, infect, antagonize, gratify, grieve, stun, animate. While language is regularly used to inspire to action, some verbal statements, either written or oral, are themselves the performing of an action (as in promising, swearing, bequeathing). Another use of speech, if anything more common than that of provoking actions, is to provoke further speech. But speech can silence, too. This indeed is how it must be: without the polarity of silence, the whole system of language would fail. And beyond its generic function as the dialectical opposite of speech, silence—like speech—also has more specific, less inevitable uses.

One use for silence: certifying the absence or renunciation of thought. Silence is often employed as a magical or mimetic procedure in repressive social relationships, as in the Jesuit regulations about speaking to superiors and in the disciplining of children. (This should not be confused with the practice of certain monastic disciplines, such as the Trappist order, in which silence is both an ascetic act and bears witness to the condition of being perfectly "full.")

Another, apparently opposed, use for silence: certifying the completion of thought. In the words of Karl Jaspers, "He who has the final answers can no longer speak to the other, breaking off genuine communication for the sake of what he believes in."

Still another use for silence: providing time for the continuing or exploring of thought. Notably, speech closes off thought. (An example: the enterprise of criticism, in which there seems no way for a critic not to assert that a given artist is *this,* is *that,* etc.) But if one decides an issue isn't closed, it's not. This is presumably the rationale behind the voluntary experiments in silence that some contemporary spiritual athletes have undertaken, and the element of wisdom in the otherwise mainly authoritarian, philistine silence of the orthodox Freudian psychoanalyst. Silence keeps things "open."

Still another use for silence: furnishing or aiding speech to attain its maximum integrity or seriousness. Everyone has experienced how, when punctuated by long silences, words weigh more; they become almost palpable. Or how, when one talks less, one begins feeling more fully one's physical presence in a given space. Silence undermines "bad speech," by which I mean dissociated speech—speech dissociated from the body (and, therefore, from feeling), speech not organically informed by the sensuous presence and concrete particularity of the speaker and by the individual occasion for using language. Unmoored from the body, speech deteriorates. It becomes false, inane, ignoble, weightless. Silence can inhibit or counteract this tendency, providing a kind of ballast, monitoring and even correcting language when it becomes inauthentic.

Given these perils to the authenticity of language (which doesn't depend on the character of any isolated statement or even group of statements, but on the relation of speaker, utterance, and situation), the imaginary project of saying clearly "everything that can be said" suggested by Wittgenstein's remarks looks fearfully complicated. (How much time would one have? Would one have to speak quickly?) The philosopher's hypothetical universe of clear speech (which assigns to silence only "that whereof one cannot speak") would seem to be a moralist's, or a psychiatrist's, nightmare—at the least a place no one should lightheartedly enter. Is there anyone who *wants* to say "everything that could be said"? The psychologically plausible answer would seem to be no. But yes is plausible, too—as a rising ideal of modern culture. Isn't that what many people *do* want today—to say everything that can be said? But this aim cannot be maintained without inner conflict. In part inspired by the spread of the ideals of psychotherapy, people are yearning to say "everything" (thereby, among other results, further undermining the crumbling distinction between public and private endeavors, between information and secrets). But, in an overpopulated world being connected by global electronic communication and jet travel at a pace too rapid and violent for an organically sound person to assimilate without shock, people are also suffering from a revulsion at any further proliferation of speech and images. Such different factors as the unlimited "technological reproduction" and near universal diffusion of printed language and speech as well as images (from "news" to "art objects"), and the degeneration of public language within the realms of politics and advertising and entertainment, have produced, especially among the better-educated inhabitants of modern mass society, a devaluation of language. (I should argue, contrary to McLuhan, that a devaluation of the power and credibility of images has taken place no less profound than, and essentially similar to, that afflicting language.) And, as the prestige of language falls, that of silence rises.

I am alluding, at this point, to the sociological context of the contemporary ambivalence toward language. The matter, of course, goes much deeper than this. In addition to the specific sociological determinants, one must recognize the operation of something like a perennial discontent with language that has been formulated in each of the major civilizations of the Orient and Occident, whenever thought reaches a certain high, *excruciating* order of complexity and spiritual seriousness.

Traditionally, it has been through the religious vocabulary, with its meta-absolutes of "sacred" and "profane," "human" and "divine," that the disaffection with language itself has been charted. In particular, the antecedents of art's dilemmas and strategies are to be found in the radical wing of the mystical tradition. (Among Christian texts: the *Mystica Theologia* of Dionysius the Areopagite, the anonymous *Cloud of Unknowing*, the writings of Jakob Boehme and Meister Eckhart; and parallels in Zen, Taoist, and Sufi texts.) The mystical tradition has always recognized, in Norman Brown's phrase, "the neurotic character of language." (According to Boehme, Adam spoke a language different from all known languages. It was "sensual speech," the unmediated expressive instrument of the senses, proper to beings integrally part of sensuous nature—that is, still employed by all the animals except that sick animal, man. This, which Boehme calls the only "natural language," the sole language free from distortion and illusion, is what man will speak again when he recovers paradise.) But, in our time, the most striking developments of such ideas have been made by artists (and certain psychotherapists) rather than by the timid legatees of the religious traditions.

Explicitly in revolt against what is deemed the desiccated, categorized life of the ordinary mind, the artist issues his own call for a revision of language. A good deal of contemporary art is moved by this quest for a consciousness purified of contaminated language and, in some versions, of the distortions produced by conceiving the world exclusively in conventional verbal (in their debased sense, "rational" or "logical") terms. Art itself becomes a kind of counterviolence, seeking to loosen the grip upon consciousness of the habits of lifeless, static verbalization, presenting models of "sensual speech."

If anything, the volume of discontent has been turned up since the arts inherited the problem of language from religious discourse. It's not just that words, ultimately, are inadequate to the highest aims of consciousness; or even that they get in the way. Art expresses a double discontent. We lack words, and we have too many of them. It raises two complaints about language. Words are too crude. And words are also too busy—inviting a hyperactivity of consciousness that is not only dysfunctional, in terms of human capacities of feeling and acting, but actively deadens the mind and blunts the senses.

Language is demoted to the status of an event. Something takes place in time, a voice speaking which points to the before and to what comes after an utterance: silence. Silence, then, is both the precondition of speech and the result or aim of properly directed speech. On this model, the artist's activity is the creating or establishing of silence; the efficacious artwork leaves silence in its wake. Silence, administered by the artist, is part of a program of perceptual and cultural therapy, often on the model of shock therapy rather than of persuasion. Even if the artist's medium is words, he can share in this task: language can be employed to check language, to express muteness. Mallarmé thought it was the job of poetry, using words, to clean up our word-clogged reality—by creating silences around things. Art must mount a full-scale attack on language itself, by means of language and its surrogates, on behalf of the standard of silence.

XIV

In the end, the radical critique of consciousness (first delineated by the mystical tradition, now administered by unorthodox psychotherapy and high modernist art) always lays the blame on language. Consciousness, experienced as a burden, is conceived of as the memory of all the words that have ever been said.

Krishnamurti claims that we must give up psychological, as distinct from factual, memory. Otherwise, we keep filling up the new with the old, closing off experience by hooking each experience onto the last.

We must destroy continuity (which is insured by psychological memory), by going to the *end* of each emotion or thought.

And after the end, what supervenes (for a while) is silence.

XV

In his Fourth Duino Elegy, Rilke gives a metaphoric statement of the problem of language and recommends a procedure for approaching as near the horizon of silence as he considers feasible. A prerequisite of "emptying out" is to be able to perceive what one is "full of," what words and mechanical gestures one is stuffed with, like a doll; only then, in polar confrontation with the doll, does the "angel" appear, a figure representing an equally inhuman though "higher" possibility, that of an entirely unmediated, translinguistic apprehension. Neither doll nor angel, human beings remain situated within the kingdom of language. But for nature, then things, then other people, then the textures of ordinary life to be experienced from a stance other than the crippled one of mere spectatorship, language must regain its chastity. As Rilke describes it in the Ninth Elegy, the redemption of language (which is to say, the redemption of the world through its interiorization in consciousness) is a long, infinitely arduous task. Human beings are so "fallen" that they must start with the simplest linguistic act: the naming of things. Perhaps no more than this minimal function can be preserved from the general corruption of discourse. Language may very well have to remain within a permanent state of reduction. Though perhaps, when this spiritual exercise of confining language to naming is perfected, it may be possible to pass on to other, more ambitious uses of language, nothing must be attempted which will allow consciousness to become reestranged from itself.

For Rilke the overcoming of the alienation of consciousness is conceivable; and not, as in the radical myths of the mystics, through transcending language altogether. It suffices to cut back drastically the scope and use of language. A tremendous spiritual preparation (the contrary of "alienation") is required for this deceptively simple act of naming. It is nothing less than the scouring and harmonious sharpening of the senses (the very opposite of such violent projects, with roughly the same end and informed by the same hostility to verbal-rational culture, as "systematically deranging the senses").

Rilke's remedy lies halfway between exploiting the numbness of language as a gross, fully installed cultural institution and yielding to the suicidal vertigo of pure silence. But this middle ground of reducing language to naming can be claimed in quite another way than his. Contrast the benign nominalism proposed by Rilke (and proposed and practiced by Francis Ponge) with the brutal nominalism adopted by many other artists. The more familiar recourse of modern art to the aesthetics of the inventory is not made—as in Rilke—with an eye to "humanizing" things, but rather to confirming their inhumanity, their impersonality, their indifference to and separateness from human concerns. (Examples of the "inhumane" preoccupation with naming: Roussel's *Impressions of Africa;* the silk-screen paintings and early films of Andy Warhol; the early novels of Robbe-Grillet, which attempt to confine the function of language to bare physical description and location.)

Rilke and Ponge assume that there *are* priorities: rich as opposed to vacuous objects, events with a certain allure. (This is the incentive for trying to peel back language, allowing the "things" themselves to speak.) More decisively, they assume that if there are states of false (language-clogged) consciousness, there are also authentic states of consciousness—which it's the function of art to promote. The alternative view denies the traditional hierarchies of interest and meaning, in which some things have more "significance" than others. The distinction between true and false experience, true and false consciousness is also denied: in principle, one should desire to pay attention to everything. It's this view, most elegantly formulated by Cage though its practice is found everywhere, that leads to the art of the inventory, the catalogue, surfaces; also "chance." The function of art isn't to sanction any specific experience, except the state of being open to the multiplicity of experience—which ends in practice by a decided stress on things usually considered trivial or unimportant.

The attachment of contemporary art to the "minimal" narrative principle of the catalogue or inventory seems almost to parody the capitalist world view, in which the environment is atomized into "items" (a category embracing things and persons, works of art and natural organisms), and in which every item is a commodity—that is, a discrete, portable object. A general leveling of value is encouraged in the art of inventory, which is itself only one of the possible approaches to an ideally uninflected discourse. Traditionally, the effects of an artwork have been unevenly distributed, to induce in the audience a certain sequence of experience: first arousing, then manipulating, and eventually fulfilling emotional expectations. What is proposed now is a discourse without emphases in this traditional sense. (Again, the principle of the stare as opposed to the look.)

Such art could also be described as establishing great "distance" (between spectator and art object, between the spectator and his emotions). But, psychologically, distance often is linked with the most intense state of feeling, in which the coolness or impersonality with which something is treated measures the insatiable interest that thing has for us. The distance that a great deal of "anti-humanist" art proposes is actually equivalent to obsession—an aspect of the involvement in "things" of which the "humanist" nominalism of Rilke has no intimation.

XVI

"There is something strange in the acts of writing and speaking," Novalis wrote in 1799. "The ridiculous and amazing mistake people make is to believe they use words in relation to things. They are unaware of the nature of language—which is to be its own and only concern, making it so fertile and splendid a mystery. When someone talks just for the sake of talking he is saying the most original and truthful thing he can say."

Novalis's statement may help explain an apparent paradox: that in the era of the widespread advocacy of art's silence, an increasing number of works of art babble. Verbosity and repetitiveness are particularly noticeable in the temporal arts of prose fiction, music, film, and dance, many of which cultivate a kind of ontological stammer—facilitated by their refusal of the incentives for a clean, anti-redundant discourse supplied by linear, beginning-middle-and-end construction. But actually, there's no contradiction. For the contemporary appeal for silence has never indicated merely a hostile dismissal of language. It also signifies a very high estimate of language—of its powers, of its past health, and of the current dangers it poses to a free consciousness. From this intense and ambivalent valuation proceeds the impulse for a discourse that appears both irrepressible (and, in principle, interminable) and strangely inarticulate, painfully reduced. Discernible in the fictions of Stein, Burroughs, and Beckett is the subliminal idea that it might be possible to outtalk language, or to talk oneself into silence.

This is not a very promising strategy, considering what results might reasonably be anticipated from it. But perhaps not so odd, when one observes how often the aesthetic of silence appears alongside a barely controlled abhorrence of the void.

Accommodating these two contrary impulses may produce the need to fill up all the spaces with objects of slight emotional weight or with large areas of barely modulated color or evenly detailed objects, or to spin a discourse with as few possible inflections, emotive variations, and risings and fallings of emphasis. These procedures seem analogous to the behavior of an obsessional neurotic warding off a danger. The acts of such a person must be repeated in the identical form, because the danger remains the same; and they must be repeated endlessly, because the danger never seems to go away. But the emotional fires feeding the art discourse analogous to obsessionalism may be turned down so low one can almost forget they're there. Then all that's left to the ear is a kind of steady hum or drone. What's left to the eye is the neat filling of a space with things, or, more accurately, the patient transcription of the surface detail of things.

In this view, the "silence" of things, images, and words is a prerequisite for their proliferation. Were they endowed with a more potent, individual charge, each of the various elements of the artwork would claim more psychic space and then their total number might have to be reduced.

XVII

Sometimes the accusation against language is not directed against all of language but only against the written word. Thus, Tristan Tzara urged the burning of all books and libraries to bring about a new era of oral legends. And McLuhan, as everyone knows, makes the sharpest distinction between written language (which exists in "visual space") and oral speech (which exists in "auditory space"), praising the psychic and cultural advantages of the latter as the basis for sensibility.

If written language is singled out as the culprit, what will be sought is not so much the reduction as the metamorphosis of language into something looser, more intuitive, less organized and inflected, non-linear (in McLuhan's terminology) and—noticeably—more verbose. But, of course, it is just these qualities that characterize many of the great prose narratives of our time. Joyce, Stein, Gadda, Laura Riding, Beckett, and Burroughs employ a language whose norms and energies come from oral speech, with its circular repetitive movements and essentially first-person voice.

"Speaking for the sake of speaking is the formula of deliverance," Novalis said. (Deliverance from what? From speaking? From art?)

In my opinion, Novalis has succinctly described the proper approach of the writer to language and offered the basic criterion for literature as an art. But to what extent oral speech is the privileged model for the speech of literature as an art is still an open question.

XVIII

A corollary of the growth of this conception of art's language as autonomous and self-sufficient (and, in the end, self-reflective) is a decline in "meaning" as traditionally sought in works of art. "Speaking for the sake of speaking" forces us to relocate the meaning of linguistic or para-linguistic statements. We are led to abandon meaning (in the sense of references to entities outside the artwork) as the criterion for the language of art in favor of "use." (Wittgenstein's famous thesis, "the meaning is the use," can and should be rigorously applied to art.)

"Meaning" partially or totally converted into "use" is the secret behind the widespread strategy of *literalness*, a major development of the aesthetics of silence. A variant on this: hidden literality, exemplified by such different writers as Kafka and Beckett. The narratives of Kafka and Beckett seem puzzling because they appear to invite the reader to ascribe high-powered symbolic and allegorical meanings to them and, at the same time, repel such ascriptions. Yet, when the narrative is examined, it discloses no more than what it literally means. The power of their language derives precisely from the fact that the meaning is so bare.

The effect of such bareness is often a kind of anxiety—like the anxiety produced when familiar things aren't in their place or playing their accustomed role. One may be made as anxious by unexpected literalness as by the Surrealists' "disturbing" objects and unexpected scale and condition of objects conjoined in an imaginary landscape. Whatever is wholly mysterious is at once both psychically relieving and anxiety-provoking. (A perfect machine for agitating this pair of contrary emotions: the Bosch drawing in a Dutch museum that shows trees furnished with two ears at the sides of their trunks, as if they were listening to the forest, while the forest floor is strewn with eyes.) Before a fully conscious work of art, one feels something like the mixture of anxiety, detachment, pruriency, and relief that a physically sound person feels when he glimpses an amputee. Beckett speaks favorably of a work of art which would be a "total object, complete with missing parts, instead of partial object. Question of degree."

But exactly what is a totality and what constitutes completeness in art (or anything else)? That problem is, in principle, unresolvable. Whatever way a work of art is, it could have been—could be—different. The necessity of *these* parts in this order is never given; it is conferred.

The refusal to admit this essential contingency (or openness) is what inspires the audience's will to confirm the closedness of a work by interpreting it, and what creates the feeling common among reflective artists and critics that the artwork is always somehow in arrears of or inadequate to its "subject." But unless one is committed to the idea that art "expresses" something, these procedures and attitudes are far from inevitable.

XIX

This tenacious concept of art as "expression" has given rise to the most common, and dubious, version of the notion of silence—which invokes the idea of "the ineffable." The theory supposes that the province of art is "the beautiful," which implies effects of unspeakableness, indescribability, ineffability. Indeed, the search to express the inexpressible is taken as the very criterion of art; and sometimes becomes the occasion for a strict—and to my mind untenable—distinction between prose literature and poetry. It is from this position that Valéry advanced his famous argument (repeated in a quite different context by Sartre) that the novel is not, strictly speaking, an art form at all. His reason is that since the aim of prose is to communicate, the use of language in prose is perfectly straightforward. Poetry, being an art, should have quite different aims: to express an experience which is essentially ineffable; using language to express muteness. In contrast to prose writers, poets are engaged in subverting their own instrument and seeking to pass beyond it.

This theory, so far as it assumes that art is concerned with beauty, is not very interesting. (Modern aesthetics is crippled by its dependence upon this essentially vacant concept. As if art were "about" beauty, as science is "about" truth!) But even if the theory dispenses with the notion of beauty, there is still a more serious objection. The view that expressing the ineffable is an essential function of poetry (considered as a paradigm of all the arts) is naïvely unhistorical. The ineffable, while surely a perennial category of consciousness, has certainly not always made its home in the arts. Its traditional shelter was in religious discourse and, secondarily (as Plato relates in his Seventh Epistle), in philosophy. The fact that contemporary artists are concerned with silence—and, therefore, in one extension, with the ineffable—must be understood historically, as a consequence of the prevailing contemporary myth of the "absoluteness" of art. The value placed on silence doesn't arise by virtue of the *nature* of art, but derives from the contemporary ascription of certain "absolute" qualities to the art object and to the activity of the artist.

The extent to which art *is* involved with the ineffable is more specific, as well as contemporary: art, in the modern conception, is always connected with systematic transgressions of a formal sort. The systematic violation of older formal conventions practiced by modern artists gives their work a certain aura of the unspeakable—for instance, as the audience uneasily senses the negative presence of what else could be, but isn't being, said; and as any "statement" made in an aggressively new or difficult form tends to seem equivocal or merely vacant. But these features of ineffability must not be acknowledged at the expense of one's awareness of the positivity of the work of art. Contemporary art, no matter how much it has defined itself by a taste for negation, can still be analyzed as a set of assertions of a formal kind.

For instance, each work of art gives us a form of paradigm or model of *knowing* something, an epistemology. But viewed as a spiritual project, a vehicle of aspirations toward an absolute, what any work of art supplies is a specific model for meta-social or meta-ethical *tact,* a standard of decorum. Each artwork indicates the unity of certain preferences about what can and cannot be said (or represented). At the same time that it may make a tacit proposal for upsetting previously consecrated rulings on what can be said (or represented), it issues its own set of limits.

XX

Contemporary artists advocate silence in two styles: loud and soft.

The loud style is a function of the unstable antithesis of "plenum" and "void." The sensuous, ecstatic, translinguistic apprehension of the plenum is notoriously fragile: in a terrible, almost instantaneous plunge it can collapse into the void of negative silence. With all its awareness of risk-taking (the hazards of spiritual nausea, even of madness), this advocacy of silence tends to be frenetic and over-generalizing. It is also frequently apocalyptic and must endure the indignity of all apocalyptic thinking: namely, to prophesy the end, to see the day come, to outlive it, and then to set a new date for the incineration of consciousness and the definitive pollution of language and exhaustion of the possibilities of art discourse.

The other way of talking about silence is more cautious. Basically, it presents itself as an extension of a main feature of traditional classicism: the concern with modes of propriety, with standards of seemliness. Silence is only "reticence" stepped up to the nth degree. Of course, in the translation of this concern from the matrix of traditional classical art, the tone has changed—from didactic seriousness to ironic open-mindedness. But while the clamorous style of proclaiming the rhetoric of silence may seem more passionate, its more subdued advocates (like Cage, Johns) are saying something equally drastic. They are reacting to the same idea of art's absolute aspirations (by programmatic disavowals of art); they share the same disdain for the "meanings" established by bourgeois-rationalist culture, indeed for culture itself in the familiar sense. What is voiced by the Futurists, some of the Dada artists, and Burroughs as a harsh despair and perverse vision of apocalypse is no less serious for being proclaimed in a polite voice and as a sequence of playful affirmations. Indeed, it could be argued that silence is likely to remain a viable notion for modern art and consciousness only if deployed with a considerable, near-systematic irony.

XXI

It is in the nature of all spiritual projects to tend to consume themselves—exhausting their own sense, the very meaning of the terms in which they are couched. (This is why "spirituality" must be continually reinvented.) All genuinely ultimate projects of consciousness eventually become projects for the unraveling of thought itself.

Art conceived as a spiritual project is no exception. As an abstracted and fragmented replica of the positive nihilism expounded by the radical religious myths, the serious art of our time has moved increasingly toward the most excruciating inflections of consciousness. Conceivably, irony is the only feasible counterweight to this grave use of art as the arena for the ordeal of consciousness. The present prospect is that artists will go on abolishing art, only to resurrect it in a more retracted version. As long as art bears up under the pressure of chronic interrogation, it would seem desirable that some of the questions have a certain playful quality.

But this prospect depends, perhaps, on the viability of irony itself.

From Socrates on, there are countless witnesses to the value of irony for the private individual: as a complex, serious method of seeking and holding one's truth, and as a means of saving one's sanity. But as irony becomes the good taste of what is, after all, an essentially collective activity—the making of art—it may prove less serviceable.

One need not judge as categorically as Nietzsche, who thought the spread of irony throughout a culture signified the flood tide of decadence and the approaching end of that culture's vitality and powers. In the post-political, electronically connected cosmopolis in which all serious modern artists have taken out premature citizenship, certain organic connections between culture and "thinking" (and art is certainly now, mainly, a form of thinking) appear to have been broken, so that Nietzsche's diagnosis may need to be modified. But if irony has more positive resources than Nietzsche acknowledged, there still remains a question as to how far the resources of irony can be stretched. It seems unlikely that the possibilities of continually undermining one's assumptions can go on unfolding indefinitely into the future, without being eventually checked by despair or by a laugh that leaves one without any breath at all.

(1967)

The Pornographic Imagination

No one should undertake a discussion of pornography before acknowledging the pornograph*ies*—there are at least three—and before pledging to take them on one at a time. There is a considerable gain in truth if pornography as an item in social history is treated quite separately from pornography as a psychological phenomenon (according to the usual view, symptomatic of sexual deficiency or deformity in both the producers and the consumers), and if one further distinguishes from both of these another pornography: a minor but interesting modality or convention within the arts.

It's the last of the three pornographies that I want to focus upon. More narrowly, upon the literary genre for which, lacking a better name, I'm willing to accept (in the privacy of serious intellectual debate, not in the courts) the dubious label of pornography. By literary genre I mean a body of work belonging to literature considered as an art, and to which inherent standards of artistic excellence pertain. From the standpoint of social and psychological phenomena, all pornographic texts have the same status; they are documents. But from the standpoint of art, some of these texts may well become something else. Not only do Pierre Louÿs's *Trois Filles de leur Mère*, Georges Bataille's *Histoire de l'Oeil* and *Madame Edwarda*, the pseudonymous *Story of O* and *The Image* belong to literature, but it can be made clear why these books, all five of them, occupy a much higher rank as literature than *Candy* or Oscar Wilde's *Teleny* or the Earl of Rochester's *Sodom* or Apollinaire's *The Debauched Hospodar* or Cleland's *Fanny Hill*. The avalanche of pornographic potboilers marketed for two centuries under and now, increasingly, over the counter no more impugns the status as literature of the first group of porno-graphic books than the proliferation of books of the caliber of *The Valley of the Dolls* throws into question the credentials of *Anna Kar-enina* and *The Man Who Loved Children*. The ratio of authentic lit-erature to trash in pornography may be somewhat lower than the ratio of novels of genuine literary merit to the entire volume of sub-literary fiction produced for mass taste. But it is probably no lower than, for instance, that of another somewhat shady sub-genre with a few first-rate books to its credit, science fiction. (As literary forms, pornography and science fiction resemble each other in several inter-esting ways.) Anyway, the quantitative measure supplies a trivial standard. Relatively uncommon as they may be, there are writings which it seems reasonable to call pornographic—assuming that the stale label has any use at all—which, at the same time, cannot be refused accreditation as serious literature.

The point would seem to be obvious. Yet, apparently, that's far from being the case. At least in England and America, the reasoned scru-tiny and assessment of pornography is held firmly within the limits of the discourse employed by psychologists, sociologists, historians, jurists, professional moralists, and social critics. Pornography is a mal-ady to be diagnosed and an occasion for judgment. It's something one is for or against. And taking sides about pornography is hardly like being for or against aleatoric music or Pop Art, but quite a bit like being for or against legalized abortion or federal aid to parochial schools. In fact, the same fundamental approach to the subject is shared by recent eloquent defenders of society's right and obligation to censor dirty books, like George P. Elliott and George Steiner, and those like Paul Goodman, who foresee pernicious consequences of a policy of censorship far worse than any harm done by the books themselves. Both the libertarians and the would-be censors agree in reducing pornography to pathological symptom and problematic so-cial commodity. A near-unanimous consensus exists as to what por-nography is—this being identified with notions about the *sources* of the impulse to produce and consume these curious goods. When viewed as a theme for psychological analysis, pornography is rarely seen as anything more interesting than texts which illustrate a de-plorable arrest in normal adult sexual development. In this view, all pornography amounts to is the representation of the fantasies of in-fantile sexual life, these fantasies having been edited by the more skilled, less innocent consciousness of the masturbatory adolescent, for purchase by so-called adults. As a social phenomenon—for instance, the boom in the production of pornography in the societies of Western Europe and America since the eighteenth century—the approach is no less unequivocally clinical. Pornography becomes a group pathology, the disease of a whole culture, about whose cause everyone is pretty well agreed. The mounting output of dirty books is attributed to a festering legacy of Christian sexual repression and to sheer physiological ignorance, these ancient disabilities being now compounded by more proximate historical events, the impact of drastic dislocations in traditional modes of family and political order and unsettling change in the roles of the sexes. (The problem of pornography is one of "the dilemmas of a society in transition," Goodman said in an essay several years ago.) Thus, there is a fairly complete consensus about the *diagnosis* of pornography itself. The disagreements arise only in the estimate of the psychological and social *consequences* of its dissemination, and therefore in the formulating of tactics and policy.

The more enlightened architects of moral policy are undoubtedly prepared to admit that there is something like a "pornographic imagination," although only in the sense that pornographic works are tokens of a radical failure or deformation of the imagination. And they may grant, as Goodman, Wayland Young, and others have suggested, that there also exists a "pornographic society": that, indeed, ours is a flourishing example of one, a society so hypocritically and repressively constructed that it must inevitably produce an effusion of pornography as both its logical expression and its subversive, demotic antidote. But nowhere in the Anglo-American community of letters have I seen it argued that some pornographic books are interesting and important works of art. So long as pornography is treated as only a social and psychological phenomenon and a locus for moral concern, how could such an argument ever be made?

II

There's another reason, apart from this categorizing of pornography as a topic of analysis, why the question whether or not works of pornography can be literature has never been genuinely debated. I mean the view of literature itself maintained by most English and American critics—a view which in excluding pornographic writings *by definition* from the precincts of literature excludes much else besides.

Of course, no one denies that pornography constitutes a branch of literature in the sense that it appears in the form of printed books of fiction. But beyond that trivial connection, no more is allowed. The fashion in which most critics construe the nature of prose literature, no less than their view of the nature of pornography, inevitably puts pornography in an adverse relation to literature. It is an airtight case, for if a pornographic book is defined as one not belonging to literature (and vice versa), there is no need to examine individual books.

Most mutually exclusive definitions of pornography and literature rest on four separate arguments. One is that the utterly single-minded way in which works of pornography address the reader, proposing to arouse him sexually, is antithetical to the complex function of literature. It may then be argued that pornography's aim, inducing sexual excitement, is at odds with the tranquil, detached involvement evoked by genuine art. But this turn of the argument seems particularly unconvincing, considering the respected appeal to the reader's moral feelings intended by "realistic" writing, not to mention the fact that some certified masterpieces (from Chaucer to Lawrence) contain passages that do properly excite readers sexually. It is more plausible just to emphasize that pornography still possesses only one "intention," while any genuinely valuable work of literature has many.

Another argument, made by Adorno among others, is that works of pornography lack the beginning-middle-and-end form characteristic of literature. A piece of pornographic fiction concocts no better than a crude excuse for a beginning; and once having begun, it goes on and on and ends nowhere.

Another argument: pornographic writing can't evidence any care for its means of expression as such (the concern of literature), since the aim of pornography is to inspire a set of nonverbal fantasies in which language plays a debased, merely instrumental role.

Last and most weighty is the argument that the subject of literature is the relation of human beings to each other, their complex feelings and emotions; pornography, in contrast, disdains fully formed persons (psychology and social portraiture), is oblivious to the question of motives and their credibility, and reports only the motiveless tireless transactions of depersonalized organs.

Simply extrapolating from the conception of literature maintained by most English and American critics today, it would follow that the literary value of pornography has to be nil. But these paradigms don't stand up to close analysis in themselves, nor do they even fit their subject. Take, for instance, *Story of O*. Though the novel is clearly obscene by the usual standards, and more effective than many in arousing a reader sexually, sexual arousal doesn't appear to be the sole function of the situations portrayed. The narrative does have a definite beginning, middle, and end. The elegance of the writing hardly gives the impression that its author considered language a bothersome necessity. Further, the characters do possess emotions of a very intense kind, although obsessional and indeed wholly asocial ones; characters do have motives, though they are not psychiatrically or socially "normal" motives. The characters in *Story of O* are endowed with a "psychology" of a sort, one derived from the psychology of lust. And while what can be learned of the characters within the situations in which they are placed is severely restricted—to modes of sexual concentration and explicitly rendered sexual behavior—O and her partners are no more reduced or foreshortened than the characters in many non-pornographic works of contemporary fiction.

Only when English and American critics evolve a more sophisticated view of literature will an interesting debate get underway. (In the end, this debate would be not only about pornography but about the whole body of contemporary literature insistently focused on extreme situations and behavior.) The difficulty arises because so many critics continue to identify with prose literature itself the particular literary conventions of "realism" (what might be crudely associated with the major tradition of the nineteenth-century novel). For examples of alternative literary modes, one is not confined only to much of the greatest twentieth-century writing—to *Ulysses,* a book not about characters but about media of transpersonal exchange, about all that lies outside individual psychology and personal need; to French Surrealism and its most recent offspring, the New Novel; to German "expressionist" fiction; to the Russian post-novel represented by Biely's *St. Petersburg* and by Nabokov; or to the non-linear, tenseless narratives of Stein and Burroughs. A definition of literature that faults a work for being rooted in "fantasy" rather than in the realistic rendering of how lifelike persons in familiar situations live with each other couldn't even handle such venerable conventions as the pastoral, which depicts relations between people that are certainly reductive, vapid, and unconvincing.

An uprooting of some of these tenacious clichés is long overdue: it will promote a sounder reading of the literature of the past as well as put critics and ordinary readers better in touch with contemporary literature, which includes zones of writing that structurally resemble pornography. It is facile, virtually meaningless, to demand that literature stick with the "human." For the matter at stake is not "human" versus "inhuman" (in which choosing the "human" guarantees instant moral self-congratulation for both author and reader) but an infinitely varied register of forms and tonalities for transposing *the human voice* into prose narrative. For the critic, the proper question is not the relationship between the book and "the world" or "reality" (in which each novel is judged as if it were a unique item, and in which the world is regarded as a far less complex place than it is) but the complexities of consciousness itself, as the medium through which a world exists at all and is constituted, and an approach to single books of fiction which doesn't slight the fact that they exist in dialogue with each other. From this point of view, the decision of the old novelists to depict the unfolding of the destinies of sharply individualized "characters" in familiar, socially dense situations within the conventional notation of chronological sequence is only one of many possible decisions, possessing no inherently superior claim to the allegiance of serious readers. There is nothing innately more "human" about these procedures. The presence of realistic characters is not, in itself, something wholesome, a more nourishing staple for the moral sensibility.

The only sure truth about characters in prose fiction is that they are, in Henry James's phrase, "a compositional resource." The presence of human figures in literary art can serve many purposes. Dramatic tension or three-dimensionality in the rendering of personal and social relations is often *not* a writer's aim, in which case it doesn't help to insist on that as a generic standard. Exploring ideas is as authentic an aim of prose fiction, although by the standards of novelistic realism this aim severely limits the presentation of lifelike persons. The constructing or imaging of something inanimate, or of a portion of the world of nature, is also a valid enterprise, and entails an appropriate rescaling of the human figure. (The form of the pastoral involves both these aims: the depiction of ideas and of nature. Persons are used only to the extent that they constitute a certain kind of landscape, which is partly a stylization of "real" nature and partly a neo-Platonic landscape of ideas.) And equally valid as a subject for prose narrative are the extreme states of human feeling and consciousness, those so peremptory that they exclude the mundane flux of feelings and are only contingently linked with concrete persons— which is the case with pornography.

One would never guess from the confident pronouncements on the nature of literature by most American and English critics that a vivid debate on this issue had been proceeding for several generations. "It seems to me," Jacques Rivière wrote in the *Nouvelle Revue Française* in 1924, "that we are witnessing a very serious crisis in the concept of what literature is." One of several responses to "the problem of the possibility and the limits of literature," Rivière noted, is the marked tendency for "art (if even the word can still be kept) to become a completely non-human activity, a super-sensory function, if I may use that term, a sort of creative astronomy." I cite Rivière not because his essay "Questioning the Concept of Literature" is particularly definitive but to recall an ensemble of radical notions about literature which were almost critical commonplaces forty years ago in European literary magazines.

To this day, though, that ferment remains alien, unassimilated, and persistently misunderstood in the English and American world of letters: suspected as issuing from a collective cultural failure of nerve, frequently dismissed as outright perversity or obscurantism or creative sterility. The better English-speaking critics, however, could hardly fail to notice how much great twentieth-century literature subverts those ideas received from certain of the great nineteenth-century novelists on the nature of literature which they continue to echo in 1967. But the critics' awareness of genuinely new literature was usually tendered in a spirit much like that of the rabbis a century before the beginning of the Christian era who, humbly acknowledging the spiritual inferiority of their own age to the age of the great prophets, nevertheless firmly closed the canon of prophetic books and declared—with more relief, one suspects, than regret—the era of prophecy ended. So has the age of what in Anglo-American criticism is still called, astonishingly enough, experimental or avant-garde writing been repeatedly declared closed. The ritual celebration of each contemporary genius's undermining of the older notions of literature was often accompanied by the nervous insistence that the writing brought forth was, alas, the last of its noble, sterile line. Now, the results of this intricate, one-eyed way of looking at modern literature have been several decades of unparalleled interest and brilliance in English and American—particularly American—criticism. But it is an interest and brilliance reared on bankruptcy of taste and something approaching a fundamental dishonesty of method. The critics' retrograde awareness of the impressive new claims staked out by modern literature, linked with their chagrin over what was usually designated as the rejection of reality and the failure of the self endemic in that literature, indicates the precise point at which most talented Anglo-American literary criticism leaves off considering structures of literature and transposes itself into criticism of culture.

I don't wish to repeat here the arguments that I have advanced elsewhere on behalf of a different critical approach. Still, some allusion to that approach needs to be made. To discuss even a single work of the radical nature of *Histoire de l'Oeil* raises the question of literature itself, of prose narrative considered as an art form. And books

like those of Bataille could not have been written except for that ag-
onized reappraisal of the nature of literature which has been preoccupying literary Europe for more than half a century; but lacking
that context, they must prove almost unassimilable for English and
American readers—except as "mere" pornography, inexplicably fancy
trash. If it is even necessary to take up the issue of whether or not
pornography and literature are antithetical, if it is at all necessary to
assert that works of pornography *can* belong to literature, then the
assertion must imply an overall view of what art is.

To put it very generally: art (and art-making) is a form of consciousness; the materials of art are the variety of forms of consciousness. By no *aesthetic* principle can this notion of the materials of art
be construed as excluding even the extreme forms of consciousness
that transcend social personality or psychological individuality.

In daily life, to be sure, we may acknowledge a moral obligation to
inhibit such states of consciousness in ourselves. The obligation seems
pragmatically sound, not only to maintain social order in the widest
sense but to allow the individual to establish and maintain a humane
contact with other persons (though that contact can be renounced,
for shorter or longer periods). It's well known that when people venture into the far reaches of consciousness, they do so at the peril of
their sanity, that is, of their humanity. But the "human scale" or humanistic standard proper to ordinary life and conduct seems misplaced when applied to art. It oversimplifies. If within the last century art conceived as an autonomous activity has come to be invested
with an unprecedented stature—the nearest thing to a sacramental
human activity acknowledged by secular society—it is because one
of the tasks art has assumed is making forays into and taking up
positions on the frontiers of consciousness (often very dangerous to
the artist as a person) and reporting back what's there. Being a freelance explorer of spiritual dangers, the artist gains a certain license
to behave differently from other people; matching the singularity of
his vocation, he may be decked out with a suitably eccentric life style,
or he may not. His job is inventing trophies of his experiences—objects and gestures that fascinate and enthrall, not merely (as prescribed by older notions of the artist) edify or entertain. His principal
means of fascinating is to advance one step further in the dialectic of
outrage. He seeks to make his work repulsive, obscure, inaccessible;
in short, to give what is, or seems to be, *not* wanted. But however
fierce may be the outrages the artist perpetrates upon his audience,
his credentials and spiritual authority ultimately depend on the audience's sense (whether something known or inferred) of the out-

rages he commits upon himself. The exemplary modern artist is a broker in madness.

The notion of art as the dearly purchased outcome of an immense spiritual risk, one whose cost goes up with the entry and participation of each new player in the game, invites a revised set of critical standards. Art produced under the aegis of this conception certainly is not, cannot be, "realistic." But words like "fantasy" or "surrealism," that only invert the guidelines of realism, clarify little. Fantasy too easily declines into "mere" fantasy; the clincher is the adjective "infantile." Where does fantasy, condemned by psychiatric rather than artistic standards, end and imagination begin?

Since it is hardly likely that contemporary critics seriously mean to bar prose narratives that are unrealistic from the domain of literature, one suspects that a special standard is being applied to sexual themes. This becomes clearer if one thinks of another kind of book, another kind of "fantasy." The ahistorical dream-like landscape where action is situated, the peculiarly congealed time in which acts are performed—these occur almost as often in science fiction as they do in pornography. There is nothing conclusive in the well-known fact that most men and women fall short of the sexual prowess that people in pornography are represented as enjoying; that the size of organs, number and duration of orgasms, variety and feasibility of sexual powers, and amount of sexual energy all seem grossly exaggerated. Yes, and the spaceships and the teeming planets depicted in science-fiction novels don't exist either. The fact that the site of narrative is an ideal *topos* disqualifies neither pornography nor science fiction from being literature. Such negations of real, concrete, three-dimensional social time, space, and personality—and such "fantastic" enlargements of human energy—are rather the ingredients of another kind of literature, founded on another mode of consciousness.

The materials of the pornographic books that count as literature are, precisely, one of the extreme forms of human consciousness. Undoubtedly, many people would agree that the sexually obsessed consciousness can, in principle, enter into literature as an art form. Literature about lust? Why not? But then they usually add a rider to the agreement which effectually nullifies it. They require that the author have the proper "distance" from his obsessions for their rendering to count as literature. Such a standard is sheer hypocrisy, revealing once again that the values commonly applied to pornography are, in the end, those belonging to psychiatry and social affairs rather than to art. (Since Christianity upped the ante and concentrated on sexual behavior as the root of virtue, everything pertaining to sex has been a "special case" in our culture, evoking peculiarly inconsistent attitudes.) Van Gogh's paintings retain their status as art even if it seems his manner of painting owed less to a conscious choice of representational means than to his being deranged and actually seeing reality the way he painted it. Similarly, *Histoire de l'Oeil* does not become case history rather than art because, as Bataille reveals in the extraordinary autobiographical essay appended to the narrative, the book's obsessions are indeed his own.

What makes a work of pornography part of the history of art rather than of trash is not distance, the superimposition of a consciousness more conformable to that of ordinary reality upon the "deranged consciousness" of the erotically obsessed. Rather, it is the originality, thoroughness, authenticity, and power of that deranged consciousness itself, as incarnated in a work. From the point of view of art, the exclusivity of the consciousness embodied in pornographic books is in itself neither anomalous nor anti-literary.

Nor is the purported aim or effect, whether it is intentional or not, of such books—to excite the reader sexually—a defect. Only a degraded and mechanistic idea of sex could mislead someone into thinking that being sexually stirred by a book like *Madame Edwarda* is a simple matter. The singleness of intention often condemned by critics is, when the work merits treatment as art, compounded of many resonances. The physical sensations involuntarily produced in someone reading the book carry with them something that touches upon the reader's whole experience of his humanity—and his limits as a personality and as a body. Actually, the singleness of pornography's intention is spurious. But the aggressiveness of the intention is not. What seems like an end is as much a means, startlingly and oppressively concrete. The end, however, is less concrete. Pornography is one of the branches of literature—science fiction is another—aiming at disorientation, at psychic dislocation.

In some respects, the use of sexual obsessions as a subject for literature resembles the use of a literary subject whose validity far fewer people would contest: religious obsessions. So compared, the familiar fact of pornography's definite, aggressive impact upon its readers looks somewhat different. Its celebrated intention of sexually stimulating readers is really a species of proselytizing. Pornography that is serious literature aims to "excite" in the same way that books which render an extreme form of religious experience aim to "convert."

III

Two French books recently translated into English, *Story of O* and *The Image,* conveniently illustrate some issues involved in this topic, barely explored in Anglo-American criticism, of pornography as literature.

Story of O by Pauline Réage appeared in 1954 and immediately became famous, partly due to the patronage of Jean Paulhan, who wrote the preface. It was widely believed that Paulhan himself had written the book—perhaps because of the precedent set by Bataille, who had contributed an essay (signed with his own name) to his *Madame Edwarda* when it was first published in 1937 under the pseudonym Pierre Angelique, and also because the name Pauline suggested Paulhan. But Paulhan has always denied that he wrote *Story of O,* insisting that it was indeed written by a woman, someone previously unpublished and living in another part of France, who insisted on remaining unknown. While Paulhan's story did not halt speculation, the conviction that he was the author eventually faded. Over the years, a number of more ingenious hypotheses, attributing the book's authorship to other notables on the Paris literary scene, gained credence and then were dropped. The real identity of Pauline Réage remains one of the few well-kept secrets in contemporary letters.

The Image was published two years later, in 1956, also under a pseudonym, Jean de Berg. To compound the mystery, it was dedicated to and had a preface by Pauline Réage, who has not been heard from since. (The preface by Réage is terse and forgettable; the one by Paulhan is long and very interesting.) But gossip in Paris literary circles about the identity of Jean de Berg is more conclusive than the detective work on Pauline Réage. One rumor only, which names the wife of an influential younger novelist, has swept the field.

It is not hard to understand why those curious enough to speculate about the two pseudonyms should incline toward some name from the established community of letters in France. For either of these books to be an amateur's one-shot seems scarcely conceivable. Different as they are from each other, *Story of O* and *The Image* both evince a quality that can't be ascribed simply to an abundance of the usual writerly endowments of sensibility, energy, and intelligence. Such gifts, very much in evidence, have themselves been processed through a dialogue of artifices. The somber self-consciousness of the narratives could hardly be further from the lack of control and craft usually considered the expression of obsessive lust. Intoxicating as is their subject (if the reader doesn't cut off and find it just funny or sinister), both narratives are more concerned with the use of erotic material than with the expression of it. And this use is preeminently—there is no other word for it—literary. The imagination pursuing its outrageous pleasures in *Story of O* and *The Image* remains firmly anchored to certain notions of the *formal* consummation of intense feeling, of procedures for exhausting an experience, that connect as much with literature and recent literary history as with the ahistorical domain of eros. And why not? Experiences aren't pornographic; only images and representations—structures of the imagination—are. That is why a pornographic book often can make the reader think of, mainly, other pornographic books, rather than sex unmediated—and this not necessarily to the detriment of his erotic excitement.

For instance, what resonates throughout *Story of O* is a voluminous body of pornographic or "libertine" literature, mostly trash, in both French and English, going back to the eighteenth century. The most obvious reference is to Sade. But here one must not think only of the writings of Sade himself, but of the reinterpretation of Sade by French literary intellectuals after World War II, a critical gesture perhaps comparable in its importance and influence upon educated literary taste and upon the actual direction of serious fiction in France to the reappraisal of James launched just before World War II in the United States, except that the French reappraisal has lasted longer and seems to have struck deeper roots. (Sade, of course, had never been forgotten. He was read enthusiastically by Flaubert, Baudelaire, and most of the other radical geniuses of French literature of the late nineteenth century. He was one of the patron saints of the Surrealist movement, and figures importantly in the thought of Breton. But it was the discussion of Sade after 1945 that really consolidated his position as an inexhaustible point of departure for radical thinking about the human condition. The well-known essay of Beauvoir, the indefatigable scholarly biography undertaken by Gilbert Lely, and writings of Blanchot, Paulhan, Bataille, Klossowski, and Leiris are the most eminent documents of the postwar reevaluation which secured this astonishingly hardy modification of French literary sensibility. The quality and theoretical density of the French interest in Sade remains virtually incomprehensible to English and American literary intellectuals, for whom Sade is perhaps an exemplary figure in the history of psychopathology, both individual and social, but inconceivable as someone to be taken seriously as a thinker.)

But what stands behind *Story of O* is not only Sade, both the problems he raised and the ones raised in his name. The book is also rooted in the conventions of the libertine potboilers written in nineteenth-century France, typically situated in a fantasy England populated by brutal aristocrats with enormous sexual equipment and violent tastes, along the axis of sadomasochism, to match. The name of O's second lover-proprietor, Sir Stephen, clearly pays homage to this period fantasy, as does the figure of Sir Edmond of *Histoire de l'Oeil*. And it should be stressed that the allusion to a stock type of pornographic trash stands, as a literary reference, on exactly the same footing as the anachronistic setting of the main action, which is lifted straight from Sade's sexual theater. The narrative opens in Paris (O joins her lover René in a car and is driven around) but most of the subsequent action is removed to more familiar if less plausible territory: that conveniently isolated château, luxuriously furnished and lavishly staffed with servants, where a clique of rich men congregate and to which women are brought as virtual slaves to be the objects, shared in common, of the men's brutal and inventive lust. There are whips and chains, masks worn by the men when the women are admitted to their presence, great fires burning in the hearth, unspeakable sexual indignities, floggings and more ingenious kinds of physical mutilation, several lesbian scenes when the excitement of the orgies in the great drawing room seems to flag. In short, the novel comes equipped with some of the creakiest items in the repertoire of pornography.

How seriously can we take this? A bare inventory of the plot might give the impression that *Story of O* is not so much pornography as meta-pornography, a brilliant parody. Something similar was urged in defense of *Candy* when it was published here several years ago, after some years of modest existence in Paris as a more or less official dirty book. *Candy* wasn't pornography, it was argued, but a spoof, a witty burlesque of the conventions of cheap pornographic narrative. My own view is that *Candy* may be funny, but it's still pornography. For pornography isn't a form that can parody itself. It is the nature of the pornographic imagination to prefer ready-made conventions of character, setting, and action. Pornography is a theater of types, never of individuals. A parody of pornography, so far as it has any real competence, always remains pornography. Indeed, parody is one common form of pornographic writing. Sade himself often used it, inverting the moralistic fictions of Richardson in which female virtue always triumphs over male lewdness (either by saying no or by dying afterwards). With *Story of O*, it would be more accurate to speak of a use rather than of a parody of Sade.

The tone alone of *Story of O* indicates that whatever in the book might be read as parody or antiquarianism—a mandarin pornography?—is only one of several elements forming the narrative. (Although sexual situations encompassing all the expectable variations of lust are graphically described, the prose style is rather formal, the level of language dignified and almost chaste.) Features of the Sadean staging are used to shape the action, but the narrative's basic line differs fundamentally from anything Sade wrote. For one thing, Sade's work has a built-in open-endedness or principle of insatiability. His *120 Days of Sodom,* probably the most ambitious pornographic book ever conceived (in terms of scale), a kind of summa of the pornographic imagination; stunningly impressive and upsetting, even in the truncated form, part narrative and part scenario, in which it has survived. (The manuscript was accidentally rescued from the Bastille after Sade had been forced to leave it behind when he was transferred in 1789 to Charenton, but Sade believed until his death that his masterpiece had been destroyed when the prison was razed.) Sade's express train of outrages tears along an interminable but level track. His descriptions are too schematic to be sensuous. The fictional actions are illustrations, rather, of his relentlessly repeated ideas. Yet these polemical ideas themselves seem, on reflection, more like principles of a dramaturgy than a substantive theory. Sade's ideas— of the person as a thing or an object, of the body as a machine and of the orgy as an inventory of the hopefully indefinite possibilities of several machines in collaboration with each other—seem mainly designed to make possible an endless, non-culminating kind of ultimately affectless activity. In contrast, *Story of O* has a definite movement; a logic of events, as opposed to Sade's static principle of the catalogue or encyclopedia. This plot movement is strongly abetted by the fact that, for most of the narrative, the author tolerates at least a vestige of "the couple" (O and René, O and Sir Stephen)—a unit generally repudiated in pornographic literature.

And, of course, the figure of O herself is different. Her feelings, however insistently they adhere to one theme, have some modulation and are carefully described. Although passive, O scarcely resembles those ninnies in Sade's tales who are detained in remote castles to be tormented by pitiless noblemen and satanic priests. And O is represented as active, too: literally active, as in the seduction of Jacqueline, and more important, profoundly active in her own passivity. O resembles her Sadean prototypes only superficially. There is no personal consciousness, except that of the author, in Sade's books. But O does possess a consciousness, from which vantage point her story is told. (Although written in the third person, the narrative never departs from O's point of view or understands more than she understands.) Sade aims to neutralize sexuality of all its personal associations, to represent a kind of impersonal—or pure—sexual encounter. But the narrative of Pauline Réage does show O reacting in quite different ways (including love) to different people, notably to René, to Sir Stephen, to Jacqueline, and to Anne-Marie.

Sade seems more representative of the major conventions of pornographic writing. So far as the pornographic imagination tends to make one person interchangeable with another and all people interchangeable with things, it's not functional to describe a person as O is described—in terms of a certain state of her will (which she's trying to discard) and of her understanding. Pornography is mainly populated by creatures like Sade's Justine, endowed with neither will nor intelligence nor even, apparently, memory. Justine lives in a perpetual state of astonishment, never learning anything from the strikingly repetitious violations of her innocence. After each fresh betrayal she gets in place for another round, as uninstructed by her experience as ever, ready to trust the next masterful libertine and have her trust rewarded by a renewed loss of liberty, the same indignities, and the same blasphemous sermons in praise of vice.

For the most part, the figures who play the role of sexual objects in pornography are made of the same stuff as one principal "humour" of comedy. Justine is like Candide, who is also a cipher, a blank, an eternal naïf incapable of learning anything from his atrocious ordeals. The familiar structure of comedy which features a character who is a still center in the midst of outrage (Buster Keaton is a classic image) crops up repeatedly in pornography. The personages in pornography, like those of comedy, are seen only from the outside, behavioristically. By definition, they can't be seen in depth, so as truly to engage the audience's feelings. In much of comedy, the joke resides precisely in the *disparity* between the understated or anesthetized feeling and a large outrageous event. Pornography works in a similar fashion. The gain produced by a deadpan tone, by what seems to the reader in an ordinary state of mind to be the incredible *under*reacting of the erotic agents to the situations in which they're placed, is not the release of laughter. It's the release of a sexual reaction, originally voyeuristic but probably needing to be secured by an underlying direct identification with one of the participants in the sex act. The emotional flatness of pornography is thus neither a failure of artistry nor an index of principled inhumanity. The arousal of a sexual response in the reader *requires* it. Only in the absence of directly stated emotions can the reader of pornography find room for his own responses. When the event narrated comes already festooned with the author's explicitly avowed sentiments, by which the reader may be stirred, it then becomes harder to be stirred by the event itself.*

*This is clear in the case of Genet's books, which, despite the explicitness of the sexual experiences related, are not sexually arousing for most readers. What the reader knows (and Genet has stated it many times) is that Genet himself was sexually excited

Silent film comedy offers many illustrations of how the formal principle of continual agitation or perpetual motion (slapstick) and that of the deadpan really converge to the same end—a deadening or neutralization or distancing of the audience's emotions, its ability to identify in a "humane" way and to make moral judgments about situations of violence. The same principle is at work in all pornography. It's not that the characters in pornography cannot conceivably possess any emotions. They can. But the principles of underreacting and frenetic agitation make the emotional climate self-canceling, so that the basic tone of pornography is affectless, emotionless.

However, degrees of this affectlessness can be distinguished. Justine is the stereotype sex-object figure (invariably female, since most pornography is written by men or from the stereotyped male point of view): a bewildered victim, whose consciousness remains unaltered by her experiences. But O is an adept; whatever the cost in pain and fear, she is grateful for the opportunity to be initiated into a mystery. That mystery is the loss of the self. O learns, she suffers, she changes. Step by step she becomes more what she is, a process identical with the emptying out of herself. In the vision of the world presented by *Story of O,* the highest good is the transcendence of personality. The plot's movement is not horizontal, but a kind of ascent through degradation. O does not simply become identical with her sexual availability, but wants to reach the perfection of becoming an object. Her condition, if it can be characterized as one of dehumanization, is not to be understood as a by-product of her enslavement to René, Sir Stephen, and the other men at Roissy, but as the point of her situation, something she seeks and eventually attains. The terminal image for her achievement comes in the last scene of the book: O is led to a party, mutilated, in chains, unrecognizable, costumed (as an owl)— so convincingly no longer human that none of the guests thinks of speaking to her directly.

O's quest is neatly summed up in the expressive letter which serves her for a name. "O" suggests a cartoon of her sex, not her individual sex but simply woman; it also stands for a nothing. But what *Story of O* unfolds is a spiritual paradox, that of the full void and of the vacuity that is also a plenum. The power of the book lies exactly in the anguish stirred up by the continuing presence of this paradox.

while writing *The Miracle of the Rose, Our Lady of the Flowers,* etc. The reader makes an intense and unsettling contact with Genet's erotic excitement, which is the energy that propels these metaphor-studded narratives; but, at the same time, the author's excitement precludes the reader's own. Genet was correct when he said that his books were not pornographic.

Pauline Réage raises, in a far more organic and sophisticated manner than Sade does with his clumsy expositions and discourses, the question of the status of human personality itself. But whereas Sade is interested in the obliteration of personality from the viewpoint of power and liberty, the author of *Story of O* is interested in the obliteration of personality from the viewpoint of happiness. (The closest statement of this theme in English literature: certain passages in Lawrence's *The Lost Girl*.)

For the paradox to gain real significance, however, the reader must entertain a view of sex different from that held by most enlightened members of the community. The prevailing view—an amalgam of Rousseauist, Freudian, and liberal social thought—regards the phenomenon of sex as a perfectly intelligible, although uniquely precious, source of emotional and physical pleasure. What difficulties arise come from the long deformation of the sexual impulses administered by Western Christianity, whose ugly wounds virtually everyone in this culture bears. First, guilt and anxiety. Then the reduction of sexual capacities—leading if not to virtual impotence or frigidity, at least to the depletion of erotic energy and the repression of many natural elements of sexual appetite (the "perversions"). Then the spillover into public dishonesties in which people tend to respond to news of the sexual pleasures of others with envy, fascination, revulsion, and spiteful indignation. It's from this pollution of the sexual health of the culture that a phenomenon like pornography is derived.

I don't quarrel with the historical diagnosis contained in this account of the deformations of Western sexuality. Nevertheless, what seems to me decisive in the complex of views held by most educated members of the community is a more questionable assumption—that human sexual appetite is, if untampered with, a natural pleasant function; and that "the obscene" is a convention, the fiction imposed upon nature by a society convinced there is something vile about the sexual functions and, by extension, about sexual pleasure. It's just these assumptions that are challenged by the French tradition represented by Sade, Lautréamont, Bataille, and the authors of *Story of O* and *The Image*. Their work suggests that the obscene is a primal notion of human consciousness, something much more profound than the backwash of a sick society's aversion to the body. Human sexuality is, quite apart from Christian repressions, a highly questionable phenomenon, and belongs, at least potentially, among the extreme rather than the ordinary experiences of humanity. Tamed as it may be, sexuality remains one of the demonic forces in human consciousness—pushing us at intervals close to taboo and dangerous desires, which range from the impulse to commit sudden arbitrary violence upon another person to the voluptuous yearning for the extinction of one's consciousness, for death itself. Even on the level of simple physical sensation and mood, making love surely resembles having an epileptic fit at least as much as, if not more than, it does eating a meal or conversing with someone. Everyone has felt (at least in fantasy) the erotic glamour of physical cruelty and an erotic lure in things that are vile and repulsive. These phenomena form part of the genuine spectrum of sexuality, and if they are not to be written off as mere neurotic aberrations, the picture looks different from the one promoted by enlightened public opinion, and less simple.

One could plausibly argue that it is for quite sound reasons that the whole capacity for sexual ecstasy is inaccessible to most people— given that sexuality is something, like nuclear energy, which may prove amenable to domestication through scruple, but then again may not. That few people regularly, or perhaps ever, experience their sexual capacities at this unsettling pitch doesn't mean that the extreme is not authentic, or that the possibility of it doesn't haunt them anyway. (Religion is probably, after sex, the second oldest resource which human beings have available to them for blowing their minds. Yet, among the multitudes of the pious, the number who have ventured very far into that state of consciousness must be fairly small, too.) There is, demonstrably, something incorrectly designed and potentially disorienting in the human sexual capacity—at least in the capacities of man-in-civilization. Man, the sick animal, bears within him an appetite which can drive him mad. Such is the understanding of sexuality—as something beyond good and evil, beyond love, beyond sanity; as a resource for ordeal and for breaking through the limits of consciousness—that informs the French literary canon I've been discussing.

Story of O, with its project for completely transcending personality, entirely presumes this dark and complex vision of sexuality so far removed from the hopeful view sponsored by American Freudianism and liberal culture. The woman who is given no other name than O progresses simultaneously toward her own extinction as a human being and her fulfillment as a sexual being. It is hard to imagine how anyone would ascertain whether there exists truly, empirically, anything in "nature" or human consciousness that supports such a split. But it seems understandable that the possibility has always haunted man, as accustomed as he is to decrying such a split.

O's project enacts, on another scale, that performed by the existence of pornographic literature itself. What pornographic literature does is precisely to drive a wedge between one's existence as a full human being and one's existence as a sexual being—while in ordinary life a healthy person is one who prevents such a gap from opening up. Normally we don't experience, at least don't want to experience, our sexual fulfillment as distinct from or opposed to our personal fulfillment. But perhaps in part they are distinct, whether we like it or not. Insofar as strong sexual feeling does involve an obsessive degree of attention, it encompasses experiences in which a person can feel he is losing his "self." The literature that goes from Sade through Surrealism to these recent books capitalizes on that mystery; it isolates the mystery and makes the reader aware of it, invites him to participate in it.

This literature is both an invocation of the erotic in its darkest sense and, in certain cases, an exorcism. The devout, solemn mood of *Story of O* is fairly unrelieved; a work of mixed moods on the same theme, a journey toward the estrangement of the self from the self, is Buñuel's film *L'Age d'Or*. As a literary form, pornography works with two patterns—one equivalent to tragedy (as in *Story of O*) in which the erotic subject-victim heads inexorably toward death, and the other equivalent to comedy (as the *The Image*) in which the obsessional pursuit of sexual exercise is rewarded by a terminal gratification, union with the uniquely desired sexual partner.

IV

The writer who renders a darker sense of the erotic, its perils of fascination and humiliation, than anyone else is Bataille. His *Histoire de l'Oeil* (first published in 1928) and *Madame Edwarda** qualify as pornographic texts insofar as their theme is an all-engrossing sexual quest that annihilates every consideration of persons extraneous to their roles in the sexual dramaturgy, and the fulfillment of this quest is depicted graphically. But this description conveys nothing of the extraordinary quality of these books. For sheer explicitness about sex organs and acts is not necessarily obscene; it only becomes so when delivered in a particular tone, when it has acquired a certain moral resonance. As it happens, the sparse number of sex acts and quasi-sexual defilements related in Bataille's novellas can hardly compete with the interminable mechanistic inventiveness of the *120 Days of*

---

*Unfortunately, the sole translation available in English of what purports to be *Madame Edwarda,* that included in *The Olympia Reader,* pp. 662–72, published by Grove Press in 1965, gives just half the work. Only the *récit* is translated. But *Madame Edwarda* isn't a *récit* padded out with a preface also by Bataille. It is a two-part invention—essay and *récit*—and one part is almost unintelligible without the other.

Sodom. Yet because Bataille possessed a finer and more profound sense of transgression, what he describes seems somehow more potent and outrageous than the most lurid orgies staged by Sade.

One reason that *Histoire de l'Oeil* and *Madame Edwarda* make such a strong and upsetting impression is that Bataille understood more clearly than any other writer I know of that what pornography is really about, ultimately, isn't sex but death. I am not suggesting that every pornographic work speaks, either overtly or covertly, of death. Only works dealing with that specific and sharpest inflection of the themes of lust, "the obscene," do. It's toward the gratifications of death, succeeding and surpassing those of eros, that every truly obscene quest tends. (An example of a pornographic work whose subject is not the "obscene" is Louÿs's jolly saga of sexual insatiability, *Trois Filles de leur Mère*. *The Image* presents a less clear-cut case. While the enigmatic transactions between the three characters are charged with a sense of the obscene—more like a premonition, since the obscene is reduced to being only a constituent of voyeurism—the book has an unequivocally happy ending, with the narrator finally united with Claire. But *Story of O* takes the same line as Bataille, despite a little intellectual play at the end: the book closes ambiguously, with several lines to the effect that two versions of a final suppressed chapter exist, in one of which O received Sir Stephen's permission to die when he was about to discard her. Although this double ending satisfyingly echoes the book's opening, in which two versions "of the same beginning" are given, it can't, I think, lessen the reader's sense that O is death-bound, whatever doubts the author expresses about her fate.)

Bataille composed most of his books, the chamber music of pornographic literature, in *récit* form (sometimes accompanied by an essay). Their unifying theme is Bataille's own consciousness, a consciousness in an acute, unrelenting state of agony; but as an equally extraordinary mind in an earlier age might have written a theology of agony, Bataille has written an erotics of agony. Willing to tell something of the autobiographical sources of his narratives, he appended to *Histoire de l'Oeil* some vivid imagery from his own outrageously terrible childhood. (One memory: his blind, syphilitic, insane father trying unsuccessfully to urinate.) Time has neutralized these memories, he explains; after many years, they have largely lost their power over him and "can only come to life again, deformed, hardly recognizable, having in the course of this deformation taken on an obscene meaning." Obscenity, for Bataille, simultaneously revives his most painful experiences and scores a victory over that pain. The obscene, that is to say, the extremity of erotic experience, is the root of vital energies. Human beings, he says in the essay part of *Madame Edwarda,* live only through excess. And pleasure depends on "perspective," or giving oneself to a state of "open being," open to death as well as to joy. Most people try to outwit their own feelings; they want to be receptive to pleasure but keep "horror" at a distance. That's foolish, according to Bataille, since horror reinforces "attraction" and excites desire.

What Bataille exposes in extreme erotic experience is its subterranean connection with death. Bataille conveys this insight not by devising sex acts whose consequences are lethal, thereby littering his narratives with corpses. (In the terrifying *Histoire de l'Oeil,* for instance, only one person dies; and the book ends with the three sexual adventurers, having debauched their way through France and Spain, acquiring a yacht in Gibraltar to pursue their infamies elsewhere.) His more effective method is to invest each action with a weight, a disturbing gravity, that feels authentically "mortal."

Yet, despite the obvious differences of scale and finesse of execution, the conceptions of Sade and Bataille have some resemblances. Like Bataille, Sade was not so much a sensualist as someone with an intellectual project: to explore the scope of transgression. And he shares with Bataille the same ultimate identification of sex and death. But Sade could never have agreed with Bataille that "the truth of eroticism is tragic." People often die in Sade's books. But these deaths always seem unreal. They're no more convincing than those mutilations inflicted during the evening's orgies from which the victims recover completely the next morning following the use of a wondrous salve. From the perspective of Bataille, a reader can't help being caught up short by Sade's bad faith about death. (Of course, many pornographic books that are much less interesting and accomplished than those of Sade share this bad faith.)

Indeed, one might speculate that the fatiguing repetitiveness of Sade's books is the consequence of his imaginative failure to confront the inevitable goal or haven of a truly systematic venture of the pornographic imagination. Death is the only end to the odyssey of the pornographic imagination when it becomes systematic; that is, when it becomes focused on the pleasures of transgression rather than mere pleasure itself. Since he could not or would not arrive at his ending, Sade stalled. He multiplied and thickened his narrative; tediously reduplicated orgiastic permutations and combinations. And his fictional alter egos regularly interrupted a bout of rape or buggery to deliver to their victims his latest reworkings of lengthy sermons on what real

"Enlightenment" means—the nasty truth about God, society, nature, individuality, virtue. Bataille manages to eschew anything resembling the counter-idealisms which are Sade's blasphemies (and which thereby perpetuate the banished idealism lying behind those fantasies); his blasphemies are autonomous.

Sade's books, the Wagnerian music dramas of pornographic literature, are neither subtle nor compact. Bataille achieves his effects with far more economical means: a chamber ensemble of non-interchangeable personages, instead of Sade's operatic multiplication of sexual virtuosi and career victims. Bataille renders his radical negatives through extreme compression. The gain, apparent on every page, enables his lean work and gnomic thought to go further than Sade's. Even in pornography, less can be more.

Bataille also has offered distinctly original and effective solutions to one perennial problem of pornographic narration: the ending. The most common procedure has been to end in a way that lays no claim to any internal necessity. Hence, Adorno could judge it the mark of pornography that it has neither beginning nor middle nor end. But Adorno is being unperceptive. Pornographic narratives do end—admittedly with abruptness and, by conventional novel standards, without motivation. This is not necessarily objectionable. (The discovery, midway in a science-fiction novel, of an alien planet may be no less abrupt or unmotivated.) Abruptness, an endemic facticity of encounters and chronically renewing encounters, is not some unfortunate defect of the pornographic narration which one might wish removed in order for the books to qualify as literature. These features are constitutive of the very imagination or vision of the world which goes into pornography. They supply, in many cases, exactly the ending that's needed.

But this doesn't preclude other types of endings. One notable feature of *Histoire de l'Oeil* and, to a lesser extent, *The Image*, considered as works of art, is their evident interest in more systematic or rigorous kinds of ending which still remain within the terms of the pornographic imagination—not seduced by the solutions of a more realistic or less abstract fiction. Their solution, considered very generally, is to construct a narrative that is, from the beginning, more rigorously controlled, less spontaneous and lavishly descriptive.

In *The Image* the narrative is dominated by a single metaphor, "the image" (though the reader can't understand the full meaning of the title until the end of the novel). At first, the metaphor appears to have a clear single application. "Image" seems to mean "flat" object or "two-dimensional surface" or "passive reflection"—all referring to the girl Anne whom Claire instructs the narrator to use freely for his own sexual purposes, making the girl into "a perfect slave." But the book is broken exactly in the middle (Section V in a short book of ten sections) by an enigmatic scene that introduces another sense of "image." Claire, alone with the narrator, shows him a set of strange photographs of Anne in obscene situations; and these are described in such a way as to insinuate a mystery in what has been a brutally straightforward, if seemingly unmotivated, situation. From this caesura to the end of the book, the reader will have simultaneously to carry the awareness of the fictionally actual "obscene" situation being described and to keep attuned to hints of an oblique mirroring or duplication of that situation. That burden (the two perspectives) will be relieved only in the final pages of the book, when, as the title of the last section has it, "Everything Resolves Itself." The narrator discovers that Anne is not the erotic plaything of Claire donated gratuitously to him, but Claire's "image" or "projection," sent out ahead to teach the narrator how to love *her*.

The structure of *Histoire de l'Oeil* is equally rigorous, and more ambitious in scope. Both novels are in the first person; in both, the narrator is male, and one of a trio whose sexual interconnections constitute the story of the book. But the two narratives are organized on very different principles. Jean de Berg describes how something came to be known that was not known by the narrator; all the pieces of action are clues, bits of evidence; and the ending is a surprise. Bataille is describing an action that is really intrapsychic: three people sharing (without conflict) a single fantasy, the acting out of a collective perverse will. The emphasis in *The Image* is on behavior, which is opaque, unintelligible. The emphasis in *Histoire de l'Oeil* is on fantasy first, and then on its correlation with some spontaneously "invented" act. The development of the narrative follows the phases of acting out. Bataille is charting the stages of the gratification of an erotic obsession which haunts a number of commonplace objects. His principle of organization is thus a spatial one: a series of things, arranged in a definite sequence, are tracked down and exploited, in some convulsive erotic act. The obscene playing with or defiling of these objects, and of people in their vicinity, constitutes the action of the novella. When the last object (the eye) is used up in a transgression more daring than any preceding, the narrative ends. There can be no revelation or surprises in the story, no new "knowledge," only further intensifications of what is already known. These seemingly unrelated elements really are related; indeed, all versions of the same thing. The egg in the first chapter is simply the earliest version of the eyeball plucked from the Spaniard in the last.

Each specific erotic fantasy is also a generic fantasy—of performing what is "forbidden"—which generates a surplus atmosphere of excruciating restless sexual intensity. At times the reader seems to be witness to a heartless debauched fulfillment; at other times, simply in attendance at the remorseless progress of the negative. Bataille's works, better than any others I know of, indicate the aesthetic possibilities of pornography as an art form: *Histoire de l'Oeil* being the most accomplished artistically of all the pornographic prose fictions I've read, and *Madame Edwarda* the most original and powerful intellectually.

To speak of the aesthetic possibilities of pornography as an art form and as a form of thinking may seem insensitive or grandiose when one considers what acutely miserable lives people with a full-time specialized sexual obsession usually lead. Still, I would argue that pornography yields more than the truths of individual nightmare. Convulsive and repetitious as this form of the imagination may be, it does generate a vision of the world that can claim the interest (speculative, aesthetic) of those who are not erotomanes. Indeed, this interest resides in precisely what are customarily dismissed as the *limits* of pornographic thinking.

V

The prominent characteristics of all products of the pornographic imagination are their energy and their absolutism.

The books generally called pornographic are those whose primary, exclusive, and overriding preoccupation is with the depiction of sexual "intentions" and "activities." One could also say sexual "feelings," except that the word seems redundant. The feelings of the personages deployed by the pornographic imagination are, at any given moment, either identical with their "behavior" or else a preparatory phase, that of "intention," on the verge of breaking into "behavior" unless physically thwarted. Pornography uses a small crude vocabulary of feeling, all relating to the prospects of action: feeling one would like to act (lust); feeling one would not like to act (shame, fear, aversion). There are no gratuitous or non-functioning feelings; no musings, whether speculative or imagistic, which are irrelevant to the business at hand. Thus, the pornographic imagination inhabits a universe that is, however repetitive the incidents occurring within it, incomparably economical. The strictest possible criterion of relevance applies: everything must bear upon the erotic situation.

The universe proposed by the pornographic imagination is a total universe. It has the power to ingest and metamorphose and translate all concerns that are fed into it, reducing everything into the one negotiable currency of the erotic imperative. All action is conceived of as a set of sexual *exchanges*. Thus, the reason why pornography refuses to make fixed distinctions between the sexes or allow any kind of sexual preference or sexual taboo to endure can be explained "structurally." The bisexuality, the disregard for the incest taboo, and other similar features common to pornographic narratives function to multiply the possibilities of exchange. Ideally, it should be possible for everyone to have a sexual connection with everyone else.

Of course the pornographic imagination is hardly the only form of consciousness that proposes a total universe. Another is the type of imagination that has generated modern symbolic logic. In the total universe proposed by the logician's imagination, all statements can be broken down or chewed up to make it possible to rerender them in the form of the logical language; those parts of ordinary language that don't fit are simply lopped off. Certain of the well-known states of the religious imagination, to take another example, operate in the same cannibalistic way, engorging all materials made available to them for retranslation into phenomena saturated with the religious polarities (sacred and profane, etc.).

The latter example, for obvious reasons, touches closely on the present subject. Religious metaphors abound in a good deal of modern erotic literature—notably in Genet—and in some works of pornographic literature, too. *Story of O* makes heavy use of religious metaphors for the ordeal that O undergoes. O "wanted to believe." Her drastic condition of total personal servitude to those who use her sexually is repeatedly described as a mode of salvation. With anguish and anxiety, she surrenders herself; and "henceforth there were no more hiatuses, no dead time, no remission." While she has, to be sure, entirely lost her freedom, O has gained the right to participate in what is described as virtually a sacramental rite.

> The word "open" and the expression "opening her legs" were, on her lover's lips, charged with such uneasiness and power that she could never hear them without experiencing a kind of internal prostration, a sacred submission, as though a god, and not he, had spoken to her.

Though she fears the whip and other cruel mistreatments before they are inflicted on her, "yet when it was over she was happy to have gone through it, happier still if it had been especially cruel and prolonged." The whipping, branding, and mutilating are described (from the point of view of *her* consciousness) as ritual ordeals which test the faith of someone being initiated into an ascetic spiritual discipline. The "perfect submissiveness" that her original lover and then Sir Stephen demand of her echoes the extinction of the self explicitly required of a Jesuit novice or Zen pupil. O is "that absentminded person who has yielded up her will in order to be totally remade," to be made fit to serve a will far more powerful and authoritative than her own.

As might be expected, the straightforwardness of the religious metaphors in *Story of O* has evoked some correspondingly straight readings of the book. The novelist Mandiargues, whose preface precedes Paulhan's in the American translation, doesn't hesitate to describe *Story of O* as "a mystic work," and therefore "not, strictly speaking, an erotic book." What *Story of O* depicts "is a complete spiritual transformation, what others would call an *ascesis*." But the matter is not so simple. Mandiargues is correct in dismissing a psychiatric analysis of O's state of mind that would reduce the book's subject to, say, "masochism." As Paulhan says, "the heroine's ardor" is totally inexplicable in terms of the conventional psychiatric vocabulary. The fact that the novel employs some of the conventional motifs and trappings of the theater of sadomasochism has itself to be explained. But Mandiargues has fallen into an error almost as reductive and only slightly less vulgar. Surely, the only alternative to the psychiatric reductions is not the religious vocabulary. But that only these two foreshortened alternatives exist testifies once again to the bone-deep denigration of the range and seriousness of sexual experience that still rules this culture, for all its much-advertised new permissiveness.

My own view is that Pauline Réage wrote an erotic book. The notion implicit in *Story of O* that eros is a sacrament is not the "truth" behind the literal (erotic) sense of the book—the lascivious rites of enslavement and degradation performed upon O—but, exactly, a metaphor for it. Why say something stronger, when the statement can't really *mean* anything stronger? But despite the virtual incomprehensibility to most educated people today of the substantive experience behind religious vocabulary, there is a continuing piety toward the grandeur of emotions that went into that vocabulary. The religious imagination survives for most people as not just the primary but virtually the only credible instance of an imagination working in a total way.

No wonder, then, that the new or radically revamped forms of the total imagination which have arisen in the past century—notably, those of the artist, the erotomane, the left revolutionary, and the madman—have chronically borrowed the prestige of the religious vocabulary. And total experiences, of which there are many kinds, tend again and again to be apprehended only as revivals or translations of the religious imagination. To try to make a fresh way of talking at the most serious, ardent, and enthusiastic level, heading off the religious encapsulation, is one of the primary intellectual tasks of future thought. As matters stand, with everything from *Story of O* to Mao reabsorbed into the incorrigible survival of the religious impulse, all thinking and feeling gets devalued. (Hegel made perhaps the grandest attempt to create a post-religious vocabulary, out of philosophy, that would command the treasures of passion and credibility and emotive appropriateness that were gathered into the religious vocabulary. But his most interesting followers steadily undermined the abstract meta-religious language in which he had bequeathed his thought, and concentrated instead on the specific social and practical applications of his revolutionary form of process-thinking, historicism. Hegel's failure lies like a gigantic disturbing hulk across the intellectual landscape. And no one has been big enough, pompous enough, or energetic enough since Hegel to attempt the task again.)

And so we remain, careening among our overvaried choices of kinds of total imagination, of species of total seriousness. Perhaps the deepest spiritual resonance of the career of pornography in its "modern" Western phase under consideration here (pornography in the Orient or the Moslem world being something very different) is this vast frustration of human passion and seriousness since the old religious imagination, with its secure monopoly on the total imagination, began in the late eighteenth century to crumble. The ludicrousness and lack of skill of most pornographic writing, films, and painting is obvious to everyone who has been exposed to them. What is less often remarked about the typical products of the pornographic imagination is their pathos. Most pornography—the books discussed here cannot be excepted—points to something more general than even sexual damage. I mean the traumatic failure of modern capitalist society to provide authentic outlets for the perennial human flair for high-temperature visionary obsessions, to satisfy the appetite for exalted self-transcending modes of concentration and seriousness. The need of human beings to transcend "the personal" is no less profound than the need to be a person, an individual. But this society serves that need poorly. It provides mainly demonic vocabularies in which to situate that need and from which to initiate action and construct rites of behavior. One is offered a choice among vocabularies of thought and action which are not merely self-transcending but self-destructive.

VI

But the pornographic imagination is not just to be understood as a form of psychic absolutism—some of whose products we might be able to regard (in the role of connoisseur, rather than client) with more sympathy or intellectual curiosity or aesthetic sophistication.

Several times before in this essay I have alluded to the possibility that the pornographic imagination says something worth listening to, albeit in a degraded and often unrecognizable form. I've urged that this spectacularly cramped form of the human imagination has, nevertheless, its peculiar access to some truth. This truth—about sensibility, about sex, about individual personality, about despair, about limits—can be shared when it projects itself into art. (Everyone, at least in dreams, has inhabited the world of the pornographic imagination for some hours or days or even longer periods of his life; but only the full-time residents make the fetishes, the trophies, the art.) That discourse one might call the poetry of transgression is also knowledge. He who transgresses not only breaks a rule. He goes somewhere that the others are not; and he knows something the others don't know.

Pornography, considered as an artistic or art-producing form of the human imagination, is an expression of what William James called "morbid-mindedness." But James was surely right when he gave as part of the definition of morbid-mindedness that it ranged over "a wider scale of experience" than healthy-mindedness.

What can be said, though, to the many sensible and sensitive people who find depressing the fact that a whole library of pornographic reading material has been made, within the last few years, so easily available in paperback form to the very young? Probably one thing: that their apprehension is justified, but may not be in scale. I am not addressing the usual complainers, those who feel that since sex after all *is* dirty, so are books reveling in sex (dirty in a way that a genocide screened nightly on TV, apparently, is not). There still remains a sizable minority of people who object to or are repelled by pornography not because they think it's dirty but because they know that pornography can be a crutch for the psychologically deformed and a brutalization of the morally innocent. I feel an aversion to pornography for those reasons, too, and am uncomfortable about the consequences of its increasing availability. But isn't the worry somewhat misplaced? What's really at stake? A concern about the uses of knowledge itself. There's a sense in which *all* knowledge is dangerous, the reason being that not everyone is in the same condition as knowers or potential knowers. Perhaps most people don't need "a wider scale of experience." It may be that, without subtle and extensive psychic preparation, any widening of experience and consciousness is destructive for most people. Then we must ask what justifies the reckless unlimited confidence we have in the present mass availability of other kinds of knowledge, in our optimistic acquiescence in the transformation of and extension of human capacities by machines. Pornography is only one item among the many dangerous commodities being circulated in this society and, unattractive as it may be, one of the less lethal, the less costly to the community in terms of human suffering. Except perhaps in a small circle of writer-intellectuals in France, pornography is an inglorious and mostly despised department of the imagination. Its mean status is the very antithesis of the considerable spiritual prestige enjoyed by many items which are far more noxious.

In the last analysis, the place we assign to pornography depends on the goals we set for our own consciousness, our own experience. But the goal A espouses for his consciousness may *not* be one he's pleased to see B adopt, because he judges that B isn't qualified or experienced or subtle enough. And B may be dismayed and even indignant at A's adopting goals that he himself professes; when A holds them, they become presumptuous or shallow. Probably this chronic mutual suspicion of our neighbor's capacities—suggesting, in effect, a hierarchy of competence with respect to human consciousness— will never be settled to everyone's satisfaction. As long as the quality of people's consciousness varies so greatly, how could it be?

In an essay on the subject some years ago, Paul Goodman wrote: "The question is not *whether* pornography, but the quality of the pornography." That's exactly right. One could extend the thought a good deal further. The question is not *whether* consciousness or *whether* knowledge, but the quality of the consciousness and of the knowledge. And that invites consideration of the quality or fineness of the human subject—the most problematic standard of all. It doesn't seem inaccurate to say most people in this society who aren't actively mad are, at best, reformed or potential lunatics. But is anyone supposed to act on this knowledge, even genuinely live with it? If so many are teetering on the verge of murder, dehumanization, sexual deformity and despair, and we were to act on that thought, then censorship much more radical than the indignant foes of pornography ever envisage seems in order. For if that's the case, not only pornography but all forms of serious art and knowledge—in other words, all forms of truth—are suspect and dangerous.

(*1967*)

Godard

It may be true that one has to choose between ethics and aesthetics, but it is no less true that, whichever one chooses, one will always find the other at the end of the road. For the very definition of the human condition should be in the mise en scène *itself.*

—GODARD

$\quad$The great culture heroes of our time have shared two qualities: they have all been ascetics in some exemplary way, and also great destroyers. But this common profile has permitted two different yet equally compelling attitudes toward "culture" itself. Some—like Duchamp, Wittgenstein, and Cage—bracket their art and thought with a disdainful attitude toward high culture and the past, or at least maintain an ironic posture of ignorance or incomprehension. Others—like Joyce, Picasso, Stravinsky, and Godard—exhibit a hypertrophy of appetite for culture (though often more avid for cultural debris than for museum-consecrated achievements); they proceed by voraciously scavenging in culture, proclaiming that nothing is alien to their art.

This essay was written when Godard had made fifteen feature films, the first being *A Bout de Souffle* (*Breathless*) in 1959. The succeeding films, in order, are: *Le Petit Soldat* (1960); *Une Femme est une Femme* (*A Woman Is a Woman*) (1961); *Vivre sa Vie* (*My Life to Live*) (1962); *Les Carabiniers* (1963); *Le Mépris* (*Contempt*) (1963); *Bande à Part* (*Band of Outsiders*) (1964); *Une Femme Mariée* (*A Married Woman*) (1964); *Alphaville* (1965); *Pierrot le Fou* (1965); *Masculin Féminin* (1966); *Made in U.S.A.* (1966); *Deux ou Trois Choses que je sais d'elle* (*Two or Three Things That I Know About Her*) (1966), *La Chinoise* (1967); and *Weekend* (1968). In addition, five shorts were made between 1954 and 1958, of which the most interesting are two from 1958: *Charlotte et son Jules* and *Une Histoire d'Eau*. The first of the seven sketches he had done up to this time was an episode in *Les Sept Pechés Capitaux* (1961); the most recent three were all made in 1967: *Anticipation,* in *Le Plus Vieux Métier du Monde;* a section of *Far from Vietnam,* the corporate film edited by Chris Marker; and an episode from the Italian-produced *Gospel 70.*

From cultural appetite on this scale comes the creation of work that is on the order of a subjective compendium: casually encyclopedic, anthologizing, formally and thematically eclectic, and marked by a rapid turnover of styles and forms. Thus, one of the most striking features of Godard's work is its daring efforts at hybridization, its insouciant mixtures of tonalities, themes, and narrative methods. Techniques from literature, theater, painting, and television mingle freely in his work, alongside witty, impertinent allusions to movie history itself. The elements often seem contradictory—as when (in the recent films) a collage method of narration drawn from advanced painting and poetry is combined with the bare, hard-staring, neo-realist aesthetic of television (cf. the interviews, filmed in frontal close-up and medium shot, in *A Married Woman, Masculine Feminine,* and *Deux ou Trois Choses*); or when Godard uses highly stylized visual compositions (such as the recurrent blues and reds in *A Woman Is a Woman, Contempt, Pierrot le Fou, La Chinoise,* and *Weekend*) at the same time that he seems eager to promote the look of improvisation and to conduct an unremitting search for the "natural" manifestations of personality before the truth-exacting eye of the camera. But, however jarring these mergers are in principle, the results Godard gets from them turn out to be something harmonious, plastically and ethically engaging, and emotionally tonic.

The consciously reflective—more precisely, reflexive—aspect of Godard's films is the key to their energies. His work constitutes a formidable meditation on the *possibilities* of cinema, which is to restate what I have already argued, that he enters the history of film as its first consciously destructive figure. Put otherwise, one might note that Godard is probably the first major director to enter the cinema on the level of commercial production with an explicitly critical intention. "I'm still as much of a critic as I ever was during the time of *Cahiers du Cinéma,*" he has declared. (Godard wrote regularly for that magazine between 1956 and 1959, and still occasionally contributes to it.) "The only difference is that instead of writing criticism, I now film it." Elsewhere, he describes *Le Petit Soldat* as an "auto-critique," and that word, too, applies to all of Godard's films.

But the extent to which Godard's films speak in the first person, and contain elaborate and often humorous reflections on the cinema as a means, is not a private whim but one elaboration of a well-established tendency of the arts to become more self-conscious, more self-referring. Like every important body of work in the canon of modern culture, Godard's films are simply what they are and also events that push their audience to reconsider the meaning and scope of the art form of which they are instances; they're not only works of art, but meta-artistic activities aimed at reorganizing the audience's entire sensibility. Far from deploring the tendency, I believe that the most promising future of films as an art lies in this direction. But the manner in which films continue into the end of the twentieth century as a serious art, becoming more self-regarding and critical, still permits a great deal of variation. Godard's method is far removed from the solemn, exquisitely conscious, self-annihilating structures of Bergman's great film *Persona*. Godard's procedures are much more lighthearted, playful, often witty, sometimes flippant, sometimes just silly. Like any gifted polemicist (which Bergman is not), Godard has the courage to simplify himself. This simplistic quality in much of Godard's work is as much a kind of generosity toward his audience as an aggression against them; and, partly, just the overflow of an inexhaustibly vivacious sensibility.

The attitude that Godard brings to the film medium is often called, disparagingly, "literary." What's usually meant by this charge, as when Satie was accused of composing literary music or Magritte of making literary painting, is a preoccupation with ideas, with conceptualization, at the expense of the sensual integrity and emotional force of the work—more generally, the habit (a kind of bad taste, it's supposed) of violating the essential unity of a given art form by introducing alien elements into it. That Godard has boldly addressed the task of representing or embodying abstract ideas as no other filmmaker has done before him is undeniable. Several films even include guest intellectual appearances: a fictional character falls in with a real philosopher (the heroine of *My Life to Live* interrogates Brice Parain in a café about language and sincerity; in *La Chinoise*, the Maoist girl disputes with Francis Jeanson on a train about the ethics of terrorism); a critic and filmmaker delivers a speculative soliloquy (Roger Leenhardt on intelligence, ardent and compromising, in *A Married Woman*); a grand old man of film history has a chance to reinvent his own somewhat tarnished personal image (Fritz Lang as himself, a chorus figure meditating on German poetry, Homer, movie-making, and moral integrity, in *Contempt*). On their own, many of Godard's characters muse aphoristically to themselves or engage their friends on such topics as the difference between the Right and the Left, the nature of cinema, the mystery of language, and the spiritual void underlying the satisfactions of the consumer society. Moreover, Godard's films are not only idea-ridden, but many of his characters are ostentatiously literate. Indeed, from the numerous references to books, mentions of writers' names, and quotations and longer excerpts from literary texts scattered throughout his films, Godard gives the impression of being engaged in an unending agon with the very fact of literature—which he attempts to settle partially by incorporating literature and literary identities into his films. And, apart from his original use of it as a cinematic object, Godard is concerned with literature both as a model for film and as the revival and alternative to film. In interviews and in his own critical writings, the relation between cinema and literature is a recurrent theme. One of the differences Godard stresses is that literature exists "as art from the very start" but cinema doesn't. But he also notes a potent similarity between the two arts: that "we novelists and filmmakers are condemned to an analysis of the world, of the real; painters and musicians aren't."

By treating cinema as above all an exercise in intelligence, Godard rules out any neat distinction between "literary" and "visual" (or cinematic) intelligence. If film is, in Godard's laconic definition, the "analysis" of something "with images and sounds," there can be no impropriety in making literature a subject for cinematic analysis. Alien to movies as this kind of material may seem, at least in such profusion, Godard would no doubt argue that books and other vehicles of cultural consciousness are part of the world; therefore, they belong in films. Indeed, by putting on the same plane the fact that people read and think and go seriously to the movies and the fact that they cry and run and make love, Godard has disclosed a new vein of lyricism and pathos for cinema: in bookishness, in genuine cultural passion, in intellectual callowness, in the misery of someone strangling in his own thoughts. (An instance of Godard's original way with a more familiar subject, the poetry of loutish illiteracy, is the twelve-minute sequence in *Les Carabiniers* in which the soldiers unpack their picture-postcard trophies.) His point is that no material is inherently unassimilable. But what's required is that literature indeed undergo its transformation into material, just like anything else. All that can be given are literary extracts, shards of literature. In order to be absorbed by cinema, literature must be dismantled or broken into wayward units; then Godard can appropriate a portion of the intellectual "content" of any book (fiction or nonfiction), borrow from the public domain of culture any contrasting tone of voice (noble or vulgar), invoke in an instant any diagnosis of contemporary malaise that is thematically relevant to his narrative, no matter how inconsistent it may be with the psychological scope or mental competence of the characters as already established.

Thus, so far as Godard's films are "literary" in some sense, it seems clear that his alliance with literature is based on quite different interests from those which linked earlier experimental filmmakers to the advanced writing of their time. If Godard envies literature, it is not so much for the formal innovations carried out in the twentieth century as for the heavy burden of explicit ideation accommodated within prose literary forms. Whatever notions Godard may have gotten from reading Faulkner or Beckett or Mayakovsky for formal inventions in cinema, his introduction of a pronounced literary taste (his own?) into his films serves mainly as a means for assuming a more public voice or elaborating more general statements. While the main tradition of avant-garde filmmaking has been a "poetic" cinema (films, like those made by the Surrealists in the 1920s and 1930s, inspired by the emancipation of modern poetry from storylike narrative and sequential discourse to the direct presentation and sensuous, polyvalent association of ideas and images), Godard has elaborated a largely anti-poetic cinema, one of whose chief literary models is the prose essay. Godard has even said: "I consider myself an essay writer. I write essays in the form of novels, or novels in the form of essays."

Notice that Godard has here made the novel interchangeable with film—apt in a way, since it is the tradition of the novel that weighs most heavily upon cinema, and the example of what the novel has recently become that spurs Godard. "I've found an idea for a novel," mumbles the hero of *Pierrot le Fou* at one point, in partial self-mockery assuming the quavering voice of Michel Simon. "Not to write the life of a man, but only life, life itself. What there is between people, space . . . sound and colors . . . There must be a way of achieving that; Joyce tried, but one must, must be able . . . to do better." Surely, Godard is here speaking for himself as a filmmaker, and he appears confident that film can accomplish what literature cannot, literature's incapacity being partly due to the less favorable *critical* situation into which each important literary work is deposited. I have spoken of Godard's work as consciously destructive of old cinematic conventions. But this task of demolition is executed with the élan of someone working in an art form experienced as young, on the threshold of its greatest development rather than at its end. Godard views the destruction of old rules as a constructive effort—in contrast to the received view of the current destiny of literature. As he has written, "literary critics often praise works like *Ulysses* or *Endgame* because they exhaust a certain genre, they close the doors on it. But in the cinema we are always praising works which *open* doors."

The relation to models offered by literature illuminates a major part of the history of cinema. Film, both protected and patronized by virtue of its dual status as mass entertainment and as art form, remains the last bastion of the values of the nineteenth-century novel and theater. Hence, the standard criticism leveled against Godard is that his plots are undramatic, arbitrary, often simply incoherent; and that his films generally are emotionally cold, static except for a busy surface of senseless movements, top-heavy with undramatized ideas, unnecessarily obscure. What his detractors don't grasp, of course, is that Godard doesn't want to do what they reproach him for not doing. Thus, audiences at first took the jump cuts in *Breathless* to be a sign of amateurishness, or a perverse flouting of self-evident rules of cinematic technique; actually, what looks as though the camera had stopped inadvertently for a few seconds in the course of a shot and then started up again was an effect Godard deliberately obtained in the cutting room, by snipping pieces out of perfectly smooth takes. (If one sees *Breathless* today, however, the once obtrusive cutting and the oddities of the hand-held camera are almost invisible, so widely imitated are these techniques now.) No less deliberate is Godard's disregard for the formal conventions of film narration based on the nineteenth-century novel—cause-and-effect sequences of events, climactic scenes, logical denouements. At the Cannes Film Festival several years ago, Godard entered into debate with Georges Franju, one of France's most talented and idiosyncratic senior filmmakers. "But surely, Monsieur Godard," the exasperated Franju is reported to have said, "you do at least acknowledge the necessity of having a beginning, middle, and end in your films." "Certainly," Godard replied. "But not necessarily in that order."

Godard's insouciance seems to me quite justified. For what is truly surprising is that film directors have not for some time, by exploiting the fact that whatever is "shown" (and heard) in the film experience is unremittingly *present,* made themselves more independent of what are essentially novelistic notions of narrative. But, as I have indicated, until now the only well-understood alternative has been to break completely with the formal structures of prose fiction, to dispense altogether with "story" and "characters." This alternative, practiced entirely outside the commercial cinema industries, resulted in the "abstract" film or the "poetic" film based on the association of images. In contrast, Godard's method is still a narrative one, though divorced from the literalism and reliance on psychological explanation that most people associate with the serious novel. Because they modify, rather than make a complete rupture with, the conventions of prose fiction underlying the main tradition of cinema, Godard's films strike many as more puzzling than the forthright "poetic" or "abstract" films of the official cinematic avant-garde.

Thus, it is precisely the presence, not the absence, of story in Godard's films that gives rise to the standard criticism of them. Unsatisfactory as his plots may be to many people, it would hardly be correct to describe Godard's films as plotless—like, say, Djiga Vertov's *The Man with the Camera,* the two silent films of Buñuel (*L'Age d'Or, Un Chien Andalou*), or Kenneth Anger's *Scorpio Rising,* films in which a story line has been completely discarded as the narrative framework. Like all ordinary feature films, Godard's films show an interrelated group of fictional characters located in a recognizable, consistent environment: in his case, usually contemporary and urban (Paris). But while the sequence of events in a Godard film suggests a fully articulated story, it doesn't add up to one; the audience is presented with a narrative line that is partly erased or effaced (the structural equivalent of the jump cut). Disregarding the traditional novelist's rule of explaining things as fully as they seem in need of explanation, Godard provides simplistic motives or frequently just leaves the motives unexplained; actions are often opaque, and fail to issue into consequences; occasionally the dialogue itself is not entirely audible. (There are other films, like Rossellini's *Journey to Italy* and Resnais's *Muriel,* that employ a comparably "unrealistic" system of narration in which the story is decomposed into disjunct objectified elements; but Godard, the only director with a whole body of work along these lines, has suggested more of the diverse routes for "abstracting" from an ostensibly realistic narrative than any other director. It is important, too, to distinguish various structures of abstracting—as, for instance, between the systematically "indeterminate" plot of Bergman's *Persona* and the "intermittent" plots of Godard's films.)

Although Godard's narrative procedures apparently owe less to cinematic models than to literary ones (at least, he never mentions the avant-garde past of cinema in interviews and statements but often mentions as models the work of Joyce, Proust, and Faulkner), he has never attempted, nor does it seem conceivable that he will attempt in the future, a transposition into film of any of the serious works of contemporary post-novelistic fiction. On the contrary, like many directors, Godard prefers mediocre, even sub-literary material, finding that easier to dominate and transform by the *mise en scène.* "I don't really like telling a story," Godard has written, somewhat simplifying the matter. "I prefer to use a kind of tapestry, a background on which I can embroider my own ideas. But I generally do need a story. A conventional one serves as well, perhaps even best." Thus, Godard has ruthlessly described the novel on which *Contempt* was based,

Moravia's *Ghost at Noon,* as "a nice novel for a train journey, full of old-fashioned sentiments. But it is with this kind of novel that one can make the best films." Although *Contempt* stays close to Moravia's story, Godard's films usually show few traces of their literary origins. (At the other extreme and more typical is *Masculine Feminine,* which bears no recognizable relation to the stories by Maupassant, "La Femme de Paul" and "La Signe," from which Godard drew his original inspiration.)

Whether text or pretext, most of the novels that Godard has chosen as his point of departure are heavily plotted action stories. He has a particular fondness for American kitsch: *Made in U.S.A.* was based on *The Jugger* by Richard Stark, *Pierrot le Fou* on *Obsession* by Lionel White, and *Band of Outsiders* on Dolores Hitchens's *Fool's Gold.* Godard resorts to popular American narrative conventions as a fertile, solid base for his own anti-narrative inclinations. "The Americans know how to tell stories very well; the French not at all. Flaubert and Proust don't know how to narrate; they do something else." Although that something else is plainly what Godard is after too, he has discerned the utility of starting from crude narrative. One allusion to this strategy is the memorable dedication of *Breathless:* "To Monogram Pictures." (In its original version, *Breathless* had no credit titles whatever, and the first image of the film was preceded only by this terse salute to Hollywood's most prolific purveyors of low-budget, quickie action pictures during the 1930s and early 1950s.) Godard wasn't being impudent or flippant here—or only a little bit. Melodrama is one of the integral resources of his plotting. Think of the comic-strip quest of *Alphaville;* the gangster-movies romanticism of *Breathless, Band of Outsiders,* and *Made in U.S.A.;* the spy-thriller ambiance of *Le Petit Soldat* and *Pierrot le Fou.* Melodrama—which is characterized by the exaggeration, the frontality, the opaqueness of "action"—provides a framework for both intensifying and transcending traditional realistic procedures of serious film narrative, but in a way which isn't necessarily condemned (as the Surrealist films were) to seeming esoteric. By adapting familiar, secondhand, vulgar materials—popular myths of action and sexual glamour—Godard gains a considerable freedom to "abstract" without losing the possibility of a commercial theater audience.

That such familiar materials do lend themselves to this kind of abstracting treatment—even contain the germ of it—had been amply demonstrated by one of the first great directors, Louis Feuillade, who worked in the debased form of the crime serial (*Fantômas, Les Vampires, Judex, Ti Minh*). Like the sub-literary model from which he drew, these serials (the greatest of which were done between 1913 and 1916) grant little to the standards of verisimilitude. Devoid of any concern for psychology, which was already beginning to make its appearance in films in the work of Griffith and De Mille, the story is populated by largely interchangeable characters and so crammed with incident that it can be followed only in a general way. But these are not the standards by which the films should be judged. What counts in Feuillade's serials is their formal and emotional values, which are produced by a subtle juxtaposition of the realistic and the highly improbable. The realism of the films lies in their look (Feuillade was one of the first European directors to do extensive location shooting); the implausibility comes from the wild nature of the actions inscribed on this physical space and the unnaturally speeded-up rhythms, formal symmetries, and repetitiveness of the action. In the Feuillade films, as in certain early Lang and early Hitchcock films, the director has carried the melodramatic narrative to absurd extremes, so that the action takes on a hallucinatory quality. Of course, this degree of abstraction of realistic material into the logic of fantasy requires a generous use of ellipses. If time patterns and space patterns and the abstract rhythms of action are to predominate, the action itself must be "obscure." In one sense, such films clearly have stories—of the most direct, action-packed kind. But in another sense, that of the continuity and consistency and ultimate intelligibility of incidents, the story has no importance at all. The loss of the sparse intertitles on some of the Feuillade films which have survived in only a single print seems hardly to matter, just as the formidable impenetrability of the plots of Hawks's *The Big Sleep* and Aldrich's *Kiss Me Deadly* doesn't matter either, indeed seems quite satisfying. Such film narratives attain their emotional and aesthetic weight precisely through this incomprehensibility, as the "obscurity" of certain poets isn't a deficiency in their work but an important technical means for accumulating and compounding relevant emotions and for establishing different levels and units of "sense." The obscurity of Godard's plots (*Made in U.S.A.* ventures furthest in this direction) is equally functional, part of the program of abstracting his materials.

Yet at the same time, these materials being what they are, Godard retains some of the vivacity of his simplistic literary and film models. Even as he employs the narrative conventions of the Série Noire novels and the Hollywood thrillers, transposing them into abstract elements, Godard has responded to their casual, sensuous energy and has introduced some of that into his own work. One result is that most of his films give the impression of speed, verging sometimes on haste. By comparison, Feuillade's temperament seems more dogged. On a few essentially limited themes (like ingenuity, ruthlessness, physical grace), Feuillade's films present a seemingly inexhaustible number of formal variations. His choice of the open-ended serial form is thus entirely appropriate. After the twenty episodes of *Les Vampires*, nearly seven hours of projection time, it's clear there was no necessary end to the exploits of the stupendous Musidora and her gang of masked bandits, any more than the exquisitely matched struggle between arch-criminal and arch-detective in *Judex* need ever terminate. The rhythm of incident Feuillade establishes is subject to indefinitely prolonged repetition and embellishment, like a sexual fantasy elaborated in secret over a long period of time. Godard's films move to a quite different rhythm; they lack the unity of fantasy, along with its obsessional gravity and its tireless, somewhat mechanistic repetitiveness.

The difference may be accounted for by the fact that the hallucinatory, absurd, abstracted action tale, while a central resource for Godard, doesn't control the form of his films as it did for Feuillade. Although melodrama remains one term of Godard's sensibility, what has increasingly emerged as the opposing term is the resources of fact. The impulsive, dissociated tone of melodrama contrasts with the gravity and controlled indignation of the sociological exposé (note the recurrent theme of prostitution that appears in what is virtually Godard's first film, the short *Une Femme Coquette*, which he made in 1955, and continues in *My Life to Live, A Married Woman, Deux ou Trois Choses,* and *Anticipation*) and the even cooler tones of straight documentary and quasi-sociology (in *Masculine Feminine, Deux ou Trois Choses, La Chinoise*).

Though Godard has toyed with the idea of the serial form, as in the end of *Band of Outsiders* (which promises a sequel, never made, relating further adventures of its hero and heroine in Latin America) and in the general conception of *Alphaville* (proposed as the latest adventure of a French serial hero, Lemmy Caution), Godard's films don't relate unequivocally to any single genre. The open-endedness of Godard's films doesn't mean the hyper-exploitation of some particular genre, as in Feuillade, but the successive devouring of genres. The counter-theme to the restless activity of the characters in Godard's films is an expressed dissatisfaction with the limits or stereotyping of "actions." Thus, in *Pierrot le Fou*, Marianne's being bored or fed up moves what there is of a plot; at one point, she says directly to the camera: "Let's leave the Jules Verne novel and go back to the *roman policier* with guns and so on." The emotional statement depicted in *A Woman Is a Woman* is summed up in the wish expressed by Belmondo's Alfredo and Anna Karina's Angela to be Gene Kelly and Cyd Charisse in a late 1940s Hollywood musical choreographed by Michael Kidd. Early in *Made in U.S.A.*, Paula Nelson comments: "Blood and mystery already. I have the feeling of moving about in a Walt Disney film starring Humphrey Bogart. Therefore, it must be a political film." But this remark measures the extent to which *Made in U.S.A.* both is and is not a political film. That Godard's characters occasionally look out of the "action" to locate themselves as actors in a film genre is only partly a piece of nostalgic first-person wit on the part of Godard the filmmaker; mainly it's an ironic disavowal of commitment to any one genre or way of regarding an action.

If the organizing principle of Feuillade's films is serial repetitiveness and obsessional elaboration, that of Godard's is the juxtaposition of contrary elements of unpredictable length and explicitness. While Feuillade's work implicitly conceives art as the gratification and prolongation of fantasy, Godard's work implies a quite different function for art: sensory and conceptual dislocation. Each of Godard's films is a totality that undermines itself, a detotalized totality (to borrow Sartre's phrase).

Instead of a narration unified by the coherence of events (a "plot") and a consistent tone (comic, serious, oneiric, affectless, or whatever), the narrative of Godard's films is regularly broken or segmented by the incoherence of events and by abrupt shifts in tone and level of discourse. Events appear to the spectator partly as converging toward a story, partly as a succession of independent tableaux.

The most obvious way Godard segments the forward-moving sequence of narration into tableaux is by explicitly theatricalizing some of his material, once more laying to rest the lively prejudice that there is an essential incompatibility between the means of theater and those of film. The conventions of the Hollywood musical, with songs and stage performances interrupting the story, supply one precedent for Godard—inspiring the general conception of *A Woman Is a Woman*, the dance trio in the café in *Band of Outsiders*, the song sequences and Vietnam protest skit performed outdoors in *Pierrot le Fou*, the singing telephone call in *Weekend*. His other model is, of course, the non-realistic and didactic theater expounded by Brecht. An aspect of Godard Brechtianizing is his distinctive style of constructing political micro-entertainments: in *La Chinoise*, the home political theater-piece acting out the American aggression in Vietnam; or the Feiffer dialogue of the two ham radio operators that opens *Deux ou Trois Choses*.

But the more profound influence of Brecht resides in those formal devices Godard uses to counteract ordinary plot development and complicate the emotional involvement of the audience. One device is the direct-to-camera declarations by the characters in many films, notably *Deux ou Trois Choses, Made in U.S.A.,* and *La Chinoise.* ("One should speak as if one were quoting the truth," says Marina Vlady at the beginning of *Deux ou Trois Choses,* quoting Brecht. "The actors must quote.") Another frequently used technique derived from Brecht is the dissection of the film narrative into short sequences: in *My Life to Live,* in addition, Godard puts on the screen prefatory synopses to each scene which describe the action to follow. The action of *Les Carabiniers* is broken into short brutal sections introduced by long titles, most of which represent cards sent home by Ulysses and Michelangelo; the titles are handwritten, which makes them a little harder to read and brings home to the movie audience the fact that it is being asked to read. Another, simpler device is the relatively arbitrary subdivision of action into numbered sequences, as when the credits of *Masculine Feminine* announce a film consisting of "fifteen precise actions" (*quinze faits précis*). A minimal device is the ironic, pseudo-quantitative statement of something, as in *A Married Woman,* with the brief monologue of Charlotte's little son explaining how to do an unspecified something in exactly ten steps; or in *Pierrot le Fou,* when Ferdinand's voice announces at the beginning of a scene: "Chapter 8. We cross France." Another example: the very title of one film, *Deux ou Trois Choses*—the lady about whom surely more than two or three things are known being the city of Paris. And, in support of these tropes of the rhetoric of disorientation, Godard practices many specifically sensorial techniques that serve to fragment the cinematic narrative. In fact, most of the familiar elements of Godard's visual and aural stylistics—rapid cutting, the use of unmatched shots, flash shots, the alternation of sunny takes with gray ones, the counterpoint of prefabricated images (signs, paintings, billboards, picture postcards, posters), the discontinuous music—function in this way.

Apart from the general strategy of "theater," perhaps Godard's most striking application of the dissociative principle is his treatment of ideas. Certainly ideas are not developed in Godard's films systematically, as they might be in a book. They aren't meant to be. In contrast to their role in Brechtian theater, ideas are chiefly formal elements in Godard's films, units of sensory and emotional stimulation. They function at least as much to dissociate and fragment as they do to indicate or illuminate the "meaning" of the action. Often the ideas, rendered in blocks of words, lie at a tangent to the action. Nana's reflections on sincerity and language in *My Life to Live,* Bruno's observations about truth and action in *Le Petit Soldat,* the articulate self-consciousness of Charlotte in *A Married Woman* and of Juliette in *Deux ou Trois Choses,* Lemmy Caution's startling aptitude for cultivated literary allusions in *Alphaville* are not functions of the realistic psychology of these characters. (Perhaps the only one of Godard's intellectually reflective protagonists who still seems "in character" when ruminating is Ferdinand in *Pierrot le Fou.*) Although Godard proposes film discourse as constantly open to ideas, ideas are only one element in a narrative form which posits an intentionally ambiguous, open, playful relation of *all* the parts to the total scheme.

Godard's fondness for interpolating literary "texts" in the action, which I have already mentioned, is one of the main variants on the presence of ideas in his films. Among the many instances: the Mayakovsky poem recited by the girl about to be executed by a firing squad in *Les Carabiniers;* the excerpt from the Poe story read aloud in the next-to-last episode in *My Life to Live;* the lines from Dante, Hölderlin, and Brecht that Lang quotes in *Contempt;* the oration from Saint-Just by a character dressed as Saint-Just in *Weekend;* the passage from Elie Faure's *History of Art* read aloud by Ferdinand to his young daughter in *Pierrot le Fou;* the lines from *Romeo and Juliet* in French translation dictated by the English teacher in *Band of Outsiders;* the scene from Racine's *Bérénice* rehearsed by Charlotte and her lover in *A Married Woman;* the quote from Fritz Lang read aloud by Camille in *Contempt;* the passages from Mao declaimed by the FLN agent in *Le Petit Soldat;* the antiphonal recitations from the little red book in *La Chinoise.* Usually someone makes an announcement before beginning to declaim, or can be seen taking up a book and reading from it. Sometimes, though, these obvious signals for the advent of a text are lacking—as with the excerpts from *Bouvard and Pécuchet* spoken by two customers in a café in *Deux ou Trois Choses,* or the long extract from *Death on the Installment Plan* delivered by the maid ("Madame Céline") in *A Married Woman.* (Although usually literary, the text may be a film: like the excerpt from Dreyer's *Jeanne d'Arc* that Nana watches in *My Life to Live,* or a minute of film shot by Godard in Sweden, reputed to be a parody of Bergman's *The Silence,* that Paul and the two girls see in *Masculine Feminine.*) These texts introduce psychologically dissonant elements into the action; they supply rhythmical variety (temporarily slowing down the action); they interrupt the action and offer ambiguous comment on it; and they also vary and extend the point of view represented in the film. The spectator is almost bound to be misled if he regards these texts simply, either as opinions of characters in the film or as samples of some unified point of view advocated by the film which presumably is dear to the director. More likely, just the opposite is or comes to be the case. Aided by "ideas" and "texts," Godard's film narratives tend to consume the points of view presented in them. Even the political ideas expressed in Godard's work—part Marxist and part anarchist in one canonical style of the postwar French intelligentsia—are subject to this rule.

Like the ideas, which function partly as divisive elements, the fragments of cultural lore embedded in Godard's films serve in part as a form of mystification and a means for refracting emotional energy. (In *Le Petit Soldat*, for instance, when Bruno says of Veronica the first time he sees her that she reminds him of a Giraudoux heroine, and later wonders whether her eyes are Renoir gray or Velásquez gray, the main impact of these references is their unverifiability by the audience.) Inevitably, Godard broaches the menace of the bastardization of culture, a theme most broadly stated in *Contempt* in the figure of the American producer with his booklet of proverbs. And, laden as his films are with furnishings of high culture, it's perhaps inevitable that Godard should also invoke the project of laying down the burden of culture—as Ferdinand does in *Pierrot le Fou* when he abandons his life in Paris for the romantic journey southward carrying only a book of old comics. In *Weekend*, Godard posits against the petty barbarism of the car-owning urban bourgeoisie the possibly cleansing violence of a rebarbarized youth, imagined as a hippie-style liberation army roaming the countryside whose principal delights seem to be contemplation, pillage, jazz, and cannibalism. The theme of cultural disburdenment is treated most fully and ironically in *La Chinoise*. One sequence shows the young cultural revolutionaries purging their shelves of all their books but the little red one. Another brief sequence shows just a blackboard at first, filled with the neatly listed names of several dozen stars of Western culture from Plato to Shakespeare to Sartre; these are then erased one by one, thoughtfully, with Brecht the last to go. The five pro-Chinese students who live together want to have only one point of view, that of Chairman Mao; but Godard shows, without insulting anyone's intelligence, how chimerical and inadequate to reality (and yet how appealing) this hope actually is. For all his native radicalism of temperament, Godard himself still appears a partisan of that other cultural revolution, ours, which enjoins the artist-thinker to maintain a multiplicity of points of view on any material.

All the devices Godard employs to keep shifting the point of view within a film can be looked at another way—as adjuncts to a positive strategy, that of overlaying a number of narrative voices, for effectively bridging the difference between first-person and third-person narration. Thus *Alphaville* opens with three samples of first-person discourse: first, a prefatory statement spoken off-camera by Godard, then a declaration by the computer-ruler Alpha 60, and only then the usual soliloquizing voice, that of the secret-agent hero, shown grimly driving his big car into the city of the future. Instead of, or in addition to, using "titles" between scenes as narrative signals (for example: *My Life to Live, A Married Woman*), Godard seems now more to favor installing a narrative voice in the film. This voice may belong to the main character: Bruno's musings in *Le Petit Soldat,* Charlotte's free-associating sub-text in *A Married Woman,* Paul's commentary in *Masculine Feminine.* It may be the director's, as in *Band of Outsiders* and *Le Grand Escroc,* the sketch from *Les Plus Belles Escroqueries du Monde* (1963). What's most interesting is when there are two voices, as in *Deux ou Trois Choses,* throughout which both Godard (whispering) and the heroine comment on the action. *Band of Outsiders* introduces the notion of a narrative intelligence which can "open a parenthesis" in the action and directly address the audience, explaining what Franz, Odile, and Arthur are really feeling at that moment; the narrator can intervene or comment ironically on the action or on the very fact of seeing a movie. (Fifteen minutes into the film, Godard off-camera says, "For the latecomers, what's happened so far is . . .") Thereby two different but concurrent times are established in the film—the time of the action shown, and the time of the narrator's reflection on what's shown—in a way which allows free passage back and forth between the first-person narration and the third-person presentation of the action.

Although the narrating voice already has a major role in some of his earliest work (for instance, the virtuoso comic monologue of the last of the pre-*Breathless* shorts, *Une Histoire d'Eau*), Godard continues to extend and complicate the task of oral narration, arriving at such recent refinements as the beginning of *Deux ou Trois Choses,* when from off-camera he introduces his leading actress, Marina Vlady, by name and then describes her as the character she will play. Such procedures tend, of course, to reinforce the self-reflexive and self-referring aspect of Godard's films, for the ultimate narrative presence is simply the fact of cinema itself; from which it follows that, for the sake of truth, the cinematic medium must be made to manifest itself before the spectator. Godard's methods for doing this range from the frequent ploy of having an actor make rapid playful asides to the

camera (i.e., to the audience) in mid-action, to the use of a bad take—
Anna Karina fumbles a line, asks if it's all right, then repeats the
line—in *A Woman Is a Woman. Les Carabiniers* only gets underway
after we hear first some coughing and shuffling and an instruction
by someone, perhaps the composer or a sound technician, on the set.
In *La Chinoise,* Godard makes the point about its being a movie by,
among other devices, flashing the clapper board on the screen from
time to time, and by briefly cutting to Raoul Coutard, the cameraman
on this as on most of Godard's films, seated behind his apparatus.
But then one immediately imagines some underling holding another
clapper while that scene was shot, and someone else who had to be
there behind another camera to photograph Coutard. It's impossible
ever to penetrate behind the final veil and experience cinema unmediated by cinema.

I have argued that one consequence of Godard's disregard for the
aesthetic rule of having a fixed point of view is that he dissolves the
distinction between first-person and third-person narration. But perhaps it would be more accurate to say that Godard proposes a new
conception of point of view, thereby staking out the possibility of
making films in the first person. By this, I don't mean simply that his
films are subjective or personal; so is the work of many other directors, particularly the cinematic avant-garde and underground. I mean
something stricter, which may indicate the originality of his achievement: namely, the way in which Godard, especially in his recent films,
has built up a narrative presence, that of the filmmaker, who is the
central *structural* element in the cinematic narrative. The first-person
filmmaker isn't an actual character within the film. That is, he is not
to be seen on the screen (except in the episode in *Far from Vietnam,*
which shows only Godard at a camera talking, intercut with snippets
from *La Chinoise*), though he is heard from time to time and one is
increasingly aware of his presence just off-camera. But this off-screen
persona is not a lucid, authorial intelligence, like the detached ob-
server-figure of many novels cast in the first person. The ultimate
first person in Godard's movies, his particular version of the filmmaker, is the person responsible for the film who stands outside it as
a mind beset by more complex, fluctuating concerns than any single
film can represent or incarnate. The most profound drama of a Godard film arises from the clash between this restless, wider consciousness of the director and the determinate, limited argument of
the particular film he's engaged in making. Therefore, each film is,
simultaneously, a creative activity and a destructive one. The director
virtually uses up his models, his sources, his ideas, his latest moral
and artistic enthusiasms—and the shape of the film consists of var-

ious means for letting the audience know that's what is happening. This dialectic has reached its furthest development so far in *Deux ou Trois Choses,* which is more radically a first-person film than any Godard has made.

The advantage of the first-person mode for cinema is presumably that it vastly augments the liberty of the filmmaker while at the same time providing incentives for greater formal rigor—the same goals espoused by all the serious post-novelists of this century. Thus Gide has Edouard, the author-protagonist of *The Counterfeiters,* condemn all previous novels because their contours are "defined," so that, however perfect, what they contain is "captive and lifeless." He wanted to write a novel that would "run freely" because he'd chosen "not to foresee its windings." But the liberation of the novel turned out to consist in writing a novel about writing a novel: presenting "literature" within literature. In a different context, Brecht discovered "theater" within theater. Godard has discovered "cinema" within cinema. However loose or spontaneous-looking or personally self-expressive his films may appear, what must be appreciated is that Godard subscribes to a severely alienated conception of his art: a cinema that eats cinema. Each film is an ambiguous event that must be simultaneously promulgated and destroyed. Godard's most explicit statement of this theme is the painful monologue of self-interrogation which was his contribution to *Far from Vietnam.* Perhaps his wittiest statement of this theme is a scene in *Les Carabiniers* (similar to the end of an early Mack Sennett two-reeler, *Mabel's Dramatic Career*) in which Michelangelo takes time off from the war to visit a movie theater, apparently for the first time, since he reacts as audiences did sixty years ago when movies first began to be shown. He follows the movements of the actors on the screen with his whole body, ducks under the seat when a train appears, and at last, driven wild by the sight of a girl taking a bath in the film within a film, bolts from his seat and rushes up to the stage. After first standing on tiptoe to try to look into the tub, then feeling tentatively for the girl along the surface of the screen, he finally tries to grab her—ripping away part of the screen within the screen, and revealing the girl and the bathroom to be a projection on a filthy wall. Cinema, as Godard says in *Le Grand Escroc,* "is the most beautiful fraud in the world."

Though all his distinctive devices serve the fundamental aim of breaking up the narrative or varying the perspective, Godard doesn't aim at a systematic variation of points of view. Sometimes, to be sure, he does elaborate a strong plastic conception—like the intricate visual patterns of the couplings of Charlotte with her lover and her husband in *A Married Woman;* and the brilliant formal metaphor of the mono-chromatic photography in three "political colors" in *Anticipation.* Still, Godard's work characteristically lacks formal rigor, a quality preeminent in all the work of Bresson and Jean-Marie Straub and in the best films of Welles and Resnais.

The jump cuts in *Breathless,* for instance, are not part of any strict overall rhythmic scheme, an observation that's confirmed by Godard's account of their rationale. "I discovered in *Breathless* that when a discussion between two people became boring and tedious one could just as well cut between the speeches. I tried it once, and it went very well, so I did the same thing right through the film." Godard may be exaggerating the casualness of his attitude in the cutting room, but his reliance upon intuition on the set is well known. For no film has a full shooting script been prepared in advance, and many films have been improvised day by day throughout large parts of the shooting; in the recent films shot with direct sound, Godard has the actors wear tiny earphones so that while they are on camera he can speak to each of them privately, feeding them their lines or posing questions which they're to answer (direct-to-camera interviews). And, though he generally uses professional actors, Godard has been in-creasingly open to incorporating accidental presences. (Examples: in *Deux ou Trois Choses,* Godard, off-camera, interviewing a young girl who worked in the beauty parlor which he'd taken over for a day of filming; Samuel Fuller talking, as himself, to Ferdinand, played by Belmondo, at a party at the beginning of *Pierrot le Fou,* because Fuller, an American director Godard admires, happened to be in Paris at the time and was visiting Godard on the set.) When using direct sound, Godard also generally keeps any natural or casual noises picked up on the sound track, even those unrelated to the action. While the results of this permissiveness are not interesting in every case, some of Godard's happiest effects have been last-minute inventions or the result of accident. The church bells tolling when Nana dies in *My Life to Live* just happened to go off, to everyone's surprise, during the shooting. The stunning scene in negative in *Alphaville* turned out that way because at the last moment Coutard told Godard there wasn't enough equipment on the set to light the scene properly (it was night); Godard decided to go ahead anyway. Godard has said that the spec-tacular ending of *Pierrot le Fou,* Ferdinand's suicide by self-dynamit-ing, "was invented on the spot, unlike the beginning, which was or-ganized. It's a sort of Happening, but one that was controlled and dominated. Two days before I began I had nothing, absolutely noth-

ing. Oh well, I did have the book. And a certain number of locations."
Godard's conviction that it is possible to absorb chance, using it as
an additional tool for developing new structures, extends beyond
making only minimal preparations for a film and keeping the conditions of shooting flexible to the editing itself. "Sometimes I have shots
that were badly filmed, because I lacked time or money," Godard has
said. "Putting them together creates a different impression; I don't
reject this; on the contrary, I try to do my best to bring out this new
idea."

Godard's openness to the aleatoric miracle is supported by his predilection for shooting on location. In his work to date—features, shorts,
and sketches all included—only his third feature, *A Woman Is a
Woman,* was shot in a studio; the rest were done in "found" locations. (The small hotel room in which *Charlotte et son Jules* takes
place was where Godard was then living; the apartment in *Deux ou
Trois Choses* belonged to a friend; and the apartment in *La Chinoise*
is where Godard lives now.) Indeed, one of the most brilliant and
haunting aspects of Godard's science-fiction fables—the sketch from
RoGoPay (1962), *Le Nouveau Monde, Alphaville,* and *Anticipation*—
is that they were filmed entirely in unretouched sites and buildings
existing around the Paris of the mid-1960s like Orly airport and the
Hotel Scribe and the new Electricity Board building. This, of course,
is exactly Godard's point. The fables about the future are at the same
time essays about today. The streak of movie-educated fantasy that
runs strong through Godard's work is always qualified by the ideal of
documentary truth.

From Godard's penchant for improvisation, for incorporating accidents, and for location shooting, one might infer a lineage from the
neo-realist aesthetic made famous by Italian films of the last twenty-
five years, starting with Visconti's *Ossessione* and *La Terra Trema*
and reaching its apogee in the postwar films of Rossellini and the
recent debut of Olmi. But Godard, although a fervent admirer of Rossellini, is not even a neo-neo-realist, and hardly aims to expel the
artifice from art. What he seeks is to conflate the traditional polarities
of spontaneous mobile thinking and finished work, of the casual jot-
ting and the fully premeditated statement. Spontaneity, casualness,
lifelikeness are not values in themselves for Godard, who is rather
interested in the *convergence* of spontaneity with the emotional discipline of abstraction (the dissolution of "subject matter"). Naturally,
the results are far from tidy. Although Godard achieved the basis of
his distinctive style very quickly (by 1958), the restlessness of his
temperament and his intellectual voracity impel him to adopt an es-

sentially exploratory posture in relation to filmmaking, in which he may answer a problem raised but not resolved in one film by starting on another. Still, viewed as a whole, Godard's work is much closer in problems and scope to the work of a radical purist and formalist in film like Bresson than to the work of the neo-realists—even though the relation with Bresson must also be drawn largely in terms of contrasts.

Bresson also achieved his mature style very quickly, but his career has throughout consisted of thoroughly premeditated, independent works conceived within the limits of his personal aesthetic of concision and intensity. Bresson's art is characterized by a pure, lyric quality, by a naturally elevated tone, and by a carefully constructed unity. He has said, in an interview conducted by Godard (*Cahiers du Cinéma* #178, May 1966), that for him "improvisation is at the base of creation in the cinema." But the look of a Bresson film is surely the antithesis of improvisation. In the finished film, a shot must be both autonomous and necessary; which means that there's only one ideally correct way of composing each shot (though it may be arrived at quite intuitively) and of editing the shots into a narrative. For all their great energy, Bresson's films project an air of formal deliberateness, of having been organized according to a relentless, subtly calculated rhythm which required their having had everything inessential cut from them. Given his austere aesthetic, it seems apt that Bresson's characteristic subject is a person either literally imprisoned or locked within an excruciating dilemma. Indeed, if one does accept narrative and tonal unity as a primary standard for film, Bresson's asceticism—his maximal use of minimal materials, the meditative "closed" quality of his films—seems to be the only truly rigorous procedure.

Godard's work exemplifies an aesthetic (and, no doubt, a temperament and sensibility) the opposite of Bresson's. The moral energy informing Godard's filmmaking, while no less powerful than Bresson's, leads to a quite different asceticism: the labor of endless self-questioning, which becomes a constitutive element in the artwork. "More and more with each film," he said in 1965, "it seems to me the greatest problem in filming is to decide where and why to begin a shot and why to end it." The point is that Godard cannot envisage anything but arbitrary solutions to his problem. While each shot is autonomous, no amount of thinking can make it necessary. Since film for Godard is preeminently an open structure, the distinction between what's essential and inessential in any given film becomes senseless. Just as no absolute, immanent standards can be discovered for determining the composition, duration, and place of a shot, there can be no truly sound reason for excluding anything from a film. This view of film as an assemblage rather than a unity lies behind the seemingly facile characterizations Godard has made of many of his recent films. *"Pierrot le Fou* isn't really a film, it's an attempt at cinema." About *Deux ou Trois Choses:* "In sum, it's not a film, it's an attempt at a film and is presented as such." *A Married Woman* is described in the main titles: "Fragments of a Film Shot in 1964"; and *La Chinoise* is subtitled "A Film in the Process of Being Made." In claiming to offer no more than "efforts" or "attempts," Godard acknowledges the structural openness or arbitrariness of his work. Each film remains a fragment in the sense that its possibilities of elaboration can never be used up. For, granted the acceptability, even desirability, of the method of juxtaposition ("I prefer simply putting things side by side"), which assembles contrary elements without reconciling them, there can indeed be no internally necessary end to a Godard film, as there is to a Bresson film. Every film must either seem broken off abruptly or else ended arbitrarily—often by the violent death in the last reel of one or more of the main characters, as in *Breathless, Le Petit Soldat, My Life to Live, Les Carabiniers, Contempt, Masculine Feminine,* and *Pierrot le Fou.*

Predictably, Godard has supported these views by pressing the relationship (rather than the distinction) between "art" and "life." Godard claims never to have had the feeling as he worked, which he thinks a novelist must have, "that I am differentiating between life and creation." The familiar mythical terrain is occupied once again: "cinema is somewhere between art and life." Of *Pierrot le Fou,* Godard has written: "Life is the subject, with 'Scope and color as its attributes. . . . Life on its own as I would like to capture it, using pan shots on nature, *plans fixes* on death, brief shots, long takes, soft and loud sounds, the movements of Anna and Jean-Paul. In short, life filling the screen as a tap fills a bathtub that is simultaneously emptying at the same rate." This, Godard claims, is how he differs from Bresson, who, when shooting a film, has "an idea of the world" that he is "trying to put on the screen or, which comes to the same thing, an idea of the cinema" he's trying "to apply to the world." For a director like Bresson, "cinema and the world are molds to be filled, while in *Pierrot* there is neither mold nor matter."

Of course Godard's films aren't bathtubs; and Godard harbors his complex sentiments about the world and his art to the same extent and in much the same way as Bresson. But despite Godard's lapse into a disingenuous rhetoric, the contrast with Bresson stands. For Bresson, who was originally a painter, it is the austerity and rigor of cinematic means which make this art (though very few movies) valuable to him. For Godard, it's the fact that cinema is so loose, promiscuous, and accommodating a medium which gives movies, even many inferior ones, their authority and promise. Film can mix forms, techniques, points of view; it can't be identified with any single leading ingredient. Indeed, what the filmmaker must show is that nothing is excluded. "One can put everything in a film," says Godard. "One must put everything in a film."

A film is conceived of as a living organism: not so much an object as a presence or an encounter—a fully historical or contemporary event, whose destiny it is to be transcended by future events. Seeking to create a cinema which inhabits the real present, Godard regularly puts into his films references to current political crises: Algeria, de Gaulle's domestic politics, Angola, the Vietnam War. (Each of his last four features includes a scene in which the main characters denounce the American aggression in Vietnam, and Godard has declared that until that war ends he'll put such a sequence into every film he makes.) The films may include even more casual references and off-the-cuff sentiments—a dig at André Malraux; a compliment to Henri Langlois, director of the Cinémathèque Française; an attack on irresponsible projectionists who show 1:66 films in Cinemascope ratio; or a plug for the unreleased movie of a fellow director and friend. Godard welcomes the opportunity to use the cinema topically, "journalistically." Using the interview style of cinema-verité and TV documentary, he can canvas characters for their opinions about the pill or the significance of Bob Dylan. Journalism can provide the basis for a film: Godard, who writes the scripts for all his movies, lists "documentation from 'Où en est la prostitution?' by Marcel Sacotte" as a source for *My Life to Live;* the story of *Deux ou Trois Choses* was suggested by a feature story, published in *Le Nouvel Observateur,* about housewives in new low-income apartment projects becoming part-time prostitutes to augment the family income.

As photography, cinema has always been an art which records temporality; but up to now this has been an inadvertent aspect of feature fiction films. Godard is the first major director who deliberately incorporates certain contingent aspects of the particular social moment when he's shooting a film—sometimes making these the frame of the film. Thus, the frame of *Masculine Feminine* is a report on the situation of French youth during three politically critical months of winter 1965, between the first presidential election and the runoff; and *La Chinoise* analyzes the faction of communist students in Paris inspired by the Maoist cultural revolution in the summer of 1967. But of course Godard does not intend to supply facts in a literal sense, the sense which denies the relevance of imagination and fantasy. In his view, "you can start either with fiction or documentary. But whichever you start with, you will inevitably find the other." Perhaps the most interesting development of his point is not the films which have the form of reportage but those which have the form of fables. The timeless universal war which is the subject of *Les Carabiniers* is illustrated by World War II documentary footage, and the squalor in which the mythic protagonists (Michelangelo, Ulysses, Cleopatra, Venus) live is concretely France today. *Alphaville* is, in Godard's words, "a fable on a realistic ground," because the intergalactic city is also, literally, Paris now.

Unworried by the issue of impurity—there are no materials unusable for film—Godard is, nevertheless, involved in an extremely purist venture: the attempt to devise a structure for films which speaks in a purer present tense. His effort is to make movies which live in the actual present, and not to tell something from the past, relate something that's already taken place. In this, of course, Godard is following a direction already taken in literature. Fiction, until recently, was the art of the past. Events told in an epic or novel are, when the reader starts the book, already (as it were) in the past. But in much of the new fiction, events pass before us as if in a present coexisting with the time of the narrative voice (more accurately, with the time in which the reader is being addressed by the narrative voice). Events exist, therefore, in the present—at least as much of the present as the reader himself inhabits. It is for this reason that such writers as Beckett, Stein, Burroughs, and Robbe-Grillet prefer actually to use the present tense, or its equivalent. (Another strategy: to make the distinction between past, present, and future time within the narration an explicit conundrum, and an insoluble one—as, for example, in certain tales of Borges and Landolfi and in *Pale Fire*.) But if the development is feasible for literature, it would seem even more apt for film to make a comparable move since, in a way, film narration knows *only* the present tense. (Everything shown is equally present, no matter when it takes place.) For film to exploit its natural liberty what was necessary was to have a much looser, less literal attachment to telling a "story." A story in the traditional sense— something that's already taken place—is replaced by a segmented situation in which the suppression of certain explicative connections between scenes creates the impression of an action continually beginning anew, unfolding in the present tense.

And, of necessity, this present tense must appear as a somewhat behaviorist, external, anti-psychological view of the human situation. For psychological understanding depends on holding in mind simultaneously the dimensions of past, present, and future. To see someone psychologically is to lay out temporal coordinates in which he is situated. An art which aims at the present tense cannot aspire to this kind of "depth" or innerness in the portrayal of human beings. The lesson is already clear from the work of Stein and Beckett; Godard demonstrates it for film.

Godard explicitly alludes to this choice only once, in connection with *My Life to Live,* which, he says, he "built . . . in tableaux to accentuate the theatrical side of the film. Besides, this division corresponded to the external view of things which best allowed me to give a feeling of what was going on inside. In other words, a contrary procedure to that used by Bresson in *Pickpocket,* in which the drama is seen from within. How can one render the 'inside'? I think, by staying prudently outside." But though there are obvious advantages to staying "outside"—flexibility of form, freedom from superimposed limiting solutions—the choice is not so clear-cut as Godard suggests. Perhaps one never goes "inside" in the sense Godard attributes to Bresson—a procedure considerably different from the reading off of motives and summing up of a character's interior life promoted by nineteenth-century novelistic realism. Indeed, by those standards, Bresson is himself considerably "outside" his characters; for instance, more involved in their somatic presence, the rhythm of their movements, the heavy weight of inexpressible feeling which they bear.

Still, Godard is right in saying that, compared with Bresson, he is "outside." One way he stays outside is by constantly shifting the point of view from which the film is told, by the juxtaposition of contrasting narrative elements: realistic alongside implausible aspects of the story, written signs interposed between images, "texts" recited aloud interrupting dialogue, static interviews as against rapid actions, interpolation of a narrator's voice explaining or commenting on the action, and so forth. A second way is by his rendering of "things" in a strenuously neutralized fashion, in contrast with Bresson's thoroughly intimate vision of things as objects used, disputed, loved, ignored, and worn out by people. Things in Bresson's films, whether a spoon, a chair, a piece of bread, a pair of shoes, are always marked by their human use. The point is *how* they are used—whether skillfully (as the prisoner uses his spoon in *Un Condamné à Mort,* and the heroine of *Mouchette* uses the saucepan and bowls to make breakfast coffee) or clumsily. In Godard's films, things display a wholly alienated character. Characteristically, they are used with indifference, neither skillfully nor clumsily; they are simply there. "Objects exist," Godard has written, "and if one pays more attention to them than to people, it is precisely because they exist more than these people. Dead objects are still alive. Living people are often already dead." Whether things can be the occasion for visual gags (like the suspended egg in *A Woman Is a Woman,* and the movie posters in the warehouse in *Made in U.S.A.*) or can introduce an element of great plastic beauty (as do the Ponge-like studies in *Deux ou Trois Choses* of the burning end of a cigarette and of bubbles separating and coming together on the surface of a hot cup of coffee), they always occur in a context of, and serve to reinforce, emotional dissociation. The most noticeable form of Godard's dissociated rendering of things is his ambivalent immersion in the allure of Pop imagery and his only partly ironic display of the symbolic currency of urban capitalism—pinball machines, boxes of detergent, fast cars, neon signs, billboards, fashion magazines. By extension, this fascination with alienated things dictates the settings of most of Godard's films: highways, airports, anonymous hotel rooms or soulless modern apartments, brightly lit modernized cafés, movie theaters. The furniture and settings of Godard's films are the landscape of alienation—whether he is displaying the pathos in the mundane facticity of the actual life of dislocated, urban persons such as petty hoodlums, discontented housewives, left-wing students, prostitutes (the everyday present) or presenting anti-utopian fantasies about the cruel future.

A universe experienced as fundamentally dehumanized or dissociated is also one conducive to rapid "associating" from one ingredient in it to another. Again, the contrast can be made with Bresson's attitude, which is rigorously non-associative and therefore concerned with the depth in any situation; in a Bresson film there are certain organically derived and mutually relevant exchanges of personal energy that flourish or exhaust themselves (either way, unifying the narrative and supplying it with an organic terminus). For Godard, there are no genuinely organic connections. In the landscape of pain, only three strictly unrelated responses of real interest are possible; violent action, the probe of "ideas," and the transcendence of sudden, arbitrary, romantic love. But each of these possibilities is understood to be revocable, or artificial. They are not acts of personal fulfillment; not so much solutions as dissolutions of a problem. It has been noted that many of Godard's films project a masochistic view of women, verging on misogyny, and an indefatigable romanticism about "the couple." It's an odd but rather familiar combination of attitudes. Such contradictions are psychological or ethical analogues to Godard's fundamental formal presuppositions. In work conceived of as open-ended, associative, composed of "fragments," constructed by the (partly alea-toric) juxtaposition of contrary elements, any principle of action or any decisive emotional resolution is bound to be an artifice (from an ethical point of view) or ambivalent (from a psychological point of view).

Each film is a provisional network of emotional and intellectual impasses. With the probable exception of his view on Vietnam, there is no attitude Godard incorporates in his films that is not simultane-ously being bracketed, and therefore criticized, by a dramatization of the gap between the elegance and seductiveness of ideas and the brutish or lyrical opaqueness of the human condition. The same sense of impasse characterizes Godard's moral judgments. For all the use made of the metaphor and the fact of prostitution to sum up contem-porary miseries, Godard's films can't be said to be "against" prostitu-tion and "for" pleasure and liberty in the unequivocal sense that Bresson's films directly extol love, honesty, courage, and dignity and deplore cruelty and cowardice.

From Godard's perspective, Bresson's work is bound to appear "rhetorical," whereas Godard is bent on destroying rhetoric by a lav-ish use of irony—the familiar outcome when a restless, somewhat dissociated intelligence struggles to cancel an irrepressible romanti-cism and tendency to moralize. In many of his films Godard deliber-ately seeks the framework of parody, of irony as contradiction. For instance, *A Woman Is a Woman* proceeds by putting an ostensibly serious theme (a woman frustrated both as wife and as would-be mother) in an ironically sentimental framework. "The subject of *A Woman Is a Woman*," Godard has said, "is a character who succeeds in resolving a certain situation, but I conceived this subject within the framework of a neo-realistic musical: an *absolute contradiction,* but that is precisely why I wanted to make the film." Another exam-ple is the lyrical treatment of a rather nasty scheme of amateur gangsterism in *Band of Outsiders,* complete with the high irony of the "happy ending" in which Odile sails away with Franz to Latin America for further, romantic adventures. Another example: the no-menclature of *Alphaville,* a film in which Godard takes up some of his most serious themes, is a collection of comic-strip identities (char-acters have names like Lemmy Caution, the hero of a famous series of French thrillers; Harry Dickson; Professor Leonard Nosferatu, al-ias von Braun; Professor Jekyll) and the lead is played by Eddie Con-stantine, the expatriate American actor whose mug has been a cliché of "B" French detective films for two decades; indeed, Godard's original title for the film was "Tarzan versus IBM." Still another example: the film Godard decided to make on the double theme of the Ben Barka and Kennedy murders, *Made in U.S.A.,* was conceived as a parodic remake of *The Big Sleep* (which had been revived at an art house in Paris in the summer of 1966), with Bogart's role of the trench-coated detective embroiled in an insoluble mystery now played by Anna Karina. The danger of such lavish use of irony is that ideas will be expressed at their point of self-caricature, and emotions only when they are mutilated. Irony intensifies what is already a considerable limitation on the emotions in the films that results from the insistence on the pure presentness of cinema narration, in which situations with less deep affect will be disproportionately represented— at the expense of vividly depicted states of grief, rage, profound erotic longing and fulfillment, and physical pain. Thus, while Bresson, at his almost unvarying best, is able to convey deep emotions without ever being sentimental, Godard, at his less effective, devises turns of plot that appear either hardhearted or sentimental (at the same time seeming emotionally flat).

Godard "straight" seems to me more successful—whether in the rare pathos he has allowed in *Masculine Feminine,* or in the hard coolness of such directly passionate films as *Les Carabiniers, Contempt, Pierrot le Fou,* and *Weekend.* This coolness is a pervasive quality of Godard's work. For all their violence of incident and sexual matter-of-factness, the films have a muted, detached relation to the grotesque and painful as well as to the seriously erotic. People are sometimes tortured and often die in Godard's films, but almost casually. (He has a particular predilection for automobile accidents: the end of *Contempt,* the wreck in *Pierrot le Fou,* the landscape of affectless highway carnage in *Weekend.*) And people are rarely shown making love, though if they are, what interests Godard isn't the sensual communion but what sex reveals "about the spaces between people." The orgiastic moments come when young people dance together or sing or play games or run—people run beautifully in Godard movies—not when they make love.

"Cinema is emotion," says Samuel Fuller in *Pierrot le Fou,* a thought one surmises that Godard shares. But emotion, for Godard, always comes accompanied by some decoration of wit, some transmuting of feeling that he clearly puts at the center of the art-making process. This accounts for part of Godard's preoccupation with language, both heard and seen on the screen. Language functions as a means of emotional distancing from the action. The pictorial element is emotional, immediate; but words (including signs, texts, stories, sayings, recitations, interviews) have a lower temperature. While images invite the spectator to identify with what is seen, the presence of words makes the spectator into a critic.

But Godard's Brechtian use of language is only one aspect of the matter. Much as Godard owes to Brecht, his treatment of language is more complex and equivocal and relates rather to the efforts of certain painters who use words actively to undermine the image, to rebuke it, to render it opaque and unintelligible. It's not simply that Godard gives language a place that no other film director has before him. (Compare the verbosity of Godard's films with Bresson's verbal severity and austerity of dialogue.) He sees nothing in the film medium that prevents one of the subjects of cinema from being language itself—as language has become the very subject of much contemporary poetry and, in a metaphoric sense, of some important painting. But it seems that language can become the subject of cinema only at that point when a filmmaker is obsessed by the problematic character of language—as Godard so evidently is. What other directors have regarded mainly as an adjunct of greater "realism" (the advantage of sound films as compared with silents) becomes in Godard's hands a virtually autonomous, sometimes subversive instrument.

I have already noted the varied ways in which Godard uses language as speech—not only as dialogue, but as monologue, as recited discourse, including quotation, and in off-screen comment and interrogation. Language is as well an important visual or plastic element in his films. Sometimes the screen is entirely filled with a printed text or lettering, which becomes the substitute for or counterpoint to a pictorial image. (Just a few examples: the stylishly elliptical credits that open each film; the postcard messages from the two soldiers in *Les Carabiniers;* the billboards, posters, record sleeves, and magazine ads in *My Life to Live, A Married Woman,* and *Masculine Feminine;* the pages from Ferdinand's journal, only part of which can be read, in *Pierrot le Fou;* the conversation with book covers in *A Woman Is a Woman;* the cover of the paperback series *Idées* used thematically in *Deux ou Trois Choses;* the Maoist slogans on the apartment walls in *La Chinoise.*) Not only does Godard not regard cinema as essentially moving photographs; for him, the fact that movies, which purport to be a pictorial medium, admit of language, precisely gives cinema its superior range and freedom compared with other art forms. Pictorial or photographic elements are in a sense only the raw materials of Godard's cinema; the transformative ingredient is language.

Thus, to cavil at Godard for the talkiness of his films is to misunderstand his materials and his intentions. It is almost as if the pictorial image had a static quality, too close to "art," that Godard wants to infect with the blight of words. In *La Chinoise,* a sign on the wall of the student Maoist commune reads: "One must replace vague ideas with clear images." But that's only one side of the issue, as Godard knows. Sometimes images are too clear, too simple. (*La Chinoise* is Godard's sympathetic, witty treatment of the arch-romantic wish to make oneself entirely simple, altogether clear.) The highly permutated dialectic between image and language is far from stable. As he declares in his own voice at the beginning of *Alphaville:* "Some things in life are too complex for oral transmission. So we make fiction out of them, to make them universal." But again, it's clear that making things universal can bring oversimplification, which must be combated by the concreteness and ambiguity of words.

Godard has always been fascinated by the opaqueness and coerciveness of language, and a recurrent feature of the film narratives is some sort of deformation of speech. At perhaps its most innocent but still oppressive stage, speech can become hysterical monologue, as in *Charlotte et son Jules* and *Une Histoire d'Eau.* Speech can become halting and incomplete, as in Godard's early use of interview passages—in *Le Grand Escroc,* and in *Breathless,* where Patricia interviews a novelist (played by the director J.-P. Melville) at Orly airport. Speech can become repetitive, as in the hallucinatory doubling of the dialogue by the quadrilingual translator in *Contempt* and, in *Band of Outsiders,* the English teacher's oddly intense repetitions of end phrases during her dictation. There are several instances of the outright dehumanization of speech—like the slow-motion croaking of the computer Alpha 60 and the mechanized impoverished speech of its catatonic human subjects in *Alphaville;* and the "broken" speech of the traveler in *Anticipation.* The dialogue may be out of step with the action, as in the antiphonal commentary in *Pierrot le Fou;* or simply fail to make sense, as in the account of "the death of logic" following a nuclear explosion over Paris in *Le Nouveau Monde.* Sometimes Godard prevents speech from being completely understood—as in the first scene in *My Life to Live,* and with the sonically harsh, partly unintelligible tape of the voice of "Richard Po—" in *Made in U.S.A.,* and in the long erotic confession at the opening of *Weekend.* Complementing these mutilations of speech and language are the many explicit discussions of language-as-a-problem in Godard's films. The puzzle about how it's possible to make moral or intellectual sense by speaking, owing to the betrayal of consciousness by language, is debated in *My Life to Live* and *A Married Woman;* the mystery of "translating" from one language to another is a theme in *Contempt* and *Band of Outsiders;* the language of the future is a subject of speculation by Guillaume and Véronique in *La Chinoise* (words will be spoken as if they were sounds and matter); the nonsensical underside of language is demonstrated in the exchange in the café between Marianne, the laborer, and the bartender in *Made in U.S.A.;* and the effort to purify language of philosophical and cultural dissociation is the explicit, main theme of *Alphaville* and *Anticipation,* the success of an individual's efforts to do this providing the dramatic resolution of both films.

At this moment in Godard's work, the problem of language appears to have become his leading motif. Behind their obtrusive verbosity, Godard's films are haunted by the duplicity and banality of language. Insofar as there is a "voice" speaking in all his films, it is one that questions all voices. Language is the widest context in which Godard's recurrent theme of prostitution must be located. Beyond its direct sociological interest for Godard, prostitution is his extended metaphor for the fate of language, that is, of consciousness itself. The coalescing of the two themes is clearest in the science-fiction nightmare of *Anticipation:* in an airport hotel some time in the future (that is, now), travelers have the choice of two kinds of temporary sexual companions, someone who makes bodily love without speaking or someone who can recite the words of love but can't take part in any physical embrace. This schizophrenia of the flesh and the soul is the menace that inspires Godard's preoccupation with language, and confers on him the painful, self-interrogatory terms of his restless art. As Natasha declares at the end of *Alphaville,* "There are words I don't know." But it's that painful knowledge, according to Godard's controlling narrative myth, that marks the beginning of her redemption, and—by an extension of the same goal—the redemption of art itself.

(February 1968)

I, etcetera

Project for a Trip to China

I

I am going to China.

I will walk across the Luhu Bridge spanning the Sham Chun River between Hong Kong and China.

After having been in China for a while, I will walk across the Luhu Bridge spanning the Sham Chun River between China and Hong Kong.

Five variables:

> Luhu Bridge
> Sham Chun River
> Hong Kong
> China
> peaked cloth caps

Consider other possible permutations.

I have never been to China.

I have always wanted to go to China. Always.

II

Will this trip appease a longing?

> Q. [stalling for time] The longing to go to China, you mean?
> A. Any longing.

Yes.

Archaeology of longings.

But it's my whole life!

Don't panic. "Confession is nothing, knowledge is everything." That's a quote but I'm not going to tell who said it.

Hints:

> —a writer
> —somebody wise
> —an Austrian (that is, a Viennese Jew)
> —a refugee
> —he died in America in 1951

Confession is me, knowledge is everybody.

Archaeology of conceptions.

Am I permitted a pun?

III

The conception of this trip is very old.

First conceived when? As far back as I can remember.

> —Investigate possibility that I was conceived in China though born in New York and brought up elsewhere (America).
> —write M.
> —telephone?

Prenatal relation to China: certain foods, perhaps. But I don't remember M. saying she actually *liked* Chinese food.

—Didn't she say that at the general's banquet she spit
the whole of the hundred-year-old egg into her nap-
kin?

Something filtering through the bloody membranes, anyway.

Myrna Loy China, *Turandot* China. Beautiful, millionaire Soong sisters from Wellesley and Wesleyan & their husbands. A landscape of
jade, teak, bamboo, fried dog.

Missionaries, foreign military advisers. Fur traders in the Gobi Desert,
among them my young father.

Chinese forms placed about the first living room I remember (we
moved away when I was six): plump ivory and rose-quartz elephants
on parade, narrow rice-paper scrolls of black calligraphy in gilded wood
frames, Buddha the Glutton immobilized under an ample lampshade
of taut pink silk. Compassionate Buddha, slim, in white porcelain.
        —Historians of Chinese art distinguish between porce-
        lain and proto-porcelain.

Colonialists collect.

Trophies brought back, left behind in homage to the other living room,
in the real Chinese house, the one I never saw. Unrepresentative,
opaque objects. In dubious taste (but I only know that now). Confusing solicitations. The birthday gift of a bracelet made of five small
tubular lengths of green jade, each tiny end capped in gold, which I
never wore.
        —Colors of jade:
                green, all sorts, notably emerald green and bluish
                    green
                white
                gray
                yellow
                brownish
                reddish
                other colors

One certainty: China inspired the first lie I remember telling. Entering the first grade, I told my classmates that I was born in China. I
think they were impressed.

270/ S U S A N   S O N T A G

I know that I wasn't born in China.

The four causes of my wanting to go to China:
       *material
       formal
       efficient
       final

The oldest country in the world: it requires years of arduous study to learn its language. The country of science fiction, where everyone speaks with the same voice. Maotsetungized.

Whose voice is the voice of the person who wants to go to China? A child's voice. Less than six years old.

Is going to China like going to the moon? I'll tell you when I get back.

Is going to China like being born again?

Forget that I was conceived in China.

IV

Not only my father and mother but Richard and Pat Nixon have been to China before me. Not to mention Marco Polo, Matteo Ricci, the Lumière brothers (or at least one of them), Teilhard de Chardin, Pearl Buck, Paul Claudel, and Norman Bethune. Henry Luce was born there. Everyone dreams of returning.
      —Did M. move from California to Hawaii three years ago to be closer to China?

After she came back for good in 1939, M. used to say, "In China, children don't talk." But her telling me that, in China, burping at the table is a polite way of showing appreciation for the meal didn't mean I could burp.

Outside the house, it seemed plausible that I'd made China up. I knew I was lying when I said at school that I was born there, but being only a small portion of a lie so much bigger and more inclusive, mine was quite forgivable. Told in the service of the bigger lie, my lie became a kind of truth. The important thing was to convince my classmates that China actually did exist.

Was the first time I told my lie after or before I announced in school that I was a half-orphan?
> —That was true.

I have always thought: China is as far as anyone can go.
> —Still true.

When I was ten, I dug a hole in the back yard. I stopped when it got to be six feet by six feet by six feet. "What are you trying to do?" said the maid. "Dig all the way to China?"

No. I just wanted a place to sit in. I laid eight-foot-long planks over the hole: the desert sun scorches. The house we lived in then was a four-room stucco bungalow on a dirt road at the edge of town. The ivory and quartz elephants had been auctioned.
> —my refuge
> —my cell
> —my study
> —my grave

Yes. I wanted to dig all the way to China. And come bursting out the other end, standing on my head or walking on my hands.

The landlord came by in his jeep one day and told M. the hole had to be filled in within twenty-four hours because it was dangerous. Anyone crossing the yard at night might fall in. I showed him how it was entirely covered by boards, solid boards, except for the small square entrance on the north side where, with difficulty, I myself could just fit through.
> —Anyway, who was going to cross the yard at night? A coyote? A lost Indian? A tubercular or asthmatic neighbor? An angry landlord?

Inside the hole, I scraped out a niche in the east wall, where I set a candle. I sat on the floor. Dirt fell through the cracks between the planks into my mouth. It was too dark to read.
> —About to jump down, I never worried that I might land on a snake or a Gila monster curled up on the floor of the hole.

I filled in the hole. The maid helped me.

Three months later I dug it again. It was easier this time, because the earth was loose. Remembering Tom Sawyer with the fence that had to be whitewashed, I got three of the five Fuller kids across the road to help me. I promised them they could sit in the hole whenever I wasn't using it.

Southwest. Southwest. My desert childhood, off-balance, dry, hot.

I have been thinking about the following Chinese equivalences:

EAST	SOUTH	CENTER	WEST	NORTH
wood	fire	earth	metal	water
blue-green	red	yellow	white	black
spring	summer	end of summer/ beginning of autumn	autumn	winter
green	red		white	black
dragon	bird		tiger	tortoise
anger	joy	sympathy	grief	fear

I would like to be in the center.

The center is earth, yellow; it lasts from the end of summer through the beginning of autumn. It has no bird, no animal.

Sympathy.

V

Invited by the Chinese government, I am going to China.

Why does everybody like China? Everybody.

Chinese things:
>   Chinese food
>   Chinese laundries
>   Chinese torture

China is certainly too big for a foreigner to understand. But so are most places.

For the moment I am not inquiring about "revolution" (Chinese revolution) but trying to grasp the meaning of patience.

And cruelty. And the endless presumption of the Occident. The bemedaled officers who led the Anglo-French occupation of Peking in 1860 probably sailed back to Europe with trunks of *chinoiserie* and respectful dreams of returning to China someday as civilians and connoisseurs.
>   —The Summer Palace, "the cathedral of Asia" (Victor
>   Hugo), pillaged and burned
>   —Chinese Gordon

Chinese patience. Who assimilates whom?

My father was sixteen when he first went to China. M. was, I think, twenty-four.

I still weep in any movie with a scene in which a father returns home after a long desperate absence, at the moment when he hugs his child. Or children.

The first Chinese object I acquired on my own was in Hanoi in May 1968. A pair of green and white canvas sneakers with "Made in China" in ridged letters on the rubber soles.

Riding around Pnom Penh in a rickshaw in April 1968, I thought of the photograph I have of my father in a rickshaw in Tientsin taken in 1931. He looks pleased, boyish, shy, absent. He is gazing into the camera.

A trip into the history of my family. I've been told that the Chinese are pleased when they learn that a visitor from Europe or America has some link with prewar China. Objection: My parents were on the wrong side. Amiable, sophisticated Chinese reply: But all foreigners who lived in China at that time were on the wrong side.

La Condition Humaine is called *Man's Fate* in English. Not convincing.

I've always liked hundred-year-old eggs. (They're duck eggs, approximately two years old, the time it takes to become an exquisite green and translucent-black cheese.

—I've always wished they *were* a hundred years old. Imagine what they might have mutated into by then.)

In restaurants in New York and San Francisco I often order a portion. The waiters inquire in their scanty English if I know what I'm ordering. I affirm that I do. The waiters go away. When the order comes, I tell my eating companions how delicious they are, but I always end up having all the slices to myself; everyone I know finds the sight of them disgusting.

Q. Didn't David try the eggs? More than once?

A. Yes. To please me.

Pilgrimage.

I'm not returning to my birthplace, but to the place where I was conceived.

When I was four, my father's partner, Mr. Chen, taught me how to eat with chopsticks. During his first and only trip to America. He said I looked Chinese.

Chinese food

Chinese torture

Chinese politeness

M. watched, approvingly. They all went back on the boat together.

China was objects. And absence. M. had a mustard-gold liquescent silk robe that belonged to a lady-in-waiting at the court of the Dowager Empress, she said.

And discipline. And taciturnity.

What was everybody doing in China all that time? My father and mother playing Great Gatsby and Daisy inside the British Concession, Mao Tse-tung thousands of miles inland marching, marching,

marching, marching, marching, marching. In the cities, millions of lean coolies smoking opium, pulling rickshaws, peeing on the sidewalks, letting themselves be pushed around by foreigners and pestered by flies.

Unlocatable "White Russians," albinos nodding over samovars as I imagined them when I was five years old.

I imagined boxers raising their heavy leather gloves to deflect the hurtling lead of Krupp cannons. No wonder they were defeated.

I am looking in an encyclopedia at a photograph whose caption reads: "Souvenir photograph of a group of Westerners with the corpses of tortured Boxers. Honghong. 1899." In the foreground, a row of decapitated Chinese bodies whose heads have rolled some distance away; it is not always clear which body each head belongs to. Seven white men standing behind them, posing for the camera. Two are wearing their safari hats; a third holds his at his right side. In the shallow-looking water behind them, several sampans. The beginning of a village on the left. Mountains in the background, lightly touched with snow.
> —The men are smiling.
> —Undoubtedly it is an eighth Westerner, their friend, who is taking the picture.

Shanghai smelling of incense and gunpowder and dung. A United States Senator (from Missouri) at the turn of the century: "With God's help, we shall raise Shanghai up and up and up until it reaches the level of Kansas City." Buffalo in the late 1930s, disemboweled by the bayonets of invading Japanese soldiers, groaning in the streets of Tientsin.

Outside the pestilential cities, here and there a sage crouches at the breast of a green mountain. A great deal of elegant geography separates each sage from his nearest counterpart. All sages are old but not all are hirsute enough to grow white beards.

Warlords, landlords; mandarins, concubines. Old China Hands. Flying Tigers.

Words that are pictures. Shadow theater. Storm Over Asia.

VI

I am interested in wisdom. I am interested in walls. China famous for both.

From the entry on China in the *Encyclopaedia Universalis* (Vol. 4, Paris, 1968, p. 306): "Dans les conversations, on aime toujours les successions de courtes phrases dont chacune est induite de la précédente, selon la méthode chinoise traditionelle de raisonnement."

Life lived by quotations. In China, the art of quotation has reached its apogee. Guidance in all tasks.

There is a woman in China, twenty-nine years old, whose right foot is on her left leg. Her name is Tsui Wen Shi. The train accident that cost her her right leg and her left foot occurred in January 1972. The operation that grafted her right foot onto her left leg took place in Peking and was performed, according to the *People's Daily*, "under the guidance of the proletarian line of Chairman Mao on matters of health, but also thanks to advanced surgical techniques."

  —The newspaper article explains why the surgeons didn't graft her left foot back on her left leg: the bones of her left foot were smashed, the right foot was intact.
  —The reader is not asked to take anything on faith. This is not a surgical miracle.

I am looking at the photograph of Tsui Wen Shi, sitting erect on a table covered with a white cloth, smiling, her hands clasping her bent left knee.

Her right foot is very large.

The flies are all gone, killed twenty years ago in the Great Fly-Killing Campaign. Intellectuals who, after criticizing themselves, were sent to the countryside to be reeducated by sharing the lot of peasants are returning to jobs in Shanghai and Peking and Canton.

Wisdom has gotten simpler, more practicable. More horizontal. The sages' bones whiten in mountain caves and the cities are clean. People are eager to tell their truth, together.

Feet long since unbound, women hold meetings to "speak bitterness" about men. Children recite anti-imperialist fairy tales. Soldiers elect and dismiss their officers. Ethnic minorities have a limited permission to be folkloric. Chou En-lai remains lean and handsome as Tyrone Power, but Mao Tse-tung now resembles the fat Buddha under the lampshade. Everyone is very calm.

VII

Three things I've been promising myself for twenty years that I would do before I die:
> —climb the Matterhorn
> —learn to play the harpsichord
> —study Chinese

Perhaps it's not too late to climb the Matterhorn. (As Mao Tse-tung swam, didactically old, eleven miles down the Yangtze?) My fussed-over lungs are sturdier today than when I was in my teens.

Richard Mallory vanished forever, behind a huge cloud, just as he was sighted nearing the top of the peak. My father, tubercular, never came back from China.

I never doubted I would go to China someday. Even when it became hard to go, impossible even, for an American.
> —Being so confident, I never considered making that one of my three projects.

David wears my father's ring. The ring, a white silk scarf with my father's initials embroidered in black silk thread, and a pigskin wallet with his name stamped in small gold letters on the inside are all I possess that belonged to him. I don't know what his handwriting was like, not even his signature. The flat signet of the ring bears his initials, too.
> —Surprising that it should just fit David's finger.

Eight variables:
> rickshaw
> my son
> my father
> my father's ring
> death

China
optimism
blue cloth jackets

The number of permutations here are impressive: epic, pathetic. Tonic.

I have some photos too, all taken before I was born. In rickshaws, on camels and boat decks, before the wall of the Forbidden City. Alone. With his mistress. With M. With his two partners, Mr. Chen and the White Russian.

It is oppressive to have an invisible father.
        Q. Doesn't David also have an invisible father?
        A. Yes, but David's father is not a dead boy.

My father keeps getting younger. (I don't know where he's buried. M. says she's forgotten.)

An unfinished pain that might, just might, get lost in the endless Chinese smile.

VIII

The most exotic place of all.

China is not a place that I—at least—can go to, just because I decide to go.

My parents decided against bringing me to China. I had to wait for the government to invite me.
        —Another government.

For meanwhile, while I was waiting, upon their China, the China of pigtails and Chiang Kai-shek and more people than can be counted, had been grafted the China of optimism, the bright future, more people than can be counted, blue cloth jackets and peaked caps.

Conception, pre-conception.

What conception of this trip can I have in advance?

A trip in search of political understanding?
　　　—"Notes toward a Definition of Cultural Revolution"?

Yes. But grounded in guesswork, vivified by misconceptions. Since I don't understand the language. Already six years older than my father when he died, I haven't climbed the Matterhorn or learned to play the harpsichord or studied Chinese.

A trip that might ease a private grief?

If so, the grief will be eased in a willful way: because I want to stop grieving. Death is unremittable, unnegotiable. Not unassimilable. But who assimilates whom? "All men must die, but death can vary in its significance. The ancient Chinese writer Szuma Chien said, 'Though death befalls all men alike, it may be heavier than Mount Tai or lighter than a feather.' "
　　　　　　　—This is not the whole of the brief quote given in *Quo-*
　　　　　　　tations from Chairman Mao Tse-tung, but it's all I
　　　　　　　need now.
　　　　　　　—Note that even in this abridged quote from Mao Tse-
　　　　　　　tung there is a quote within a quote.
　　　　　　　—The omitted final sentence of the quote makes clear
　　　　　　　that the heavy death is desirable, not the light one.

He died so far away. By visiting my father's death, I make him heavier. I will bury him myself.

I will visit a place entirely other than myself. Whether it is the future or the past need not be decided in advance.

What makes the Chinese different is that they live both in the past and in the future.

Hypothesis. Individuals who seem truly remarkable give the impression of belonging to another epoch. (Either some epoch in the past or, simply, the future.) No one extraordinary appears to be entirely contemporary. People who are contemporary don't appear at all:
　　　　　　　　　　　　　　　　　they are invisible.

Moralism is the legacy of the past, moralism rules the domain of the future. We hesitate. Wary, ironic, disillusioned. What a difficult bridge

this present has become! How many, many trips we have to undertake so as not to be empty and invisible.

IX

From *The Great Gatsby*, p. 2: "When I came back from the East last
autumn I felt that I wanted the world to be in uniform and at a sort
of moral attention forever; I wanted no more riotous excursions with
privileged glimpses into the human heart."

       —Another "East," but no matter. The quote fits.

       —Fitzgerald meant New York, not China.

       —(Much to be said about the "discovery of the modern
          function of the quotation," attributed by Hannah
          Arendt to Walter Benjamin in her essay "Walter Ben-
          jamin."

          —Facts:

             a writer

             someone brilliant

             a German [that is, a Berlin Jew]

             a refugee

             he died at the French-Spanish border in 1940

          —To Benjamin, add Mao Tse-tung and Godard.)

"When I came back from the East last autumn I felt that I wanted
the world . . ." Why shouldn't the world stand at moral attention?
Poor, bruised world.

First half of second quotation from unnamed Austrian-Jewish refugee sage who died in America: "Man as such is the problem of our
time; the problems of individuals are fading away and are even forbidden, morally forbidden."

It's not that I'm afraid of getting simple, by going to China. The truth
is simple.

I will be taken to see factories, schools, collective farms, hospitals,
museums, dams. There will be banquets and ballets. I will never be
alone. I will smile often (though I don't understand Chinese).

Second half of unidentified quote: "The personal problem of the individual has become a subject of laughter for the Gods, and they are
right in their lack of pity."

"Fight individualism," says Chairman Mao. Master moralist.

Once China meant ultimate refinements: in pottery, cruelty, astrology, manners, food, eroticism, landscape painting, the relation of thought to written sign. Now China means ultimate simplifying.

What doesn't put me off, imagining it on the eve of my departure for China, is all that talk about goodness. I don't share the anxiety I detect in everyone I know about being *too* good.
> —As if goodness brings with it a loss of energy, individuality;
> —in men, a loss of virility.

"Nice guys finish last." American saying.

"It's not hard for one to do a bit of good. What is hard is to do good all one's life and never do anything bad. . . ." (*Quotations from Chairman Mao Tse-tung*, Bantam paperback edition, p. 141.)

A teeming world of oppressed coolies and concubines. Of cruel landlords. Of arrogant mandarins, arms crossed, long fingernails sheathed inside the wide sleeves of their robes. All mutating, peaceably, into Heavenly Girl & Boy Scouts as the Red Star mounts over China.

Why *not* want to be good?

But to be good one must be simpler. Simpler, as in a return to origins. Simpler, as in a great forgetting.

X

Once, leaving China to return to the United States to visit their child (or children), my father and M. took the train. On the Trans-Siberian Railroad, ten days without a dining car, they cooked in their compartment on a Sterno stove. Since just one breathful of cigarette smoke was enough to send my father into an asthmatic attack, M., who smokes, probably spent a lot of time in the corridor.
> —I am imagining this. M. never told me this, as she did tell me the following anecdote.

After crossing Stalin's Russia, M. wanted to get out when the train stopped in Bialystok, where her mother, who had died in Los Angeles

when M. was fourteen, had been born; but in the 1930s the doors of
the coaches reserved for foreigners were sealed.

> —The train stayed for several hours in the station.
> —Old women rapped on the icy windowpane, hoping to
> sell them tepid kvass and oranges.
> —M. wept.
> —She wanted to feel the ground of her mother's far-
> away birthplace under her feet. Just once.
> —She wasn't allowed to. (She would be arrested, she
> was warned, if she asked once more to step off the
> train for a minute.)
> —She wept.
>> —She didn't tell me that she wept, but I know she
>> did. I see her.

Sympathy. Legacy of loss. Women gather to speak bitterness. I have
been bitter.

Why *not* want to be good? A change of heart. (The heart, the most
exotic place of all.)

If I pardon M., I free myself. She has still not, after all these years,
forgiven her mother for dying. I shall forgive my father. For dying.

> —Shall David forgive his? (Not for dying.) For him to
> decide.

"The problems of individuals are fading away . . ."

XI

Somewhere, some place inside myself, I am detached. I have always
been detached (in part). Always.

> —Oriental detachment?
> —pride?
> —fear of pain?

With respect to pain, I have been ingenious.

After M. returned to the United States from China in early 1939, it
took several months for her to tell me my father wasn't coming back.
I was nearly through the first grade, where my classmates believed I
had been born in China. I knew, when she asked me to come into
the living room, that it was a solemn occasion.

    —Wherever I turned, squirming on the brocaded sofa,
       there were Buddhas to distract me.
    —She was brief.
    —I didn't cry long. I was already imagining how I would
       announce this new fact to my friends.
    —I was sent out to play.
    —I didn't really believe my father was dead.

Dearest M. I cannot telephone. I am six years old. My grief falls like snowflakes on the warm soil of your indifference. You are inhaling your own pain.

Grief ripened. My lungs wavered. My will got stronger. We went to the desert.

From *Le Potomak* by Cocteau (1919 edition, p. 66): "Il était, dans la ville de Tien-Sin, un papillon."

Somehow, my father had gotten left behind in Tientsin. It became even more important to have been conceived in China.

It seems even more important to go there now. History now compounds my personal, individual reasons. Bleaches them, displaces them, annihilates them. Thanks to the labors of the greatest world-historical figure since Napoleon.

Don't languish. Pain is not inevitable. Apply the gay science of Mao: "Be united, alert, earnest, and lively" (same edition, p. 81).

What does it mean, "be alert"? Each person alertly within himself, avoiding the collective drone?
        —All very well, except for the risk of accumulating too
          many truths.
        —Think of the damage to "be united."

Degree of alertness equals the degree to which one is not lazy, avoids habits. Be vigilant.

The truth is simple, very simple. Centered. But people crave other nourishment besides the truth. Its privileged distortions, in philosophy and literature. For example.

284 / SUSAN SONTAG

I honor my cravings, and I lose patience with them.

"Literature is only impatience on the part of knowledge." (Third and last quote from unnamed Austrian-Jewish sage who died, a refugee, in America.)

Already in possession of my visa, I am impatient to leave for China. To know. Will I be stopped by a conflict with literature?

A nonexistent conflict, according to Mao Tse-tung in his Yenan lectures and elsewhere, if literature serves the people.

But we are ruled by words. (Literature tells us what is happening to words.) More to the point, we are ruled by quotations. Not only in China, but everywhere else as well. So much for the transmissibility of the past! Disunite sentences, fracture memories.
>—When my memories become slogans, I no longer need
>them. No longer believe them.
>>—Another lie?
>>—An inadvertent truth?

Death doesn't die. And the problems of literature are not fading away . . .

XII

After walking across the Luhu Bridge spanning the Sham Chun River between Hong Kong and China, I will board a train for Canton.

From then on, I am in the hands of a committee. My hosts. My gracious bureaucratic Virgil. They control my itinerary. They know what they want me to see, what they deem proper for me to see; and I shall not argue with them. But when invited to make additional suggestions, what I shall tell them is: the farther north the better. I shall come closer.

I hate the cold. My desert childhood left me an intractable lover of heat, of tropics and deserts; but for this trip I'm willing to support as much cold as is necessary.
>—China has cold deserts, like the Gobi Desert.

Mythical voyage.

Before injustice and responsibility became too clear, and strident, mythical voyages were to places outside of history. Hell, for instance. The land of the dead.

Now such voyages are entirely circumscribed by history. Mythical voyages to places consecrated by the history of real peoples, and by one's own personal history.

The result is, inevitably, literature. More than it is knowledge.

Travel as accumulation. The colonialism of the soul, any soul, however well intentioned.
   —However chaste, however bent on being good.

At the border between literature and knowledge, the soul's orchestra breaks into a loud fugue. The traveler falters, trembles. Stutters.

Don't panic. But to continue the trip, neither colonialist nor native, requires ingenuity. Travel as decipherment. Travel as disburdenment. I am taking one small suitcase, and neither typewriter nor camera nor tape recorder. Hoping to resist the temptation to bring back any Chinese objects, however shapely, or any souvenirs, however evocative. When I already have so many in my head.

How impatient I am to leave for China! Yet even before leaving, part of me has already made the long trip that brings me to its border, traveled about the country, and come out again.

After walking across the Luhu Bridge spanning the Sham Chun River between China and Hong Kong, I will board a plane for Honolulu.
   —Where I have never been, either.
   —A stop of a few days. After three years I am exhausted
    by the nonexistent literature of unwritten letters and
    unmade telephone calls that passes between me
    and M.

After which I take another plane. To where I can be alone: at least, sheltered from the collective drone. And even from the tears of things, as bestowed—be it with relief or indifference—by the interminably self-pitying individual heart.

XIII

I shall cross the Sham Chun bridge both ways.

And after that? No one is surprised. Then comes literature.
        —The impatience of knowing
        —Self-mastery
        —Impatience in self-mastery

I would gladly consent to being silent. But then, alas, I'm unlikely to know anything. To renounce literature, I would have to be really sure that I could know. A certainty that would crassly prove my ignorance.

Literature, then. Literature before and after, if need be. Which does not release me from the demands of tact and humility required for this overdetermined trip. I am afraid of betraying so many contradictory claims.

The only solution: both to know and not to know. Literature and not literature, using the same verbal gestures.

Among the so-called romantics of the last century, a trip almost always resulted in the production of a book. One traveled to Rome, Athens, Jerusalem—and beyond—in order to write about it.

Perhaps I will write the book about my trip to China before I go.

(1972)

Debriefing

. . . Frail long hair, brown with reddish lights in it, artificial-looking hair, actressy hair, the hair she had at twenty-three when I met her (I was nineteen), hair too youthful to need tinting then, but too old now to have exactly the same color; a weary, dainty body with wide wrists, shy chest, broad-bladed shoulders, pelvic bones like gulls' wings; an absent body one might be reluctant to imagine undressed, which may explain why her clothes are never less than affected and are often regal; one husband in dark phallocratic mustache; unexpectedly successful East Side restaurant owner with dim Mafia patronage, separated from and then divorced in fussy stages; two flaxenhaired children, who look as if they have two other parents, safely evacuated to grassy boarding schools. "For the fresh air," she says.

Autumn in Central Park, several years ago. Lounging under a sycamore, our bicycles paired on their sides—Julia's was hers (she had once bicycled regularly), mine was rented—she admitted to finding less time lately for doing: going to an aikido class, cooking a meal, phoning the children, maintaining love affairs. But for wondering there seemed all the time in the world—hours, whole days.

Wondering?

"About . . ." she said, looking at the ground. "Oh, I might start wondering about the relation of that leaf"—pointing to one—"to that one"—pointing to a neighbor leaf, also yellowing, its frayed tip almost perpendicular to the first one's spine. "Why are they lying there just like that? Why not some other way?"

"I'll play. 'Cause that's how they fell down from the tree."

"But there's a relation, a connection . . ."

Julia, sister, poor moneyed waif, you're crazy. (A crazy question: one that shouldn't be asked.) But I didn't say that. I said: "You shouldn't ask yourself questions you can't answer." No reply. "Even if you could answer a question like that, you wouldn't know you had."

Look, Julia. Listen, Peter Pan. Instead of leaves—that's crazy—take people. Undoubtedly, between two and five this afternoon, eighty-four embittered Viet veterans are standing on line for welfare checks in a windowless downtown office while seventeen women sit in mauve leatherette chairs in a Park Avenue surgeon's lair waiting to be examined for breast cancer. But there's no point in trying to connect these two events.

Or is there?

Julia didn't ask me what I wonder about. Such as:

What Is Wrong

A thick brownish-yellow substance has settled in everyone's lungs—it comes from too much smoking, and from history. A constriction around the chest, nausea that follows each meal.

Julia, naturally lean, has managed lately to lose more weight. She told me last week that only bread and coffee don't make her ill. "Oh, no!" I groaned—we were talking on the phone. That evening I wanted to throw out the plastic envelope of pale hamburger at the back; she wouldn't let me. "Even chicken isn't cheap any more," she murmured.

She brewed some Nescafé and we sat cross-legged on the living-room tatami; after tales of her current lover, that brute, we passed to debating Lévi-Strauss on the closing off of history. I, pious to the end, defended history. Although she still wears sumptuous caftans and treats her lungs to Balkan Sobranies, the other reason she is not eating is that she's too stingy.

One thickness of pain at a time. Julia may not want to go out "at all," but many people no longer feel like leaving their apartments "often."

This city is neither a jungle nor the moon nor the Grand Hotel. In long shot: a cosmic smudge, a conglomerate of bleeding energies.

Close up, it is a fairly legible printed circuit, a transistorized labyrinth of beastly tracks, a data bank for asthmatic voice-prints. Only some of its citizens have the right to be amplified and become audible.

A black woman in her mid-fifties, wearing a brown cloth coat darker than the brown shopping bag she is carrying, gets into a cab, sighing. "143rd and St. Nicholas." Pause. "Okay?" After the wordless, hairy young driver turns on the meter, she settles the shopping bag between her fat knees and starts crying. On the other side of the scarred plastic partition, Esau can hear her.

With more people, there are more voices to tune out.

It is certainly possible that the black woman is Doris, Julia's maid (every Monday morning), who, a decade ago, while down on St. Nicholas Avenue buying a six-pack and some macaroni salad, lost both of her small children in a fire that partly destroyed their two-room apartment. But if it is Doris, she does not ask herself why they burned up just that much and no more, why the two bodies lay next to each other in front of the TV at exactly that angle. And if it is Doris, it is certainly not Monday, Miz Julia's day, because the brown paper bag holds cast-off clothing from the woman whose seven-room apartment she's just cleaned, and Julia never throws out or gives away any of her clothes.

It's not easy to clothe oneself. Since the Easter bombing in Bloomingdale's third-floor boutique section, shoppers in large department stores are body-searched as they enter. Veined city!

If it is not Doris, Julia's Doris, then perhaps it is Doris II, whose daughter (B.A., Hunter College, 1965), having been bewitched, now lives with a woman the same age as her mother, only fatter, muscularly fat, and rich: Roberta Jorrell, the Queen of the Black Arts; internationally known monologist poet, set designer, filmmaker, voice coach, originator of the Jorrell System of body awareness, movement, and functional coordination; and initiated voodoo priestess third-class. Doris II, also a maid, has not heard from her daughter in seven years, a captivity of biblical length that the girl has been serving as assistant stage manager of the Roberta Jorrell Total Black Theater Institute; bookkeeper for Jorrell real-estate holdings in Dakar, Cap-Haïtien, and Philadelphia; decipherer and typist of the two-volume correspondence between R.J. and Bertrand Russell; and on-call body servant to the woman whom no one, not even her husband, dares address as anything other than Miss Jorrell.

After taking Doris, if she is Doris, to 143rd and St. Nicholas, the taxi driver, stopping for a red light on 131st Street, has a knife set against his throat by three brown boys—two are eleven, one is twelve—and surrenders his money. Off-duty sign blazing, he quickly returns to his garage on West Fifty-fifth Street and unwinds in a corner, on the far side of the Coke machine, with a joint.

However, if it is not Doris but Doris II whom he has dropped at 143rd and St. Nicholas, the driver is not robbed but immediately gets a fare to 173rd and Vyse Avenue. He accepts. But he is afraid of getting lost, of never finding his way back. Writhing, uncontrollable city! In the years since the city stopped offering garbage collection to Morrisania and Hunts Point, the dogs that roam the streets have been subtly turning into coyotes.

Julia doesn't bathe enough. Suffering smells.

Several days later, a middle-aged black woman carrying a brown shopping bag climbs out of a subway in Greenwich Village and accosts the first middle-aged white woman who's passing by. "Excuse me, ma'am, but can you tell me the way to the Ladies' House of Detention?" This is Doris III, whose only daughter, age twenty-two, is well into her third ninety-day sentence for being a, et cetera.

We know more than we can use. Look at all this stuff I've got in my head: rockets and Venetian churches, David Bowie and Diderot, *nuoc mam* and Big Macs, sunglasses and orgasms. How many newspapers and magazines do you read? For me, they're what candy or Quääludes or scream therapy are for my neighbors. I get my daily ration from the bilious Lincoln Brigade veteran who runs a tobacco shop on 110th Street, not from the blind news agent in the wooden pillbox on Broadway, who's nearer my apartment.

And we don't know nearly enough.

What People Are Trying to Do

All around us, as far as I can see, people are striving to be ordinary. This takes a great deal of effort. Ordinariness, generally considered to be safer, has gotten much rarer than it used to be.

Julia called yesterday to report that, an hour before, she had gone downstairs to take in her laundry. I congratulated her.

People try to be interested in the surface. Men without guns are wearing mascara, glittering, prancing. Everyone's in some kind of moral drag.

People are trying not to mind, not to mind too much. Not to be afraid.

The daughter of Doris II has actually witnessed Roberta Jorrell—stately, unflinching—dip both hands up to the wrists in boiling oil, extract some shreds of cornmeal that she kneaded into a small pancake, and then briefly reimmerse pancake and hands. No pain, no scars. She had herself prepared by twenty hours of nonstop drumming and chanting, curtseying and asyncopated hand clapping; brackish holy water was passed around in a tin cup and sipped; and her limbs were smeared with goat's blood. After the ceremony, Doris II's daughter and four other followers, including Henry, the husband of Roberta Jorrell, escorted her back to the hotel suite in Pétionville. Henry was not allowed to stay on the same floor this trip. Miss Jorrell gave instructions that she would sleep for twenty hours and was not to be awakened for any reason. Doris II's daughter washed out Miss J's bloody robes and stationed herself on a wicker stool outside the bedroom door, waiting.

I try to get Julia to come out and play with me (fifteen years have gone by since we met): see the city. On different days and nights I've offered the roller derby in Brooklyn, a dog show, F. A. O. Schwarz, the Tibetan Museum on Staten Island, a women's march, a new singles' bar, midnight-to-dawn movies at the Elgin, Sunday's La Marqueta on upper Park Avenue, a poetry reading, anything. She invariably refuses. Once I got her to a performance of *Pelléas et Mélisande* at the old Met, but we had to leave at the intermission; Julia was trembling—with boredom, she claimed. Moments after the curtain rose on the Scene One set, a clearing in a dark forest, I knew it was a mistake. "Ne me touchez pas! Ne me touchez pas!" moans the heroine, leaning dangerously into a deep well. Her first words. The well-meaning stranger and would-be rescuer—equally lost—backs off, gazing lasciviously at the heroine's long hair; Julia shudders. Lesson: don't take Mélisande to see *Pelléas et Mélisande*.

After getting out of jail, Doris III's daughter is trying to quit the life. But she can't afford to: everything's gotten so expensive. From chicken, even wings and gizzards, to the Coromandel screen, once owned by a leading couturier of the 1930s, for which Lyle's mother bids $18,000 at a Parke-Bernet auction.

People are economizing. Those who like to eat—a category that includes most people, and excludes Julia—no longer do the week's marketing in an hour at one supermarket, but must give over most of a day, exploring ten stores to assemble a shopping cart's worth of food. They, too, are wandering about the city.

The affluent, having invested in their pocket calculators, are now seeking uses for them.

Unless already in a state of thralldom, like the daughter of Doris II, people are answering ads that magicians and healers place in newspapers. "You don't have to wait for pie in the sky by-and-by when you die. If you want your pie now with ice cream on top, then see and hear Rev. Ike on TV and in person." Rev. Ike's church is not, repeat not, located in Harlem. New churches without buildings are migrating from West to East: people are worshiping the devil. On Fifty-third Street west of the Museum of Modern Art, a blond boy with a shag cut who resembles Lyle tries to interest me in the Process Church of the Final Judgment. "Have you ever heard of the Process?" When I say yes, he goes on as if I'd said no. I'll never get into the 5:30 screening if I stop to talk to him, but I hand over a buck fifty for his magazine; and he keeps up with me, telling me about free breakfast programs the Process runs for poor children, until I spin into the museum's revolving door. Breakfast programs, indeed! I thought they ate little children.

People are videotaping their bedroom feats, tapping their own telephones.

My good deed for November 12: calling Julia after a lapse of three weeks. "Hey, how are you?" "Terrible," she answered, laughing. I laughed back and said, "So am I," which wasn't exactly true. Together we laughed some more; the receiver felt sleek and warm in my hand. "Want to meet?" I asked. "Could you come to my place again? I hate leaving the apartment these days." Dearest Julia, I know that already.

I try not to reproach Julia for throwing away her children.

Lyle, who is nineteen now, called me the other morning from a phone booth at Broadway and Ninety-sixth. I tell him to come up, and he brings me a story he's just completed, the first in years, which I read. It is not as accomplished as the stories that were published when he was eleven, an undergrown baby-voiced pale boy, the Mozart of *Partisan Review;* at eleven Lyle hadn't yet taken all that acid, gone temporarily blind, been a groupie on a cross-country Rolling Stones tour, gotten committed twice by his parents, or attempted three suicides—all before finishing his junior year at Bronx Science. Lyle, with my encouragement, agrees not to burn his story.

Taki 183, Pain 145, Turok 137, Charmin 65, Think 160, Snake 128, Hondo II, Stay High 149, Cobra 151, along with several of their friends, are sending insolent messages to Simone Weil—no Jewish-American Princess she. She tells them there is no end to suffering. You think that, they answer, because you had migraines. So do you, she says tartly. Only you don't know you have them.

She also says that the only thing more hateful than a "we" is an "I"—and they go on blazoning their names on the subway cars.

What Relieves, Soothes, Helps

It's a pleasure to share one's memories. Everything remembered is dear, endearing, touching, precious. At least the past is safe—though we didn't know it at the time. We know it now. Because it's in the past; because we have survived.

Doris, Julia's Doris, has decorated her living room with photographs, toys, and clothes of her two dead children, which, each time you visit her, you have to spend the first half hour examining. Dry-eyed, she shows you everything.

A cold wind comes shuddering over the city, the temperature drops. People are cold. But at least it clears off the pollution. From my roof on Riverside Drive, squinting through the acceptable air, I can see—across New Jersey—a rim of the Ramapo hills.

It helps to say no. One evening, when I drop by Julia's apartment to retrieve a book, her psychiatrist father calls. I'm expected to answer the phone: covering the mouthpiece, I whisper, "Cambridge!"

and, across the room, she whispers back, "Say I'm not home!" He knows I'm lying. "I know Julia never goes out," he says indignantly. "She would have," I say, "if she'd known you were going to call." Julia grins—heartbreaking, childish grin—and bites into a pomegranate I've brought her.

What helps is having the same feelings for a lifetime. At a fundraising party on Beekman Place for the New Democratic Coalition's alternate mayoral candidate, I flirt with an elderly Yiddish journalist who doesn't want to talk about quotas and school boycotts in Queens. He tells me about his childhood in a shtetl ten miles from Warsaw ("Of course, you never heard of a shtetl. You're too young. It was a village where the Jews lived"). He had been inseparable from another small boy. "I couldn't live without him. He was more to me than my brothers. But, you know, I didn't like him. I hated him. Whenever we played together, he would make me so mad. Sometimes we would hurt each other with sticks." Then he goes on to tell me how, last month, a shabby old man with stiff pink ears had come into the *Forward* office, had asked for him, had come over to his desk, had stood there, had said, "Walter Abramson, you know who I am?" And how he'd gazed into the old man's eyes, scrutinized his bald skull and shopping-bag body, and suddenly knew. "You're Isaac." And the old man said, "You're right."

"After fifty years, can you imagine? Honestly, I don't know how I recognized him," said the journalist. "It wasn't something in his eyes. But I did."

What happened? "So we fell into each other's arms. And I asked him about his family, and he told me they were all killed by the Nazis. And he asked me about my family, and I told him they were all killed . . . And you know what? After fifteen minutes, everything he said infuriated me. I didn't care any more if his whole family had been killed. I didn't care if he was a poor old man. I hated him." He trembled—with vitality. "I wanted to beat him. With a stick."

Sometimes it helps to change your feelings altogether, like getting your blood pumped out and replaced. To become another person. But without magic. There's no moral equivalent to the operation that makes transsexuals happy.

A sense of humor helps. I haven't explained that Julia is funny, droll, witty—that she can make me laugh. I've made her sound like nothing but a burden.

Sometimes it helps to be paranoid. Conspiracies have the merit of making sense. It's a relief to discover your enemies, even if first you have to invent them. Roberta Jorrell, for instance, has humorlessly instructed Doris II's daughter and others on her payroll exactly how to thwart the enemies of her federally funded South Philadelphia Black Redress Center—white bankers, AMA psychiatrists, Black Panthers, cops, Maoists, and the CIA—with powders, with hexes, and with preternaturally smooth flat stones blessed by a Cuban *santera* in Miami Beach. Julia, however, doesn't think she has any enemies—as, when her current lover again refuses to leave his wife, she still doesn't understand that she isn't loved. But when she goes down on the street, which happens less and less frequently, she finds the cars menacingly unpredictable.

Flight is said to help. Dean and Shirley, Lyle's parents, having pulled out of the market last year, have bought into a condominium in Sarasota, Florida, whose City Fathers recently voted, in order to make the city more seductive to tourists, to take out all the parking meters they installed downtown five years ago. Lyle's parents don't know how many weeks a year they can actually spend in the Ringling Brothers' home town; but there's never been a decade when real-estate values haven't gone up, right? And that crazy Quiz Kid, their son, will always have his room there if he wants it.

It helps to feel guiltless about your sexual options, though it's not clear that many people actually manage this. After eventually finding his way back from Hunts Point into the well-lit grid of more familiar predators, the driver who had taken Doris II to 143rd and St. Nicholas picks up a pale, blond boy with a shag cut who also resembles Lyle and who says, as he gets into the cab, "West Street and the trucks, please."

Lately, my sexual life has become very pure. I don't want it to be like a dirty movie. (Having enjoyed a lot of dirty movies, I don't want it to be like that.)

Let's lie down together, love, and hold each other.

Meanwhile, the real Lyle has again skipped his four o'clock class, Comp. Lit. 203 ("Sade and the Anarchist Tradition"), and is sprawled in front of a TV set in the dormitory lounge. He's been watching

296 / SUSAN SONTAG

more and more television lately, with a preference for serials like *Secret Storm* and *As the World Turns*. He has also started showing up at student parties, instead of rebuffing his roommate's kindly, clumsy invitations. A good rule: Any party is depressing, if you think about it. But you don't have to think about it.

I'm happy when I dance.

Touch me.

What Is Upsetting

To read *Last Letters from Stalingrad,* and grieve for those lost, all-too-human voices among the most devilish of enemies. No one is a devil if fully heard.

To find everyone crazy—example: both Lyle and his parents. And to find the crazy particularly audible.

To be afraid.

To know that Lyle will be introduced to Roberta Jorrell next week at an elegant SoHo loft party given in her honor after her speech at New York University; be recruited by her; drop out of college; and not be heard from again for at least seven years.

To feel how desperate everyone is. Doris, Julia's Doris, is being evicted from her apartment. She not only has no money to pay a higher rent; she wants to go on living in the place where her children perished.

To learn that the government—using information that the law now requires be recorded on tape and stored indefinitely by banks, the telephone company, airlines, credit-card companies—can know more about me (my more sociable activities, anyway) than I do myself. If necessary, I could list most of the plane trips I've taken; and my old checkbook stubs are in a drawer—somewhere. But I don't remember whom I telephoned exactly four months ago at 11 a.m., and never will. I don't think it was Julia.

To find in myself the desire to stop listening to people's distress.

To be unsure of how to exercise the powers I do possess.

Julia had once fallen under the spell of an ex-ESP researcher, then a specialist in the North American Indian occult, who claimed to know how to help her. Most people who meet Julia, stunned by her vulnerability, take a crack at helping her; the pleasure of her beauty, which is the only gift Julia has ever been able to make to other people, helps too. The sorceress in question, Martha Wooten, was white, Westchester-born, crisp, a superb tennis player—rather like a gym teacher; I thought, condescendingly, she might be good for Julia, until as part of a program for freeing Julia from her demons, she had her bay at the full moon on all fours. Then I swooped back into Julia's underfurnished life, performed my old rites of counter-exorcism—reason! self-preservation! pessimism of the intellect, optimism of the will!—and Martha Wooten vanished, metamorphosed, rather, into one of the Wicked Witches of the West, setting up in Big Sur as Lady Lambda, head of the only Lucifer cult that practices deep breathing and bioenergetic analysis.

Was I right to de-bewitch her?

To be unable to change one's life. Doris III's daughter is back in jail.

To live in bad air. To have an airless life. To feel there's no ground: that there is nothing but air.

Our Prospects

Aleatoric. Repetitious. On a Monday, after taking Doris, Julia's Doris, home from cleaning Julia's apartment, the taxi driver stops to pick up three fourteen-year-old Puerto Ricans on 111th and Second Avenue. If they don't rob him, they will get in the cab, ask to be taken to the juice bar in the alley by the Fifty-ninth Street Bridge, and give him a big tip.

Not good. A hand-lettered sign pasted at eye level on the bare brick wall of a housing project on the corner of Ninetieth and Amsterdam reads, plaintively: Stop Killing.

Wounded city!

Although none of the rules for becoming more alive is valid, it is healthy to keep on formulating them.

Here's a solid conservative rule, deposited by Goethe with Ecker-mann: "Every healthy effort is directed from the inner to the outer world." Put that in your hashish pipe and smoke it.

But let's say, or suppose, we're not up to being healthy. Then there's only one way left to get to the world. We could be glad of the world, if we were flying to it for refuge.

Actually, this world isn't just one world—now. As this city is actually layers of cities. Behind the many thicknesses of pain, try to connect with the single will for pleasure that moves even in the violence of streets and beds, of jails and opera houses.

In the words of Rev. Ike, "You Can Be Happy Now." By an extraordinary coincidence, there is one day when Doris, Doris II, and Doris III—who don't know each other—may all be found under the same roof: in Rev. Ike's United Church and Science of Living Institute, attending a 3 p.m. Sunday Healing and Blessing Meeting. As for their prospects of being happy: none of the three Dorises is convinced.

Julia . . . anybody! Hey, how are you? Terrible, yes. But you laughed.

Some of us will falter, but some of us will be brave. A middle-aged black woman in a brown coat carrying a brown suitcase leaves a bank and gets into a cab. "I'm going to the Port of Authority, please." Doris II is taking the bus to Philadelphia. After seven years, she's going to confront Roberta Jorrell and try to get her daughter back.

Some of us will get more craven. Meanwhile, most of us will never know what's happening.

Let's dig through the past. Let's admire whatever, whenever we can. But people now have such grudging sympathy for the past.

If I come out to dinner in my space suit, will you wear yours? We'll look like Dale and Flash Gordon, maybe, but who cares. What everybody thinks now: one can form an alliance only with the future.

The prospects are for more of the same. As always. But I refuse.

Suppose, just suppose, leaden soul, you would try to lead an exemplary life. To be kind, honorable, helpful, just. On whose authority?

And you'll never know, that way, what you most long to know. Wisdom requires a life that is singular in another way, that's perverse. To know more, you must conjure up all the lives there are, and then leave out whatever fails to please you. Wisdom is a ruthless business.

But what about those I love? Although I don't believe my friends can't get on without me, surviving isn't so easy; and I probably can't survive without them.

If we don't help each other, forlorn demented bricklayers who've forgotten the location of the building we were putting up . . .

"Taxi!" I hail a cab during the Wednesday afternoon rush hour and ask the driver to get to Julia's address as fast as he can. Something in her voice on the phone lately . . . But she seems all right when I come in. She'd even been out the day before to take a batik (made last year) to be framed; it will be ready in a week. And when I ask to borrow a back issue of a feminist magazine that I spy, under a pile of old newspapers, on the floor, she mentions three times that I must return it soon. I promise to come by next Monday. Reassured by the evidence of those petty forms that Julia's hold on life often takes, I'm ready to leave. But then she asks me to stay on, just a few minutes more, which means that it's changing; she wants to talk sadness. On cue, like an old vaudevillian, I go into my routines of secular ethical charm. They seem to work. She promises to try.

What I'm Doing

I leave the city often. But I always come back.

I made Lyle give me his story—his only copy, of course—knowing that, despite his promise, if I returned it to him, he'd burn it, as he's burned everything he's written since he was fifteen. I've given it to a magazine editor I know.

I exhort, I interfere. I'm impatient. For God's sake, it isn't *that* hard to live. One of the pieces of advice I give is: Don't suffer future pain. And whether or not the other person heeds my advice, at least I've learned something from what was said. I give fairly good advice to myself.

That late Wednesday afternoon I told Julia how stupid it would be if she committed suicide. She agreed. I thought I was convincing.

Two days later she left her apartment again and killed herself, showing me that she didn't mind doing something stupid.

I would. Even when I announce to friends that I'm going to do something stupid, I don't really think it is.

I want to save my soul, that timid wind.

Some nights, I dream of dragging Julia back by her long hair, just as she's about to jump into the river. Or I dream she's already in the river: I am standing on my roof, facing New Jersey; I look down and see her floating by, and I leap from the roof, half falling, half swooping like a bird, and seize her by the hair and pull her out.

Julia, darling Julia, you weren't supposed to lean any farther into the well—daring anyone with good intentions to come closer, to save you, to be kind. You were at least supposed to die in a warm bed—mute; surrounded by the guilty, clumsy people who adored you, leaving them frustrated and resentful of you to the end.

I'm not thinking of what the lordly polluted Hudson did to your body before you were found.

Julia, plastic face in the waxy casket, how could you be as old as you were? You're still the twenty-three-year-old who started an absurdly pedantic conversation with me on the steps of Widener Library—so thin; so prettily affected; so electric; so absent; so much younger than I, who was four years younger than you; so tired already; so exasperating; so moving. I want to hit you.

How I groaned under the burden of our friendship. But your death is heavier.

Why you went under while others, equally absent from their lives, survive is a mystery to me.

Say we are all asleep. Do we want to wake up?

Is it fair if I wake up and you, most of you, don't? Fair! you sneer. What's fair got to do with it? It's every soul for itself. But I didn't want to wake up without you.

You're the tears in things, I'm not. You weep for me, I'll weep for you. Help me, I don't want to weep for myself. I'm not giving up.

Sisyphus, I. I cling to my rock, you don't have to chain me. Stand back! I roll it up—up, up. And . . . down we go. I knew that would happen. See, I'm on my feet again. See, I'm starting to roll it up again. Don't try to talk me out of it. Nothing, nothing could tear me away from this rock.

(1973)

Under the Sign
of Saturn

Fascinating Fascism

I

First Exhibit. Here is a book of 126 splendid color photographs by Leni Riefenstahl, certainly the most ravishing book of photographs published anywhere in recent years. In the intractable mountains of the southern Sudan live about eight thousand aloof, godlike Nuba, emblems of physical perfection, with large, well-shaped, partly shaven heads, expressive faces, and muscular bodies that are depilated and decorated with scars; smeared with sacred gray-white ash, the men prance, squat, brood, wrestle on the arid slopes. And here is a fascinating layout of twelve black-and-white photographs of Riefenstahl on the back cover of *The Last of the Nuba*, also ravishing, a chronological sequence of expressions (from sultry inwardness to the grin of a Texas matron on safari) vanquishing the intractable march of aging. The first photograph was taken in 1927 when she was twenty-five and already a movie star, the most recent are dated 1969 (she is cuddling a naked African baby) and 1972 (she is holding a camera), and each of them shows some version of an ideal presence, a kind of imperishable beauty, like Elisabeth Schwarzkopf's, that only gets gayer and more metallic and healthier-looking with old age. And here is a biographical sketch of Riefenstahl on the dust jacket, and an introduction (unsigned) entitled "How Leni Riefenstahl came to study the Mesakin Nuba of Kordofan"—full of disquieting lies.

The introduction, which gives a detailed account of Riefenstahl's pilgrimage to the Sudan (inspired, we are told, by reading Hemingway's *The Green Hills of Africa* "one sleepless night in the mid-1950s"), laconically identifies the photographer as "something of a

mythical figure as a film-maker before the war, half-forgotten by a
nation which chose to wipe from its memory an era of its history."
Who (one hopes) but Riefenstahl herself could have thought up this
fable about what is mistily referred to as "a nation" which for some
unnamed reason "chose" to perform the deplorable act of cowardice
of forgetting "an era"—tactfully left unspecified—"of its history"?
Presumably, at least some readers will be startled by this coy allusion
to Germany and the Third Reich.

Compared with the introduction, the jacket of the book is positively
expansive on the subject of the photographer's career, parroting mis-
information that Riefenstahl has been dispensing for the last twenty
years.

> It was during Germany's blighted and momentous 1930s that Leni Rie-
> fenstahl sprang to international fame as a film director. She was born in
> 1902, and her first devotion was to creative dancing. This led to her par-
> ticipation in silent films, and soon she was herself making—and starring
> in—her own talkies, such as *The Mountain* (1929).
>
> These tensely romantic productions were widely admired, not least by
> Adolf Hitler, who, having attained power in 1933, commissioned Riefen-
> stahl to make a documentary on the Nuremberg Rally in 1934.

It takes a certain originality to describe the Nazi era as "Germany's
blighted and momentous 1930s," to summarize the events of 1933 as
Hitler's "having attained power," and to assert that Riefenstahl, most
of whose work was in its own decade correctly identified as Nazi
propaganda, enjoyed "international fame as a film director," ostensibly like her contemporaries Renoir, Lubitsch, and Flaherty. (Could
the publishers have let LR write the jacket copy herself? One hesitates to entertain so unkind a thought, although "her first devotion
was to creative dancing" is a phrase few native speakers of English
would be capable of.)

The facts are, of course, inaccurate or invented. Not only did Riefenstahl not make—or star in—a talkie called *The Mountain* (1929).
No such film exists. More generally: Riefenstahl did not first simply
participate in silent films and then, when sound came in, begin directing and starring in her own films. In all nine films she ever acted
in, Riefenstahl was the star; and seven of these she did not direct.
These seven films were: *The Holy Mountain* (*Der heilige Berg*, 1926),
The Big Jump (*Der grosse Sprung*, 1927), *The Fate of the House of
Habsburg* (*Das Schicksal derer von Habsburg*, 1929), *The White Hell
of Pitz Palü* (*Die weisse Hölle von Piz Palü*, 1929)—all silents—followed by *Avalanche* (*Stürme über dem Montblanc*, 1930), *White*

Frenzy (Der weisse Rausch, 1931), and *S.O.S. Iceberg (S.O.S. Eisberg,* 1932–1933). All but one were directed by Arnold Fanck, *auteur* of hugely successful Alpine epics since 1919, who made only two more films, both flops, after Riefenstahl left him to strike out on her own as a director in 1932. (The film not directed by Fanck is *The Fate of the House of Habsburg,* a royalist weepie made in Austria in which Riefenstahl played Marie Vetsera, Crown Prince Rudolf's companion at Mayerling. No print seems to have survived.)

Fanck's pop-Wagnerian vehicles for Riefenstahl were not just "tensely romantic." No doubt thought of as apolitical when they were made, these films now seem in retrospect, as Siegfried Kracauer has pointed out, to be an anthology of proto-Nazi sentiments. Mountain climbing in Fanck's films was a visually irresistible metaphor for unlimited aspiration toward the high mystic goal, both beautiful and terrifying, which was later to become concrete in Führer-worship. The character that Riefenstahl generally played was that of a wild girl who dares to scale the peak that others, the "valley pigs," shrink from. In her first role, in the silent *The Holy Mountain* (1926), that of a young dancer named Diotima, she is wooed by an ardent climber who converts her to the healthy ecstasies of Alpinism. This character underwent a steady aggrandizement. In her first sound film, *Avalanche* (1930), Riefenstahl is a mountain-possessed girl in love with a young meteorologist, whom she rescues when a storm strands him in his observatory on Mont Blanc.

Riefenstahl herself directed six films, the first of which, *The Blue Light (Das blaue Licht,* 1932), was another mountain film. Starring in it as well, Riefenstahl played a role similar to the ones in Fanck's films for which she had been so "widely admired, not least by Adolf Hitler," but allegorizing the dark themes of longing, purity, and death that Fanck had treated rather scoutishly. As usual, the mountain is represented as both supremely beautiful and dangerous, that majestic force which invites the ultimate affirmation of and escape from the self—into the brotherhood of courage and into death. The role Riefenstahl devised for herself is that of a primitive creature who has a unique relation to a destructive power: only Junta, the rag-clad outcast girl of the village, is able to reach the mysterious blue light radiating from the peak of Mount Cristallo, while other young villagers, lured by the light, try to climb the mountain and fall to their deaths. What eventually causes the girl's death is not the impossibility of the goal symbolized by the mountain but the materialist, prosaic spirit of envious villagers and the blind rationalism of her lover, a well-meaning visitor from the city.

The next film Riefenstahl directed after *The Blue Light* was not "a documentary on the Nuremberg Rally in 1934"—Riefenstahl made four nonfiction films, not two, as she has claimed since the 1950s and as most current whitewashing accounts of her repeat—but *Victory of the Faith* (*Sieg des Glaubens,* 1933), celebrating the first National Socialist Party Congress held after Hitler seized power. Then came the first of two works which did indeed make her internationally famous, the film on the next National Socialist Party Congress, *Triumph of the Will* (*Triumph des Willens,* 1935)—whose title is never mentioned on the jacket of *The Last of the Nuba*—after which she made a short film (eighteen minutes) for the army, *Day of Freedom: Our Army* (*Tag der Freiheit: Unsere Wehrmacht,* 1935), that depicts the beauty of soldiers and soldiering for the Führer. (It is not surprising to find no mention of this film, a print of which was found in 1971; during the 1950s and 1960s, when Riefenstahl and everyone else believed *Day of Freedom* to have been lost, she had it dropped from her filmography and refused to discuss it with interviewers.)

The jacket copy continues:

> Riefenstahl's refusal to submit to Goebbels' attempt to subject her visualisation to his strictly propagandistic requirements led to a battle of wills which came to a head when Riefenstahl made her film of the 1936 Olympic Games, *Olympia.* This, Goebbels attempted to destroy; and it was only saved by the personal intervention of Hitler.
>
> With two of the most remarkable documentaries of the 1930s to her credit, Riefenstahl continued making films of her devising, unconnected with the rise of Nazi Germany, until 1941, when war conditions made it impossible to continue.
>
> Her acquaintance with the Nazi leadership led to her arrest at the end of the Second World War: she was tried twice, and acquitted twice. Her reputation was in eclipse, and she was half forgotten—although to a whole generation of Germans her name had been a household word.

Except for the bit about her having once been a household word in Nazi Germany, not one part of the above is true. To cast Riefenstahl in the role of the individualist-artist, defying philistine bureaucrats and censorship by the patron state ("Goebbels' attempt to subject her visualisation to his strictly propagandistic requirements") should seem like nonsense to anyone who has seen *Triumph of the Will*—a film whose very conception negates the possibility of the filmmaker's having an aesthetic conception independent of propaganda. The facts, denied by Riefenstahl since the war, are that she made *Triumph of the Will* with unlimited facilities and unstinting official cooperation (there was never any struggle between the filmmaker and the German minister of propaganda). Indeed, Riefenstahl was, as she relates in the short book about the making of *Triumph of the Will,* in on the planning of the rally—which was from the start conceived as the set of a film spectacle.* *Olympia*—a three-and-a-half-hour film in two parts, *Festival of the People (Fest der Völker)* and *Festival of Beauty (Fest der Schönheit)*—was no less an official production. Riefenstahl has maintained in interviews since the 1950s that *Olympia* was commissioned by the International Olympic Committee, produced by her own company, and made over Goebbels's protests. The truth is that *Olympia* was commissioned and entirely financed by the Nazi government (a dummy company was set up in Riefenstahl's name because it was thought unwise for the government to appear as the producer) and facilitated by Goebbels's ministry at every stage of the shooting; † even the plausible-sounding legend of Goebbels objecting to her footage of the triumphs of the black American track star Jesse Owens is untrue. Riefenstahl worked for eighteen months on the editing, finishing in time so that the film could have its world premiere on April 29, 1938, in Berlin, as part of the festivities for Hitler's forty-ninth birthday; later that year *Olympia* was the principal German entry at the Venice Film Festival, where it won the Gold Medal.

More lies: to say that Riefenstahl "continued making films of her devising, unconnected with the rise of Nazi Germany, until 1941." In 1939 (after returning from a visit to Hollywood, the guest of Walt Disney), she accompanied the invading Wehrmacht into Poland as a uniformed army war correspondent with her own camera team; but there is no record of any of this material surviving the war. After *Olympia* Riefenstahl made exactly one more film, *Tiefland* (*Lowland*), which she began in 1941—and, after an interruption, resumed in 1944 (in the Barrandov Film Studios in Nazi-occupied Prague), and finished in 1954. Like *The Blue Light,* *Tiefland* opposes lowland

*Leni Riefenstahl, *Hinter den Kulissen des Reichparteitag-Films* (Munich, 1935). A photograph on page 31 shows Hitler and Riefenstahl bending over some plans, with the caption: "The preparations for the Party Congress were made hand in hand with the preparations for the camera work." The rally was held on September 4–10; Riefenstahl relates that she began work in May, planning the film sequence by sequence, and supervising the construction of elaborate bridges, towers, and tracks for the cameras. In late August, Hitler came to Nuremberg with Viktor Lutze, head of the SA, "for an inspection and to give final instructions." Her thirty-two cameramen were dressed in SA uniforms throughout the shooting, "a suggestion of the Chief of Staff [Lutz], so that no one will disturb the solemnity of the image with his civilian clothing." The SS supplied a team of guards.

†See Hans Barkhausen, "Footnote to the History of Riefenstahl's 'Olympia,'" *Film Quarterly,* Fall 1974—a rare act of informed dissent amid the large number of tributes to Riefenstahl that have appeared in American and Western European film magazines during the last few years.

or valley corruption to mountain purity, and once again the protagonist (played by Riefenstahl) is a beautiful outcast. Riefenstahl prefers
to give the impression that there were only two documentaries in a
long career as a director of fiction films, but the truth is that four of
the six films she directed were documentaries made for and financed
by the Nazi government.

It is hardly accurate to describe Riefenstahl's professional relationship to and intimacy with Hitler and Goebbels as "her acquaintance
with the Nazi leadership." Riefenstahl was a close friend and companion of Hitler's well before 1932; she was a friend of Goebbels, too:
no evidence supports Riefenstahl's persistent claim since the 1950s
that Goebbels hated her, or even that he had the power to interfere
with her work. Because of her unlimited personal access to Hitler,
Riefenstahl was precisely the only German filmmaker who was not
responsible to the Film Office (Reichsfilmkammer) of Goebbels's
ministry of propaganda. Last, it is misleading to say that Riefenstahl
was "tried twice, and acquitted twice" after the war. What happened
is that she was briefly arrested by the Allies in 1945 and two of her
houses (in Berlin and Munich) were seized. Examinations and court
appearances started in 1948, continuing intermittently until 1952,
when she was finally "de-Nazified" with the verdict: "No political
activity in support of the Nazi regime which would warrant punishment." More important: whether or not Riefenstahl deserved a prison
sentence, it was not her "acquaintance" with the Nazi leadership but
her activities as a leading propagandist for the Third Reich that were
at issue.

The jacket copy of *The Last of the Nuba* summarizes faithfully the
main line of the self-vindication which Riefenstahl fabricated in the
1950s and which is most fully spelled out in the interview she gave
to *Cahiers du Cinéma* in September 1965. There she denied that any
of her work was propaganda—calling it cinema verité. "Not a single
scene is staged," Riefenstahl says of *Triumph of the Will.* "Everything is genuine. And there is no tendentious commentary for the
simple reason that there is no commentary at all. It is *history—pure
history.*" We are a long way from that vehement disdain for "the
chronicle-film," mere "reportage" or "filmed facts," as being unwor-
thy of the event's "heroic style" which is expressed in her book on
the making of the film.*

* If another source is wanted—since Riefenstahl now claims (in an interview in the
German magazine *Filmkritik,* August 1972) that she didn't write a single word of
Hinter den Kulissen des Reichparteitag-Films, or even read it at the time—there is an
interview in the *Völkischer Beobachter,* August 26, 1933, about her filming of the 1933
Nuremberg rally, where she makes similar declarations.

Although *Triumph of the Will* has no narrative voice, it does open
with a written text heralding the rally as the redemptive culmination
of German history. But this opening statement is the least original of
the ways in which the film is tendentious. It has no commentary
because it doesn't need one, for *Triumph of the Will* represents an
already achieved and radical transformation of reality: history become
theater. How the 1934 Party convention was staged was partly determined by the decision to produce *Triumph of the Will*—the historic
event serving as the set of a film which was then to assume the
character of an authentic documentary. Indeed, when some of the
footage of Party leaders at the speakers' rostrum was spoiled, Hitler
gave orders for the shots to be refilmed; and Streicher, Rosenberg,
Hess, and Frank histrionically repledged their fealty to the Führer
weeks later, without Hitler and without an audience, on a studio set
built by Speer. (It is altogether correct that Speer, who built the gigantic site of the rally on the outskirts of Nuremberg, is listed in the
credits of *Triumph of the Will* as architect of the film.) Anyone who
defends Riefenstahl's films as documentaries, if documentary is to be
distinguished from propaganda, is being ingenuous. In *Triumph of
the Will,* the document (the image) not only is the record of reality
but is one reason for which the reality has been constructed, and
must eventually supersede it.

The rehabilitation of proscribed figures in liberal societies does not
happen with the sweeping bureaucratic finality of the *Soviet Encyclopedia,* each new edition of which brings forward some hitherto
unmentionable figures and lowers an equal or greater number through
the trap door of nonexistence. Our rehabilitations are smoother, more

---

Riefenstahl and her apologists always talk about *Triumph of the Will* as if it were an
independent "documentary," often citing technical problems encountered while filming to prove she had enemies among the Party leadership (Goebbels's hatred), as if
such difficulties were not a normal part of filmmaking. One of the more dutiful reruns
of the myth of Riefenstahl as mere documentarist—and political innocent—is the *Filmguide to "Triumph of the Will"* published in the Indiana University Press Filmguide
Series, whose author, Richard Meram Barsam, concludes his preface by expressing
his "gratitude to Leni Riefenstahl herself, who cooperated in many hours of interviews,
opened her archive to my research, and took a genuine interest in this book." Well
might she take an interest in a book whose opening chapter is "Leni Riefenstahl and
the Burden of Independence," and whose theme is "Riefenstahl's belief that the artist
must, at all costs, remain independent of the material world. In her own life, she has
achieved artistic freedom, but at a great cost." Etc.

As an antidote, let me quote an unimpeachable source (at least he's not here to say
he didn't write it)—Adolf Hitler. In his brief preface to *Hinter den Kulissen,* Hitler
describes *Triumph of the Will* as "a totally unique and incomparable glorification of
the power and beauty of our Movement." And it is.

insinuative. It is not that Riefenstahl's Nazi past has suddenly become acceptable. It is simply that, with the turn of the cultural wheel, it no longer matters. Instead of dispensing a freeze-dried version of history from above, a liberal society settles such questions by waiting for cycles of taste to distill out the controversy.

The purification of Leni Riefenstahl's reputation of its Nazi dross has been gathering momentum for some time, but it has reached some kind of climax this year, with Riefenstahl the guest of honor at a new cinéphile-controlled film festival held in the summer in Colorado and the subject of a stream of respectful articles and interviews in newspapers and on TV, and now with the publication of *The Last of the Nuba*. Part of the impetus behind Riefenstahl's recent promotion to the status of a cultural monument surely owes to the fact that she is a woman. The 1973 New York Film Festival poster, made by a well-known artist who is also a feminist, showed a blond doll-woman whose right breast is encircled by three names: Agnès Leni Shirley. (That is, Varda, Riefenstahl, Clarke.) Feminists would feel a pang at having to sacrifice the one woman who made films that everybody acknowledges to be first-rate. But the strongest impetus behind the change in attitude toward Riefenstahl lies in the new, ampler fortunes of the idea of the beautiful.

The line taken by Riefenstahl's defenders, who now include the most influential voices in the avant-garde film establishment, is that she was always concerned with beauty. This, of course, has been Riefenstahl's own contention for some years. Thus the *Cahiers du Cinéma* interviewer set Riefenstahl up by observing fatuously that what *Triumph of the Will* and *Olympia* "have in common is that they both give form to a certain reality, itself based on a certain idea of form. Do you see anything peculiarly German about this concern for form?" To this, Riefenstahl answered:

> I can simply say that I feel spontaneously attracted by everything that is beautiful. Yes: beauty, harmony. And perhaps this care for composition, this aspiration to form is in effect something very German. But I don't know these things myself, exactly. It comes from the unconscious and not from my knowledge. . . . What do you want me to add? Whatever is purely realistic, slice-of-life, which is average, quotidian, doesn't interest me. . . . I am fascinated by what is beautiful, strong, healthy, what is living. I seek harmony. When harmony is produced I am happy. I believe, with this, that I have answered you.

That is why *The Last of the Nuba* is the last, necessary step in Riefenstahl's rehabilitation. It is the final rewrite of the past; or, for her partisans, the definitive confirmation that she was always a beauty freak rather than a horrid propagandist.* Inside the beautifully produced book, photographs of the perfect, noble tribe. And on the jacket, photographs of "my perfect German woman" (as Hitler called Riefenstahl), vanquishing the slights of history, all smiles.

Admittedly, if the book were not signed by Riefenstahl one would not necessarily suspect that these photographs had been taken by the most interesting, talented, and effective artist of the Nazi era. Most people who leaf through *The Last of the Nuba* will probably see it as one more lament for vanishing primitives—the greatest example remains Lévi-Strauss in *Tristes Tropiques* on the Bororo Indians in Brazil—but if the photographs are examined carefully, in conjunction with the lengthy text written by Riefenstahl, it becomes clear that they are continuous with her Nazi work. Riefenstahl's particular slant is revealed by her choice of this tribe and not another: a people she describes as acutely artistic (everyone owns a lyre) and beautiful (Nuba men, Riefenstahl notes, "have an athletic build rare in any other African tribe"); endowed as they are with "a much stronger sense of spiritual and religious relations than of worldly and material matters," their principal activity, she insists, is ceremonial. *The Last of the Nuba* is about a primitivist ideal: a portrait of a people subsisting in a pure harmony with their environment, untouched by "civilization."

All four of Riefenstahl's commissioned Nazi films—whether about Party congresses, the Wehrmacht, or athletes—celebrate the rebirth of the body and of community, mediated through the worship of an irresistible leader. They follow directly from the films of Fanck in which she starred and her own *The Blue Light*. The Alpine fictions are tales of longing for high places, of the challenge and ordeal of the elemental, the primitive; they are about the vertigo before power, symbolized by the majesty and beauty of mountains. The Nazi films are epics of achieved community, in which everyday reality is transcended through ecstatic self-control and submission; they are about the triumph of power. And *The Last of the Nuba,* an elegy for the soon-to-be extinguished beauty and mystic powers of primitives whom

*This is how Jonas Mekas (*The Village Voice,* October 31, 1974) salutes the publication of *The Last of the Nuba:* "Riefenstahl continues her celebration—or is it a search?— of the classical beauty of the human body, the search which she began in her films. She is interested in the ideal, in the monumental." Mekas in the same paper on November 7, 1974: "And here is my own final statement on Riefenstahl's films: If you are an idealist, you'll see idealism in her films; if you are a classicist, you'll see in her films an ode to classicism; if you are a Nazi, you'll see in her films Nazism."

Riefenstahl calls "her adopted people," is the third in her triptych of fascist visuals.

In the first panel, the mountain films, heavily dressed people strain upward to prove themselves in the purity of the cold; vitality is identified with physical ordeal. For the middle panel, the films made for the Nazi government: *Triumph of the Will* uses overpopulated wide shots of massed figures alternating with close-ups that isolate a single passion, a single perfect submission: in a temperate zone clean-cut people in uniforms group and regroup, as if they were seeking the perfect choreography to express their fealty. In *Olympia*, the richest visually of all her films (it uses both the verticals of the mountain films and the horizontal movements characteristic of *Triumph of the Will*), one straining, scantily clad figure after another seeks the ecstasy of victory, cheered on by ranks of compatriots in the stands, all under the still gaze of the benign Super-Spectator, Hitler, whose presence in the stadium consecrates this effort. (*Olympia*, which could as well have been called *Triumph of the Will*, emphasizes that there are no easy victories.) In the third panel, *The Last of the Nuba*, the almost naked primitives, awaiting the final ordeal of their proud heroic community, their imminent extinction, frolic and pose under the scorching sun.

It is Götterdämmerung time. The central events in Nuba society are wrestling matches and funerals: vivid encounters of beautiful male bodies and death. The Nuba, as Riefenstahl interprets them, are a tribe of aesthetes. Like the henna-daubed Masai and the so-called Mudmen of New Guinea, the Nuba paint themselves for all important social and religious occasions, smearing on a white-gray ash which unmistakably suggests death. Riefenstahl claims to have arrived "just in time," for in the few years since these photographs were taken the glorious Nuba have been corrupted by money, jobs, clothes. (And, probably, by war—which Riefenstahl never mentions, since what she cares about is myth not history. The civil war that has been tearing up that part of the Sudan for a dozen years must have scattered new technology and a lot of detritus.)

Although the Nuba are black, not Aryan, Riefenstahl's portrait of them evokes some of the larger themes of Nazi ideology: the contrast between the clean and the impure, the incorruptible and the defiled, the physical and the mental, the joyful and the critical. A principal accusation against the Jews within Nazi Germany was that they were urban, intellectual, bearers of a destructive corrupting "critical spirit." The book bonfire of May 1933 was launched with Goebbels's cry: "The age of extreme Jewish intellectualism has now ended, and the success of the German revolution has again given the right of way to the German spirit." And when Goebbels officially forbade art criticism in November 1936, it was for having "typically Jewish traits of character": putting the head over the heart, the individual over the community, intellect over feeling. In the transformed thematics of latter-day fascism, the Jews no longer play the role of defiler. It is "civilization" itself.

What is distinctive about the fascist version of the old idea of the Noble Savage is its contempt for all that is reflective, critical, and pluralistic. In Riefenstahl's casebook of primitive virtue, it is hardly—as in Lévi-Strauss—the intricacy and subtlety of primitive myth, social organization, or thinking that is being extolled. Riefenstahl strongly recalls fascist rhetoric when she celebrates the ways the Nuba are exalted and unified by the physical ordeals of their wrestling matches, in which the "heaving and straining" Nuba men, "huge muscles bulging," throw one another to the ground—fighting not for material prizes but "for the renewal of the sacred vitality of the tribe." Wrestling and the rituals that go with it, in Riefenstahl's account, bind the Nuba together. Wrestling

> is the expression of all that distinguishes the Nuba way of life. . . . Wrestling generates the most passionate loyalty and emotional participation in the team's supporters, who are, in fact, the entire "non-playing" population of the village. . . . Its importance as the expression of the total outlook of the Mesakin and Korongo cannot be exaggerated; it is the expression in the visible and social world of the invisible world of the mind and of the spirit.

In celebrating a society where the exhibition of physical skill and courage and the victory of the stronger man over the weaker are, as she sees it, the unifying symbols of the communal culture—where success in fighting is the "main aspiration of a man's life"—Riefenstahl seems hardly to have modified the ideas of her Nazi films. And her portrait of the Nuba goes further than her films in evoking one aspect of the fascist ideal: a society in which women are merely breeders and helpers, excluded from all ceremonial functions, and represent a threat to the integrity and strength of men. From the "spiritual" Nuba point of view (by the Nuba Riefenstahl means, of course, males), contact with women is profane; but, ideal society that this is supposed to be, the women know their place.

> The fiancées or wives of the wrestlers are as concerned as the men to avoid any intimate contact . . . their pride at being the bride or wife of a strong wrestler supersedes their amorousness.

Lastly, Riefenstahl is right on target with her choice as a photographic subject of a people who "look upon death as simply a matter of fate—which they do not resist or struggle against," of a society whose most enthusiastic and lavish ceremonial is the funeral. Viva la muerte.

It may seem ungrateful and rancorous to refuse to cut loose *The Last of the Nuba* from Riefenstahl's past, but there are salutary lessons to be learned from the continuity of her work as well as from that curious and implacable recent event—her rehabilitation. The careers of other artists who became fascists, such as Céline and Benn and Marinetti and Pound (not to mention those, like Pabst and Pirandello and Hamsun, who embraced fascism in the decline of their powers), are not instructive in a comparable way. For Riefenstahl is the only major artist who was completely identified with the Nazi era and whose work, not only during the Third Reich but thirty years after its fall, has consistently illustrated many themes of fascist aesthetics.

Fascist aesthetics include but go far beyond the rather special celebration of the primitive to be found in *The Last of the Nuba*. More generally, they flow from (and justify) a preoccupation with situations of control, submissive behavior, extravagant effort, and the endurance of pain; they endorse two seemingly opposite states, egomania and servitude. The relations of domination and enslavement take the form of a characteristic pageantry: the massing of groups of people; the turning of people into things; the multiplication or replication of things; and the grouping of people/things around an all-powerful, hypnotic leader-figure or force. The fascist dramaturgy centers on the orgiastic transactions between mighty forces and their puppets, uniformly garbed and shown in ever swelling numbers. Its choreography alternates between ceaseless motion and a congealed, static, "virile" posing. Fascist art glorifies surrender, it exalts mindlessness, it glamorizes death.

Such art is hardly confined to works labeled as fascist or produced under fascist governments. (To cite films only: Walt Disney's *Fantasia,* Busby Berkeley's *The Gang's All Here,* and Kubrick's *2001* also strikingly exemplify certain formal structures and themes of fascist art.) And, of course, features of fascist art proliferate in the official art of communist countries—which always presents itself under the banner of realism, while fascist art scorns realism in the name of "idealism." The tastes for the monumental and for mass obeisance to the hero are common to both fascist and communist art, reflecting the view of all totalitarian regimes that art has the function of "immortalizing" its leaders and doctrines. The rendering of movement in grandiose and rigid patterns is another element in common, for such choreography rehearses the very unity of the polity. The masses are made to take form, be design. Hence mass athletic demonstrations, a choreographed display of bodies, are a valued activity in all totalitarian countries; and the art of the gymnast, so popular now in Eastern Europe, also evokes recurrent features of fascist aesthetics; the holding in or confining of force; military precision.

In both fascist and communist politics, the will is staged publicly, in the drama of the leader and the chorus. What is interesting about the relation between politics and art under National Socialism is not that art was subordinated to political needs, for this is true of dictatorships both of the right and of the left, but that politics appropriated the rhetoric of art—art in its late romantic phase. (Politics is "the highest and most comprehensive art there is," Goebbels said in 1933, "and we who shape modern German policy feel ourselves to be artists . . . the task of art and the artist [being] to form, to give shape, to remove the diseased and create freedom for the healthy.") What is interesting about art under National Socialism are those features which make it a special variant of totalitarian art. The official art of countries like the Soviet Union and China aims to expound and reinforce a utopian morality. Fascist art displays a utopian aesthetics— that of physical perfection. Painters and sculptors under the Nazis often depicted the nude, but they were forbidden to show any bodily imperfections. Their nudes look like pictures in physique magazines: pinups which are both sanctimoniously asexual and (in a technical sense) pornographic, for they have the perfection of a fantasy. Riefenstahl's promotion of the beautiful and the healthy, it must be said, is much more sophisticated than this; and never witless, as it is in other Nazi visual art. She appreciates a range of bodily types—in matters of beauty she is not racist—and in *Olympia* she does show some effort and strain, with its attendant imperfections, as well as stylized, seemingly effortless exertions (such as diving, in the most admired sequence of the film).

In contrast to the asexual chasteness of official communist art, Nazi art is both prurient and idealizing. A utopian aesthetics (physical perfection; identity as a biological given) implies an ideal eroticism: sexuality converted into the magnetism of leaders and the joy of followers. The fascist ideal is to transform sexual energy into a "spiritual" force, for the benefit of the community. The erotic (that is, women) is always present as a temptation, with the most admirable response being a heroic repression of the sexual impulse. Thus Riefenstahl explains why Nuba marriages, in contrast to their splendid funerals, involve no ceremonies or feasts.

> A Nuba man's greatest desire is not union with a woman but to be a good wrestler, thereby affirming the principle of abstemiousness. The Nuba dance ceremonies are not sensual occasions but rather "festivals of chastity"—of containment of the life force.

Fascist aesthetics is based on the containment of vital forces; movements are confined, held tight, held in.

Nazi art is reactionary, defiantly outside the century's mainstream of achievement in the arts. But just for this reason it has been gaining a place in contemporary taste. The left-wing organizers of a current exhibition of Nazi painting and sculpture (the first since the war) in Frankfurt have found, to their dismay, the attendance excessively large and hardly as serious-minded as they had hoped. Even when flanked by didactic admonitions from Brecht and by concentration-camp photographs, what Nazi art reminds these crowds of is—other art of the 1930s, notably Art Deco. (Art Nouveau could never be a fascist style; it is, rather, the prototype of that art which fascism defines as decadent; the fascist style at its best is Art Deco, with its sharp lines and blunt massing of material, its petrified eroticism.) The same aesthetic responsible for the bronze colossi of Arno Breker—Hitler's (and, briefly, Cocteau's) favorite sculptor—and of Josef Thorak also produced the muscle-bound Atlas in front of Manhattan's Rockefeller Center and the faintly lewd monument to the fallen doughboys of World War I in Philadelphia's Thirtieth Street railroad station.

To an unsophisticated public in Germany, the appeal of Nazi art may have been that it was simple, figurative, emotional; not intellectual; a relief from the demanding complexities of modernist art. To a more sophisticated public, the appeal is partly to that avidity which is now bent on retrieving all the styles of the past, especially the most pilloried. But a revival of Nazi art, following the revivals of Art Nouveau, Pre-Raphaelite painting, and Art Deco, is most unlikely. The painting and sculpture are not just sententious; they are astonishingly meager as art. But precisely these qualities invite people to look at Nazi art with knowing and sniggering detachment, as a form of Pop Art.

Riefenstahl's work is free of the amateurism and naïveté one finds in other art produced in the Nazi era, but it still promotes many of the same values. And the same very modern sensibility can appreciate her as well. The ironies of Pop sophistication make for a way of looking at Riefenstahl's work in which not only its formal beauty but its political fervor are viewed as a form of aesthetic excess. And alongside this detached appreciation of Riefenstahl is a response, whether conscious or unconscious, to the subject itself, which gives her work its power.

Triumph of the Will and *Olympia* are undoubtedly superb films (they may be the two greatest documentaries ever made), but they are not really important in the history of cinema as an art form. Nobody making films today alludes to Riefenstahl, while many filmmakers (including myself) regard Dziga Vertov as an inexhaustible provocation and source of ideas about film language. Yet it is arguable that Vertov—the most important figure in documentary films—never made a film as purely effective and thrilling as *Triumph of the Will* or *Olympia*. (Of course, Vertov never had the means at his disposal that Riefenstahl had. The Soviet government's budget for propaganda films in the 1920s and early 1930s was less than lavish.)

In dealing with propagandistic art on the left and on the right, a double standard prevails. Few people would admit that the manipulation of emotion in Vertov's later films and in Riefenstahl's provides similar kinds of exhilaration. When explaining why they are moved, most people are sentimental in the case of Vertov and dishonest in the case of Riefenstahl. Thus Vertov's work evokes a good deal of moral sympathy on the part of his cinéphile audiences all over the world; people consent to be moved. With Riefenstahl's work, the trick is to filter out the noxious political ideology of her films, leaving only their "aesthetic" merits. Praise of Vertov's films always presupposes the knowledge that he was an attractive person and an intelligent and original artist-thinker, eventually crushed by the dictatorship which he served. And most of the contemporary audience for Vertov (as for Eisenstein and Pudovkin) assumes that the film propagandists in the early years of the Soviet Union were illustrating a noble ideal, however much it was betrayed in practice. But praise of Riefenstahl has no such recourse, since nobody, not even her rehabilitators, has managed to make Riefenstahl seem even likable; and she is no thinker at all.

More important, it is generally thought that National Socialism stands only for brutishness and terror. But this is not true. National Socialism—more broadly, fascism—also stands for an ideal or rather ideals that are persistent today under the other banners: the ideal of life as art, the cult of beauty, the fetishism of courage, the dissolution of alienation in ecstatic feelings of community; the repudiation of the intellect; the family of man (under the parenthood of leaders). These ideals are vivid and moving to many people, and it is dishonest as well as tautological to say that one is affected by *Triumph of the Will* and *Olympia* only because they were made by a filmmaker of genius. Riefenstahl's films are still effective because, among other reasons, their longings are still felt, because their content is a romantic ideal to which many continue to be attached and which is expressed in such diverse modes of cultural dissidence and propaganda for new forms of community as the youth/rock culture, primal therapy, anti-psychiatry, Third World camp-following, and belief in the occult. The exaltation of community does not preclude the search for absolute leadership; on the contrary, it may inevitably lead to it. (Not surprisingly, a fair number of the young people now prostrating themselves before gurus and submitting to the most grotesquely autocratic discipline are former anti-authoritarians and anti-elitists of the 1960s.)

Riefenstahl's current de-Nazification and vindication as indomitable priestess of the beautiful—as a filmmaker and, now, as a photographer—do not augur well for the keenness of current abilities to detect the fascist longings in our midst. Riefenstahl is hardly the usual sort of aesthete or anthropological romantic. The force of her work being precisely in the continuity of its political and aesthetic ideas, what is interesting is that this was once seen so much more clearly than it seems to be now, when people claim to be drawn to Riefenstahl's images for their beauty of composition. Without a historical perspective, such connoisseurship prepares the way for a curiously absentminded acceptance of propaganda for all sorts of destructive feelings—feelings whose implications people are refusing to take seriously. Somewhere, of course, everyone knows that more than beauty is at stake in art like Riefenstahl's. And so people hedge their bets—admiring this kind of art, for its undoubted beauty, and patronizing it, for its sanctimonious promotion of the beautiful. Backing up the solemn choosy formalist appreciations lies a larger reserve of appreciation, the sensibility of camp, which is unfettered by the scruples of high seriousness: and the modern sensibility relies on continuing trade-offs between the formalist approach and camp taste.

Art which evokes the themes of fascist aesthetic is popular now, and for most people it is probably no more than a variant of camp. Fascism may be merely fashionable, and perhaps fashion with its irrepressible promiscuity of taste will save us. But the judgments of taste themselves seem less innocent. Art that seemed eminently worth defending ten years ago, as a minority or adversary taste, no longer seems defensible today, because the ethical and cultural issues it raises have become serious, even dangerous, in a way they were not then. The hard truth is that what may be acceptable in elite culture may not be acceptable in mass culture, that tastes which pose only innocuous ethical issues as the property of a minority become corrupting when they become more established. Taste is context, and the context has changed.

II

Second Exhibit. Here is a book to be purchased at airport magazine stands and in "adult" bookstores, a relatively cheap paperback, not an expensive coffee-table item appealing to art lovers and the *bien-pensant* like *The Last of the Nuba*. Yet both books share a certain community of moral origin, a root preoccupation: the same preoccupation at different stages of evolution—the ideas that animate *The Last of the Nuba* being less out of the moral closet than the cruder, more efficient idea that lies behind *SS Regalia*. Though *SS Regalia* is a respectable British-made compilation (with a three-page historical preface and notes in the back), one knows that its appeal is not scholarly but sexual. The cover already makes that clear. Across the large black swastika of an SS armband is a diagonal yellow stripe which reads "Over 100 Brilliant Four-Color Photographs Only $2.95," exactly as a sticker with the price on it used to be affixed—part tease, part deference to censorship—on the cover of pornographic magazines, over the model's genitalia.

There is a general fantasy about uniforms. They suggest community, order, identity (through ranks, badges, medals, things which declare who the wearer is and what he has done: his worth is recognized), competence, legitimate authority, the legitimate exercise of violence. But uniforms are not the same thing as photographs of uniforms—which are erotic materials and photographs of SS uniforms are the units of a particularly powerful and widespread sexual fantasy. Why the SS? Because the SS was the ideal incarnation of fascism's overt assertion of the righteousness of violence, the right to have total power over others and to treat them as absolutely inferior. It was in the SS that this assertion seemed most complete, because they acted it out in a singularly brutal and efficient manner; and because they dramatized it by linking themselves to certain aesthetic standards. The SS was designed as an elite military community that would be not only supremely violent but also supremely beautiful. (One is not likely to come across a book called "SA Regalia." The SA, whom the SS replaced, were not known for being any less brutal than their successors, but they have gone down in history as beefy, squat, beerhall types; mere brownshirts.)

SS uniforms were stylish, well-cut, with a touch (but not too much) of eccentricity. Compare the rather boring and not very well cut American army uniform: jacket, shirt, tie, pants, socks, and lace-up shoes—essentially civilian clothes no matter how bedecked with medals and badges. SS uniforms were tight, heavy, stiff and included gloves to confine the hands and boots that made legs and feet feel heavy, encased, obliging their wearer to stand up straight. As the back cover of SS *Regalia* explains:

> The uniform was black, a colour which had important overtones in Germany. On that, the SS wore a vast variety of decorations, symbols, badges to distinguish rank, from the collar runes to the death's-head. The appearance was both dramatic and menacing.

The cover's almost wistful come-on does not quite prepare one for the banality of most of the photographs. Along with those celebrated black uniforms, SS troopers were issued almost American-army-looking khaki uniforms and camouflage ponchos and jackets. And besides the photographs of uniforms, there are pages of collar patches, cuff bands, chevrons, belt buckles, commemorative badges, regimental standards, trumpet banners, field caps, service medals, shoulder flashes, permits, passes—few of which bear either the notorious runes or the death's-head; all meticulously identified by rank, unit, and year and season of issue. Precisely the innocuousness of practically all of the photographs testifies to the power of the image: one is handling the breviary of a sexual fantasy. For fantasy to have depth, it must have detail. What, for example, was the color of the travel permit an SS sergeant would have needed to get from Trier to Lübeck in the spring of 1944? One needs all the documentary evidence.

If the message of fascism has been neutralized by an aesthetic view of life, its trappings have been sexualized. This eroticization of fascism can be remarked in such enthralling and devout manifestations as Mishima's *Confessions of a Mask* and *Sun and Steel,* and in films like Kenneth Anger's *Scorpio Rising* and, more recently and far less interestingly, in Visconti's *The Damned* and Cavani's *The Night Porter.* The solemn eroticizing of fascism must be distinguished from a sophisticated playing with cultural horror, where there is an element of the put-on. The poster Robert Morris made for his recent show at the Castelli Gallery is a photograph of the artist, naked to the waist, wearing dark glasses, what appears to be a Nazi helmet, and a spiked steel collar, attached to which is a stout chain which he holds in his manacled, uplifted hands. Morris is said to have considered this to be the only image that still has any power to shock: a singular virtue to those who take for granted that art is a sequence of ever-fresh gestures of provocation. But the point of the poster is its own negation. Shocking people in the context also means inuring them, as Nazi material enters the vast repertory of popular iconography usable for the ironic commentaries of Pop Art. Still, Nazism fascinates in a way other iconography staked out by the Pop sensibility (from Mao Tse-tung to Marilyn Monroe) does not. No doubt, some part of the general rise of interest in fascism can be set down as a product of curiosity. For those born after the early 1940s, bludgeoned by a lifetime's palaver, pro and con, about communism, it is fascism—the great conversation piece of their parents' generation—which represents the exotic, the unknown. Then there is a general fascination among the young with horror, with the irrational. Courses dealing with the history of fascism are, along with those on the occult (including vampirism), among the best attended these days on college campuses. And beyond this the definitely sexual lure of fascism, which SS *Regalia* testifies to with unabashed plainness, seems impervious to deflation by irony or overfamiliarity.

In pornographic literature, films, and gadgetry throughout the world, especially in the United States, England, France, Japan, Scandinavia, Holland, and Germany, the SS has become a referent of sexual adventurism. Much of the imagery of far-out sex has been placed under the sign of Nazism. Boots, leather, chains, Iron Crosses on gleaming torsos, swastikas, along with meat hooks and heavy motorcycles, have become the secret and most lucrative paraphernalia of eroticism. In the sex shops, the baths, the leather bars, the brothels, people are dragging out their gear. But why? Why has Nazi Germany, which was a sexually repressive society, become erotic? How could a regime which persecuted homosexuals become a gay turn-on?

A clue lies in the predilections of the fascist leaders themselves for sexual metaphors. Like Nietzsche and Wagner, Hitler regarded leadership as sexual mastery of the "feminine" masses, as rape. (The expression of the crowds in *Triumph of the Will* is one of ecstasy; the leader makes the crowd come.) Left-wing movements have tended to be unisex, and asexual in their imagery. Right-wing movements, however puritanical and repressive the realities they usher in, have an erotic surface. Certainly Nazism is "sexier" than communism (which is not to the Nazis' credit, but rather shows something of the nature and limits of the sexual imagination).

Of course, most people who are turned on by SS uniforms are not signifying approval of what the Nazis did, if indeed they have more than the sketchiest idea of what that might be. Nevertheless, there are powerful and growing currents of sexual feeling, those that generally go by the name of sadomasochism, which make playing at Nazism seem erotic. These sadomasochistic fantasies and practices are to be found among heterosexuals as well as homosexuals, although it is among male homosexuals that the eroticizing of Nazism is most visible. S-m, not swinging, is the big sexual secret of the last few years.

Between sadomasochism and fascism there is a natural link. "Fascism is theater," as Genet said.* As is sadomasochistic sexuality: to be involved in sadomasochism is to take part in a sexual theater, a staging of sexuality. Regulars of sadomasochistic sex are expert costumers and choreographers as well as performers, in a drama that is all the more exciting because it is forbidden to ordinary people. Sadomasochism is to sex what war is to civil life: the magnificent experience. (Riefenstahl put it: "Whatever is purely realistic, slice-of-life, which is average, quotidian, doesn't interest me.") As the social contract seems tame in comparison with war, so fucking and sucking come to seem merely nice, and therefore unexciting. The end to which all sexual experience tends, as Bataille insisted in a lifetime of writing, is defilement, blasphemy. To be "nice," as to be civilized, means being alienated from this savage experience—which is entirely staged.

Sadomasochism, of course, does not just mean people hurting their sexual partners, which has always occurred—and generally means men beating up women. The perennial drunken Russian peasant thrashing his wife is just doing something he feels like doing (because he is unhappy, oppressed, stupefied; and because women are

* It was Genet, in his novel *Funeral Rites,* who provided one of the first texts that showed the erotic allure fascism exercised on someone who was not a fascist. Another description is by Sartre, an unlikely candidate for these feelings himself, who may have heard about them from Genet. In *La Mort dans l'âme* (1949), the third novel in his four-part *Les Chemins de la liberté,* Sartre describes one of his protagonists experiencing the entry of the German army into Paris in 1940: "[Daniel] was not afraid, he yielded trustingly to those thousands of eyes, he thought 'Our conquerors!' and he was supremely happy. He looked them in the eye, he feasted on their fair hair, their sunburned faces with eyes which looked like lakes of ice, their slim bodies, their incredibly long and muscular hips. He murmured: 'How handsome they are!' . . . Something had fallen from the sky: it was the ancient law. The society of judges had collapsed, the sentence had been obliterated; those ghostly little khaki soldiers, the defenders of the rights of man, had been routed. . . . An unbearable, delicious sensation spread through his body; he could hardly see properly; he repeated, gasping, 'As if it were butter—they're entering Paris as if it were butter.' . . . He would like to have been a woman to throw them flowers."

handy victims). But the perennial Englishman in a brothel being whipped is re-creating an experience. He is paying a whore to act out a piece of theater with him, to reenact or reevoke the past—experiences of his schooldays or nursery which now hold for him a huge reserve of sexual energy. Today it may be the Nazi past that people invoke, in the theatricalization of sexuality, because it is those images (rather than memories) from which they hope a reserve of sexual energy can be tapped. What the French call "the English vice" could, however, be said to be something of an artful affirmation of individuality; the playlet referred, after all, to the subject's own case history. The fad for Nazi regalia indicates something quite different: a response to an oppressive freedom of choice in sex (and in other matters), to an unbearable degree of individuality; the rehearsal of enslavement rather than its reenactment.

The rituals of domination and enslavement being more and more practiced, the art that is more and more devoted to rendering their themes, are perhaps only a logical extension of an affluent society's tendency to turn every part of people's lives into a taste, a choice; to invite them to regard their very lives as a (life) style. In all societies up to now, sex has mostly been an activity (something to do, without thinking about it). But once sex becomes a taste, it is perhaps already on its way to becoming a self-conscious form of theater, which is what sadomasochism is about: a form of gratification that is both violent and indirect, very mental.

Sadomasochism has always been the furthest reach of the sexual experience: when sex becomes most purely sexual, that is, severed from personhood, from relationships, from love. It should not be surprising that it has become attached to Nazi symbolism in recent years. Never before was the relation of masters and slaves so consciously aestheticized. Sade had to make up his theater of punishment and delight from scratch, improvising the decor and costumes and blasphemous rites. Now there is a master scenario available to everyone. The color is black, the material is leather, the seduction is beauty, the justification is honesty, the aim is ecstasy, the fantasy is death.

(1974)

The *Salmagundi*
Interview

• • • • •

Interviewer: In "On Style," written in 1965, you wrote: "To call Leni Riefenstahl's *Triumph of the Will* and *Olympia* masterpieces is not to gloss over Nazi propaganda with aesthetic lenience . . . [but] these two films of Riefenstahl (unique among works of Nazi artists) transcend the categories of propaganda or even reportage. And we find ourselves—to be sure, rather uncomfortably—seeing 'Hitler' and not Hitler, the '1936 Olympics' and not the 1936 Olympics. Through Riefenstahl's genius as a filmmaker, the 'content' has—let us even assume, against her intentions—come to play a purely formal role." And you continue: "A work of art, so far as it is a work of art, cannot—whatever the artist's personal intention—advocate anything at all." Yet, in the Riefenstahl essay published a few months ago, you refer to *Triumph of the Will* as "a film whose very conception negates the possibility of the filmmaker's having an aesthetic conception independent of propaganda." At the very least, these two statements contrast with each other. Is there also a continuity between the two essays?

Sontag: A continuity, it seems to me, in that both statements illustrate the richness of the form-content distinction, as long as one is careful always to use it against itself. My point in 1965 was about the

A slightly abridged version of an interview conducted in April 1975, and published in the quarterly *Salmagundi*, No. 31–32 (Fall 1975–Winter 1976). The interviewers were Robert Boyars, editor of the magazine, and Maxine Bernstein.

formal implications of content, while the recent essay examines the content implicit in certain ideas of form. One of the main assertions of "On Style" is that the formalist and the historicist approaches are not in competition with each other, but are complementary—and equally indispensable. That's where Riefenstahl comes in. Because her work speaks for values that have received an official seal of disapproval, it offers a vivid test of the exchanges between form and content. Knowing that *Triumph of the Will* and *Olympia* might be considered exceptions to the general argument I was making about the ways in which content functions as form, it seemed necessary to point out that even those films also illustrate the process whereby—as in any other bold and complex work of art—content functions as form. I wasn't discussing the complementary process, how form functions as content. When I set out, early this year, to treat Riefenstahl's work at some length, and with *that* approach, I arrived at an analysis that was simply more interesting, as well as more concrete—and that rather overwhelms the summary as well as formalist use I had made of her work in 1965. The paragraph about Riefenstahl in "On Style" is correct—as far as it goes. It just doesn't go very far. While it is true that her films in some sense transcend the propaganda for which they are the vehicle, their specific qualities show how their aestheticizing conception is itself identical with a certain brand of propaganda.

I'm still working with the thesis about the relation of art to the moral sense that is advanced in "On Style." But my understanding of the moral services that works of art perform is less abstract than it was in 1965. And I know more about totalitarianism and about the aesthetics with which it is compatible, which it actually generates, than I did then. One of the experiences that made me more interested in the, so to speak, "contentual" implications of form (without lessening my interest in the formal implications of content) was seeing—three years after I wrote "On Style"—several of the mass spectacle films made in China in the 1960s. One film led to another, inside my head—from *The East Is Red* to, say, Eisenstein's *Alexander Nevsky,* Walt Disney's *Fantasia,* the choreographed patterning of bodies as objects in Busby Berkeley musicals, Kubrick's *2001.* What these films exemplify is a major form of the modern aesthetic imagination which—as I've learned since the Riefenstahl essay was published—Siegfried Kracauer had explored as early as 1927, in an essay called "The Mass Ornament," and Walter Benjamin had summed up a few years later, when he described fascism as an aestheticization of political life.

It's not enough to say that an aesthetics is, or eventually becomes, a politics. What aesthetics? What politics? The key to understanding "fascist aesthetics," I think, is seeing that a "communist aesthetics" is probably a contradiction in terms. Hence, the mediocrity and staleness of the art promoted in communist countries. And when official art in the Soviet Union and China isn't resolutely old-fashioned, it is, objectively, fascist. Unlike the ideal communist society, which is totally didactic—turning every institution into a school—the fascist ideal is to mobilize everybody into a kind of national *Gesamtkunstwerk:* making the whole society into a theater. This is the most far-reaching way in which aesthetics becomes a politics. It becomes a politics of the lie. As Nietzsche said, "To experience a thing as beautiful means: to experience it necessarily wrongly." In the nineteenth century, ideologues of provocation and transvaluation like Nietzsche and Wilde expounded on "the aesthetic view of the world," one of whose superiorities was that it was supposed to be the most generous and large-spirited view, a form of civility, beyond politics. The evolution of fascism in the twentieth century has taught us that they were wrong. As it turns out, "the aesthetic view of the world" is extremely hospitable to many of the uncivilized ideas and dissociated yearnings that were made explicit in fascism, and which also have great currency in our consumer culture. Yet it is clear—China has made it very clear—that the moralism of *serious* communist societies not only wipes out the autonomy of the aesthetic but makes it impossible to produce art (in the modern sense) at all. A six-week trip to China in 1973 convinced me—if I needed convincing—that the autonomy of the aesthetic is something to be protected, and cherished, as indispensable nourishment to intelligence. But a decade-long residence in the 1960s, with its inexorable conversion of moral and political radicalisms into "style," has convinced me of the perils of overgeneralizing the aesthetic view of the world.

I would still argue that a work of art, qua work of art, cannot advocate anything. But since no work of art is in fact only a work of art, it's often more complicated than that. In "On Style" I was trying to recast the truths expressed in Wilde's calculatedly outrageous preface to *The Picture of Dorian Gray* and Ortega y Gasset's more sober overstatement of the same polemic against philistinism in *The Dehumanization of Art*—by not tacitly separating or actually opposing—as Wilde and Ortega do—aesthetic and moral response. Ten years after "On Style," this is still the position I write from. But I have more historical flesh on my bones now. Though I continue to be as besotted an aesthete and as obsessed a moralist as I ever was, I've come

332 / SUSAN SONTAG

to appreciate the limitations—and the indiscretion—of generalizing either the aesthete's or the moralist's view of the world without a much denser notion of historical context. Since you've been quoting me to myself, let me quote myself back to you. I say in that essay of 1965 that "awareness of style as a problematic and isolable element in a work of art has emerged in the audience for art only at certain historical moments—as a front behind which other issues, ultimately ethical and political, are being debated." The essays I've been writing recently are attempts to take that point further, to make it concrete— as it applies to my own work, as well as to that of others.

Interviewer: When the poet Adrienne Rich attacked the essay on Riefenstahl for disregarding feminist values, you replied: "Applied to a particular historical subject, the feminist passion yields conclusions which, however true, are extremely general. . . . Most of history, alas, is 'patriarchal history.' So distinctions will have to be made. . . . Virtually everything deplorable in human history furnishes material for a restatement of the feminist plaint . . . just as every story of a life could lead to a reflection on our common mortality and the vanity of human wishes. But if the point is to have meaning some of the time, it can't be made all the time."* What are the times when the point should be made? Are there certain events, or "movements," or works of art that are more reasonable subjects for feminist criticism?

Sontag: I want armies of women and men to be pointing out the omnipresence of sexist stereotypes in the language, behavior, and imagery of our society. If that's what you mean by feminist criticism, then whenever it's practiced—and however coarsely—it's always of some value. But I'd like to see a few platoons of intellectuals who are also feminists doing their bit in the war against misogyny in their own way, letting the feminist implications be residual or implicit in their work, without risking being charged by their sisters with desertion. I don't like party lines. They make for intellectual monotony and bad prose. Let me put it very simply, though not—I hope—too plaintively. There are many intellectual tasks, and different levels of discourse. If there *is* a question of appropriateness, it's not because some events or works of art are more "reasonable" targets, but because people who reason in public have—and ought to exercise—options about how many and how complex are the points they want to make. And where, in what form, and to what audience they make them.

*"Feminism and Fascism: An Exchange," *The New York Review of Books*, Vol. XXII, No. 4, March 20, 1975.

Rich complained that I had failed to say that Nazi Germany was, after all, the culmination of a sexist and patriarchal society. She was assuming, of course, that the values of Riefenstahl's films were Nazi values. So was I. That's why I wanted to discuss the question: in *what* sense does Riefenstahl's work embody Nazi values? *Why* are these films—and *The Last of the Nuba*—interesting and persuasive? I think it was permissible to assume that the audience for whom I wrote my essay is aware of the derogation of women not only in Nazi ideology, but in the main tradition of German letters and thought from Luther to Nietzsche to Freud and Jung.

It's not the appropriateness of feminist criticism which needs to be rethought, but its level—its demands for intellectual simplicity, advanced in the name of ethical solidarity. These demands have convinced many women that it is undemocratic to raise questions about "quality"—the quality of feminist discourse, if it is sufficiently militant, and the quality of works of art, if these are sufficiently warmhearted and self-revealing. Hatred of the intellect is one of the recurrent themes of modernist protest in art and in morals. Though actually quite inimical to effective political action, it seems like a political statement. Both avant-garde art and feminism have made large use of, and sometimes seem to be parodies of, the languages of failed political movements. As advanced art, in the 1910s, inherited the rhetoric of Anarchism (and baptized it Futurism), feminism, in the late 1960s, inherited another political rhetoric on the wane, that of *gauchisme*. One common denominator of New Left polemics was its zeal for pitting hierarchy against equality, theory against practice, intellect (cold) against feeling (warm). Feminists have tended to perpetuate these philistine characterizations of hierarchy, theory, and intellect. What was denounced in the 1960s as bourgeois, repressive, and elitist was discovered to be phallocratic, too. That kind of second-hand militancy may appear to serve feminist goals in the short run. But it means a surrender to callow notions of art and of thought and the encouragement of a genuinely repressive moralism.

Interviewer: In 1967 you wrote a long, admiring essay on Ingmar Bergman's *Persona.** It has since become common to attack Bergman as a technically reactionary force in world cinema. Feminist critics complain that his films regularly project "negative" images of women which promise no useful encouragement to people in need of positive identity images. Do you share any of these views of Bergman as a reactionary artist, aesthetically or politically?

* In *Styles of Radical Will.*

Sontag: I am extremely reluctant to attack anyone as a reactionary artist. That's the weapon of the repressive and ignorant officialdom in you-know-which countries, where "reactionary" is also associated with a kind of pessimistic content or (using the phrase you cite) with not providing "positive images." Being very attached to the benefits of pluralism in the arts and of factionalism in politics, I've grown allergic to the words "reactionary" and "progressive." Such judgments always support ideological conformity, encourage intolerance—even if they aren't originally formulated to do that. As for Bergman, I'd say that anyone who reduces his work to its neo-Strindbergian views of women has jettisoned the idea of art and of complex standards of judgment. (If correctness of attitude counted most, Alexander Room's *Bed and Sofa,* full of appealing feminist intuitions, would be a greater film than Pudovkin's macho epic *Storm over Asia.*).

The harsh indictment of Bergman simply inverts the slack standards that prevail in much of feminist criticism. To those critics who rate films according to whether they make moral reparations, it must seem snobbish to cavil about the low quality of most recent movies made by women which do convey positive images. And what's happening when an attack on someone for not supplying "useful encouragement to people" is bolstered by calling him "technically reactionary" and "old-fashioned"? (Presumably, this is how these critics hope to show they are not behaving like stodgy cultural commissars.) I wouldn't call Bergman old-fashioned. But, despite some brilliant narrative inventions in his two best films, *The Silence* and *Persona,* his work doesn't suggest any fruitful development. He is an obsessional artist, the worst kind to imitate. Like Stein and Bacon and Jancsco, Bergman is one of those oppressively memorable geniuses of the artistic dead end, who go very far with a limited material—refining it when they are inspired, repeating it and parodying themselves when they aren't.

Interviewer: Many people have observed the "scandalous" fact that the sentiment of being for most great artists has been decidedly conservative, that their attachment to the past has been much more passionate than their feeling for things yet to be. Is there something about works of art which almost demands that their creators have a preservative, therefore conservative, relation to the world in which they live, even when committed to this or that "radical" policy. Perhaps in this sense art itself, whatever the artist's personal politics, is objectively conservative, therefore reactionary . . .

Sontag: "Reactionary" again! This feels like another version of the same question, so I'll try to answer in a different way. I doubt that there is anything more conservative or reactionary about artists than there is about people. And why shouldn't people be naturally conservative? That the past necessarily weighs more on the axis of human consciousness is perhaps a greater liability to the individual than to society, but how could it be otherwise? Where is the scandal? To be scandalized by the normal is always demagogic. And it is only normal that we are aware of ourselves as persons in a historical continuum, with indefinite thicknesses of past behind us, the present a razor's edge, and the future—well, problematic is one damp word for it. Dividing time into Past, Present & Future suggests that reality is distributed equally among three parts, but in fact the past is the most real of all. The future is inevitably, an accumulation of loss, and dying is something we do all our lives. If artists are memory specialists, professional curators of consciousness, they are only practicing—willfully, obsessionally—a prototypical devoutness. There is a tilt in the very experience of living which always gives memory an advantage over amnesia.

To reproach artists for having an insufficiently radical relation to the world has to be a complaint about art as such. And to reproach art is, in more than one way, like reproaching consciousness itself for being a burden. For consciousness can be conscious of itself, as Hegelians quaintly say, only through its sense of the past. And art is the most general condition of the Past in the present. To become past is, in one version, to become art. (The arts that most literally illustrate this mutation are architecture and photography.) The pathos that all works of art reek of comes from their historicity. From the way they are overtaken by physical decay and stylistic obsolescence. And from whatever is mysterious, partly (and forever) veiled about them. And simply from our awareness, with each work, that no one would or could ever do exactly *that* again. Perhaps no work of art *is* art. It can only *become* art, when it is part of the past. In this normative sense, a "contemporary" work of art would be a contradiction—except so far as we can, in the present, assimilate the present to the past.

Interviewer: And yet a great many contemporary liberationists, radicals of various kinds, have demanded that works of art be new, that they cut loose from the inherited props and furnishings of the familiar material world.

Sontag: But wouldn't that be like peeling off one's own skin? And doesn't demanding that artists throw away their toys—that is, the world—mean wanting them not to be artists any more? Such a talent for jettisoning everything has to be extremely rare. And its promised benefits have yet to be demonstrated. The clean sweep being proposed as a goal for radical therapy as well as art (and, by extension, for politics) suggests that "liberation" can be very confining. That is, it seems regressive in relation to the full range of our possibilities— among which civilization tries, to almost everyone's dissatisfaction, to arbitrate. The price we would pay for liberation in that undialectical sense is at least as steep as the price we've been paying for civilization. If we are indeed going to be forced to choose between defensive fantasies of liberation and ruling corruptions of civilization, let's work fast to soften the harshness of that choice. It's sobering to realize that both options seemed just as morally defective a century ago when Henry James made his prescient, melancholy analysis of our post-1960s cultural dilemmas in *The Princess Casamassima,* with imaginary London anarchists anticipating American New Left and countercultural ideologues.

You seem to be talking about a politicized version of the classic modernist demand on Art (Making It New), but then the only difference between the Poundian demand and the more recent imperatives is a radical politics, and I'm not sure that the language in which this politics is declared should be taken at face value. Question the self-designated radicals who appear to be calling for a cultural *tabula rasa,* and I think you'd find that they are seldom as modernist as their rhetoric would imply. The way you've formulated their protest seems to me to confuse a moralistic political radicalism (assumed to be a Good Thing) with an amoral revolt against the inherited past that is in full complicity with the status quo. Much of radical dissent is animated by a kind of restorationism—the wish to reconstitute communal pleasures and civic virtues that have been wiped out to make possible the very real *tabula rasa* of our consumer society. A radical in the sense you describe would be Andy Warhol, the ideally passive avatar of an economy in which everything of the past is scheduled to be traded in for newer goods.

Interviewer: What do you make of this assertion by the sociologist Philip Rieff: "Never before has there been such a general shifting of sides as now among intellectuals in the United States and England. Many have gone over to the enemy without realizing that they, self-considered the cultural elite, have actually become spokesmen for what Freud called the instinctual [mass]." Insofar as some of your own work in the mid-sixties attempted to legitimate an easier relation between popular culture and the elite, would you say that you had "gone over to the enemy"?

Sontag: [Laughter]

Interviewer: What?

Sontag: Of course I wouldn't say that.

Interviewer: Well, do you think it is useful to draw a distinction between "the cultural elite" and "the instinctual mass"?

Sontag: No. I think the distinction is a vulgar one. By ignoring the difference between the descriptive and prescriptive senses of culture, it can't give a properly specific meaning to either. There are several senses in which "culture" doesn't equal "elite." (Anyway, there are elites—not one, but many.) And I don't think that "instinctual" and "mass" go together—even if Le Bon and Freud did say so. The distinction suggests a contempt for the instincts, a facile pessimism about people, and a lack of passion for the arts (as distinct from ideas) that is not confirmed by my own instincts, pessimism, passions.

Intellectuals who want to defend our poor sick culture should resist the all-too-understandable temptation to fume about the unlettered masses and accuse other intellectuals of joining the enemy. If I'm leery of talking about a cultural elite, it's not because I don't care about culture but because I think the notion is virtually unusable and should be retired. For instance, it doesn't explain anything about the cultural mix I was writing about in the mid-sixties—a particularly vivid moment in a century-long set of exchanges between different levels of culture, different elites. Early modernists like Rimbaud, Stravinsky, Apollinaire, Joyce, and Eliot had showed how "high culture" could assimilate shards of "low culture" (*The Waste Land, Ulysses,* etc. etc.). By the 1960s the popular arts, notably film and rock music, had taken up the abrasive themes and some of the "difficult" techniques (like collage) that had hitherto been the fare of a restricted cultural elite, if you will—the university-educated, museum-going cosmopolitan audience for the avant-garde or experimental arts. That low culture was an important ingredient in the modernist takeover of high culture, that the modernist sensibility had created new boundaries for popular culture and was eventually incorporated into it—these are subjects that nobody who has cared for culture can ignore or should fail to treat with high seriousness. Is trying to understand something—in this instance, a process that had been going on at least since Baudelaire—legitimizing it? It hardly needed me to offer that legitimacy. And the 1960s seems rather late to stop identifying culture with some Masterpiece Theatre of World History and to respond—on the basis of contemporary experience, and moved by pleasure rather than resentment—to how complex the destiny of high culture has become since Matthew Arnold whistled in the dark on Dover Beach. The notion of culture implied by Rieff's distinction seems to me awfully middlebrow, and plausible only to someone who has never been really immersed in or derived intense pleasure from contemporary poetry and music and painting. Does culture here mean art? (And what art?) Does it mean thought? They're not the same, and culture isn't exactly synonymous with either. Toryish labels like "cultural elite" and "instinctual mass" do not tell us anything useful about how to protect that endangered species, "high" standards. Diagnoses of cultural sickness made in such general and self-congratulatory terms become a symptom of the problem, not part of the answer.

Interviewer: In 1964, in your essay "Notes on Camp," you wrote: "I am strongly drawn to camp, and almost as strongly offended by it. That is why I want to talk about it, and why I can." And you continued: "To name a sensibility, to draw its contours and to recount its history, requires a deep sympathy modified by revulsion." Could you tell us something more about that dual set of attitudes—sympathy/revulsion—particularly in relation to what you call "the corny flamboyance of femaleness" embodied in certain actresses? And how do such responses relate to your feminist sensibility?

Sontag: Like the recent essays on photography, "Notes on Camp" grew out of speculations of a rather general order. How "to name a sensibility," how "to draw its contours, to recount its history"—that was the problem I started from, and then looked for an example, a model. And it seemed more interesting not to pick Sensibility X from among those heaped with ethical or aesthetic laurels, and to evoke instead a sensibility that was exotic and in obvious ways minor, even despised—as the rather quirky notion of a sensibility had itself been slighted, in favor of that tidier fiction, an "idea."

Morbidity was my first choice. I stayed with that for a while, attempting to systematize a long-term fascination with mortuary sculpture, architecture, inscriptions, and other such wistful lore that eventually found an unsystematic place in *Death Kit* and *Promised Lands*. But the material was too detailed, and cumbersome to describe, so I switched to camp, which had the advantage of being familiar as well as marginal, and could be illustrated in a more rapid and comprehensible way. Camp, I knew, was a sensibility that many people were tuned in to, although they might have no name for it. As for myself: by deciding to write "Notes on Camp" instead of "Notes on Death," I was choosing to humor the part of my seriousness that was being zapped and loosened up and made more sociable by camp wit, rather than to fortify the part of my wit that got regularly choked off by seizures of morbidity. Compared to morbidity, camp was hard to pin down. It was, in fact, a rich example of how a sensibility can have divergent meanings, can have a latent content that is more complex than—and often different from—its manifest one.

Which brings me to the question of ambivalence. I've dawdled in the culture graveyard, enjoying what camp taste could effect in the way of ironic resurrections, just as I've stopped to pay my respects to real death, in real cemeteries, off the country roads and in the cities of three continents. And it is in the nature of such detours that some sights fascinate, while others repel. The theme you single out—the parodistic rendering of women—usually left me cold. But I can't say that I was simply offended. For I was often amused and, so far as I needed to be, liberated. I think that the camp taste for the theatrically feminine did help undermine the credibility of certain stereotyped femininities—by exaggerating them, by putting them between quotation marks. Making something corny of femaleness is one way of creating distance from the stereotype. Camp's extremely sentimental relation to beauty is no help to women, but its irony is: ironizing about the sexes is one small step toward depolarizing them. In this sense the diffusion of camp taste in the early sixties should probably be credited with a considerable if inadvertent role in the upsurge of feminist consciousness in the late 1960s.

Interviewer: What about women like Mae West, an old-style sex queen who didn't, apparently, strike audiences the way you suggest?

Sontag: I think she did. Whether or not she started with the oldest of blandishments, her glory was as a new-style sex queen—that is, the impersonator of one. Unlike Sarah Bernhardt's style, which audiences at a certain moment stopped being able to take straight, Mae West's was appreciated from the beginning as a sort of parody. Let-

ting oneself, self-consciously, be beguiled by such robust, shrill, vulgar parody is the last step in a century-long evolution—and progressive democratization—of the aestheticism whose broader history and
implications are sketched in "Notes on Camp" but which has had its
most knowing reception from the milieu in which the word "camp"
appeared some fifty years ago. (Although scholars of slang disagree
as much about the origin of "camp" as they do about "O.K.," I assume that it derives from *camper*—which the Oxford French Dictio-
nary translates as "to posture boldly.") And it was in the 1920s that
a kind of deconstruction of the stereotypes of femininity gets underway, a mocking challenge to sexism that complements the moralistic
call for justice and reparations to women that had found its voice in
the 1890s in, say, Shaw's essays and George Gissing's novel *The Odd
Women*. What I am arguing is that today's feminist consciousness
has a long and complicated history, of which the diffusion of male
homosexual taste is a part—including its sometimes witless put-downs
of and delirious homage to the "feminine." Feminists have been less
quick at seeing this than some of their opponents—for example,
Wyndham Lewis, whose novel-diatribe *The Childermass*, written in
the late twenties, contains a long speech about how the naturally
feminine and the masculine are being subverted jointly by homosexuals and by suffragettes. (Contemporary homosexuality is denounced
as "a branch of the Feminist Revolution.") And Lewis was not wrong
to link them.

Interviewer: In "The Pornographic Imagination," written in 1967, you
describe the heroine of *Story of O* as a woman who "progresses simultaneously toward her own extinction as a human being and her
fulfillment as a sexual being." You then wonder "how anyone would
ascertain whether there exists, truly, empirically, anything in 'nature'
or human consciousness that supports such a split." It seems to me
that the loss of self in exchange for sexual fulfillment might be viewed
as an allegory of the new feminist awareness. That is, in exchange
for "fulfillment as women," women have often surrendered their
identities as autonomous individuals. Do you agree there might be
more to *Story of O* than you saw in 1967? Could that book be considered a peculiarly political work whose meaning could be enriched
by the feminist perspective?

Sontag: Though I'd agree that one can extract useful lessons from all
sorts of unpromising material, O's destiny seems to me an unlikely
allegory of either feminist awareness or, simply, the age-old subjec-
tion of women. My interest in *Story of O* was, still would be, in its

candor about the demonic side of sexual fantasy. The violence of the imagination that it consecrates—and does not at all deplore—cannot be confined within the optimistic and rationalist perceptions of mainstream feminism. Pornography's form of utopistic thinking is, like most of science fiction, a negative utopia. Since the writers who have insisted on how fierce, disruptive, and antinomian an energy sexuality (potentially, ideally) is are mostly men, it's commonly supposed that this form of the imagination must discriminate against women. I don't think it does, necessarily. (It could discriminate against men, as in Monique Wittig's celebrations of unfettered sexual energy.)

What distinguishes the work of "the pornographic imagination" from other accounts of the erotic life is that it treats sexuality as an extreme situation. That means that what pornography depicts is, in one obvious sense, quite unrealistic. Sexual energy is not endlessly renewable; sex acts cannot be tirelessly repeated. But in another sense pornography is rudely accurate about important realities of desire. That voluptuousness does mean surrender, and that sexual surrender pursued imaginatively enough, experienced immoderately enough, does erode pride of individuality and mocks the notion that the will could ever be free—these are truths about sexuality itself and what it may, naturally, become. Because it is such an *ascesis* to live completely for voluptuousness, only a few women and men ever do pursue pleasure to this terminal extreme. The fantasy of sexual apocalypse is common enough, however—indisputably, a means for intensifying sexual pleasure. And what that tells us about the inhuman, as it were, character of intense pleasure is still being slighted by the humanist "revisionist" Freudianism that most feminists feel comfortable with, which minimizes the intractable powers of unconscious or irrational feeling.

You propose a political view of the book in place of my tentative idea about something "in 'nature,' or in human consciousness." But I would still reaffirm that speculation. There seems to be something inherently defective or self-frustrating in the way the sexual impulse works in human beings—for instance, an essential (that is, normal), not accidental (that is, neurotic), link between sexual energy and obsession. It appears likely that the full development of our sexual being does clash with the full development of our consciousness. Instead of supposing that *all* our sexual discontent is part of a tax sexuality pays for being civilized, it may be more correct to assume that we are, first of all, sick by nature—and that it is our being, to begin with, what Nietzsche called "sick animals," that makes us civilization-producing animals.

It is the innate incongruence between important achievements in

342 / SUSAN SONTAG

the realms of sexual fulfillment and of individual consciousness that is exacerbated by the enlarged use to which sexuality has been put in modern, secular culture. As the credibility of religious experience has declined, erotic experience has not only gotten an inflated, even grandiose significance, but is itself now subjected to standards of credibility (thereby attaching a whole new sort of anxiety to sexual performance). In particular, the quest for the experience of complete psychic surrender now no longer enclosed within traditional religious forms has become increasingly, and restlessly, attached to the mind-blowing character of the orgasm. The myths of total sexual fulfill-ment dramatized in *Story of O* concern that peculiarly modern *via negativa*. Evidence about the feelings and sexual tastes in our culture before it was wholly secularized, and in other cultures past and pre-sent, suggests that voluptuousness was rarely pursued in this way, as the organon to transcend individual consciousness. Perhaps only when sexuality is invested with that ideological burden, as it is now, does it also become a real, and not just a potential, danger to person-hood and to individuation.

Interviewer: In his book *Fellow Teachers,* Philip Rieff writes: "True criticism is constituted, first, by repeating what is already known. The great teacher is he who, because he carries in himself what is already known, can transfer it to his student; that inwardness is his absolute and irreducible authority. If a student fails to re-cognize that authority, then he is not a student." Obviously, the authoritative knowing Rieff invokes has nothing to do with the expertise of the specialist. What do you take him to mean by it, and would you agree that, according to Rieff's definition, there are very few students in our institutions of higher learning?

Sontag: Precious few students, according to that definition—yes. But perhaps still more than enough, since—again following Philip Rieff's definition—there are probably *no* professors. The authority of the pro-fessoriat being invoked here goes no further back than Wilhelmine Germany. That there are very few students in the prescriptive sense (devoted, talented lovers of learning) is surely as well known as that there are many more students in the descriptive sense (bodies in classrooms), liberal-arts education having assumed those functions which, precisely, make it harder than it was a generation ago to as-sign so-called difficult books and to expound complex ideas without back talk from students. But Philip Rieff does not make his case against mass education more convincing by overstating it. When in

Western intellectual history did the college teacher have "an absolute and irreducible authority"? Even in the great ages of faith, which one might suppose well-stocked with models for the pedagogue as dictator, a closer look discloses a reassuring ferment of dissent, of heterodoxy, of questioning what was "already known." Fiat cannot restore to the office of the teacher (now irrevocably secular, transmitting a plurality of "traditions") an absolute authority that both the teacher and what is being taught do not have—if they ever did.

The genuine historical pressures to lower the standards for higher learning that do exist aren't weakened by declaring what words *ought* to mean—defining a teacher as one who teaches authoritatively, a student as one who accepts the authority of the teacher. Perhaps one should take Philip Rieff's definitions as evidence that the fight to maintain the highest standards really is a lost cause. If the decline of first-rate teaching in universities really is irreversible, as it probably is, then one should expect exactly such a defense of the *ancien régime* as is projected by these empty definitions of great teacher and great student. Making a virtue of its own historical inappropriateness, Philip Rieff's authoritarian theory of the university parallels the authoritarian theory of the bourgeois state advanced in Germany and France in the late nineteenth and early twentieth centuries. Whereas, traditionally, a teacher had authority by virtue of a particular doctrine, a "teaching," what is proposed here is a very modern, contentless notion of authority: not the authority of, say, the Nicene Creed, but the authority of—authority. The substance of the teacher's authority having been eroded, only its form remains. Authority itself ("that inwardness") is made the defining characteristic of the great teacher. Perhaps one only stakes out such a large, truculent claim to authority when one doesn't, can't possibly, have it. Even in the Maoist conception of the relation between leaders and masses, the authority of the Great Teacher does not derive, tautologically, from his authority, but from his wisdom—a much-advertised part of which consists in overturning "what is already known." But Philip Rieff's notion of the teacher has more in common with the Maoist pedagogic conception than with the main tradition of Western activity and high culture that he thinks he's defending against barbarous students: it is formulated in a fashion as dismissive of independence of thought as Maoism.

To define a teacher primarily in terms of the idea of authority seems to me grossly inadequate to the standards of that elite education for which Philip Rieff is proselytizing. That the definition encourages wishful thinking and licenses personal arrogance is relatively unim-

344 / SUSAN SONTAG

portant. What is important is that it leaves out virtually all the teacherly virtues. Wisdom, as I've already mentioned. And the Socratic pedagogic eros. Forget about humility—if that is too radical, or it sounds mawkish. But what about skepticism?

A little skepticism about what one "carries" in oneself, if one is well-educated, might be especially useful—to balance the temptations of self-righteousness. As someone who, like Philip Rieff, had the good fortune to do undergraduate work in the most ambitious and the most successful authoritarian program of education ever devised in this country—the Hutchins-era College of the University of Chicago—I remain as much as he, I would think, a partisan of the nonelective curriculum. But I'm aware that all such forms of consensus about "great" books and "perennial" problems, once stabilized, tend to deteriorate eventually into something philistine. The real life of the mind is always at the frontiers of "what is already known." Those great books don't only need custodians and transmitters. To stay alive, they also need adversaries. The most interesting ideas are heresies.

Interviewer: I would like to link "The Pornographic Imagination" with your essay on Riefenstahl, where you discuss the aesthetics of totalitarian art. To what extent is *Story of O* a totalitarian work? Or an ironic commentary upon such a work? Is there a connection between this tale of total female submission and Riefenstahl's work, with its focus on obeisance to an all-powerful leader?

Sontag: I don't find *Story of O* ironic, either about totalitarianism or about the Sadean literary tradition of which it is a self-conscious but exquisitely limited modernization. Is it a totalitarian work? The connection that could be drawn between *Story of O* and the eroticized politics of Nazism seems a fortuitous one—and extraneous to the book and the intentions of the woman who wrote it, pseudonymously—however easily it springs to mind now, especially since the sadomasochistic dramaturgy started going in for Nazi drag. And there is still another difference worth noting, the one between the eroticism of a political event (real or, say, in a film) and the eroticism of a private life (real or fictional). Hitler, when he used sexual metaphors to express the authority of leaders and the obeisance of masses, in characterizing leadership as violation could only *compare* the masses to a woman. (But O *is* one woman, and the book is about an individual salvation, through the erotic, which is profoundly anti-political, as all forms of mysticism and neo-mysticism are.) Measured against submission and fulfillment in a real erotic situation, the eroticism of

Hitler's notion of leadership (as rape) and of followership (as surrender) is a cheat, a fake.

As there is a difference between an idea, mediated by a metaphor, and an experience (real or fictional), the metaphors used by the modern regimes that have sought to create total ideological consensus have different degrees of closeness to or distance from practical reality. In the communist view of how leaders lead masses, the metaphor is one not of sexual domination but of teachership: the teacher who has authority and the masses who are students of the teacher. Although this metaphor makes Maoist rhetoric very attractive, almost as attractive as Nazi rhetoric is repellent, its result is probably a much more total system of control over minds and bodies. While the eroticized politics of fascism is, after all, a pseudo-eroticism, the pedagogic politics of communism is a real and effective process of teaching.

Interviewer: In 1964, you wrote an essay on science-fiction films called "The Imagination of Disaster."* Have you reflected about science fiction since then—for example, about the idea of intelligence proposed in Arthur Clarke's *Childhood's End?* Can you make a connection between "the imagination of disaster" and "the pornographic imagination"? And between leaders and followers in fascist aesthetics?

Sontag: That essay, among others, could be seen as one phase of an argument about modes of authoritarian feeling and perception. (And the argument isn't only to be found in my essays. For instance, *Duet for Cannibals* and *Brother Carl,* the two films I made in Sweden, and two recent stories, "Old Complaints Revisited" and "Doctor Jekyll," are fictional treatments of the private lives of leaders and followers.) Science fiction—about which I hope to write a better essay someday—is full of authoritarian ideas, ideas that have much in common with those developed in other contemporary contexts (like pornography), illustrating typical forms of the authoritarian imagination. Clarke's fable is one of the abler examples of science fiction's characteristic polemic on behalf of an authoritarian ideal of intelligence. The romantic protest against the assassin mind, a leading theme of art and thought since the early nineteenth century, gradually became a self-fulfilling prophecy as, in the twentieth century, technocratic, purely instrumental ideas of the mind took over, which made intelligence seem hopelessly inadequate to a social and psychological dis-

* In *Against Interpretation.*

order experienced as more menacing than ever. Science fiction promotes the idea of a superior or "higher" intelligence that will impose order on human affairs and messy emotions and, thereby, end childhood—that is, history. Pornography, like the fascist mass spectacle, looks to the abolition of mind (in an ideal choreography of bodies, of dominators and the dominated).

We live in a culture in which intelligence is denied relevance altogether, in a search for radical innocence, or is defended as an instrument of authority and repression. In my view, the only intelligence worth defending is critical, dialectical, skeptical, desimplifying. An intelligence which aims at the definitive resolution (that is, suppression) of conflict, which justifies manipulation—always, of course, for other people's good, as in the argument brilliantly made by Dostoevsky's Grand Inquisitor, which haunts the main tradition of science fiction—is not *my* normative idea of intelligence. Not surprisingly, contempt for intelligence goes with the contempt for history. And history is, yes, tragic. But I'm not able to support any idea of intelligence which aims at bringing history to an end—substituting for the tragedy that makes civilization at least possible the nightmare or the Good Dream of eternal barbarism.

I am assuming that the defense of civilization implies the defense of an intelligence that is not authoritarian. But all contemporary defenders of civilization must be aware—though I don't think it helps to say it often—that this civilization, already so far overtaken by barbarism, *is* at an end, and nothing we do will put it back together again. So, in the culture of transition out of which we can try to make sense, fighting off the twin afflictions of hyperaesthesia and passivity, no position can be a comfortable one or should be complacently held. Perhaps the most instructive discussion of the questions of intelligence and innocence, civilization and barbarism, responsibility to the truth and responsibility to people's needs is in the libretto of Schönberg's *Moses and Aaron*. Dostoevsky does not let Jesus answer the Grand Inquisitor's monologue, although the whole novel is supposed to give us, does give us, the material to construe that answer. But Moses and Aaron do answer each other's arguments. And although Schönberg uses both dramaturgy and music to stack the whole opera against the view Aaron represents, and for the Word of Moses, in the actual debate between them he set their arguments at parity. So the debate is unresolved, as it really is, for these questions are fiercely complicated. Moses and Aaron are both right. And any serious argument about culture—which has to be, finally, an argument about truth—must honor that complexity.

(1975)

On Photography

The Image-World

Reality has always been interpreted through the reports given by images; and philosophers since Plato have tried to loosen our dependence on images by evoking the standard of an image-free way of apprehending the real. But when, in the mid-nineteenth century, the standard finally seemed attainable, the retreat of old religious and political illusions before the advance of humanistic and scientific thinking did not—as anticipated—create mass defections to the real. On the contrary, the new age of unbelief strengthened the allegiance to images. The credence that could no longer be given to realities understood *in the form of* images was now being given to realities understood *to be* images, illusions. In the preface to the second edition (1843) of *The Essence of Christianity,* Feuerbach observes about "our era" that it "prefers the image to the thing, the copy to the original, the representation to the reality, appearance to being"—while being aware of doing just that. And his premonitory complaint has been transformed in the twentieth century into a widely agreed-on diagnosis: that a society becomes "modern" when one of its chief activities is producing and consuming images, when images that have extraordinary powers to determine our demands upon reality and are themselves coveted substitutes for firsthand experience become indispensable to the health of the economy, the stability of the polity, and the pursuit of private happiness.

Feuerbach's words—he is writing a few years after the invention of the camera—seem, more specifically, a presentiment of the impact of photography. For the images that have virtually unlimited authority in a modern society are mainly photographic images; and the scope of that authority stems from the properties peculiar to images taken by cameras.

Such images are indeed able to usurp reality because first of all a photograph is not only an image (as a painting is an image), an interpretation of the real; it is also a trace, something directly stenciled off the real, like a footprint or a death mask. While a painting, even one that meets photographic standards of resemblance, is never more than the stating of an interpretation, a photograph is never less than the registering of an emanation (light waves reflected by objects)—a material vestige of its subject in a way that no painting can be. Between two fantasy alternatives, that Holbein the Younger had lived long enough to have painted Shakespeare or that a prototype of the camera had been invented early enough to have photographed him, most Bardolators would choose the photograph. This is not just because it would presumably show what Shakespeare really looked like, for even if the hypothetical photograph were faded, barely legible, a brownish shadow, we would probably still prefer it to another glorious Holbein. Having a photograph of Shakespeare would be like having a nail from the True Cross.

Most contemporary expressions of concern that an image-world is replacing the real one continue to echo, as Feuerbach did, the Platonic depreciation of the image: true insofar as it resembles something real, sham because it is no more than a resemblance. But this venerable naïve realism is somewhat beside the point in the era of photographic images, for its blunt contrast between the image ("copy") and the thing depicted (the "original")—which Plato repeatedly illustrates with the example of a painting—does not fit a photograph in so simple a way. Neither does the contrast help in understanding image-making at its origins, when it was a practical, magical activity, a means of appropriating or gaining power over something. The further back we go in history, as E. H. Gombrich has observed, the less sharp is the distinction between images and real things; in primitive societies, the thing and its image were simply two different, that is, physically distinct, manifestations of the same energy or spirit. Hence, the supposed efficacy of images in propitiating and gaining control over powerful presences. Those powers, those presences were present in *them*.

For defenders of the real from Plato to Feuerbach to equate image with mere appearance—that is, to presume that the image is absolutely distinct from the object depicted—is part of that process of desacralization which separates us irrevocably from the world of sacred times and places in which an image was taken to participate in the reality of the object depicted. What defines the originality of photography is that, at the very moment in the long, increasingly secular history of painting when secularism is entirely triumphant, it revives—in wholly secular terms—something like the primitive status of images. Our irrepressible feeling that the photographic process is something magical has a genuine basis. No one takes an easel painting to be in any sense co-substantial with its subject; it only represents or refers. But a photograph is not only like its subject, a homage to the subject. It is part of, an extension of that subject; and a potent means of acquiring it, of gaining control over it.

Photography is acquisition in several forms. In its simplest form, we have in a photograph surrogate possession of a cherished person or thing, a possession which gives photographs some of the character of unique objects. Through photographs, we also have a consumer's relation to events, both to events which are part of our experience and to those which are not—a distinction between types of experience that such habit-forming consumership blurs. A third form of acquisition is that, through image-making and image-duplicating machines, we can acquire something as information (rather than experience). Indeed, the importance of photographic images as the medium through which more and more events enter our experience is, finally, only a by-product of their effectiveness in furnishing knowledge disassociated from and independent of experience.

This is the most inclusive form of photographic acquisition. Through being photographed, something becomes part of a system of information, fitted into schemes of classification and storage which range from the crudely chronological order of snapshot sequences pasted in family albums to the dogged accumulations and meticulous filing needed for photography's uses in weather forecasting, astronomy, microbiology, geology, police work, medical training and diagnosis, military reconnaissance, and art history. Photographs do more than redefine the stuff of ordinary experience (people, things, events, whatever we see—albeit, differently, often inattentively—with natural vision) and add vast amounts of material that we never see at all. Reality as such is redefined—as an item for exhibition, as a record for scrutiny, as a target for surveillance. The photographic exploration and duplication of the world fragments continuities and feeds the pieces into an interminable dossier, thereby providing possibilities of control that could not even be dreamed of under the earlier system of recording information: writing.

That photographic recording is always, potentially, a means of control was already recognized when such powers were in their infancy. In 1850, Delacroix noted in his *Journal* the success of some "experiments in photography" being made at Cambridge, where astronomers were photographing the sun and the moon and had managed to obtain a pinhead-size impression of the star Vega. He added the following "curious" observation:

> Since the light of the star which was daguerreotyped took twenty years to traverse the space separating it from the earth, the ray which was fixed on the plate had consequently left the celestial sphere a long time before Daguerre had discovered the process by means of which we have just gained control of this light.

Leaving behind such puny notions of control as Delacroix's, photography's progress has made ever more literal the senses in which a photograph gives control over the thing photographed. The technology that has already minimized the extent to which the distance separating photographer from subject affects the precision and magnitude of the image; provided ways to photograph things which are unimaginably small as well as those, like stars, which are unimaginably far; rendered picture-taking independent of light itself (infrared photography) and freed the picture-object from its confinement to two dimensions (holography); shrunk the interval between sighting the picture and holding it in one's hands (from the first Kodak, when it took weeks for a developed roll of film to be returned to the amateur photographer, to the Polaroid, which ejects the image in a few seconds); not only got images to move (cinema) but achieved their simultaneous recording and transmission (video)—this technology has made photography an incomparable tool for deciphering behavior, predicting it, and interfering with it.

Photography has powers that no other image-system has ever enjoyed because, unlike the earlier ones, it is *not* dependent on an image maker. However carefully the photographer intervenes in setting up and guiding the image-making process, the process itself remains an optical-chemical (or electronic) one, the workings of which are automatic, the machinery for which will inevitably be modified to provide still more detailed and, therefore, more useful maps of the real. The mechanical genesis of these images, and the literalness of the powers they confer, amounts to a new relationship between image and reality. And if photography could also be said to restore the most primitive relationship—the partial identity of image and object—the potency of the image is now experienced in a very different way. The primitive notion of the efficacy of images presumes that images possess the qualities of real things, but our inclination is to attribute to real things the qualities of an image.

As everyone knows, primitive people fear that the camera will rob them of some part of their being. In the memoir he published in 1900, at the end of a very long life, Nadar reports that Balzac had a similar "vague dread" of being photographed. His explanation, according to Nadar, was that

> every body in its natural state was made up of a series of ghostly images superimposed in layers to infinity, wrapped in infinitesimal films. . . . Man never having been able to create, that is to make something material from an apparition, from something impalpable, or to make from nothing, an object—each Daguerreian operation was therefore going to lay hold of, detach, and use up one of the layers of the body on which it focused.

It seems fitting for Balzac to have had this particular brand of trepidation—"Was Balzac's fear of the Daguerreotype real or feigned?" Nadar asks. "It was real . . ."—since the procedure of photography is a materializing, so to speak, of what is most original in his procedure as a novelist. The Balzacian operation was to magnify tiny details, as in a photographic enlargement, to juxtapose incongruous traits or items, as in a photographic layout: made expressive in this way, any one thing can be connected with everything else. For Balzac, the spirit of an entire milieu could be disclosed by a single material detail, however paltry or arbitrary-seeming. The whole of a life may be summed up in a momentary appearance.* And a change in appearances is a change in the person, for he refused to posit any "real" person ensconced behind these appearances. Balzac's fanciful theory, expressed to Nadar, that a body is composed of an infinite series of "ghostly images," eerily parallels the supposedly realistic theory expressed in his novels, that a person is an aggregate of appearances,

---

* I am drawing on the account of Balzac's realism in Erich Auerbach's *Mimesis*. The passage that Auerbach analyzes from the beginning of *Le Père Goriot* (1834)—Balzac is describing the dining room of the Vauquer pension at seven in the morning and the entry of Madame Vauquer—could hardly be more explicit (or proto-Proustian). "Her whole person," Balzac writes, "explains the pension, as the pension implies her person. . . . The short-statured woman's blowsy *embonpoint* is the product of the life here, as typhoid is the consequence of the exhalations of a hospital. Her knitted wool petticoat, which is longer than her outer skirt (made of an old dress), and whose wadding is escaping by the gaps in the splitting material, sums up the drawing-room, the dining room, the little garden, announces the cooking and gives an inkling of the boarders. When she is there, the spectacle is complete."

appearances which can be made to yield, by proper focusing, infinite layers of significance. To view reality as an endless set of situations which mirror each other, to extract analogies from the most dissimilar things, is to anticipate the characteristic form of perception stimulated by photographic images. Reality itself has started to be understood as a kind of writing, which has to be decoded—even as photographed images were themselves first compared to writing. (Niepce's name for the process whereby the image appears on the plate was heliography, sun-writing; Fox Talbot called the camera "the pencil of nature.")

The problem with Feuerbach's contrast of "original" with "copy" is its static definitions of reality and image. It assumes that what is real persists, unchanged and intact, while only images have changed: shored up by the most tenuous claims to credibility, they have somehow become more seductive. But the notions of image and reality are complementary. When the notion of reality changes, so does that of the image, and vice versa. "Our era" does not prefer images to real things out of perversity but partly in response to the ways in which the notion of what is real has been progressively complicated and weakened, one of the early ways being the criticism of reality as façade which arose among the enlightened middle classes in the last century. (This was of course the very opposite of the effect intended.) To reduce large parts of what has hitherto been regarded as real to mere fantasy, as Feuerbach did when he called religion "the dream of the human mind" and dismissed theological ideas as psychological projections; or to inflate the random and trivial details of everyday life into ciphers of hidden historical and psychological forces, as Balzac did in his encyclopedia of social reality in novel form—these are themselves ways of experiencing reality as a set of appearances, an image.

Few people in this society share the primitive dread of cameras that comes from thinking of the photograph as a material part of themselves. But some trace of the magic remains: for example, in our reluctance to tear up or throw away the photograph of a loved one, especially of someone dead or far away. To do so is a ruthless gesture of rejection. In *Jude the Obscure* it is Jude's discovery that Arabella has sold the maple frame with the photograph of himself in it which he gave her on their wedding day that signifies to Jude "the utter death of every sentiment in his wife" and is "the conclusive little stroke to demolish all sentiment in him." But the true modern primitivism is not to regard the image as a real thing; photographic images are hardly that real. Instead, reality has come to seem more and more like what we are shown by cameras. It is common now for people to insist about their experience of a violent event in which they were caught up—a plane crash, a shoot-out, a terrorist bombing—that "it seemed like a movie." This is said, other descriptions seeming insufficient, in order to explain how real it was. While many people in non-industrialized countries still feel apprehensive when being photographed, divining it to be some kind of trespass, an act of disrespect, a sublimated looting of the personality or the culture, people in industrialized countries seek to have their photographs taken—feel that they are images, and are made real by photographs.

A steadily more complex sense of the real creates its own compensatory fervors and simplifications, the most addictive of which is picture-taking. It is as if photographers, responding to an increasingly depleted sense of reality, were looking for a transfusion—traveling to new experiences, refreshing the old ones. Their ubiquitous activities amount to the most radical, and the safest, version of mobility. The urge to have new experiences is translated into the urge to take photographs: experience seeking a crisis-proof form.

As the taking of photographs seems almost obligatory to those who travel about, the passionate collecting of them has special appeal for those confined—either by choice, incapacity, or coercion—to indoor space. Photograph collections can be used to make a substitute world, keyed to exalting or consoling or tantalizing images. A photograph can be the starting point of a romance (Hardy's Jude had already fallen in love with Sue Bridehead's photograph before he met her), but it is more common for the erotic relation to be not only created by but understood as limited to the photographs. In Cocteau's *Les Enfants Terribles,* the narcissistic brother and sister share their bedroom, their "secret room," with images of boxers, movie stars, and murderers. Isolating themselves in their lair to live out their private legend, the two adolescents put up these photographs, a private pantheon. On one wall of cell No. 426 in Fresnes Prison in the early 1940s Jean Genet pasted the photographs of twenty criminals he had clipped from newspapers, twenty faces in which he discerned "the sacred sign of the monster," and in their honor wrote *Our Lady of the Flowers;* they served as his muses, his models, his erotic talismans. "They watch over my little routines," writes Genet—conflating reverie, masturbation, and writing—and "are all the family I have and my only friends." For stay-at-homes, prisoners, and the self-imprisoned, to live among the photographs of glamorous strangers is a sentimental response to isolation and an insolent challenge to it.

J. G. Ballard's novel *Crash* (1973) describes a more specialized collecting of photographs in the service of sexual obsession: photographs of car accidents which the narrator's friend Vaughan collects
while preparing to stage his own death in a car crash. The acting out
of his erotic vision of car death is anticipated and the fantasy itself
further eroticized by the repeated perusal of these photographs. At
one end of the spectrum, photographs are objective data; at the other
end, they are items of psychological science fiction. And as in even
the most dreadful, or neutral-seeming, reality a sexual imperative can
be found, so even the most banal photograph-document can mutate
into an emblem of desire. The mug shot is a clue to a detective, an
erotic fetish to a fellow thief. To Hofrat Behrens, in *The Magic Mountain*, the pulmonary X-rays of his patients are diagnostic tools. To
Hans Castorp, serving an indefinite sentence in Behrens's sanatorium, and made lovesick by the enigmatic, unattainable Clavdia
Chauchat, "Clavdia's X-ray portrait, showing not her face, but the
delicate bony structure of the upper half of her body, and the organs
of the thoracic cavity, surrounded by the pale, ghostlike envelope of
flesh," is the most precious of trophies. The "transparent portrait" is
a far more intimate vestige of his beloved than the Hofrat's painting
of Clavdia, that "exterior portrait," which Hans had once gazed at
with such longing.

Photographs are a way of imprisoning reality, understood as recalcitrant, inaccessible; of making it stand still. Or they enlarge a reality
that is felt to be shrunk, hollowed out, perishable, remote. One can't
possess reality, one can possess (and be possessed by) images—as,
according to Proust, most ambitious of voluntary prisoners, one can't
possess the present but one can possess the past. Nothing could be
more unlike the self-sacrificial travail of an artist like Proust than the
effortlessness of picture-taking, which must be the sole activity resulting in accredited works of art in which a single movement, a touch
of the finger, produces a complete work. While the Proustian labors
presuppose that reality is distant, photography implies instant access
to the real. But the results of this practice of instant access are another way of creating distance. To possess the world in the form of
images is, precisely, to reexperience the unreality and remoteness of
the real.

The strategy of Proust's realism presumes distance from what is
normally experienced as real, the present, in order to reanimate what
is usually available only in a remote and shadowy form, the past—
which is where the present becomes in his sense real, that is, something that can be possessed. In this effort photographs were of no
help. Whenever Proust mentions photographs, he does so disparag-

ingly: as a synonym for a shallow, too exclusively visual, merely voluntary relation to the past, whose yield is insignificant compared with the deep discoveries to be made by responding to cues given by all the senses—the technique he called "involuntary memory." One can't imagine the Overture to *Swann's Way* ending with the narrator's coming across a snapshot of the parish church at Combray and the savoring of *that* visual crumb, instead of the taste of the humble madeleine dipped in tea, making an entire part of his past spring into view. But this is not because a photograph cannot evoke memories (it can, depending on the quality of the viewer rather than of the photograph) but because of what Proust makes clear about his own demands upon imaginative recall, that it be not just extensive and accurate but give the texture and essence of things. And by considering photographs only so far as he could use them, as an instrument of memory, Proust somewhat misconstrues what photographs are: not so much an instrument of memory as an invention of it or a replacement.

It is not reality that photographs make immediately accessible, but images. For example, now all adults can know exactly how they and their parents and grandparents looked as children—a knowledge not available to anyone before the invention of cameras, not even to that tiny minority among whom it was customary to commission paintings of their children. Most of these portraits were less informative than any snapshot. And even the very wealthy usually owned just one portrait of themselves or any of their forebears as children, that is, an image of one moment of childhood, whereas it is common to have many photographs of oneself, the camera offering the possibility of possessing a complete record, at all ages. The point of the standard portraits in the bourgeois household of the eighteenth and nineteenth centuries was to confirm an ideal of the sitter (proclaiming social standing, embellishing personal appearance); given this purpose, it is clear why their owners did not feel the need to have more than one. What the photograph-record confirms is, more modestly, simply that the subject exists; therefore, one can never have too many.

The fear that a subject's uniqueness was leveled by being photographed was never so frequently expressed as in the 1850s, the years when portrait photography gave the first example of how cameras could create instant fashions and durable industries. In Melville's *Pierre,* published at the start of the decade, the hero, another fevered champion of voluntary isolation,

considered with what infinite readiness now, the most faithful portrait of any one could be taken by the Daguerreotype, whereas in former times a faithful portrait was only within the power of the moneyed, or mental aristocrats of the earth. How natural then the inference, that instead of, as in old times, immortalizing a genius, a portrait now only *dayalized* a dunce. Besides, when every body has his portrait published, true distinction lies in not having yours published at all.

But if photographs demean, paintings distort in the opposite way: they make grandiose. Melville's intuition is that all forms of portraiture in the business civilization are compromised; at least, so it appears to Pierre, a paragon of alienated sensibility. Just as a photograph is too little in a mass society, a painting is too much. The nature of a painting, Pierre observes, makes it

> better entitled to reverence than the man; inasmuch as nothing belittling can be imagined concerning the portrait, whereas many unavoidably belittling things can be fancied as touching the man.

Even if such ironies can be considered to have been dissolved by the completeness of photography's triumph, the main difference between a painting and a photograph in the matter of portraiture still holds. Paintings invariably sum up; photographs usually do not. Photographic images are pieces of evidence in an ongoing biography or history. And one photograph, unlike one painting, implies that there will be others.

"Ever—the Human Document to keep the present and the future in touch with the past," said Lewis Hine. But what photography supplies is not only a record of the past but a new way of dealing with the present, as the effects of the countless billions of contemporary photograph-documents attest. While old photographs fill out our mental image of the past, the photographs being taken now transform what is present into a mental image, like the past. Cameras establish an inferential relation to the present (reality is known by its traces), provide an instantly retroactive view of experience. Photographs give mock forms of possession: of the past, the present, even the future. In Nabokov's *Invitation to a Beheading* (1938), the prisoner Cincinnatus is shown the "photohoroscope" of a child cast by the sinister M'sieur Pierre: an album of photographs of little Emmie as an infant, then a small child, then pre-pubescent, as she is now, then—by retouching and using photographs of her mother—of Emmie the adolescent, the bride, the thirty-year-old, concluding with a photograph at age forty, Emmie on her deathbed. A "parody of the work of time" is what Nabokov calls this exemplary artifact; it is also a parody of the work of photography.

Photography, which has so many narcissistic uses, is also a powerful instrument for depersonalizing our relation to the world; and the two uses are complementary. Like a pair of binoculars with no right or wrong end, the camera makes exotic things near, intimate; and familiar things small, abstract, strange, much farther away. It offers, in one easy, habit-forming activity, both participation and alienation in our own lives and those of others—allowing us to participate, while confirming alienation. War and photography now seem inseparable, and plane crashes and other horrific accidents always attract people with cameras. A society which makes it normative to aspire never to experience privation, failure, misery, pain, dread disease, and in which death itself is regarded not as natural and inevitable but as a cruel, unmerited disaster, creates a tremendous curiosity about these events—a curiosity that is partly satisfied through picture-taking. The feeling of being exempt from calamity stimulates interest in looking at painful pictures, and looking at them suggests and strengthens the feeling that one is exempt. Partly it is because one is "here," not "there," and partly it is the character of inevitability that all events acquire when they are transmuted into images. In the real world, something *is* happening and no one knows what is *going* to happen. In the image-world, it *has* happened, and it *will* forever happen in that way.

Knowing a great deal about what is in the world (art, catastrophe, the beauties of nature) through photographic images, people are frequently disappointed, surprised, unmoved when they see the real thing. For photographic images tend to subtract feeling from something we experience at first hand and the feelings they do arouse are, largely, not those we have in real life. Often something disturbs us more in photographed form than it does when we actually experience it. In a hospital in Shanghai in 1973, watching a factory worker with advanced ulcers have nine-tenths of his stomach removed under acupuncture anesthesia, I managed to follow the three-hour procedure (the first operation I'd ever observed) without queasiness, never once feeling the need to look away. In a movie theater in Paris a year later, the less gory operation in Antonioni's China documentary *Chung Kuo* made me flinch at the first cut of the scalpel and avert my eyes several times during the sequence. One is vulnerable to disturbing events in the form of photographic images in a way that one is not to the real thing. That vulnerability is part of the distinctive passivity of someone who is a spectator twice over, spectator of events already shaped, first by the participants and second by the image maker. For the real operation I had to get scrubbed, don a surgical gown, then stand alongside the busy surgeons and nurses with my roles to play: inhibited adult, well-mannered guest, respectful witness. The movie operation precludes not only this modest participation but whatever is active in spectatorship. In the operating room, I am the one who changes focus, who makes the close-ups and the medium shots. In the theater, Antonioni has already chosen what parts of the operation I can watch; the camera looks for me—and obliges me to look, leaving as my only option not to look. Further, the movie condenses something that takes hours to a few minutes, leaving only interesting parts presented in an interesting way, that is, with the intent to stir or shock. The dramatic is dramatized, by the didactics of layout and montage. We turn the page in a photo magazine, a new sequence starts in a movie, making a contrast that is sharper than the contrast between successive events in real time.

Nothing could be more instructive about the meaning of photography for us—as, among other things, a method of hyping up the real—than the attacks on Antonioni's film in the Chinese press in early 1974. They make a negative catalogue of all the devices of modern photography, still and film.* While for us photography is intimately connected with discontinuous ways of seeing (the point is precisely to see the whole by means of a part—an arresting detail, a striking way of cropping), in China it is connected only with continuity. Not only are there proper subjects for the camera, those which are positive, inspirational (exemplary activities, smiling people, bright weather), and orderly, but there are proper ways of photographing, which derive from notions about the moral order of space that preclude the very idea of photographic seeing. Thus Antonioni was reproached for photographing things that were old, or old-fashioned— "he sought out and took dilapidated walls and blackboard newspapers discarded long ago"; paying "no attention to big and small tractors

---

* See *A Vicious Motive, Despicable Tricks—A Criticism of Antonioni's Anti-China Film "China"* (Peking: Foreign Languages Press, 1974), an eighteen-page pamphlet (unsigned) which reproduces an article that appeared in the paper *Renminh Ribao* on January 30, 1974; and "Repudiating Antonioni's Anti-China Film," *Peking Review,* No. 8 (February 22, 1974), which supplies abridged versions of three other articles published that month. The aim of these articles is not, of course, to expound a view of photography—their interest on that score is inadvertent—but to construct a model ideological enemy, as in other mass educational campaigns staged during this period. Given this purpose, it was as unnecessary for the tens of millions mobilized in meetings held in schools, factories, army units, and communes around the country to "Criticize Antonioni's Anti-China Film" to have actually seen *Chung Kuo* as it was for the participants in the "Criticize Lin Piao and Confucius" campaign of 1976 to have read a text of Confucius.

working in the fields, [he] chose only a donkey pulling a stone roller"—and for showing undecorous moments—"he disgustingly filmed people blowing their noses and going to the latrine"—and undisciplined movement—"instead of taking shots of pupils in the classroom in our factory-run primary school, he filmed the children running out of the classroom after a class." And he was accused of denigrating the right subjects by his way of photographing them: by using "dim and dreary colors" and hiding people in "dark shadows"; by treating the same subject with a variety of shots—"there are sometimes long-shots, sometimes close-ups, sometimes from the front, and sometimes from behind"—that is, for not showing things from the point of view of a single, ideally placed observer; by using high and low angles—"The camera was intentionally turned on this magnificent modern bridge from very bad angles in order to make it appear crooked and tottering"; and by not taking enough full shots—"He racked his brain to get such close-ups in an attempt to distort the people's image and uglify their spiritual outlook."

Besides the mass-produced photographic iconography of revered leaders, revolutionary kitsch, and cultural treasures, one often sees photographs of a private sort in China. Many people possess pictures of their loved ones, tacked to the wall or stuck under the glass on top of the dresser or office desk. A large number of these are the sort of snapshots taken here at family gatherings and on trips; but none is a candid photograph, not even of the kind that the most unsophisticated camera user in this society finds normal—a baby crawling on the floor, someone in mid-gesture. Sports photographs show the team as a group, or only the most stylized balletic moments of play: generally, what people do with the camera is assemble for it, then line up in a row or two. There is no interest in catching a subject in movement. This is, one supposes, partly because of certain old conventions of decorum in conduct and imagery. And it is the characteristic visual taste of those at the first stage of camera culture, when the image is defined as something that can be stolen from its owner; thus, Antonioni was reproached for "forcibly taking shots against people's wishes," like "a thief." Possession of a camera does not license intrusion, as it does in this society whether people like it or not. (The good manners of a camera culture dictate that one is supposed to pretend not to notice when one is being photographed by a stranger in a public place as long as the photographer stays at a discreet distance—that is, one is supposed neither to forbid the picture-taking nor to start posing.) Unlike here, where we pose where we can and yield when we must, in China taking pictures is always a ritual; it always involves posing and, necessarily, consent. Someone who "deliberately stalked people who were unaware of his intention to film them" was depriving people and things of their right to pose, in order to look their best.

Antonioni devoted nearly all of the sequence in *Chung Kuo* about Peking's Tien An Men Square, the country's foremost goal of political pilgrimage, to the pilgrims waiting to be photographed. The interest to Antonioni of showing Chinese performing that elementary rite, having a trip documented by the camera, is evident: the photograph and being photographed are favorite contemporary subjects for the camera. To his critics, the desire of visitors to Tien An Men Square for a photograph souvenir

> is a reflection of their deep revolutionary feelings. But with bad intentions, Antonioni, instead of showing this reality, took shots only of people's clothing, movement, and expressions: here, someone's ruffled hair; there, people peering, their eyes dazzled by the sun; one moment, their sleeves; another, their trousers. . . .

The Chinese resist the photographic dismemberment of reality. Close-ups are not used. Even the postcards of antiquities and works of art sold in museums do not show part of something; the object is always photographed straight on, centered, evenly lit, and in its entirety.

We find the Chinese naïve for not perceiving the beauty of the cracked peeling door, the picturesqueness of disorder, the force of the odd angle and the significant detail, the poetry of the turned back. We have a modern notion of embellishment—beauty is not inherent in anything; it is to be found, by another way of seeing—as well as a wider notion of meaning, which photography's many uses illustrate and powerfully reinforce. The more numerous the variations of something, the richer its possibilities of meaning: thus, more is said with photographs in the West than in China today. Apart from whatever is true about *Chung Kuo* as an item of ideological merchandise (and the Chinese are not wrong in finding the film condescending), Antonioni's images simply mean *more* than any images the Chinese release of themselves. The Chinese don't want photographs to mean very much or to be very interesting. They do not want to see the world from an unusual angle, to discover new subjects. Photographs are supposed to display what has already been described. Photography for us is a double-edged instrument for producing clichés (the French word that means both trite expression and photographic negative) and for serving up "fresh" views. For the Chinese authorities, there are only clichés—which they consider not to be clichés but "correct" views.

In China today, only two realities are acknowledged. We see reality as hopelessly and interestingly plural. In China, what is defined as an issue for debate is one about which there are "two lines," a right one and a wrong one. Our society proposes a spectrum of discontinuous choices and perceptions. Theirs is constructed around a single, ideal observer; and photographs contribute their bit to the Great Monologue. For us, there are dispersed, interchangeable "points of view"; photography is a polylogue. The current Chinese ideology defines reality as a historical process structured by recurrent dualisms with clearly outlined, morally colored meanings; the past, for the most part, is simply judged as bad. For us, there are historical processes with awesomely complex and sometimes contradictory meanings; and arts which draw much of their value from our consciousness of time as history, like photography. (This is why the passing of time adds to the aesthetic value of photographs, and the scars of time make objects more rather than less enticing to photographers.) With the idea of history, we certify our interest in knowing the greatest number of things. The only use the Chinese are allowed to make of their history is didactic: their interest in history is narrow, moralistic, deforming, uncurious. Hence, photography in our sense has no place in their society.

The limits placed on photography in China only reflect the character of their society, a society unified by an ideology of stark, unremitting conflict. Our unlimited use of photographic images not only reflects but gives shape to this society, one unified by the denial of conflict. Our very notion of the world—the capitalist twentieth century's "one world"—is like a photographic overview. The world is "one" not because it is united but because a tour of its diverse contents does not reveal conflict but only an even more astounding diversity. This spurious unity of the world is affected by translating its contents into images. Images are always compatible, or can be made compatible, even when the realities they depict are not.

Photography does not simply reproduce the real, it recycles it—a key procedure of a modern society. In the form of photographic images, things and events are put to new uses, assigned new meanings, which go beyond the distinctions between the beautiful and the ugly, the true and the false, the useful and the useless, good taste and bad. Photography is one of the chief means for producing that quality ascribed to things and situations which erases these distinctions: "the interesting." What makes something interesting is that it can be seen to be like, or analogous to, something else. There is an art and there are fashions of seeing things in order to make them interesting; and to supply this art, these fashions, there is a steady recycling of the artifacts and tastes of the past. Clichés, recycled, become meta-clichés. The photographic recycling makes clichés out of unique objects, distinctive and vivid artifacts out of clichés. Images of real things are interlayered with images of images. The Chinese circumscribe the uses of photography so that there are no layers or strata of images, and all images reinforce and reiterate each other.* We make of photography a means by which, precisely, anything can be said, any purpose served. What in reality is discrete, images join. In the form of a photograph the explosion of an A-bomb can be used to advertise a safe.

To us, the difference between the photographer as an individual eye and the photographer as an objective recorder seems fundamental, the difference often regarded, mistakenly, as separating photography as art from photography as document. But both are logical extensions of what photography means: note-taking on, potentially, everything in the world, from every possible angle. The same Nadar who took the most authoritative celebrity portraits of his time and did the first photo-interviews was also the first photographer to take aerial views; and when he performed "the Daguerreian operation" on Paris from a balloon in 1855 he immediately grasped the future benefit of photography to warmakers.

Two attitudes underlie this presumption that anything in the world is material for the camera. One finds that there is beauty or at least interest in everything, seen with an acute enough eye. (And the aestheticizing of reality that makes everything, anything, available to

*The Chinese concern for the reiterative function of images (and of words) inspires the distributing of additional images, photographs that depict scenes in which, clearly, no photographer could have been present; and the continuing use of such photographs suggests how slender is the population's understanding of what photographic images and picture-taking imply. In his book *Chinese Shadows,* Simon Leys gives an example from the "Movement to Emulate Lei Feng," a mass campaign of the mid-1960s to inculcate the ideals of Maoist citizenship built around the apotheosis of an Unknown Citizen, a conscript named Lei Feng who died at twenty in a banal accident. Lei Feng Exhibitions organized in the large cities included "photographic documents, such as 'Lei Feng helping an old woman to cross the street,' 'Lei Feng secretly [sic] doing his comrade's washing,' 'Lei Feng giving his lunch to a comrade who forgot his lunch box,' and so forth," with, apparently, nobody questioning "the providential presence of a photographer during the various incidents in the life of that humble, hitherto unknown soldier." In China, what makes an image true is that it is good for people to see it.

the camera is what also permits the coopting of any photograph, even one of an utterly practical sort, as art.) The other treats everything as the object of some present or future use, as matter for estimates, decisions, and predictions. According to one attitude, there is nothing that should not be *seen;* according to the other, there is nothing that should not be *recorded.* Cameras implement an aesthetic view of reality by being a machine-toy that extends to everyone the possibility of making disinterested judgments about importance, interest, beauty. (*"That* would make a good picture.") Cameras implement the instrumental view of reality by gathering information that enables us to make a more accurate and much quicker response to whatever is going on. The response may of course be either repressive or benevolent: military reconnaissance photographs help snuff out lives, X-rays help save them.

Though these two attitudes, the aesthetic and the instrumental, seem to produce contradictory and even incompatible feelings about people and situations, that is the altogether characteristic contradiction of attitude which members of a society that divorces public from private are expected to share in and live with. And there is perhaps no activity which prepares us so well to live with these contradictory attitudes as does picture-taking, which lends itself so brilliantly to both. On the one hand, cameras arm vision in the service of power—of the state, of industry, of science. On the other hand, cameras make vision expressive in that mythical space known as private life. In China, where no space is left over from politics and moralism for expressions of aesthetic sensibility, only some things are to be photographed and only in certain ways. For us, as we become further detached from politics, there is more and more free space to fill up with exercises of sensibility such as cameras afford. One of the effects of the newer camera technology (video, instant movies) has been to turn even more of what is done with cameras in private to narcissistic uses—that is, to self-surveillance. But such currently popular uses of image-feedback in the bedroom, the therapy session, and the weekend conference seem far less momentous than video's potential as a tool for surveillance in public places. Presumably, the Chinese will eventually make the same instrumental uses of photography that we do, except, perhaps, this one. Our inclination to treat character as equivalent to behavior makes more acceptable a widespread public installation of the mechanized regard from the outside provided by cameras. China's far more repressive standards of order require not only monitoring behavior but changing hearts; there, surveillance is internalized to a degree without precedent, which suggests a more limited future in their society for the camera as a means of surveillance.

China offers the model of one kind of dictatorship, whose master idea is "the good," in which the most unsparing limits are placed on all forms of expression, including images. The future may offer another kind of dictatorship, whose master idea is "the interesting," in which images of all sorts, stereotyped and eccentric, proliferate. Something like this is suggested in Nabokov's *Invitation to a Beheading*. Its portrait of a model totalitarian state contains only one, omnipresent art: photography—and the friendly photographer who hovers around the hero's death cell turns out, at the end of the novel, to be the headsman. And there seems no way (short of undergoing a vast historical amnesia, as in China) of limiting the proliferation of photographic images. The only question is whether the function of the image-world created by cameras could be other than it is. The present function is clear enough, if one considers in what contexts photographic images are seen, what dependencies they create, what antagonisms they pacify—that is, what institutions they buttress, whose needs they really serve.

A capitalist society requires a culture based on images. It needs to furnish vast amounts of entertainment in order to stimulate buying and anesthetize the injuries of class, race, and sex. And it needs to gather unlimited amounts of information, the better to exploit natural resources, increase productivity, keep order, make war, give jobs to bureaucrats. The camera's twin capacities, to subjectivize reality and to objectify it, ideally serve these needs and strengthen them. Cameras define reality in the two ways essential to the workings of an advanced industrial society: as a spectacle (for masses) and as an object of surveillance (for rulers). The production of images also furnishes a ruling ideology. Social change is replaced by a change in images. The freedom to consume a plurality of images and goods is equated with freedom itself. The narrowing of free political choice to free economic consumption requires the unlimited production and consumption of images.

The final reason for the need to photograph everything lies in the very logic of consumption itself. To consume means to burn, to use up—and, therefore, to need to be replenished. As we make images and consume them, we need still more images; and still more. But images are not a treasure for which the world must be ransacked; they are precisely what is at hand wherever the eye falls. The possession of a camera can inspire something akin to lust. And like all credible forms of lust, it cannot be satisfied: first, because the possibilities of photography are infinite; and, second, because the project is finally self-devouring. The attempts by photographers to bolster up a depleted sense of reality contribute to the depletion. Our oppressive sense of the transience of everything is more acute since cameras gave us the means to "fix" the fleeting moment. We consume images at an ever faster rate and, as Balzac suspected cameras used up layers of the body, images consume reality. Cameras are the antidote and the disease, a means of appropriating reality and a means of making it obsolete.

The powers of photography have in effect de-Platonized our understanding of reality, making it less and less plausible to reflect upon our experience according to the distinction between images and things, between copies and originals. It suited Plato's derogatory attitude toward images to liken them to shadows—transitory, minimally informative, immaterial, impotent co-presences of the real things which cast them. But the force of photographic images comes from their being material realities in their own right, richly informative deposits left in the wake of whatever emitted them, potent means for turning the tables on reality—for turning *it* into a shadow. Images are more real than anyone could have supposed. And just because they are an unlimited resource, one that cannot be exhausted by consumerist waste, there is all the more reason to apply the conservationist remedy. If there can be a better way for the real world to include the one of images, it will require an ecology not only of real things but of images as well.

(*1977*)

FROM

I, etcetera

Unguided Tour

I took a trip to see the beautiful things. Change of scenery. Change of heart. And do you know?

What?

They're still there.

Ah, but they won't be there for long.

I know. That's why I went. To say goodbye. Whenever I travel, it's always to say goodbye.

Tile roofs, timbered balconies, fish in the bay, the copper clock, shawls drying on the rocks, the delicate odor of olives, sunsets behind the bridge, ocher stone. "Gardens, parks, forests, woods, canals, private lakes, with huts, villas, gates, garden seats, gazebos, alcoves, grottoes, hermitages, triumphal arches, chapels, temples, mosques, banqueting houses, rotundas, observatories, aviaries, greenhouses, icehouses, fountains, bridges, boats, cascades, baths." The Roman amphitheater, the Etruscan sarcophagus. The monument to the 1914–18 war dead in every village square. You don't see the military base. It's out of town, and not on the main road.

Omens. The cloister wall has sprung a long diagonal crack. The water level is rising. The marble saint's nose is no longer aquiline.

This spot. Some piety always brings me back to this spot. I think of all the people who were here. Their names scratched into the bottom of the fresco.

Vandals!

Yes. Their way of being here.

372 / S U S A N   S O N T A G

The proudest of human-made things dragged down to the condition of natural things. Last Judgment.

You can't lock up all the things in museums.

Aren't there any beautiful things in your own country?

No. Yes. Fewer.

Did you have guidebooks, maps, timetables, stout shoes?

I read the guidebooks when I got home. I wanted to stay with my—

Immediate impressions?

You could call them that.

But you did see the famous places. You didn't perversely neglect them.

I did see them. As conscientiously as I could while protecting my ignorance. I don't want to know more than I know, don't want to get more attached to them than I already am.

How did you know where to go?

By playing my memory like a roulette wheel.

Do you remember what you saw?

Not much.

It's too sad. I can't love the past that's trapped within my memory like a souvenir.

Object lessons. Grecian urns. A pepper-mill Eiffel Tower. Bismarck beer mug. Bay-of-Naples-with-Vesuvius scarf. David-by-Michelangelo cork tray.

No souvenirs, thanks. Let's stay with the real thing.

The past. Well, there's always something ineffable about the past, don't you think?

In all its original glory. The indispensable heritage of a woman of culture.

I agree. Like you, I don't consider devotion to the past a form of snobbery. Just one of the more disastrous forms of unrequited love.

I was being wry. I'm a fickle lover. It's not love that the past needs in order to survive, it's an absence of choices.

And armies of the well-off, immobilized by vanity, greed, fear of scandal, and the inefficiency and discomfort of travel. Women carrying parasols and pearl handbags, with mincing steps, long skirts, shy eyes. Mustached men in top hats, lustrous hair parted on the left side, garters holding up their silk socks. Seconded by footmen, cobblers, ragpickers, blacksmiths, buskers, printer's devils, chimney sweeps, lacemakers, midwives, carters, milkmaids, stonemasons, coachmen, turnkeys, and sacristans. As recently as that. All gone. The people. And their pomp and circumstance.

Is that what you think I went to see?

Not the people. But their places, their beautiful things. You said they were still there. The hut, the hermitage, the grotto, the park, the castle. An aviary in the Chinese style. His Lordship's estate. A delightful seclusion in the midst of his impenetrable woods.

I wasn't happy there.

What did you feel?

Regret that the trees were being cut down.

So you have a hazy vision of natural things. From too much indulgence in the nervous, metallic pleasures of cities.

Unequal to my passions, I fled the lakes, I fled the woods, I fled the fields pulsing with glowworms, I fled the aromatic mountains.

Provincial blahs. Something less solitary is what you need.

I used to say: Landscapes interest me only in relation to human beings. Ah, loving someone would give life to all this . . . But the emotions that human beings inspire in us also sadly resemble each other. The more that places, customs, the circumstances of adventures are changed, the more we see that we amidst them are unchanging. I know all the reactions I shall have. Know all the words that I am going to utter again.

You should have taken me along instead.

You mean him. Yes, of course I wasn't alone. But we quarreled most of the time. He plodding, I odious.

They say. They say a trip is a good time for repairing a damaged love.

Or else it's the worst. Feelings like shrapnel half worked out of the wound. Opinions. And competition of opinions. Desperate amatory exercises back at the hotel on golden summer afternoons. Room service.

How did you let it get that dreary? You were so hopeful.

Rubbish! Prisons and hospitals are swollen with hope. But not charter flights and luxury hotels.

But you were moved. Sometimes.

Maybe it was exhaustion. Sure I was. I am. The inside of my feelings is damp with tears.

And the outside?

Very dry. Well—as dry as is necessary. You can't imagine how tiring it is. That double-membraned organ of nostalgia, pumping the tears in. Pumping them out.

Qualities of depth and stamina.

And discrimination. When one can summon them.

I'm bushed. They aren't all beautiful, the beautiful things. I've never seen so many squabbly Cupids and clumsy Graces.

Here's a café. *In the café.* The village priest playing the pinball machine. Nineteen-year-old sailors with red pompons watching. Old gent with amber worry beads. Proprietor's granddaughter doing her homework at a deal table. Two hunters buying picture postcards of stags. He says: You can drink the acidic local wine, become a little less odious, unwind.

Monsieur René says it closes at five.

Each picture. "Each picture had beneath it a motto of some good intention. Seeing that I was looking carefully at these noble images, he said: 'Here everything is natural.' The figures were clothed like living men and women, though they were far more beautiful. Much light, much darkness, men and women who are and yet are not."

Worth a detour? Worth a trip! It's a remarkable collection. Still possessed its aura. The things positively importuned.

The baron's zeal in explaining. His courteous manner. He stayed all through the bombardment.

A necessary homogeneity. Or else some stark, specific event.

I want to go back to that antique store.

"The ogival arch of the doorway is Gothic, but the central nave and the flanking wings—"

You're hard to please.

Can't you imagine traveling not to accumulate pleasures but to make them rarer?

Satiety is not my problem. Nor is piety.

There's nothing left but to wait for our meals, like animals.

Are you catching a cold? Drink this.

I'm perfectly all right. I beg you, don't buy the catalogue. Or the postcard-size reproductions. Or the sailor sweater.

Don't be angry, but—did you tip Monsieur René?

Say to yourself fifty times a day: I am not a connoisseur, I am not a romantic wanderer, I am not a pilgrim.

You say it.

"A permanent part of mankind's spiritual goods."

Translate that for me. I forgot my phrase book.

Still, you saw what you came to see.

The old victory of arrangement over accumulation.

But sometimes you were happy. Not just in spite of things.

Barefoot on the mosaic floor of the baptistery. Clambering above the flying buttresses. Irradiated by a Baroque monstrance shimmering indistinctly in the growing dusk of the cathedral. Effulgence of things. Voluminous. Resplendent. Unutterable bliss.

You send postcards on which you write "Bliss." Remember? You sent one to me.

I remember. Don't stop me. I'm flying. I'm prowling. Epiphany. Hot tears. Delirium. Don't stop me. I stroke my delirium like the balls of the comely waiter.

You want to make me jealous.

Don't stop me. His dainty skin, his saucy laughter, his way of whistling, the succulent dampness of his shirt. We went into a shed behind the restaurant. And I said: Enter, sir, this body. This body is your castle, your cabin, your hunting lodge, your villa, your carriage, your luxury liner, your drawing room, your kitchen, your speedboat, your toolshed . . .

Do you often do that sort of thing when he's around?

Him? He was napping at the hotel. A mild attack of heliophobia.

In the hotel. Back at the hotel, I woke him up. He had an erection. I seated myself on his loins. The nub, the hub, the fulcrum. Gravitational lines of force. In a world of perfect daylight. Indeed, a high-noon world, in which objects cast no shadows.

Only the half wise will despise these sensations.

I'm turning. I'm a huge steering wheel, unguided by any human hand. I'm turning . . .

And the other pleasures? The ones you came for.

"In the entire visible world there is hardly a more powerful mood-impression than that experienced within one of the Gothic cathedrals just as the sun is setting."

Pleasures of the eye. They, too, must be emphasized.

"The eye can see nothing beyond those glimmering figures that hover overhead to the west in stern, solemn rows as the burning evening sun falls across them."

Messengers of temporal and spiritual infinity.

"The sensation of fire permeates all, and the colors sing out, rejoicing and sobbing."

There, in truth, is a different world.

I found a wonderful old Baedeker, with lots of things that aren't in the Michelin. *Let's.* Let's visit the caves. Unless they're closed.

Let's visit the World War I cemetery.

Let's watch the regatta.

This spot. He committed suicide right here, by the lake. With his fiancée. In 1811.

I seduced a waiter in the restaurant by the port two days ago. *He said.* He said his name was Arrigo.

I love you. And my heart is pounding.

So is mine.

What's important is that we're strolling in this arcade together.

That we're strolling. That we're looking. That it's beautiful.

Object lessons. Give me that suitcase, it's heavy.

One must be careful not to wonder if these pleasures are superior to last year's pleasures. They never are.

That must be the seduction of the past again. But just wait until now becomes then. You'll see how happy we were.

I'm not expecting to be happy. *Complaints.* I've already seen it. I'm sure it'll be full. It's too far. You're driving too fast, I can't see anything. Only two showings of the movie, at seven and at nine. There's a strike, I can't telephone. This damned siesta, nothing's open between one and four. If everything came out of this suitcase, I don't understand why I can't cram it all back in.

You'll soon stop fretting over these mingy impediments. You'll realize you're carefree, without obligations. And then the unease will start.

Like those upper-middle-class Protestant folk who experience revelations, become hysterical, suffer breakdowns under the disorienting impact of Mediterranean light and Mediterranean manners. You're still thinking about the waiter.

I said I love you, I trust you, I didn't mind.

You shouldn't. I don't want that kind of revelation. I don't want to satisfy my desire, I want to exacerbate it. I want to resist the temptation of melancholy, my dear. If you only knew how much.

Then you must stop this flirtation with the past invented by poets and curators. We can forget about their old things. We can buy their postcards, eat their food, admire their sexual nonchalance. We can march in their workers' festivals and sing the "Internationale," for even we know the words.

I'm feeling perfectly all right.

I think it's safe to. Pick up hitchhikers, drink unbottled water, try to score some hash in the piazza, eat the mussels, leave the camera in the car, hang out in waterfront bars, trust the hotel concierge to make the reservation, don't you?

Something. Don't you want to do something?

Does every country have a tragic history except ours?

This spot. See? There's a commemorative plaque. Between the windows.

Ruined. Ruined by too many decades of intrepid appreciation. Nature, the whore, cooperates. The crags of the Dolomites made too pink by the sun, the water of the lagoon made too silver by the moon, the blue skies of Greece (or Sicily) made too deep a blue by the arch in a white wall.

Ruins. These are ruins left from the last war.

Antiquarian effrontery: our pretty dwelling.

It was a convent, built according to a plan drawn up by Michelangelo. Turned into a hotel in 1927. Don't expect the natives to take care of the beautiful things.

I don't.

They say. They say they're going to fill in the canal and make it a highway, sell the duchess's rococo chapel to a sheik in Kuwait, build a condominium on that bluff with a stand of pine, open a boutique in the fishing village, put a sound-and-light show in the ghetto. It's going fast. International Committee. Attempting to preserve. Under the patronage of His Excellency and the Honorable. Going fast. You'll have to run.

Will I have to run?

Then let them go. Life is not a race.

Or else it is.

Any more. Isn't it a pity they don't write out the menus in purple ink any more. That you can't put your shoes outside the hotel room at night. *Remember*. Those outsize bills, the kind they had until the devaluation. *Last time*. There weren't as many cars last time, were there?

How could you stand it?

It was easier than it sounds. With an imagination like a pillar of fire. And a heart like a pillar of salt.

And you want to break the tie.

Right.

Lot's wife!

But his lover.

I told you. I told you, you should have taken me along instead.

Lingering. In the basilica. In the garden behind the inn. In the spice market. In bed, in the middle of the golden afternoon.

Because. It's because of the fumes from the petrochemical factories nearby. It's because they don't have enough guards for the museums.

"Two groups of statuary, one depicting virtuous toil, the other unbridled licentiousness."

Do you realize how much prices have gone up? Appalling inflation. I can't conceive how people here manage. With rents almost as high as back home and salaries half.

"On the left of the main road, the Tomb of the Reliefs (the so-called Tomba Bella) is entered. On the walls round the niches and on the pillars, the favorite objects of the dead and domestic articles are reproduced in painted stucco relief: dogs, helmets, swords, leggings, shields, knapsacks and haversacks, bowls, a jug, a couch, pincers, a saw, knives, kitchen vessels and utensils, coils of rope, etc."

I'm sure. I'm sure she was a prostitute. Did you look at her shoes? I'm sure they're giving a concert in the cathedral tonight. *Plus they said.* Three stars, I'm sure they said it had three stars.

This spot. This is where they shot the scene in that movie.

Quite unspoiled. I'm amazed. I was expecting the worst.

They rent mules.

Of course. Every wage earner in the country gets five weeks' paid vacation.

The women age so quickly.

Nice. It's the second summer for the Ministry of Tourism's "Be Nice" campaign. This country where ruined marvels litter the ground.

It says. It says it's closed for restoration. It says you can't swim there any more.

Pollution.

They said.

I don't care. Come on in. The water's almost as warm as the Caribbean.

I want you, I feel you. Lick my neck. Slip off your trunks. Let me . . .

Let's. Let's go back to the hotel.

"The treatment of space in Mannerist architecture and painting shows this change from the 'closed' Renaissance world order to the 'open,' 'loose,' and deviating motions in the Mannerist universe."

What are you trying to tell me?

"The harmony, intelligibility, and coherence of the Renaissance world view were inherent in the symmetrical courtyards of Italian palaces."

I don't want to flatter my intelligence with evidence.

If you don't want to look at the painting, look at me.

See the sign? You can't take the boat that way. We're getting near the nuclear-submarine base.

Reports. Five cases of cholera have been reported.

This piazza has been called a stage for heroes.

It gets much cooler at night. You have to wear a sweater.

Thanks to the music festival every summer. You should see this place in the winter. It's dead.

The trial is next week, so now they're having demonstrations. Can't you see the banner? And listen to that song.

Let's not. I'm sure it's a clip joint.

Covered with flies. That poor child. Did you see?

Omens. The power failure yesterday. New graffiti on the monument this morning. Tanks grinding along the boulevard at noon. *They say.* They say the radar at the airport has been out for the last seventy-two hours.

They say the dictator has recovered from his heart attack.

No, bottled water. Hardier folk. Quite different vegetation.

And the way they treat women here! Beasts of burden. Hauling those sacks up azure hills on which—

They're building a ski station.

They're phasing out the leprosarium.

Look at his face. He's trying to talk to you.

Of course we could live here, privileged as we are. It isn't our country. I don't even mind being robbed.

"The sun having mounted and the heat elsewhere too extreme for us, we have retired to the shade of an oasis."

Sometimes I did love him. Still, in a certain hour of mental fatigue . . .

At the mercy of your moods.

My undaunted caresses. My churlish silences.

You were trying to mend an error.

I was trying to change my plight.

I told you, you should have taken me along instead.

It wouldn't have been different. I went on from there alone. I would have left you, too.

Mornings of departure. With everything prepared. Sun rising over the most majestic of bays (Naples, Rio, or Hong Kong).

But you could decide to stay. Make new arrangements. Would that make you feel free? Or would you feel you'd spurned something irreplaceable?

The whole world.

That's because it's later rather than earlier. "In the beginning, all the world was America."

They said. Sharks, I think they said.

Not the hydrofoil. I know it's faster, but they make me sick.

"The sun having mounted and the heat elsewhere too extreme for us, we have retired to the tree-shaded courtyard." It's not that I loved him. But in a certain hour of physical fatigue . . .

At the mercy of your moods.

Contented sometimes. Even blissful.
Doesn't sound like it. Sounds like struggling to savor.
Maybe. Loss of judgment in the necropolis.
Reports. There's a civil war raging in the north. The Liberation Front's leader is still in exile. Rumors that the dictator has had a stroke. But everything seems so—
Calm?
I guess . . . calm.

This spot. On this spot they massacred three hundred students.
I'd better go with you. You'll have to bargain.
I'm starting to like the food. You get used to it after a while. Don't you?
In the oldest paintings there is a complete absence of chiaroscuro.
I feel well here. There's not so much to see.
"Below the molding, small leafy trees, from which hang wreaths, ribbons, and various objects, alternate with figures of men dancing. One man is lying on the ground, playing the double flute."
Cameras. The women don't like to be photographed.
We may need a guide.
It's a book on the treasures they unearthed. Pictures, bronzes, and lamps.
That's the prison where they torture political suspects. Terror incognita.
How far from the beginning are we? When did we first start to feel the wound?
This staunchless wound, the great longing for another place. To make this place another.
In a mosque at Damietta stands a column that, if you lick it until your tongue bleeds, will cure you of restlessness. It must bleed.
A curious word, wanderlust. I'm ready to go.
I've already gone. Regretfully, exultantly. A prouder lyricism. It's not Paradise that's lost.
Advice. Move along, let's get cracking, don't hold me down, he travels fastest who travels alone. Let's get the show on the road. Get up, slugabed. I'm clearing out of here. Get your ass in gear. Sleep faster, we need the pillow.
She's racing, he's stalling.
If I go this fast, I won't see anything. If I slow down—
Everything. —then I won't have seen everything before it disappears.

Everywhere. I've been everywhere. I haven't been everywhere, but it's on my list.

Land's end. But there's water, O my heart. And salt on my tongue.

The end of the world. This is not the end of the world.

(1978)

Under the Sign of Saturn

Under the Sign of Saturn

In most of the portrait photographs he is looking down, his right hand to his face. The earliest one I know shows him in 1927—he is thirty-five—with dark curly hair over a high forehead, mustache above a full lower lip: youthful, almost handsome. With his head lowered, his jacketed shoulders seem to start behind his ears; his thumb leans against his jaw; the rest of the hand, cigarette between bent index and third fingers, covers his chin; the downward look through his glasses—the soft, daydreamer's gaze of the myopic—seems to float off to the lower left of the photograph.

In a picture from the late 1930s, the curly hair has hardly receded, but there is no trace of youth or handsomeness; the face has widened and the upper torso seems not just high but blocky, huge. The thicker mustache and the pudgy folded hand with thumb tucked under cover his mouth. The look is opaque, or just more inward: he could be thinking—or listening. ("He who listens hard doesn't see," Benjamin wrote in his essay on Kafka.) There are books behind his head.

In a photograph taken in the summer of 1938, on the last of several visits he made to Brecht in exile in Denmark after 1933, he is standing in front of Brecht's house, an old man at forty-six, in white shirt, tie, trousers with watch chain: a slack, corpulent figure, looking truculently at the camera.

Another picture, from 1937, shows Benjamin in the Bibliothèque Nationale in Paris. Two men, neither of whose face can be seen, share a table some distance behind him. Benjamin sits in the right foreground, probably taking notes for the book on Baudelaire and nineteenth-century Paris he had been writing for a decade. He is consulting a volume he holds open on the table with his left hand—his eyes can't be seen—looking, as it were, into the lower right edge of the photograph.

His close friend Gershom Scholem has described his first glimpse of Benjamin in Berlin in 1913, at a joint meeting of a Zionist youth group and Jewish members of the Free German Student Association, of which the twenty-one-year-old Benjamin was a leader. He spoke "extempore without so much as a glance at his audience, staring with a fixed gaze at a remote corner of the ceiling which he harangued with much intensity, in a style incidentally that was, as far as I remember, ready for print."

He was what the French call *un triste*. In his youth he seemed marked by "a profound sadness," Scholem wrote. He thought of himself as a melancholic, disdaining modern psychological labels and invoking the traditional astrological one: "I came into the world under the sign of Saturn—the star of the slowest revolution, the planet of detours and delays. . . ." His major projects, the book published in 1928 on the German baroque drama (the *Trauerspiel;* literally, sorrow-play) and his never completed *Paris, Capital of the Nineteenth Century,* cannot be fully understood unless one grasps how much they rely on a theory of melancholy.

Benjamin projected himself, his temperament, into all his major subjects, and his temperament determined what he chose to write about. It was what he saw in subjects, such as the seventeenth-century baroque plays (which dramatize different facets of "Saturnine acedia") and the writers about whose work he wrote most brilliantly—Baudelaire, Proust, Kafka, Karl Kraus. He even found the Saturnine element in Goethe. For, despite the polemic in his great (still untranslated) essay on Goethe's *Elective Affinities* against interpreting a writer's work by his life, he did make selective use of the life in his deepest meditations on texts: information that disclosed the melancholic, the solitary. (Thus, he describes Proust's "loneliness which pulls the world down into its vortex"; explains how Kafka, like Klee, was "essentially solitary"; cites Robert Walser's "horror of success in life.") One cannot use the life to interpret the work. But one can use the work to interpret the life.

Two short books of reminiscences of his Berlin childhood and student years, written in the early 1930s and unpublished in his lifetime, contain Benjamin's most explicit self-portrait. To the nascent melancholic, in school and on walks with his mother, "solitude appeared to me as the only fit state of man." Benjamin does not mean solitude in a room—he was often sick as a child—but solitude in the great metropolis, the busyness of the idle stroller, free to daydream, observe, ponder, cruise. The mind who was to attach much of the nineteenth century's sensibility to the figure of the *flâneur,* personified by that superbly self-aware melancholic Baudelaire, spun much of his own sensibility out of his phantasmagorical, shrewd, subtle relation to cities. The street, the passage, the arcade, the labyrinth are recurrent themes in his literary essays and, notably, in the projected book on nineteenth-century Paris, as well as in his travel pieces and reminiscences. (Robert Walser, for whom walking was the center of his reclusive life and marvelous books, is a writer to whom one particularly wishes Benjamin had devoted a longer essay.) The only book of a discreetly autobiographical nature published in his lifetime was titled *One-Way Street.* Reminiscences of self are reminiscences of a place, and how he positions himself in it, navigates around it.

"Not to find one's way about in a city is of little interest," begins his still untranslated *A Berlin Childhood Around the Turn of the Century.* "But to lose one's way in a city, as one loses one's way in a forest, requires practice. . . . I learned this art late in life: it fulfilled the dreams whose first traces were the labyrinths on the blotters of my exercise books." This passage also occurs in *A Berlin Chronicle,* after Benjamin suggests how much practice it took to get lost, given an original sense of "impotence before the city." His goal is to be a competent street-map reader who knows how to stray. And to locate himself, with imaginary maps. Elsewhere in *Berlin Chronicle* Benjamin relates that for years he had played with the idea of mapping his life. For this map, which he imagined as gray, he had devised a colorful system of signs that "clearly marked in the houses of my friends and girl friends, the assembly halls of various collectives, from the 'debating chambers' of the Youth Movement to the gathering places of the communist youth, the hotel and brothel rooms that I knew for one night, the decisive benches in the Tiergarten, the ways to different schools and the graves that I saw filled, the sites of prestigious cafés whose long-forgotten names daily crossed our lips." Once, waiting for someone in the Café des Deux Magots in Paris, he relates, he managed to draw a diagram of his life: it was like a labyrinth, in which each important relationship figures as "an entrance to the maze."

The recurrent metaphors of maps and diagrams, memories and dreams, labyrinths and arcades, vistas and panoramas, evoke a certain vision of cities as well as a certain kind of life. Paris, Benjamin writes, "taught me the art of straying." The revelation of the city's true nature came not in Berlin but in Paris, where he stayed frequently throughout the Weimar years, and lived as a refugee from 1933 until his suicide while trying to escape from France in 1940—more exactly, the Paris reimagined in the Surrealist narratives (Breton's *Nadja,* Aragon's *Le Paysan de Paris*). With these metaphors, he is indicating a general problem about orientation, and erecting a standard of difficulty and complexity. (A labyrinth is a place where one gets lost.) He is also suggesting a notion about the forbidden, and how to gain access to it: through an act of the mind that is the same as a physical act. "Whole networks of streets were opened up under the auspices of prostitution," he writes in *Berlin Chronicle,* which begins by invoking an Ariadne, the whore who leads this son of rich parents for the first time across "the threshold of class." The metaphor of the labyrinth also suggests Benjamin's idea of obstacles thrown up by his own temperament.

The influence of Saturn makes people "apathetic, indecisive, slow," he writes in *The Origin of German Trauerspiel* (1928). Slowness is one characteristic of the melancholic temperament. Blundering is another, from noticing too many possibilities, from not noticing one's lack of practical sense. And stubbornness, from the longing to be superior—on one's own terms. Benjamin recalls his stubbornness during childhood walks with his mother, who would turn insignificant items of conduct into tests of his aptitude for practical life, thereby reinforcing what was inept ("my inability even today to make a cup of coffee") and dreamily recalcitrant in his nature. "My habit of seeming slower, more maladroit, more stupid than I am, had its origin in such walks, and has the great attendant danger of making me think myself quicker, more dexterous, and shrewder than I am." And from this stubbornness comes, "above all, a gaze that appears to see not a third of what it takes in."

One-Way Street distills the experiences of the writer and lover (it is dedicated to Asja Lacis, who "cut it through the author"),* experiences that can be guessed at in the opening words on the writer's situation, which sound the theme of revolutionary moralism, and the

---

*Asja Lacis and Benjamin met in Capri in the summer of 1924. She was a Latvian communist revolutionary and theater director, assistant to Brecht and to Piscator, with whom Benjamin wrote "Naples" in 1925 and for whom he wrote "Program for a Proletarian Children's Theater" in 1928. It was Lacis who got Benjamin an invitation to Moscow in the winter of 1926–27 and who introduced him to Brecht in 1929. Benjamin hoped to marry her when he and his wife were finally divorced in 1930. But she returned to Riga and later spent ten years in a Soviet camp.

final "To the Planetarium," a paean to the technological wooing of nature and to sexual ecstasy. Benjamin could write about himself more directly when he started from memories, not contemporary experiences; when he writes about himself as a child. At that distance, childhood, he can survey his life as a space that can be mapped. The candor and the surge of painful feelings in *Berlin Childhood* and *Berlin Chronicle* become possible precisely because Benjamin has adopted a completely digested, analytical way of relating the past. It evokes events for the reactions to the events, places for the emotions one has deposited in the places, other people for the encounter with oneself, feelings and behavior for intimations of future passions and failures contained in them. Fantasies of monsters loose in the large apartment while his parents entertain their friends prefigure his revulsion against his class; the dream of being allowed to sleep as long as he wants, instead of having to get up early to go to school, will be fulfilled when—after his book on the *Trauerspiel* failed to qualify him for a university lectureship—he realizes that "his hopes of a position and a secure livelihood had always been in vain"; his way of walking with his mother, "with pedantic care" keeping one step behind her, prefigures his "sabotage of real social existence."

Benjamin regards everything he chooses to recall in his past as prophetic of the future, because the work of memory (reading oneself backward, he called it) collapses time. There is no chronological ordering of his reminiscences, for which he disavows the name of autobiography, because time is irrelevant. ("Autobiography has to do with time, with sequence and what makes up the continuous flow of life," he writes in *Berlin Chronicle*. "Here, I am talking of a space, of moments and discontinuities.") Benjamin, the translator of Proust, wrote fragments of an opus that could be called *A la recherche des espaces perdus*. Memory, the staging of the past, turns the flow of events into tableaux. Benjamin is not trying to recover his past but to understand it: to condense it into its spatial forms, its premonitory structures.

For the baroque dramatists, he writes in *The Origin of German Trauerspiel*, "chronological movement is grasped and analyzed in a spatial image." The book on the *Trauerspiel* is not only Benjamin's first account of what it means to convert time into space; it is where he explains most clearly what feeling underlies this move. Awash in melancholic awareness of "the disconsolate chronicle of world history," a process of incessant decay, the baroque dramatists seek to escape from history and restore the "timelessness" of paradise. The seventeenth-century baroque sensibility had a "panoramatic" conception of history: "history merges into the setting." In *Berlin Childhood* and *Berlin Chronicle,* Benjamin merges his life into a setting. The successor to the baroque stage set is the Surrealist city: the metaphysical landscape in whose dream-like spaces people have "a brief, shadowy existence," like the nineteen-year-old poet whose suicide, the great sorrow of Benjamin's student years, is condensed in the memory of rooms that the dead friend inhabited.

Benjamin's recurrent themes are, characteristically, means of spatializing the world: for example, his notion of ideas and experiences as ruins. To understand something is to understand its topography, to know how to chart it. And to know how to get lost.

For the character born under the sign of Saturn, time is the medium of constraint, inadequacy, repetition, mere fulfillment. In time, one is only what one is: what one has always been. In space, one can be another person. Benjamin's poor sense of direction and inability to read a street map become his love of travel and his mastery of the art of straying. Time does not give one much leeway: it thrusts us forward from behind, blows us through the narrow funnel of the present into the future. But space is broad, teeming with possibilities, positions, intersections, passages, detours, U-turns, dead ends, one-way streets. Too many possibilities, indeed. Since the Saturnine temperament is slow, prone to indecisiveness, sometimes one has to cut one's way through with a knife. Sometimes one ends by turning the knife against oneself.

The mark of the Saturnine temperament is the self-conscious and unforgiving relation to the self, which can never be taken for granted. The self is a text—it has to be deciphered. (Hence, this is an apt temperament for intellectuals.) The self is a project, something to be built. (Hence, this is an apt temperament for artists and martyrs, those who court "the purity and beauty of a failure," as Benjamin says of Kafka.) And the process of building a self and its works is always too slow. One is always in arrears to oneself.

Things appear at a distance, come forward slowly. In *Berlin Childhood,* he speaks of his "propensity for seeing everything I care about approach me from far away"—the way, often ill as a child, he imagined the hours approaching his sickbed. "This is perhaps the origin of what others call patience in me, but which in truth does not resemble any virtue." (Of course, others did experience it as patience, as a virtue. Scholem has described him as "the most patient human being I ever came to know.")

But something like patience is needed for the melancholic's labors of decipherment. Proust, as Benjamin notes, was excited by "the secret language of the salons"; Benjamin was drawn to more compact codes. He collected emblem books, liked to make up anagrams, played with pseudonyms. His taste for pseudonyms well antedates his need as a German-Jewish refugee, who from 1933 to 1936 continued to publish reviews in German magazines under the name of Detlev Holz, the name he used to sign the last book to appear in his lifetime, *Deutsche Menschen,* published in Switzerland in 1936. In the amazing text written in Ibiza in 1933, "Agesilaus Santander," Benjamin speaks of his fantasy of having a secret name; the name of this text— which turns on the figure in the Klee drawing he owned, "Angelus Novus"—is, as Scholem has pointed out, an anagram of *Der Angelus Santanas.* He was an "uncanny" graphologist, Scholem reports, though "later on he tended to conceal his gift."

Dissimulation, secretiveness appear a necessity to the melancholic. He has complex, often veiled relations with others. These feelings of superiority, of inadequacy, of baffled feeling, of not being able to get what one wants, or even name it properly (or consistently) to oneself—these can be, it is felt they ought to be, masked by friendliness, or the most scrupulous manipulation. Using a word that was also applied to Kafka by those who knew him, Scholem speaks of "the almost Chinese courtesy" that characterized Benjamin's relations with people. But one is not surprised to learn, of the man who could justify Proust's "invectives against friendship," that Benjamin could also drop friends brutally, as he did his comrades from the Youth Movement, when they no longer interested him. Nor is one surprised to learn that this fastidious, intransigent, fiercely serious man could also flatter people he probably did not think his equals, that he could let himself be "baited" (his own word) and condescended to by Brecht on his visits to Denmark. This prince of the intellectual life could also be a courtier.

Benjamin analyzed both roles in *The Origin of German Trauerspiel* by the theory of melancholy. One characteristic of the Saturnine temperament is slowness: "The tyrant falls on account of the sluggishness of his emotions." "Another trait of the predominance of Saturn," says Benjamin, is "faithlessness." This is represented by the character of the courtier in baroque drama, whose mind is "fluctuation itself." The manipulativeness of the courtier is partly a "lack of character"; partly it "reflects an inconsolable, despondent surrender to an impenetrable conjunction of baleful constellations [that] seem to have taken on a massive, almost thing-like cast." Only someone identifying with this sense of historical catastrophe, this degree of despondency, would have explained why the courtier is not to be despised. His faithlessness to his fellow men, Benjamin says, corresponds to the "deeper, more contemplative faith" he keeps with material emblems.

What Benjamin describes could be understood as simple pathology: the tendency of the melancholic temperament to project its inner torpor outward, as the immutability of misfortune, which is experienced as "massive, almost thing-like." But his argument is more daring: he perceives that the deep transactions between the melancholic and the world always take place with things (rather than with people); and that these are genuine transactions, which reveal meaning. Precisely because the melancholy character is haunted by death, it is melancholics who best know how to read the world. Or, rather, it is the world which yields itself to the melancholic's scrutiny, as it does to no one else's. The more lifeless things are, the more potent and ingenious can be the mind which contemplates them.

If this melancholy temperament is faithless to people, it has good reason to be faithful to things. Fidelity lies in accumulating things—which appear, mostly, in the form of fragments or ruins. ("It is common practice in baroque literature to pile up fragments incessantly," Benjamin writes.) Both the baroque and Surrealism, sensibilities with which Benjamin felt a strong affinity, see reality as things. Benjamin describes the baroque as a world of things (emblems, ruins) and spatialized ideas ("Allegories are, in the realm of thought, what ruins are in the realm of things"). The genius of Surrealism was to generalize with ebullient candor the baroque cult of ruins; to perceive that the nihilistic energies of the modern era make everything a ruin or fragment—and therefore collectible. A world whose past has become (by definition) obsolete, and whose present churns out instant antiques, invites custodians, decoders, and collectors.

As one kind of collector himself, Benjamin remained faithful to things—as things. According to Scholem, building his library, which included many first editions and rare books, was "his most enduring personal passion." Inert in the face of thing-like disaster, the melancholy temperament is galvanized by the passions aroused by privileged objects. Benjamin's books were not only for use, professional tools; they were contemplative objects, stimuli for reverie. His library evokes "memories of the cities in which I found so many things: Riga, Naples, Munich, Danzig, Moscow, Florence, Basel, Paris . . . memories of the rooms where these books had been housed. . . ." Bookhunting, like the sexual hunt, adds to the geography of pleasure—another reason for strolling about in the world. In collecting, Benjamin experienced what in himself was clever, successful, shrewd,

unabashedly passionate. "Collectors are people with a tactical instinct"—like courtiers.

Apart from first editions and baroque emblem books, Benjamin
specialized in children's books and books written by the mad. "The
great works which meant so much to him," reports Scholem, "were
placed in bizarre patterns next to the most out-of-the-way writings
and oddities." The odd arrangement of the library is like the strategy
of Benjamin's work, in which a Surrealist-inspired eye for the treasures of meaning in the ephemeral, discredited, and neglected worked
in tandem with his loyalty to the traditional canon of learned taste.

He liked finding things where nobody was looking. He drew from
the obscure, disdained German baroque drama elements of the modern (that is to say, his own) sensibility: the taste for allegory, Surrealist shock effects, discontinuous utterance, the sense of historical
catastrophe. "These stones were the bread of my imagination," he
wrote about Marseilles—the most recalcitrant of cities to that imagination, even when helped by a dose of hashish. Many expected references are absent in Benjamin's work—he didn't like to read what
everybody was reading. He preferred the doctrine of the four temper-
aments as a psychological theory to Freud. He preferred being a communist, or trying to be one, without reading Marx. This man who
read virtually everything, and had spent fifteen years sympathizing
with revolutionary communism, had barely looked into Marx until
the late 1930s.

His sense of strategy was one of his points of identification with
Kafka, a kindred would-be tactician, who "took precautions against
the interpretation of his writing." The whole point of the Kafka stories, Benjamin argues, is that they have *no* definite, symbolic meaning. And he was fascinated by the very different, un-Jewish sense of
ruse practiced by Brecht, the anti-Kafka of his imagination. (Predictably, Brecht disliked Benjamin's great essay on Kafka intensely.)
Brecht, with the little wooden donkey near his desk from whose neck
hung the sign "I, too, must understand it," represented for Benjamin,
an admirer of esoteric religious texts, the possibly more potent ruse
of reducing complexity, of making everything clear. Benjamin's
"masochistic" (the word is Siegfried Kracauer's) relation to Brecht,
which most of his friends deplored, shows the extent to which he
was fascinated by this possibility.

Benjamin's propensity is to go against the usual interpretation. "All
the decisive blows are struck left-handed," as he says in *One-Way
Street*. Precisely because he saw that "all human knowledge takes
the form of interpretation," he understood the importance of being

against interpretation wherever it is obvious. His most common strategy is to drain symbolism out of some things, like the Kafka stories or Goethe's *Elective Affinities* (texts where everybody agrees it is there), and pour it into others, where nobody suspects its existence (such as the German baroque plays, which he reads as allegories of historical pessimism). "Each book is a tactic," he wrote. In a letter to a friend, he claimed for his writings, only partly facetiously, forty-nine levels of meaning. For moderns as much as for cabalists, nothing is straightforward. Everything is—at the least—difficult. "Ambiguity displaces authenticity in all things," he wrote in *One-Way Street*. What is most foreign to Benjamin is anything like ingenuousness: "the 'unclouded,' 'innocent' eye has become a lie."

Much of the originality of Benjamin's arguments owes to his microscopic gaze (as his friend and disciple Theodor Adorno called it), combined with his indefatigable command over theoretical perspectives. "It was the small things that attracted him most," writes Scholem. He loved old toys, postage stamps, picture postcards, and such playful miniaturizations of reality as the winter world inside a glass globe that snows when it is shaken. His own handwriting was almost microscopic, and his never realized ambition, Scholem reports, was to get a hundred lines on a sheet of paper. (The ambition was realized by Robert Walser, who used to transcribe the manuscripts of his stories and novels as micrograms, in a truly microscopic script.) Scholem relates that when he visited Benjamin in Paris in August 1927 (the first time the two friends had seen each other since Scholem emigrated to Palestine in 1923), Benjamin dragged him to an exhibit of Jewish ritual objects at the Musée Cluny to show him "two grains of wheat on which a kindred soul had inscribed the complete Shema Israel." *

To miniaturize is to make portable—the ideal form of possessing things for a wanderer, or a refugee. Benjamin, of course, was both a wanderer, on the move, and a collector, weighed down by things; that is, passions. To miniaturize is to conceal. Benjamin was drawn

---

*Scholem argues that Benjamin's love for the miniature underlies his taste for brief literary utterances, evident in *One-Way Street*. Perhaps; but books of this sort were common in the 1920s, and it was in a specifically Surrealist montage style that these short independent texts were presented. *One-Way Street* was published by Ernst Rowohlt in Berlin, in booklet form with typography intended to evoke advertising shock effects; the cover was a photographic montage of aggressive phrases in capital letters from newspaper announcements, ads, official and odd signs. The opening passage, in which Benjamin hails "prompt language" and denounces "the pretentious, universal gesture of the book," does not make much sense unless one knows what kind of book *One-Way Street* was designed to be.

to the extremely small as he was to whatever had to be deciphered: emblems, anagrams, handwriting. To miniaturize means to make useless. For what is so grotesquely reduced is, in a sense, liberated from its meaning—its tininess being the outstanding thing about it. It is both a whole (that is, complete) and a fragment (so tiny, the wrong scale). It becomes an object of disinterested contemplation or reverie. Love of the small is a child's emotion, one colonized by Surrealism. The Paris of the Surrealists is "a little world," Benjamin observes; so is the photograph, which Surrealist taste discovered as an enigmatic, even perverse, rather than a merely intelligible or beautiful, object, and about which Benjamin wrote with such originality. The melancholic always feels threatened by the dominion of the thing-like, but Surrealist taste mocks these terrors. Surrealism's great gift to sensibility was to make melancholy cheerful.

"The only pleasure the melancholic permits himself, and it is a powerful one, is allegory," Benjamin wrote in *The Origin of German Trauerspiel*. Indeed, he asserted, allegory is the way of reading the world typical of melancholics, and quoted Baudelaire: "Everything for me becomes allegory." The process which extracts meaning from the petrified and insignificant, allegory, is the characteristic method of the German baroque drama and of Baudelaire, Benjamin's major subjects; and, transmuted into philosophical argument and the micrological analysis of things, the method Benjamin practiced himself.

The melancholic sees the world itself become a thing: refuge, solace, enchantment. Shortly before his death, Benjamin was planning an essay about miniaturization as a device of fantasy. It seems to have been a continuation of an old plan to write on Goethe's "The New Melusina" (in *Wilhelm Meister*), which is about a man who falls in love with a woman who is actually a tiny person, temporarily granted normal size, and unknowingly carries around with him a box containing the miniature kingdom of which she is the princess. In Goethe's tale, the world is reduced to a collectible thing, an object, in the most literal sense.

Like the box in Goethe's tale, a book is not only a fragment of the world but itself a little world. The book is a miniaturization of the world, which the reader inhabits. In *Berlin Chronicle*, Benjamin evokes his childhood rapture: "You did not read books through; you dwelt, abided between their lines." To reading, the delirium of the child, was eventually added writing, the obsession of the adult. The most praiseworthy way of acquiring books is by writing them, Benjamin remarks in an essay called "Unpacking My Library." And the best way to understand them is also to enter their space: one never really understands a book unless one copies it, he says in *One-Way Street,* as one never understands a landscape from an airplane but only by walking through it.

"The amount of meaning is in exact proportion to the presence of death and the power of decay," Benjamin writes in the *Trauerspiel* book. This is what makes it possible to find meaning in one's own life, in "the dead occurrences of the past which are euphemistically known as experience." Only because the past is dead is one able to read it. Only because history is fetishized in physical objects can one understand it. Only because the book is a world can one enter it. The book for him was another space in which to stroll. For the character born under the sign of Saturn, the true impulse when one is being looked at is to cast down one's eyes, look in a corner. Better, one can lower one's head to one's notebook. Or put one's head behind the wall of a book.

It is characteristic of the Saturnine temperament to blame its undertow of inwardness on the will. Convinced that the will is weak, the melancholic may make extravagant efforts to develop it. If these efforts are successful, the resulting hypertrophy of will usually takes the form of a compulsive devotion to work. Thus Baudelaire, who suffered constantly from "acedia, the malady of monks," ended many letters and his *Intimate Journals* with the most impassioned pledges to work more, to work uninterruptedly, to do nothing but work. (Despair over "every defeat of the will"—Baudelaire's phrase again—is a characteristic complaint of modern artists and intellectuals, particularly of those who are both.) One is condemned to work; otherwise, one might not do anything at all. Even the dreaminess of the melancholic temperament is harnessed to work, and the melancholic may try to cultivate phantasmagorical states, like dreams, or seek the access to concentrated states of attention offered by drugs. Surrealism simply puts a positive accent on what Baudelaire experienced so negatively: it does not deplore the guttering of volition but raises it to an ideal, proposing that dream states may be relied on to furnish all the material needed for work.

Benjamin, always working, always trying to work more, speculated a good deal on the writer's daily existence. *One-Way Street* has several sections which offer recipes for work: the best conditions, timing, utensils. Part of the impetus for the large correspondence he conducted was to chronicle, report on, confirm the existence of work. His instincts as a collector served him well. Learning was a form of collecting, as in the quotations and excerpts from daily reading which

Benjamin accumulated in notebooks that he carried everywhere and from which he would read aloud to friends. Thinking was also a form of collecting, at least in its preliminary stages. He conscientiously logged stray ideas; developed mini-essays in letters to friends; re-wrote plans for future projects; noted his dreams (several are re-counted in *One-Way Street*); kept numbered lists of all the books he read. (Scholem recalls seeing, on his second and last visit to Benja-min in Paris, in 1938, a notebook of current reading in which Marx's *Eighteenth Brumaire* is listed as No. 1649.)

How does the melancholic become a hero of will? Through the fact that work can become like a drug, a compulsion. ("Thinking which is an eminent narcotic," he wrote in the essay on Surrealism.) In fact, melancholics make the best addicts, for the true addictive experience is always a solitary one. The hashish sessions of the late 1920s, su-pervised by a doctor friend, were prudent stunts, not acts of self-surrender; material for the writer, not escape from the exactions of the will. (Benjamin considered the book he wanted to write on hash-ish one of his most important projects.)

The need to be solitary—along with bitterness over one's loneli-ness—is characteristic of the melancholic. To get work done, one must be solitary—or, at least, not bound to any permanent relationship. Benjamin's negative feelings about marriage are clear in the essay on Goethe's *Elective Affinities*. His heroes—Kierkegaard, Baudelaire, Proust, Kafka, Kraus—never married; and Scholem reports that Ben-jamin came to regard his own marriage (he was married in 1917, estranged from his wife after 1921, and divorced in 1930) "as fatal to himself." The world of nature, and of natural relationships, is per-ceived by the melancholic temperament as less than seductive. The self-portrait in *Berlin Childhood* and *Berlin Chronicle* is of a wholly alienated son; as husband and father (he had a son, born in 1918, who emigrated to England with Benjamin's ex-wife in the mid-1930s), he appears to have simply not known what to do with these relation-ships. For the melancholic, the natural, in the form of family ties, introduces the falsely subjective, the sentimental; it is a drain on the will, on one's independence; on one's freedom to concentrate on work. It also presents a challenge to one's humanity to which the melan-cholic knows, in advance, he will be inadequate.

The style of work of the melancholic is immersion, total concentra-tion. Either one is immersed, or attention floats away. As a writer, Benjamin was capable of extraordinary concentration. He was able to research and write *The Origin of German Trauerspiel* in two years; some of it, he boasts in *Berlin Chronicle,* was written in long evenings at a café, sitting close to a jazz band. But although Benjamin wrote prolifically—in some periods turning out work every week for the German literary papers and magazines—it proved impossible for him to write a normal-sized book again. In a letter in 1935, Benjamin speaks of "the Saturnine pace" of writing *Paris, Capital of the Nineteenth Century*, which he had begun in 1927 and thought could be finished in two years. His characteristic form remained the essay. The melancholic's intensity and exhaustiveness of attention set natural limits to the length at which Benjamin could develop his ideas. His major essays seem to end just in time, before they self-destruct.

His sentences do not seem to be generated in the usual way; they do not entail. Each sentence is written as if it were the first, or the last. ("A writer must stop and restart with every new sentence," he says in the Prologue to *The Origin of German Trauerspiel*.) Mental and historical processes are rendered as conceptual tableaux; ideas are transcribed in extremis and the intellectual perspectives are vertiginous. His style of thinking and writing, incorrectly called aphoristic, might better be called freeze-frame baroque. This style was torture to execute. It was as if each sentence had to say everything, before the inward gaze of total concentration dissolved the subject before his eyes. Benjamin was probably not exaggerating when he told Adorno that each idea in his book on Baudelaire and nineteenth-century Paris "had to be wrested away from a realm in which madness lies."*

Something like the dread of being stopped prematurely lies behind these sentences as saturated with ideas as the surface of a baroque painting is jammed with movement. In a letter to Adorno in 1935, Benjamin describes his transports when he first read Aragon's *Le Paysan de Paris*, the book that inspired *Paris, Capital of the Nineteenth Century*: "I would never read more than two or three pages in bed of an evening because the pounding of my heart was so loud that I had to let the book fall from my hands. What a warning!" Cardiac failure is the metaphoric limit of Benjamin's exertions and passions. (He suffered from a heart ailment.) And cardiac sufficiency is a metaphor he offers for the writer's achievement. In the essay in praise of Karl Kraus, Benjamin writes:

> If style is the power to move freely in the length and breadth of linguistic thinking without falling into banality, it is attained chiefly by the car-

* In a letter from Adorno to Benjamin, written from New York on November 10, 1938. Benjamin and Adorno met in 1923 (Adorno was twenty), and in 1935 Benjamin started to receive a small stipend from Max Horkheimer's Institut für Sozialforschung, of which Adorno was a member.

diac strength of great thoughts, which drives the blood of language through
the capillaries of syntax into the remotest limbs.

Thinking, writing are ultimately questions of stamina. The melancholic, who feels he lacks will, may feel that he needs all the destructive energies he can muster.

"Truth resists being projected into the realm of knowledge," Benjamin writes in *The Origin of German Trauerspiel.* His dense prose
registers that resistance, and leaves no space for attacking those who
distribute lies. Benjamin considered polemic beneath the dignity of a
truly philosophical style, and sought instead what he called "the fullness of concentrated positivity"—the essay on Goethe's *Elective Affinities,* with its devastating refutation of the critic and Goethe biographer Friedrich Gundolf, being the one exception to this rule among
his major writings. But his awareness of the ethical utility of polemic
made him appreciate that one-man Viennese public institution, Karl
Kraus, a writer whose facility, stridency, love of the aphoristic, and
indefatigable polemic energies make him so unlike Benjamin.

The essay on Kraus is Benjamin's most passionate and perverse
defense of the life of the mind. "The perfidious reproach of being 'too
intelligent' haunted him throughout his life," Adorno has written.
Benjamin defended himself against this philistine defamation by
bravely raising the standard of the "inhumanity" of the intellect, when
it is properly—that is, ethically—employed. "The life of letters is existence under the aegis of mere mind as prostitution is existence under the aegis of mere sexuality," he wrote. This is to celebrate both
prostitution (as Kraus did, because mere sexuality was sexuality in a
pure state) and the life of letters, as Benjamin did, using the unlikely
figure of Kraus, because of "the genuine and demonic function of
mere mind, to be a disturber of the peace." The ethical task of the
modern writer is to be not a creator but a destroyer—a destroyer of
shallow inwardness, the consoling notion of the universally human,
dilettantish creativity, and empty phrases.

The writer as scourge and destroyer, portrayed in the figure of
Kraus, he sketched with concision and even greater boldness in the
allegorical "The Destructive Character," also written in 1931. Scholem has written that the first of several times Benjamin contemplated
suicide was in the summer of 1931. The second time was the following summer, when he wrote "Agesilaus Santander." The Apollonian
scourge whom Benjamin calls the destructive character

> is always blithely at work . . . has few needs . . . has no interest in being
> understood . . . is young and cheerful . . . and feels not that life is worth
> living but that suicide is not worth the trouble.

It is a kind of conjuration, an attempt by Benjamin to draw the destructive elements of his Saturnine character outward—so that they are not self-destructive.

Benjamin is not referring just to his own destructiveness. He thought that there was a peculiarly modern temptation to suicide. In "The Paris of the Second Empire in Baudelaire," he wrote:

> The resistance which modernity offers to the natural productive élan of a person is out of proportion to his strength. It is understandable if a person grows tired and takes refuge in death. Modernity must be under the sign of suicide, an act which seals a heroic will. . . . It is *the* achievement of modernity in the realm of passions. . . .

Suicide is understood as a response of the heroic will to the defeat of the will. The only way to avoid suicide, Benjamin suggests, is to be beyond heroism, beyond efforts of the will. The destructive character cannot feel trapped, because "he sees ways everywhere." Cheerfully engaged in reducing what exists to rubble, he "positions himself at the crossroads."

Benjamin's portrait of the destructive character would evoke a kind of Siegfried of the mind—a high-spirited, childlike brute under the protection of the gods—had this apocalyptic pessimism not been qualified by the irony always within the range of the Saturnine temperament. Irony is the positive name which the melancholic gives to his solitude, his asocial choices. In *One-Way Street* Benjamin hailed the irony that allows individuals to assert the right to lead lives independent of the community as "the most European of all accomplishments," and observed that it had completely deserted Germany. Benjamin's taste for the ironic and the self-aware put him off most of recent German culture: he detested Wagner, despised Heidegger, and scorned the frenetic vanguard movements of Weimar Germany such as Expressionism.

Passionately, but also ironically, Benjamin placed himself at the crossroads. It was important for him to keep his many "positions" open: the theological, the Surrealist/aesthetic, the communist. One position corrects another; he needed them all. Decisions, of course, tended to spoil the balance of these positions, vacillation kept everything in place. The reason he gave for his delay in leaving France, when he last saw Adorno in early 1938, was that "there are still positions here to defend."

Benjamin thought the freelance intellectual was a dying species anyway, made no less obsolete by capitalist society than by revolutionary communism; indeed, he felt that he was living in a time in which everything valuable was the last of its kind. He thought Surrealism was the last intelligent moment of the European intelligentsia, an appropriately destructive, nihilistic kind of intelligence. In his essay on Kraus, Benjamin asks rhetorically: Does Kraus stand on the frontier of a new age? "Alas, by no means. For he stands on the threshold of the Last Judgment." Benjamin is thinking of himself. At the Last Judgment, the Last Intellectual—that Saturnine hero of modern culture, with his ruins, his defiant visions, his reveries, his unquenchable gloom, his downcast eyes—will explain that he took many "positions" and defended the life of the mind to the end, as righteously and inhumanly as he could.

(1978)

Syberberg's Hitler

Wer nicht von dreitausend Jahren
Sich weiss Rechenschaft zu geben
Bleib im Dunkeln, unerfahren,
Mag von Tag zu Tage leben.

[Anyone who cannot give an account
to oneself of the past three thousand
years remains in darkness, without
experience, living from day to day.]

The Romantics thought of great art as a species of heroism, a breaking through or going beyond. Following them, adepts of the modern demanded of masterpieces that they be, in each case, an extreme case—terminal or prophetic, or both. Walter Benjamin was making a characteristic modernist judgment when he observed (writing about Proust): "All great works of literature found a genre or dissolve one." However rich in precursors, the truly great work must seem to break with an old order and really is a devastating if salutary move. Such a work extends the reach of art but also complicates and burdens the enterprise of art with new, self-conscious standards. It both excites and paralyzes the imagination.

Lately, the appetite for the truly great work has become less robust. Thus Hans-Jürgen Syberberg's *Hitler, a Film from Germany* is not only daunting because of the extremity of its achievement, but discomfiting, like an unwanted baby in the era of zero population growth. The modernism that reckoned achievement by the Romantics' grandiose aims for art (as wisdom/as salvation/as cultural subversion or revolution) has been overtaken by an impudent version of itself which has enabled modernist tastes to be diffused on an undreamed-of scale. Stripped of its heroic stature, of its claims as an adversary sensibility, modernism has proved acutely compatible with the ethos of an advanced consumer society. Art is now the name of a huge variety of satisfactions—of the unlimited proliferation, and devaluation, of satisfaction itself. Where so many blandishments flourish, bringing off a masterpiece seems a retrograde feat, a naïve form of accomplish-

404 / SUSAN SONTAG

ment. Always implausible (as implausible as justified megalomania), the Great Work is now truly odd. It proposes satisfactions that are immense, solemn, and restricting. It insists that art must be true, not just interesting; a necessity, not just an experiment. It dwarfs other work, challenges the facile eclecticism of contemporary taste. It throws the admirer into a state of crisis.

Syberberg assumes importance both for his art (*the* art of the twentieth century: film) and for his subject (*the* subject of the twentieth century: Hitler). The assumptions are familiar, crude, plausible. But they hardly prepare us for the scale and virtuosity with which he conjures up the ultimate subjects: hell, paradise lost, the apocalypse, the last days of mankind. Leavening romantic grandiosity with modernist ironies, Syberberg offers a spectacle about spectacle: evoking "the big show" called history in a variety of dramatic modes—fairy tale, circus, morality play, allegorical pageant, magic ceremony, philosophical dialogue, *Totentanz*—with an imaginary cast of tens of millions and, as protagonist, the Devil himself.

The Romantic notions of the maximal so congenial to Syberberg such as the boundless talent, the ultimate subject, and the most inclusive art—these notions confer an excruciating sense of possibility. Syberberg's confidence that his art is adequate to his great subject derives from his idea of cinema as a way of knowing that incites speculation to take a self-reflexive turn. Hitler is depicted through examining our relation to Hitler (the theme is "our Hitler" and "Hitler-in-us"), as the rightly unassimilable horrors of the Nazi era are represented in Syberberg's film as images or signs. (Its title isn't *Hitler* but, precisely, *Hitler, a Film* . . .)

To simulate atrocity convincingly is to risk making the audience passive, reinforcing witless stereotypes, confirming distance and creating fascination. Convinced that there is a morally (and aesthetically) correct way for a filmmaker to confront Nazism, Syberberg can make no use of any of the stylistic conventions of fiction that pass for realism. Neither can he rely on documents to show how it "really" was. Like its simulation as fiction, the display of atrocity in the form of photographic evidence risks being tacitly pornographic. Further, the truths it conveys, unmediated, about the past are slight. Film clips of the Nazi period cannot speak for themselves; they require a voice—explaining, commenting, interpreting. But the relation of the voice-over to a film document, like that of the caption to a still photograph, is merely adhesive. In contrast to the pseudo-objective style of narration in most documentaries, the two ruminating voices which suffuse Syberberg's film constantly express pain, grief, dismay.

Rather than devise a spectacle in the past tense, either by attempting to simulate "unrepeatable reality" (Syberberg's phrase) or by showing it in photographic document, he proposes a spectacle in the present tense—"adventures in the head." Of course, for such a devoutly anti-realist aesthetician, historical reality is, by definition, unrepeatable. Reality can only be grasped indirectly—seen reflected in a mirror, staged in the theater of the mind. Syberberg's synoptic drama is radically subjective, without being solipsistic. It is a ghostly film—haunted by his great cinematic models (Méliès, Eisenstein) and anti-models (Riefenstahl, Hollywood); by German Romanticism; and, above all, by the music of Wagner and the case of Wagner. A posthumous film, in the era of cinema's unprecedented mediocrity—full of cinéphile myths, about cinema as the ideal space of the imagination and cinema history as an exemplary history of the twentieth century (the martyrdom of Eisenstein by Stalin, the excommunication of von Stroheim by Hollywood); and of cinéphile hyperboles: he designates Riefenstahl's *Triumph of the Will* as Hitler's "only lasting monument, apart from the newsreels of his war." One of the film's conceits is that Hitler, who never visited the front and watched the war every night through newsreels, was a kind of moviemaker. Germany, a Film by Hitler.

Syberberg has cast his film as a phantasmagoria: the meditative-sensuous form favored by Wagner which distends time and results in works that the unpassionate find overlong. Its length is suitably exhaustive—seven hours; and, like the *Ring*, it is a tetralogy. The titles of its four parts are: *Hitler, a Film from Germany; A German Dream; The End of a Winter's Tale; We, Children of Hell*. A film, a dream, a tale. Hell.

In contrast to the lavish De Mille-like décors that Wagner projected for his tetralogy, Syberberg's film is a cheap fantasy. The large sound studio in Munich where the film was shot in 1977 (in twenty days—after four years of preparation) is furnished as a surreal landscape. The wide shot of the set at the beginning of the film displays many of the modest props that will recur in different sequences, and suggests the multiple uses Syberberg will make of this space: as a space of rumination (the wicker chair, the plain table, the candelabra); a space of theatrical assertion (the canvas director's chair, the giant black megaphone, the upturned mask); a space of emblems (models of the polyhedron in Dürer's *Melencolia I,* and of the ash tree from the set of the first production of *Die Walküre*); a space of moral judgment (a large globe, a life-size rubber sex-doll); a space of melancholy (the dead leaves strewn on the floor).

This allegory-littered wasteland (as limbo, as the moon) is designed to hold multitudes, in their contemporary, that is posthumous, form. It is really the land of the dead, a cinematic Valhalla. Since all the characters of the Nazi catastrophe-melodrama are dead, what we see are their ghosts—as puppets, as spirits, as caricatures of themselves. Carnivalesque skits alternate with arias and soliloquies, narratives, reveries. The two ruminating presences (André Heller, Harry Baer) keep up, on screen and off, an endless intellectual melody—lists, judgments, questions, historical anecdotes, as well as multiple characterizations of the film and the consciousness behind it.

The muse of Syberberg's historic epic is cinema itself ("the world of our inner projections"), represented on the wasteland set by Black Maria, the tarpaper shack built for Thomas Edison in 1893 as the first film studio. By invoking cinema as Black Maria, that is, recalling the artisanal simplicity of its origins, Syberberg also points to his own achievement. Using a small crew, with time for only one take of many long and complex shots, this technically ingenious inventor of fantasy managed to film virtually all of what he intended as he had envisaged it; and all of it is on the screen. (Perhaps only a spectacle as underbudgeted as this one—it cost $500,000—can remain wholly responsive to the intentions and improvisations of a single creator.) Out of this ascetic way of filmmaking, with its codes of deliberate naïveté, Syberberg has made a film that is both stripped-down and lush, discursive and spectacular.

Syberberg provides spectacle out of his modest means by replicating and reusing the key elements as many times as possible. Having each actor play several roles, the convention inspired by Brecht, is an aspect of this aesthetics of multiple use. Many things appear at least twice in the film, once full-sized and once miniaturized—for example, a thing and its photograph; and all the Nazi notables appear played by actors and as puppets. Edison's Black Maria, the primal film studio, is presented in four ways: as a large structure, indeed the principal item of the master set, from which actors appear and into which they disappear; as toy structures in two sizes, the tinier on a snowy landscape inside a glass globe, which can be held in an actor's hand, shaken, ruminated upon; and in a photographic blowup of the globe.

Syberberg uses multiple approaches, multiple voices. The libretto is a medley of imaginary discourse and the ipsissima verba of Hitler, Himmler, Goebbels, Speer, and such backstage characters as Himmler's Finnish masseur Felix Kersten and Hitler's valet Karl-Wilhelm Krause. The complex sound track often provides two texts at once.

Interspersed between and intermittently overlaid on the speeches of actors—a kind of auditory back-projection—are historical sound documents, such as snatches from speeches by Hitler and Goebbels, from wartime news broadcasts by German radio and the BBC. The stream of words also includes cultural references in the form of quotations (often left unattributed), such as Einstein on war and peace, a passage from Marinetti's Futurist Manifesto—and the whole verbal polyphony swelled by excerpts from the pantheon of German music, mostly Wagner. A passage from, say, *Tristan und Isolde* or the chorus of Beethoven's Ninth is used as another kind of historical quotation which complements or comments on what is being said, simultaneously, by an actor.

On the screen, a varying stock of emblematic props and images supplies more associations. Doré engravings for the *Inferno* and the Bible, Graff's portrait of Frederick the Great, a still from Méliès's *A Trip to the Moon*, Runge's *Morning,* Caspar David Friedrich's *The Frozen Ocean* are among the visual references that appear (by a canny technique of slide projection) behind the actors. The image is constructed on the same assemblage principle as the sound track except that, while we hear many historical sound documents, Syberberg makes sparing use of visual documents from the Nazi era.

Méliès in the foreground, Lumière very much in the background. Syberberg's meta-spectacle virtually swallows up the photographic document: when we see the Nazi reality on film, it is as film. Behind a seated, ruminating actor (Heller) appears some private 8 mm. footage of Hitler—indistinct, rather unreal. Such bits of film are not used to show how anything "really" was: film clips, slides of paintings, movie stills all have the same status. Actors play in front of photographic blowups that show legendary places without people: these empty, almost abstract, oddly scaled views of Ludwig II's Venus Grotto at Linderhof, Wagner's villa in Bayreuth, the conference room in the Reich Chancellery in Berlin, the terrace of Hitler's villa in Berchtesgaden, the ovens at Auschwitz are a more stylized kind of allusion. They are also a ghostly décor rather than a "real" set, with which Syberberg can play illusionist tricks reminiscent of Méliès: having the actor appear to be walking within a deep-focus photograph, ending a scene with the actor turning and vanishing into a backdrop that had appeared to be seamless.

Nazism is known by allusion, through fantasy, in quotation. Quotations are both literal, like an Auschwitz's survivor's testimony, and, more commonly, fanciful cross-references—as when the hysterical SS man recites the child murderer's plea from Lang's *M;* or Hitler, in a tirade of self-exculpation, rising in a cobwebby toga from the grave of Richard Wagner, quotes Shylock's "If you prick us, do we not bleed?" Like the photographic images and the props, the actors are also stand-ins for the real. Most speech is monologue or monodrama, whether by a single actor talking directly to the camera, that is, the audience, or by actors half talking to themselves (as in the scene of Himmler and his masseur) or declaiming in a row (the rotting puppets in hell). As in a Surrealist tableau, the presence of the inanimate makes its ironic comment on the supposedly alive. Actors talk to, or on behalf of, puppets of Hitler, Goebbels, Goering, Himmler, Eva Braun, Speer. Several scenes set actors among department-store mannequins, or among the life-size photographic cutouts of legendary ghouls from the German silent cinema (Mabuse, Alraune, Caligari, Nosferatu) and of the archetypal Germans photographed by August Sander. Hitler is a recurrent multiform presence, depicted in memory, through burlesque, in historical travesty.

Quotations in the film; the film as a mosaic of stylistic quotations. To present Hitler in multiple guises and from many perspectives, Syberberg draws on disparate stylistic sources: Wagner, Méliès, Brechtian distancing techniques, homosexual baroque, puppet theater. This eclecticism is the mark of an extremely self-conscious, erudite, avid artist, whose choice of stylistic materials (blending high art and kitsch) is not as arbitrary as it might seem. Syberberg's film is, precisely, Surrealist in its eclecticism. Surrealism is a late variant of Romantic taste, a Romanticism that assumes a broken or posthumous world. It is Romantic taste with a leaning toward pastiche. Surrealist works proceed by conventions of dismemberment and reaggregation, in the spirit of pathos and irony; these conventions include the inventory (or open-ended list); the technique of duplication by miniaturization; the hyper-development of the art of quotation. By means of these conventions, particularly the circulation and recycling of visual and aural quotations, Syberberg's film simultaneously inhabits many places, many times—his principal device of dramatic and visual irony.

His broadest irony is to mock all this complexity by presenting his meditation on Hitler as something simple: a tale told in the presence of a child. His nine-year-old daughter is the mute somnambulistic witness, crowned by loops of celluloid, who wanders through the steam-filled landscape of hell; who begins and closes each of the film's four parts. Alice in Wonderland, the spirit of cinema—she is surely meant as these. And Syberberg also evokes the symbolism of melancholy, identifying the child with Dürer's *Melencolia:* at the film's end she is posed inside a plump tear, gazing in front of the stars. Whatever the attributions, the image owes much to Surrealist taste. The condition of the somnambulist is a convention of Surrealist narrative. The person who moves through a Surrealist landscape is typically in a dreamy, becalmed state. The enterprise that takes one through a Surrealist landscape is always quixotic—hopeless, obsessional; and, finally, self-regarding. An emblematic image in the film, one much admired by the Surrealists, is Ledoux's "Eye Reflecting the Interior of the Theater of Besançon" (1804). Ledoux's eye first appears on the set as a two-dimensional picture. Later it is a three-dimensional construction, an eye-as-theater in which one of the narrators (Baer) sees, projected at the rear, himself—in an earlier film by Syberberg, *Ludwig, Requiem for a Virgin King*, in which he played the lead. As Ledoux locates his theater in the eye, Syberberg locates his cinema inside the mind, where all associations are possible.

Syberberg's repertory of theatrical devices and images seems inconceivable without the freedoms and ironies introduced by Surrealist taste, and reflects many of its distinctive affections. Grand Guignol, puppet theater, the circus, and the films of Méliès were Surrealist passions. The taste for naïve theater and primitive cinema as well as for objects which miniaturize reality, for the art of Northern Romanticism (Dürer, Blake, Friedrich, Runge), for architecture as utopian fantasy (Ledoux) and as private delirium (Ludwig II)—the sensibility that encompasses all these is Surrealism. But there is an aspect of Surrealist taste that is alien to Syberberg—the surrender to chance, to the arbitrary; the fascination with the opaque, the meaningless, the mute. There is nothing arbitrary or aleatoric about his décor, no throw-away images or objects without emotional weight; indeed, certain relics and images in Syberberg's film have the force of personal talismans. Everything means, everything speaks. One mute presence, Syberberg's child, only sets off the film's unrelenting verbosity and intensity. Everything in the film is presented as having been already consumed by a mind.

When history takes place inside the head, public and private mythologies gain equal status. Unlike the other mega-films with whose epic ambitions it might be compared—*Intolerance, Napoleon, Ivan the Terrible I & II, 2001*—Syberberg's film is open to personal references as well as public ones. Public myths of evil are framed by the private mythologies of innocence, developed in two earlier films, *Ludwig* (1972, two hours twenty minutes) and *Karl May—In Search of Paradise Lost* (1974, three hours), which Syberberg treats as the first two parts of a trilogy on Germany that concludes with *Hitler, a Film from Germany*. Wagner's patron and victim, Ludwig II, is a recurrent figure of innocence. One of Syberberg's talismanic images—it ends *Ludwig* and is reused in the Hitler film—shows Ludwig as a bearded, weeping child. The image that opens the Hitler film is J. Lange's oil painting of the Winter Garden that the King had made on the roof of the Munich Residenz: a paradisiacal landscape of Himalayas (actually a vast backcloth), palm trees, lake, tent, gondola, which had figured throughout *Ludwig.*

Each of the three films stands on its own, but so far as they are regarded as comprising a trilogy, it is worth noting that *Ludwig* feeds more images to *Hitler, a Film from Germany* than does the second film, *Karl May.* Parts of *Karl May,* with its "real" sets and actors, come closer to linear, mimetic dramaturgy than anything in *Ludwig* or in the incomparably more ambitious and profound film on Hitler. But, like all artists with a taste for pastiche, Syberberg has only a limited feeling for what is understood as realism. The pasticheur's style is essentially a style of fantasy.

Syberberg has devised a particularly German variety of spectacle: the moralized horror show. In the excruciating banalities of the valet's narrative, in a burlesque of Chaplin's impersonation of Hitler in *The Great Dictator,* in a Grand Guignol skit about Hitler's sperm— the Devil is a familiar spirit. Hitler is even allowed to share in the pathos of miniaturization: the Hitler-puppet (dressed, undressed, reasoned with) held on a ventriloquist's knees, the cloth dog with the Hitler face, carried mournfully by the child.

The spectacle assumes familiarity with the incidents and personages of German history and culture, the Nazi regime, World War II; alludes freely to events in the three decades since Hitler's death. While the present is reduced to being the legacy of the past, the past is embellished with knowledge of its future. In *Ludwig,* this open-ended historical itinerary seems like cool (Brechtian?) irony—as when Ludwig I cites Brecht. In *Hitler, a Film from Germany* the irony of anachronism is weightier. Syberberg denies that the events of Nazism were part of the ordinary gait and demeanor of history. ("They said it was the end of the world," muses one of the puppet-masters. "And it was.") His film takes Nazism at its (Hitler's, Goebbels's) word, as a venture in apocalypse, as a cosmology of a New Ice Age, in other words as an eschatology of evil; and itself takes place at a kind of end-of-time, a Messianic time (to use Benjamin's term) which imposes the duty of trying to do justice to the dead. Hence, the long solemn roll call of the accomplices of Nazism ("Those whom we must not forget"), then of some exemplary victims—one of the several points at which the film seems to end.

Syberberg has cast his film in the first person: as the action of one artist assuming the German duty to confront fully the horror of Nazism. Like many German intellectuals of the past, Syberberg treats his Germanness as a moral vocation and regards Germany as the cockpit of European conflicts. ("The twentieth century . . . a film from Germany," says one of the ruminators.) Syberberg was born in 1935 in what was to become East Germany and left in 1953 for West Germany, where he has lived ever since; but the true provenance of his film is the extraterritorial Germany of the spirit whose first great citizen was that self-styled *romantique défroqué* Heine, and whose last great citizen was Thomas Mann. "To be the spiritual battlefield of European antagonisms—that's what it means to be German," Mann declared in his *Reflections of an Unpolitical Man,* written during World War I, sentiments that had not changed when he wrote *Doctor Faustus* as an old man in exile in the late 1940s. Syberberg's view of Nazism as the explosion of the German demonic recalls Mann, as does his unfashionable insistence on Germany's collective guilt (the theme of "Hitler-in-us"). The narrators' repeated challenge, "Who would Hitler be without us?," also echoes Mann, who wrote an essay in 1939 called "Brother Hitler" in which he argues that "the whole thing is a distorted phase of Wagnerism." Like Mann, Syberberg regards Nazism as the grotesque fulfillment—and betrayal—of German Romanticism. It may seem odd that Syberberg, who was a child during the Nazi era, shares so many themes with someone so *ancien-régime.* But there is much that is old-fashioned about Syberberg's sensibility (one consequence, perhaps, of being educated in a communist country)—including the vividness with which he identifies with that Germany whose greatest citizens have gone into exile.

Although it draws on innumerable versions and impressions of Hitler, the film offers very few ideas about Hitler. For the most part they are the theses formulated in the ruins: the thesis that "Hitler's work" was "the eruption of the satanic principle in world history" (Meinecke's *The German Catastrophe,* written two years before *Doctor Faustus*); the thesis, expressed by Horkheimer in *The Eclipse of Reason,* that Auschwitz was the logical culmination of Western progress. Starting in the 1950s, when the ruins of Europe were rebuilt, more complex theses—political, sociological, economic—prevailed about Nazism. (Horkheimer eventually repudiated his argument of 1946.) In reviving those unmodulated views of thirty years ago, their indignation, their pessimism, Syberberg's film makes a strong case for their moral appropriateness.

Syberberg proposes that we really listen to what Hitler said—to the kind of cultural revolution Nazism was, or claimed to be; to the spir-

412 / SUSAN SONTAG

itual catastrophe it was, and still is. By Hitler Syberberg does not mean only the real historical monster, responsible for the deaths of tens of millions. He evokes a kind of Hitler-substance that outlives Hitler, a phantom presence in modern culture, a protean principle of evil that saturates the present and remakes the past. Syberberg's film alludes to familiar genealogies, real and symbolic: from Romanticism to Hitler, from Wagner to Hitler, from Caligari to Hitler, from kitsch to Hitler. And, in the hyperbole of woe, he insists on some new filiations: from Hitler to pornography, from Hitler to the soulless consumer society of the Federal Republic, from Hitler to the rude coercions of the DDR. In using Hitler thus, there is some truth, some unconvincing attributions. It is true that Hitler has contaminated Romanticism and Wagner, that much of nineteenth-century German culture is, retroactively, haunted by Hitler. (As, say, nineteenth-century Russian culture is not haunted by Stalin.) But it is not true that Hitler engendered the modern, post-Hitlerian plastic consumer society. That was already well on the way when the Nazis took power. Indeed, it could be argued—contra Syberberg—that Hitler was in the long run an irrelevance, an attempt to halt the historical clock; and that communism is what ultimately mattered in Europe, not fascism. Syberberg is more plausible when he asserts that the DDR resembles the Nazi state, a view for which he has been denounced by the left in West Germany; like most intellectuals who grew up under a communist regime and moved to a bourgeois-democratic one, he is singularly free of left-wing pieties. It could also be argued that Syberberg has unduly simplified his moralist's task by the extent to which, like Mann, he identifies the inner history of Germany with the history of Romanticism.

Syberberg's notion of history as catastrophe recalls the long German tradition of regarding history eschatologically, as the history of the spirit. Comparable views today are more likely to be entertained in Eastern Europe than in Germany. Syberberg has the moral intransigence, the lack of respect for literal history, the heartbreaking seriousness of the great illiberal artists from the Russian empire—with their fierce convictions about the primacy of spiritual over material (economic, political) causation, the irrelevance of the categories "left" and "right," the existence of absolute evil. Appalled by the extensiveness of German support for Hitler, Syberberg calls the Germans "a Satanic people."

The devil story that Mann devised to sum up the Nazi demonic was narrated by someone who does not understand. Thereby Mann suggested that evil so absolute may be, finally, beyond comprehension or the grasp of art. But the obtuseness of the narrator of *Doctor Faustus* is too much insisted on. Mann's irony backfires: Serenus Zeitblom's fatuous modesty of understanding seems like Mann's confession of inadequacy, his inability to give full voice to grief. Syberberg's film about the devil, though sheathed in ironies, affirms our ability to understand and our obligation to grieve. Dedicated, as it were, to grief, the film begins and ends with Heine's lacerating words: "I think of Germany in the night and sleep leaves me, I can no longer close my eyes, I weep hot tears." Grief is the burden of the calm, rueful, musical soliloquies of Baer and Heller; neither reciting nor declaiming, they are simply speaking out, and listening to these grave, intelligent voices seething with grief is itself a civilizing experience.

The film carries without any condescension a vast legacy of information about the Nazi period. But information is assumed. The film is not designed to meet a standard of information but claims to address a (hypothetical) therapeutic ideal. Syberberg repeatedly says that his film is addressed to the German "inability to mourn," that it undertakes "the work of mourning" (*Trauerarbeit*). These phrases recall the famous essay Freud wrote deep in World War I, "Mourning and Melancholia," which connects melancholy with the inability to work through grief; and the application of this formula in an influential psychoanalytic study of postwar Germany by Alexander and Margarete Mitscherlich, *The Inability to Mourn,* published in Germany in 1967, which diagnoses the Germans as afflicted by mass melancholia, the result of the continuing denial of their collective responsibility for the Nazi past and their persistent refusal to mourn. Syberberg has appropriated the well-known Mitscherlich thesis (without ever mentioning their book), but one might doubt that his film was inspired by it. It seems more likely that Syberberg found in the notion of *Trauerarbeit* a psychological and moral justification for his aesthetics of repetition and recycling. It takes time—and much hyperbole—to work through grief.

So far as the film can be considered as an act of mourning, what is interesting is that it is conducted in the style of mourning—by exaggeration, repetition. It provides an overflow of information: the method of saturation. Syberberg is an artist of excess: thought is a kind of excess, the surplus production of ruminations, images, associations, emotions connected with, evoked by, Hitler. Hence the film's length, its circular arguments, its several beginnings, its four or five endings, its many titles, its plurality of styles, its vertiginous shifts of perspective on Hitler, from below or beyond. The most wonderful shift occurs in Part II, when the valet's forty-minute monologue with its mesmerizing trivia about Hitler's taste in underwear and shaving cream and breakfast food is followed by Heller's musings on the unreality of the idea of the galaxies. (It is the verbal equivalent of the cut in *2001* from the bone thrown in the air by a primate to the space ship—surely the most spectacular cut in the history of cinema.) Syberberg's idea is to exhaust, to empty his subject.

Syberberg measures his ambitions by the standards of Wagner, although living up to the legendary attributes of a German genius is no easy task in the consumer society of the Federal Republic. He considers that *Hitler, a Film from Germany* is not just a film, as Wagner did not want the *Ring* and *Parsifal* to be considered operas or to be part of the normal repertory of opera houses. Its defiant, seductive length, which prevents the film from being distributed conventionally, is very Wagnerian, as is Syberberg's reluctance (until recently) to let it be shown except in special circumstances, encouraging seriousness. Also Wagnerian are Syberberg's ideal of exhaustiveness and profundity; his sense of mission; his belief in art as a radical act; his taste for scandal; his polemical energies (he is incapable of writing an essay that is not a manifesto); his taste for the grandiose. Grandiosity is, precisely, Syberberg's great subject. The protagonists of his trilogy about Germany—Ludwig II, Karl May, Hitler—are all megalomaniacs, liars, reckless dreamers, virtuosi of the grandiose. (Very different sorts of documentaries Syberberg made for German television between 1967 and 1975 also express his fascination with the self-assured and self-obsessed: *Die Grafen Pocci*, about an aristocratic German family; portraits of German film stars; and the five-hour interview-film on Wagner's daughter-in-law and Hitler's friend, *The Confessions of Winifred Wagner*.)

Syberberg is a great Wagnerian, the greatest since Thomas Mann, but his attitude to Wagner and the treasures of German Romanticism is not only pious. It contains more than a bit of malice, the touch of the cultural vandal. To evoke the grandeur and the failure of Wagnerianism, *Hitler, a Film from Germany* uses, recycles, parodies elements of Wagner. Syberberg means his film to be an anti-*Parsifal*, and hostility to Wagner is one of its leitmotifs: the spiritual filiation of Wagner and Hitler. The whole film could be considered a profaning of Wagner, undertaken with a full sense of the gesture's ambiguity, for Syberberg is attempting to be both inside and outside his own deepest sources as an artist. (The graves of Wagner and Cosima behind Villa Wahnfried recur as an image; and one scene satirizes that most ineffectual of profanations, when black American GIs jitterbugged on the graves after the war.) For it is from Wagner that Syberberg's film gets its biggest boost—its immediate intrinsic claim on the sublime. As the film opens, we hear the beginning of the prelude to *Parsifal* and see the word GRAIL in fractured blocky letters. Syberberg claims that his aesthetic is Wagnerian, that is, musical. But it might be more correct to say that his film is in a mimetic relation to Wagner, and in part a parasitic one—as *Ulysses* is in a parasitic relation to the history of English literature.

Syberberg takes very literally, more literally than Eisenstein ever did, the promise of film as a synthesis of the plastic arts, music, literature, and theater—the modern fulfillment of Wagner's idea of the total work of art. (It has often been said that Wagner, had he lived in the twentieth century, would have been a filmmaker.) But the modern *Gesamtkunstwerk* tends to be an aggregation of seemingly disparate elements instead of a synthesis. For Syberberg there is always something more, and different, to say—as the two films on Ludwig he made in 1972 attest. *Ludwig, Requiem for a Virgin King,* which became the first film in his trilogy about Germany, pays delirious homage to the ironic theatricality and overripe pathos of such filmmakers as Cocteau, Carmelo Bene, and Werner Schroeter. *Theodor Hirneis,* the other film, is an austere Brechtian monodrama of ninety minutes with Ludwig's cook as its one character—it anticipates the valet's narrative in *Hitler, a Film from Germany*—and was inspired by Brecht's unfinished novel on the life of Julius Caesar narrated by his slave. Syberberg considers that he began as a disciple of Brecht, and in 1952 and 1953 filmed several of Brecht's productions in East Berlin.

According to Syberberg, his work comes from "the duality Brecht/Wagner"; that is the "aesthetic scandal" he claims to have "sought." In interviews he invariably cites both as his artistic fathers, partly (it may be supposed) to neutralize the politics of one by the politics of the other and place himself beyond issues of left and right; partly to appear more evenhanded than he is. But he is inevitably more of a Wagnerian than a Brechtian, because of the way the inclusive Wagnerian aesthetic accommodates contraries of feeling (including ethical feeling and political bias). Baudelaire heard in Wagner's music "the ultimate scream of a soul driven to its utmost limits," while Nietzsche, even after giving up on Wagner, still praised him as a great "miniaturist" and "our greatest melancholiac in music"—and both were right. Wagner's contraries reappear in Syberberg: the radical democrat and the right-wing elitist, the aesthete and the moralist, rant and rue.

Syberberg's polemical genealogy, Brecht/Wagner, obscures other influences on the film; in particular, what he owes to Surrealist ironies and images. But even the role of Wagner seems a more complex affair than Syberberg's enthrallment with the art and life of Wagner would indicate. Apart from the Wagner that Syberberg has appropriated, one is tempted to say expropriated, this Wagnerianism is, properly, an attenuated affair—a fascinatingly belated example of the art which grew out of the Wagnerian aesthetic: Symbolism. (Both Symbolism and Surrealism could be considered as late developments of the Romantic sensibility.) Symbolism was the Wagnerian aesthetic turned into a procedure of creation for all the arts; further subjectivized, pulled toward abstraction. What Wagner wanted was an ideal theater, a theater of maximal emotions purged of distractions and irrelevancies. Thus Wagner chose to conceal the orchestra of the Bayreuth Festspielhaus under a black wooden shell, and once quipped that, having invented the invisible orchestra, he wished he could invent the invisible stage. The Symbolists found the invisible stage. Events were to be withdrawn from reality, so to speak, and restaged in the ideal theater of the mind.* And Wagner's fantasy of the invisible stage was fulfilled more literally in that immaterial stage, cinema.

Syberberg's film is a magistral rendering of the Symbolist potentialities of cinema and probably the most ambitious Symbolist work of this century. He construes cinema as a kind of ideal mental activity, being both sensuous and reflective, which takes up where reality leaves off: cinema not as the fabrication of reality but as "a continuation of reality by other means." In Syberberg's meditation on history in a sound studio, events are visualized (with the aid of Surrealist conventions) while remaining in a deeper sense invisible (the Symbolist ideal). But because it lacks the stylistic homogeneity that was typical of Symbolist works, *Hitler, a Film from Germany* has a vigor that Symbolists would forgo as vulgar. Its impurities rescue the film from what was most rarefied about Symbolism without making its reach any less indeterminate and comprehensive.

The Symbolist artist is above all a mind, a creator-mind that (distilling the Wagnerian grandiosity and intensity) sees everything, that is able to permeate its subject; and eclipses it. Syberberg's meditation

* "Instead of trying to produce the largest possible reality outside himself," Jacques Rivière has written, the Symbolist artist "tries to consume as much as possible within himself. . . . he offers his mind as a kind of ideal theater where [events] can be acted out without becoming visible." Rivière's essay on Symbolism, "Le Roman d'aventure" (1913), is the best account of it I know.

on Hitler has the customary overbearingness of this mind, and the characteristic porousness of the overextended Symbolist mental structures: soft-edge arguments that begin "I think of . . . ," verbless sentences that evoke rather than explain. Conclusions are everywhere but nothing concludes. All the parts of a Symbolist narrative are simultaneous; that is, all coexist simultaneously in this superior, overbearing mind.

The function of this mind is not to tell a story (at the start the story is behind it, as Rivière pointed out) but to confer meaning in unlimited amounts. Actions, figures, individual bits of décor can have, ideally do have, multiple meanings—for example, the charge of meanings Syberberg attaches to the figure of the child. He appears to be seeking, from a more subjective standpoint, what Eisenstein prescribes with his theory of "overtonal montage." (Eisenstein, who saw himself in the tradition of Wagner and the *Gesamtkunstwerk* and in his writings quotes copiously from the French Symbolists, was the greatest exponent of Symbolist aesthetics in cinema.) The film overflows with meanings of varying accessibility, and there are further meanings from relics and talismans on the set which the audience can't possibly know about.* The Symbolist artist is not primarily interested in exposition, explanation, communication. It seems fitting that Syberberg's dramaturgy consists in talk addressed to those who cannot talk back: to the dead (one can put words in their mouths) and to one's own daughter (who has no lines). The Symbolist narrative is always a posthumous affair; its subject is precisely something that is assumed. Hence, Symbolist art is characteristically dense, difficult. Syberberg is appealing (intermittently) to another process of knowing, as is indicated by one of the film's principal emblems, Ledoux's ideal theater in the form of an eye—the Masonic eye; the eye of intelligence, of esoteric knowledge. But Syberberg wants, passionately wants his film to be understood; and in some parts it is as overexplicit as in other parts it is encoded.

The Symbolist relation of a mind to its subject is consummated when the subject is vanquished, undone, used up. Thus Syberberg's

* For example, on Baer's table Syberberg put a piece of wood from Ludwig's Hundinghütte, the fantasy refuge at Linderhof (it burned down in 1945) inspired by the designs for Act I of *Die Walküre* in the first two productions; elsewhere on the set are a stone from Bayreuth, a relic from Hitler's villa at Berchtesgaden, and other treasures. In one instance, talismans were furnished by the actor: Syberberg asked Heller to bring some objects that were precious to him, and Heller's photograph of Joseph Roth and a small Buddha can just be made out (if one knows they're there) on his table while he delivers the cosmos monologue at the end of Part II and the long monologue of Part IV.

grandest conceit is that with his film he may have "defeated" Hitler—
exorcised him. This splendidly outrageous hyperbole caps Syberberg's profound understanding of Hitler as an image. (If from *The
Cabinet of Dr. Caligari* to Hitler, then why not from Hitler to *Hitler,
a Film from Germany*? The end.) It also follows from Syberberg's
Romantic views of the sovereignty of the imagination, and his flirtation with esoteric ideas of knowing, with notions of art as magic or
spiritual alchemy, and of the imagination as a purveyor of the powers
of blackness.

Heller's monologue in Part IV leads toward a roll call of myths that
can be regarded as metaphors for the esoteric powers of cinema—
starting with Edison's Black Maria ("the black studio of our imagination"); evoking black stones (of the Kaaba; of Dürer's *Melencolia*,
the presiding image of the film's complex iconography); and ending
with a modern image: cinema as the imagination's black hole. Like a
black hole, or our fantasy about it, cinema collapses space and time.
The image perfectly describes the excruciating fluency of Syberberg's film: its insistence on occupying different spaces and times
simultaneously. It seems apt that Syberberg's private mythology of
subjective cinema concludes with an image drawn from science fiction. A subjective cinema of these ambitions and moral energy logically mutates into science fiction. Thus Syberberg's film begins with
the stars and ends, like *2001*, with the stars and a star-child.

Evoking Hitler by means of myth and travesty, fairy tales and science fictions, Syberberg conducts his own rites of deconsecration:
the Grail has been destroyed (Syberberg's anti-*Parsifal* opens and
closes with the word GRAIL—the film's true title); it is no longer
permissible to dream of redemption. Syberberg defends his mythol-
ogizing of history as a skeptic's enterprise: myth as "the mother of
irony and pathos," not myths which stimulate new systems of belief.
But someone who believes that Hitler was Germany's "fate" is hardly
a skeptic. Syberberg is the sort of artist who wants to have it both—
all—ways. The method of his film is contradiction, irony. And, exercising his ingenious talent for naïveté, he also claims to transcend
this complexity. He relishes notions of innocence and pathos—the
traditions of Romantic idealism; some nonsense around the figure of
a child (his daughter, the infant in Runge's *Morning*, Ludwig as a
bearded, weeping child); dreams of an ideal world purified of its complexity and mediocrity.

The earlier parts of Syberberg's trilogy are elegiac portraits of last-
ditch dreamers of paradise: Ludwig II, who built castles which were
stage sets and paid for Wagner's dream factory at Bayreuth; Karl May,

who romanticized American Indians, Arabs, and other exotics in his immensely popular novels, the most famous of which, *Winnetou,* chronicles the destruction of beauty and bravery by the coming of modern technological civilization. Ludwig and Karl May attract Syberberg as gallant, doomed practitioners of the Great Refusal, the refusal of modern industrial civilization. What Syberberg loathes most, such as pornography and the commercialization of culture, he identifies with the modern. (In this stance of utter superiority to the modern, Syberberg recalls the author of *Art in Crisis,* Hans Sedlmayr, with whom he studied art history at the University of Munich in the fifties.) The film is a work of mourning for the modern and what precedes it, and opposes it. If Hitler is also a "utopian," as Syberberg calls him, then Syberberg is condemned to be a post-utopian, a utopian who acknowledges that utopian feelings have been hopelessly defiled. Syberberg does not believe in a "new human being"—that perennial theme of cultural revolution on both the left and the right. For all his attraction to the credo of romantic genius, what he really believes in is Goethe and a thorough Gymnasium education.

Of course, one can find the usual contradictions in Syberberg's film—the poetry of utopia, the futility of utopia; rationalism and magic. And that only confirms what kind of film *Hitler, a Film from Germany* really is. Science fiction is precisely the genre which dramatizes the mix of nostalgia for utopia with anti-utopian fantasies and dread; the dual conviction that the world is ending and that it is on the verge of a new beginning. Syberberg's film about history is also a moral and cultural science fiction. Starship Goethe-Haus.

Syberberg manages to perpetuate in a melancholy, attenuated form something of Wagner's notions of art as therapy, as redemption, and as catharsis. He calls cinema "the most beautiful compensation" for the ravages of modern history, a kind of "redemption" to "our senses oppressed by progress." That art does in sorts redeem reality, by being better than reality—that is the ultimate Symbolist belief. Syberberg makes of cinema the last, most inclusive, most ghostly paradise. It is a view that reminds one of Godard. Syberberg's cinéphilia is another part of the immense pathos of his film; perhaps its only involuntary pathos. For whatever Syberberg says, cinema is now another lost paradise. In the era of cinema's unprecedented mediocrity, his masterpiece has something of the character of a posthumous event.

Spurning naturalism, the Romantics developed a melancholic style: intensely personal, the outreach of its tortured "I," centered on the agon of the artist and society. Mann gave the last profound expression to this romantic notion of the self's dilemma. Post-Romantics like Syberberg work in an impersonal melancholic style. What is central now is the relation between memory and the past: the clash between the possibility of remembering, of going on, and the lure of oblivion. Beckett gives one ahistorical version of this agon. Another version, obsessed with history, is Syberberg's.

To understand the past, and thereby to exorcise it, is Syberberg's largest moral ambition. His problem is that he cannot give anything up. So large is his subject—and everything Syberberg does makes it even larger—that he has to take many positions beyond it. One can find almost anything in Syberberg's passionately voluble film (short of a Marxist analysis or a shred of feminist awareness). Though he tries to be silent (the child, the stars), he can't stop talking; he's so immensely ardent, avid. As the film is ending, Syberberg wants to produce yet another ravishing image. Even when the film is finally over, he still wants to say more, and adds postscripts: the Heine epigraph, the citation of Mogadishu–Stammheim, a final oracular Syberberg-sentence, one last evocation of the Grail. The film is itself the creation of a world, from which (one feels) its creator has the greatest difficulty in extricating himself—as does the admiring spectator; this exercise in the art of empathy produces a voluptuous anguish, an anxiety about concluding. Lost in the black hole of the imagination, the filmmaker has to make everything pass before him; identifies with each, and none.

Benjamin suggests that melancholy is the origin of true—that is, just—historical understanding. The true understanding of history, he said in the last text he wrote, is "a process of empathy whose origin is indolence of the heart, acedia." Syberberg shares something of Benjamin's positive, instrumental view of melancholy, and uses symbols of melancholy to punctuate his film. But Syberberg does not have the ambivalence, the slowness, the complexity, the tension of the Saturnian temperament. Syberberg is not a true melancholic but an *exalté*. But he uses the distinctive tools of the melancholic—the allegorical props, the talismans, the secret self-references; and with his irrepressible talent for indignation and enthusiasm, he is doing "the work of mourning." The word first appears at the end of the film he made on Winifred Wagner in 1975, where we read: "This film is part of Hans-Jürgen Syberberg's *Trauerarbeit*." What we see is Syberberg smiling.

Syberberg is a genuine elegiast. But his film is tonic. The poetic, husky-voiced, diffident logorrhea of Godard's late films discloses a morose conviction that speaking will never exorcise anything; in contrast to Godard's off-camera musings, the musings of Syberberg's personae (Heller and Baer) teem with calm assurance. Syberberg, whose temperament seems the opposite of Godard's, has a supreme confidence in language, in discourse, in eloquence itself. The film tries to say everything. Syberberg belongs to the race of creators like Wagner, Artaud, Céline, the late Joyce, whose work annihilates other work. All are artists of endless speaking, endless melody—a voice that goes on and on. Beckett would belong to this race, too, were it not for some inhibitory force—sanity? elegance? good manners? less energy? deeper despair? So might Godard, were it not for the doubts he evidences about speaking, and the inhibition of feeling (both of sympathy and repulsion) that results from this sense of the impotence of speaking. Syberberg has managed to stay free of the standard doubts—doubts whose main function, now, seems to be to inhibit. The result is a film altogether exceptional in its emotional expressiveness, its great visual beauty, its sincerity, its moral passion, its concern with contemplative values.

The film tries to be everything. Syberberg's unprecedented ambition in *Hitler, a Film from Germany* is on another scale from anything one has seen on film. It is work that demands a special kind of attention and partisanship; and invites being reflected upon, reseen. The more one recognizes of its stylistic references and lore, the more the film vibrates. (Great art in the mode of pastiche invariably rewards study, as Joyce affirmed by daring to observe that the ideal reader of his work would be someone who could devote his life to it.) Syberberg's film belongs in the category of noble masterpieces which ask for fealty and can compel it. After seeing *Hitler, a Film from Germany,* there is Syberberg's film—and then there are the other films one admires. (Not too many these days, alas.) As was said ruefully of Wagner, he spoils our tolerance for the others.

(1979)

Writing Itself:
On Roland Barthes

The best poetry will be rhetorical criticism. . . .

—WALLACE STEVENS
(*in a journal of 1899*)

I rarely lose sight of myself.

—PAUL VALÉRY,
Monsieur Teste

Teacher, man of letters, moralist, philosopher of culture, connoisseur of strong ideas, protean autobiographer . . . of all the intellectual notables who have emerged since World War II in France, Roland Barthes is the one whose work I am most certain will endure. Barthes was in full flow, incessantly productive as he had been for over three decades, when he was struck by a van as he started across a street in Paris in early 1980—a death felt by friends and admirers to be excruciatingly untimely. But along with the backward look of grief comes the awareness that confers upon his large, chronically mutating body of writing, as on all major work, its retroactive completeness. The development of Barthes's work now seems logical; more than that, exhaustive. It even begins and falls silent on the same subject—that exemplary instrument in the career of consciousness, the writer's journal. As it happens, the first essay Barthes ever published celebrates the model consciousness he found in the *Journal* of André Gide, and what turned out to be the last essay published before he died offers Barthes's musings on his own journal-keeping. The symmetry, however adventitious, is an utterly appropriate one, for Barthes's writing, with its prodigious variety of subjects, has finally one great subject: writing itself.

His early themes were those of the freelance partisan of letters, on the occasions afforded by cultural journalism, literary debate, theater and book reviews. To these were added topics that originated and were recycled in seminars and from the lecture platform, for Barthes's literary career was run concurrently with a (very successful) academic one, and in part *as* an academic one. But the voice was always singular, and self-referring; the achievement is of another, larger order than can be had even by practicing, with thrilling virtuosity, the most lively and many-tracked of academic disciplines. For all his contributions to the would-be science of signs and structures, Barthes's endeavor was the quintessentially literary one: the writer organizing, under a series of doctrinal auspices, the theory of his own mind. And when the current enclosure of his reputation by the labels of semiology and structuralism crumbles, as it must, Barthes will appear, I think, as a rather traditional *promeneur solitaire,* and a greater writer than even his more fervent admirers now claim.

He always wrote full out, was always concentrated, keen, indefatigable. This dazzling inventiveness seems not just a function of Barthes's extraordinary powers as a mind, as a writer. It seems to have almost the status of a position—as if this is what critical discourse *must* be. "Literature is like phosphorus," he says in his first book, which came out in 1953, *Writing Degree Zero;* "it shines with its maximum brilliance at the moment when it attempts to die." In Barthes's view, literature is already a posthumous affair. His work affirms a standard of vehement brilliance that is indeed one ideal of a cultural moment which believes itself to be having, in several senses, the last word.

Its brilliance aside, Barthes's work has some of the specific traits associated with the style of a late moment in culture—one that presumes an endless discourse anterior to itself, that presumes intellectual sophistication: it is work that, strenuously unwilling to be boring or obvious, favors compact assertion, writing that rapidly covers a great deal of ground. Barthes was an inspired, ingenious practitioner of the essay and the anti-essay—he had a resistance to long forms. Typically, his sentences are complex, comma-ridden and colon-prone, packed with densely worded entailments of ideas deployed as if these were the materials of a supple prose. It is a style of exposition, recognizably French, whose parent tradition is to be found in the tense, idiosyncratic essays published between the two world wars in the *Nouvelle Revue Française*—a perfected version of the *NRF*'s house style which can deliver more ideas per page while retaining the brio of that style, its acuteness of timbre. His vocabulary is large, fastidious, fearlessly mandarin. Even Barthes's less fleet, more jargon-haunted writings—most of them from the 1960s—are full of flavor; he manages to make an exuberant use of neologisms. While exuding straight-ahead energy, his prose constantly reaches for the summa-tive formulation; it is irrepressibly aphoristic. (Indeed, one could go through Barthes's work extracting superb bits—epigrams, maxims— to make a small book, as has been done with Wilde and Proust.) Barthes's strengths as an aphorist suggest a sensibility gifted, before any intervention of theory, for the perception of structure. Being a method of condensed assertion by means of symmetrically counter- posed terms, the maxim or aphorism inevitably displays the symme- tries and complementarities of situations or ideas—their design, their shape. Like a markedly greater feeling for drawings than for paint- ings, a talent for aphorism is one of the signs of what could be called the formalist temperament.

The formalist temperament is just one variant of a sensibility shared by many who speculate in an era of hyper-saturated awareness. What characterizes such a sensibility is its reliance on the criterion of taste, and its proud refusal to propose anything that does not bear the stamp of subjectivity. Confidently assertive, it nevertheless insists that its assertions are no more than provisional. (To do otherwise would be . . . bad taste.) Indeed, adepts of this sensibility usually make a point of claiming and reclaiming amateur status. "In linguistics I have never been anything but an amateur," Barthes told an interviewer in 1975. Throughout his late writings Barthes repeatedly disavows the, as it were, vulgar roles of system-builder, authority, mentor, expert, in or- der to reserve for himself the privileges and freedoms of delectation: the exercise of taste for Barthes means, usually, to praise. What makes the role a choice one is his unstated commitment to finding some- thing new and unfamiliar to praise (which requires having the right dissonance with established taste); or to praising a familiar work dif- ferently.

An early example is his second book—it appeared in 1954—which is on Michelet. Through an inventory of the recurrent metaphors and themes in the great nineteenth-century historian's epic narratives, Barthes discloses a more intimate narration: Michelet's history of his own body and the "lyric resurrection of past bodies." Barthes is al- ways after another meaning, a more eccentric—often utopian—dis- course. What pleased him was to show insipid and reactionary works to be quirky and implicitly subversive; to display in the most extrav- agant projects of the imagination an opposite extreme—in his essay on Sade, a sexual ideal that was really an exercise in delirious ratio- nality; in his essay on Fourier, a rationalist ideal that was really an exercise in sensual delirium. Barthes did take on central figures of the literary canon when he had something polemical to offer: in 1960 he wrote a short book on Racine, which scandalized academic critics (the ensuing controversy ended with Barthes's complete triumph over his detractors); he also wrote on Proust and Flaubert. But more often, armed with his essentially adversary notion of the "text," he applied his ingenuity to the marginal literary subject: an unimportant "work"—say, Balzac's *Sarrasine,* Chateaubriand's *Life of Rancé*—could be a marvelous "text." Considering something as a "text" means for Barthes precisely to suspend conventional evaluations (the difference between major and minor literature), to subvert established classifi- cations (the separation of genres, the distinctions among the arts).

Though work of every form and worth qualifies for citizenship in the great democracy of "texts," the critic will tend to avoid the texts that everyone has handled, the meaning that everyone knows. The formalist turn in modern criticism—from its pristine phase, as in Shklovsky's idea of defamiliarizing, onward—dictates just this. It charges the critic with the task of discarding worn-out meanings for fresh ones. It is a mandate to scout for new meanings. *Etonne-moi.*

The same mandate is supplied by Barthes's notions of "text" and "textuality." These translate into criticism the modernist ideal of an open-ended, polysemous literature; and thereby make the critic, just like the creators of that literature, the inventor of meaning. (The aim of literature, Barthes asserts, is to put "meaning" into the world but not "a meaning.") To decide that the point of criticism is to alter and to relocate meaning—adding, subtracting, multiplying it—is in effect to base the critic's exertions on an enterprise of avoidance, and thereby to recommit criticism (if it had ever left) to the dominion of taste. For it is, finally, the exercise of taste which identifies meanings that are familiar; a judgment of taste which discriminates against such meanings as too familiar; an ideology of taste which makes of the familiar something vulgar and facile. Barthes's formalism at its most decisive, his ruling that the critic is called on to reconstitute not the "message" of a work but only its "system"—its form, its struc- ture—is perhaps best understood thus, as the liberating avoidance of the obvious, as an immense gesture of good taste.

For the modernist—that is, formalist—critic, the work with its re- ceived valuations already exists. Now, what *else* can be said? The canon of great books has been fixed. What can we add or restore to it? The "message" is already understood, or is obsolete. Let's ignore it.

Of a variety of means Barthes possessed for giving himself some- thing to say—he had an exceptionally fluent, ingenious generalizing power—the most elementary was his aphorist's ability to conjure up a vivacious duality: anything could be split either into itself and its opposite, or into two versions of itself; and one term then fielded against the other to yield an unexpected relation. The point of Voltairean travel, he remarks, is "to manifest an immobility"; Baudelaire "had to protect theatricality from the theater"; the Eiffel Tower "makes the city into a kind of Nature"—Barthes's writing is seeded with such ostensibly paradoxical, epigrammatic formulas as these, whose point is to sum something up. It is the nature of aphoristic thinking to be always in a state of concluding; a bid to have the final word is inherent in all powerful phrase-making.

Less elegant, indeed making a point of dogged explicitness, and far more powerful as an instrument for giving himself something to say, are the classifications that Barthes lays out in order to topple himself into a piece of argument—dividing into two, three, even four parts the matter to be considered. Arguments are launched by announcing that there are two main classes and two subclasses of narrative units, two ways in which myth lends itself to history, two facets of Racinean eros, two musics, two ways to read La Rochefoucauld, two kinds of writers, two forms of his own interest in photographs. That there are three types of corrections a writer makes, three Mediterraneans and three tragic sites in Racine, three levels on which to read the plates of the *Encyclopedia,* three areas of spectacle and three types of gesture in Japanese puppet theater, three attitudes toward speech and writing, equivalent to three vocations: writer, intellectual, and teacher. That there are four kinds of readers, four reasons for keeping a journal . . .

And so on. This is the codifying, frontal style of French intellectual discourse, a branch of the rhetorical tactics that the French call, not quite accurately, Cartesian. Although a few of the classifications Barthes employs are standard, such as semiology's canonical triad of signified, signifier, and sign, many are inventions devised by Barthes in order to *make* an argument, such as his assertion in a late book, *The Pleasure of the Text,* that the modern artist seeks to destroy art, "this effort taking three forms." The aim of this implacable categorizing is not just to map the intellectual territory: Barthes's taxonomies are never static. Often the point is precisely for one category to subvert the other, as do the two forms, which he calls *punctum* and *studium,* of his interest in photographs. Barthes offers classifications to keep matters open—to reserve a place for the uncodified, the enchanted, the intractable, the histrionic. He was fond of bizarre classifications, of classificatory excess (Fourier's, for example), and his boldly physical metaphors for mental life stress not topography but transformation. Drawn to hyperbole, as all aphorists are, Barthes enlists ideas in a drama, often a sensual melodrama or a faintly Gothic one. He speaks of the quiver, thrill, or shudder of meaning, of meanings that themselves vibrate, gather, loosen, disperse, quicken, shine, fold, mutate, delay, slide, separate, that exert pressure, crack, rupture, fissure, are pulverized. Barthes offers something like a poetics of thinking, which identifies the meaning of subjects with the very mobility of meaning, with the kinetics of consciousness itself; and liberates the critic as artist. The uses that binary and triadic thinking had for Barthes's imagination were always provisional, available to correction, destabilization, condensation.

As a writer he preferred short forms, and had been planning to give a seminar on them; he was particularly drawn to miniature ones, like the haiku and the quotation; and, like all true writers, what enthralled him was "the detail" (his word)—experience's model short form. Even as an essayist, Barthes mostly wrote short, and the books he did write tend to be multiples of short forms rather than "real" books, itineraries of topics rather than unified arguments. His *Michelet,* for example, keys its inventory of the historian's themes to a large number of brief excerpts from Michelet's prolific writings. The most rigorous example of the argument as an itinerary by means of quotation is *S/Z,* published in 1970, his model exegesis of Balzac's *Sarrasine.* From staging the texts of others, he passed inevitably to the staging of his own ideas. And, in the same series on great writers to which he contributed the Michelet volume, he eventually did one on himself in 1975: that dazzling oddity in the series, *Roland Barthes* by Roland Barthes. The high-velocity arrangements of Barthes's late books dramatize both his fecundity (insatiability *and* lightness) and his desire to subvert all tendencies to system-making.

An animus against the systematizers has been a recurrent feature of intellectual good taste for more than a century; Kierkegaard, Nietzsche, Wittgenstein are among the many voices that proclaim, from a superior if virtually unbearable burden of singularity, the absurdity of systems. In its strong modern form, scorn for systems is one aspect of the protest against Law, against Power itself. An older, milder refusal is lodged in the French sceptic tradition, from Montaigne to Gide: writers who are epicures of their own consciousness are likely to decry "the sclerosis of systems," a phrase Barthes used in his first essay, on Gide. And along with these refusals a distinctive modern stylistics has evolved, the prototypes of which go back at least to Sterne and the German Romantics—the invention of anti-linear forms of narration: in fiction, the destruction of the "story"; in nonfiction, the abandonment of linear argument. The presumed impossibility (or irrelevance) of producing a continuous systematic argument has led to a remodeling of the standard long forms—the treatise, the long book—and a recasting of the genres of fiction, autobiography, and essay. Of this stylistics, Barthes is a particularly inventive practitioner.

The Romantic and post-Romantic sensibility discerns in every book a first-person performance: to write is a dramatic act, subject to dramatic elaboration. One strategy is to use multiple pseudonyms, as Kierkegaard did, concealing and multiplying the figure of the author. When autobiographical, the work invariably includes avowals of reluctance to speak in the first person. One of the conventions of *Roland Barthes* is for the autobiographer to refer to himself sometimes as "I," sometimes as "he." All this, Barthes announces on the first page of this book about himself, "must be considered as if spoken by a character in a novel." Under the meta-category of performance, not only the line between autobiography and fiction is muted, but that between essay and fiction as well. "Let the essay avow itself almost a novel," he says in *Roland Barthes*. Writing registers new forms of dramatic stress, of a self-referring kind: writing becomes the record of compulsions and of resistances to write. (In the further extension of this view, writing itself becomes the writer's subject.)

For the purpose of achieving an ideal digressiveness and an ideal intensity, two strategies have been widely adopted. One is to abolish some or all of the conventional demarcations or separations of discourse, such as chapters, paragraphing, even punctuation, whatever is regarded as impeding formally the continuous production of (the writer's) voice—the run-on method favored by writers of philosophical fictions such as Hermann Broch, Joyce, Stein, Beckett. The other strategy is the opposite one: to multiply the ways in which discourse is segmented, to invent further ways of breaking it up. Joyce and Stein used this method, too; Shklovsky in his best books, from the 1920s, writes in one-sentence paragraphs. The multiple openings and closures produced by the start-and-stop method permit discourse to become as differentiated, as polyphonous, as possible. Its most common shape in expository discourse is that of short, one- or two-paragraph units separated by spaces. "Notes on . . ." is the usual literary title—a form Barthes uses in the essay on Gide, and returns to often in his later work. Much of his writing proceeds by techniques of interruption, sometimes in the form of an excerpt alternating with a disjunctive commentary, as in *Michelet* and *S/Z*. To write in fragments or sequences or "notes" entails new, serial (rather than linear) forms of arrangements. These sequences may be staged in some arbitrary way. For example, they may be numbered—a method practiced with great refinement by Wittgenstein. Or they may be given headings, sometimes ironic or overemphatic—Barthes's strategy in *Roland Barthes*. Headings allow an additional possibility: for the elements to be arranged alphabetically, to emphasize further the arbitrary character of their sequence—the method of *A Lover's Discourse* (1977), whose real title evokes the notion of the fragment; it is *Fragments d'un discours amoureux*.

Barthes's late writing is his boldest formally: all major work was organized in a serial rather than linear form. Straight essay writing was reserved for the literary good deed (prefaces, for example, of which Barthes wrote many) or journalistic whim. However, these strong forms of the late writing only bring forward a desire implicit in all of his work—Barthes's wish to have a superior relation to assertion: the relation that art has, of pleasure. Such a conception of writing excludes the fear of contradiction. (In Wilde's phrase: "A truth in art is that whose contradiction is also true.") Barthes repeatedly compared teaching to play, reading to eros, writing to seduction. His voice became more and more personal, more full of grain, as he called it; his intellectual art more openly a performance, like that of the other great anti-systematizers. But whereas Nietzsche addresses the reader in many tones, mostly aggressive—exulting, berating, coaxing, prodding, taunting, inviting complicity—Barthes invariably performs in an affable register. There are no rude or prophetic claims, no pleadings with the reader, and no efforts *not* to be understood. This is seduction as play, never violation. All of Barthes's work is an exploration of the histrionic or ludic; in many ingenious modes, a plea for savor, for a festive (rather than dogmatic or credulous) relation to ideas. For Barthes, as for Nietzsche, the point is not to teach us something in particular. The point is to make us bold, agile, subtle, intelligent, detached. And to give pleasure.

Writing is Barthes's perennial subject—indeed, perhaps no one since Flaubert (in his letters) has thought as brilliantly, as passionately as Barthes has about what writing is. Much of his work is devoted to portraits of the vocation of the writer: from the early debunking studies included in *Mythologies* (1957) of the writer as seen by others, that is, the writer as fraud, such as "The Writer on Holiday," to more ambitious essays on writers writing, that is, the writer as hero and martyr, such as "Flaubert and the Sentence," about the writer's "agony of style." Barthes's wonderful essays on writers must be considered as different versions of his great apologia for the vocation of the writer. For all his admiration for the self-punishing standards of integrity set by Flaubert, he dares to conceive of writing as a kind of happiness: the point of his essay on Voltaire ("The Last Happy Writer"), and of his portrait of Fourier, unvexed by the sense of evil. In his late work he speaks directly of his own practice, scruples, bliss.

Barthes construes writing as an ideally complex form of consciousness: a way of being both passive and active, social and asocial, present and absent in one's own life. His idea of the writer's vocation excludes the sequestration that Flaubert thought inevitable, would appear to deny any conflict between the writer's necessary inwardness and the pleasures of worldliness. It is, so to speak, Flaubert strongly amended by Gide: a more well-bred, casual rigor, an avid, guileful relation to ideas that excludes fanaticism. Indeed, the ideal self-portrait—the portrait of the self as writer—that Barthes sketched throughout his work is virtually complete in the first essay, on Gide's "work of egoism," his *Journal*. Gide supplied Barthes with the patrician model for the writer who is supple, multiple; never strident or vulgarly indignant; generous . . . but also properly egotistical; incapable of being deeply influenced. He notes how little Gide was altered by his vast reading ("so many self-recognitions"), how his "discoveries" were never "denials." And he praises the profusion of Gide's scruples, observing that Gide's "situation at the intersection of great contradictory currents has nothing facile about it. . . ." Barthes subscribes as well to Gide's idea of writing that is elusive, willing to be minor. His relation to politics also recalls Gide's: a willingness in times of ideological mobilization to take the right stands, to be political— but, finally, not: and thereby, perhaps, to tell the truth that hardly anybody else is telling. (See the short essay Barthes wrote after a trip to China in 1974.) Barthes had many affinities with Gide, and much of what he says of Gide applies unaltered to himself. How remarkable to find it all laid out—including the program of "perpetual self-correction"—well before he embarked on his career. (Barthes was twenty-seven, a patient in a sanatorium for tubercular students, when he wrote this essay in 1942 for the sanatorium's magazine; he did not enter the Paris literary arena for another five years.)

When Barthes, who began under the aegis of Gide's doctrine of psychic and moral availability, started writing regularly, Gide's important work was long over, his influence already negligible (he died in 1951); and Barthes put on the armor of postwar debate about the responsibility of literature, the terms of which were set up by Sartre—

the demand that the writer be in a militant relation to virtue, which Sartre described by the tautological notion of "commitment." Gide and Sartre were, of course, the two most influential writer-moralists of this century in France, and the work of these two sons of French Protestant culture suggests quite opposed moral and aesthetic choices. But it is just this kind of polarization that Barthes, another Protestant in revolt against Protestant moralism, seeks to avoid. Supple Gidean that he is, Barthes is eager to acknowledge the model of Sartre as well. While a quarrel with Sartre's view of literature lies at the heart of his first book, *Writing Degree Zero* (Sartre is never mentioned by name), an agreement with Sartre's view of the imagination, and its obsessional energies, surfaces in Barthes's last book, *Camera Lucida* (written "in homage" to the early Sartre, the author of *L'Imaginaire*). Even in the first book, Barthes concedes a good deal to Sartre's view of literature and language—for example, putting poetry with the other "arts" and identifying literature with prose, with argument. Barthes's view of literature in his subsequent writing was more complex. Though he never wrote on poetry, his standards for literature approached those of the poet: language that has undergone an upheaval, has been displaced, liberated from ungrateful contexts; that, so to speak, lives on its own. Although Barthes agrees with Sartre that the writer's vocation has an ethical imperative, he insists on its complexity and ambiguity. Sartre appeals to the morality of ends. Barthes invokes "the morality of form"—what makes literature a problem rather than a solution; what makes literature.

To conceive of literature as successful "communication" and position-taking, however, is a sentiment that must inevitably become conformist. The instrumental view expounded in Sartre's *What Is Literature?* (1948) makes of literature something perpetually obsolete, a vain—and misplaced—struggle between ethical good soldiers and literary purists, that is, modernists. (Contrast the latent philistinism of this view of literature with the subtlety and acuity of what Sartre had to say about visual images.) Riven by his love of literature (the love recounted in his own perfect book, *The Words*) and an evangelical contempt for literature, one of the century's great *littérateurs* spent the last years of his life insulting literature and himself with that indigent idea, "the neurosis of literature." His defense of the writer's project of commitment is no more convincing. Accused of thereby reducing literature (to politics), Sartre protested that it would be more correct to accuse him of overestimating it. "If literature isn't *everything*, it's not worth a single hour of someone's trouble," he declared in an interview in 1960. "That's what I mean by 'commitment.' " But Sartre's inflation of literature to "everything" is another brand of depreciation.

Barthes, too, might be charged with overestimating literature—with treating literature as "everything"—but at least he made a good case for doing so. For Barthes understood (as Sartre did not) that literature is first of all, last of all, language. It is language that is everything. Which is to say that all of reality is presented in the form of language—the poet's wisdom, and also the structuralist's. And Barthes takes for granted (as Sartre, with his notion of writing as communication, did not) what he calls the "radical exploration of writing" undertaken by Mallarmé, Joyce, Proust, and their successors. That no venture is valuable unless it can be conceived as a species of radicalism, radicalism thereby unhinged from any distinctive content, is perhaps the essence of what we call modernism. Barthes's work belongs to the sensibility of modernism in the extent to which it assumes the necessity of the adversary stance: literature conceived by modernist standards but not necessarily a modernist literature. Rather, all varieties of counterposition are available to it.

Perhaps the most striking difference between Sartre and Barthes is the deep one, of temperament. Sartre has an intellectually brutal, *bon enfant* view of the world, a view that wills simplicity, resolution, transparence; Barthes's view is irrevocably complex, self-conscious, refined, irresolute. Sartre was eager, too eager, to seek confrontation, and the tragedy of this great career, of the use he made of his stupendous intellect, was just his willingness to simplify himself. Barthes preferred to avoid confrontation, to evade polarization. He defines the writer as "the watcher who stands at the crossroads of all other discourses"—the opposite of an activist or a purveyor of doctrine.

Barthes's utopia of literature has an ethical character almost the opposite of Sartre's. It emerges in the connections he makes between desire and reading, desire and writing—his insistence that his own writing is, more than anything, the product of appetite. The words "pleasure," "bliss," "happiness" recur in his work with a weight, reminiscent of Gide, that is both voluptuous and subversive. As a moralist —Puritan or anti-Puritan—might solemnly distinguish sex for procreation from sex for pleasure, Barthes divides writers into those who write *something* (what Sartre meant by a writer) and the real writers, who do not write something but, rather, *write*. This intransitive sense of the verb "to write" Barthes endorses as not only the source of the writer's felicity but the model of freedom. For Barthes, it is not the commitment that writing makes to something outside of itself (to a social or moral goal) that makes literature an instrument of opposition and subversion but a certain practice of writing itself: excessive, playful, intricate, subtle, sensuous—language which can never be that of power.

Barthes's praise of writing as a gratuitous, free activity is, in one sense, a political view. He conceives of literature as a perpetual renewal of the right of individual assertion; and all rights are, finally, political ones. Still, Barthes is in an evasive relation to politics, and he is one of the great modern refusers of history. Barthes started publishing and mattering in the aftermath of World War II, which, astonishingly, he never mentions; indeed, in all his writings he never, as far as I recall, mentions the word "war." Barthes's friendly way of understanding subjects domesticates them, in the best sense. He lacks anything like Walter Benjamin's tragic awareness that every work of civilization is also a work of barbarism. The ethical burden for Benjamin was a kind of martyrdom; he could not help connecting it with politics. Barthes regards politics as a kind of constriction of the human (and intellectual) subject which has to be outwitted; in *Roland Barthes* he declares that he likes political positions "lightly held." Hence, perhaps, he was never gripped by the project that is central for Benjamin, as for all true modernists: to try to fathom the nature of "the modern." Barthes, who was not tormented by the catastrophes of modernity or tempted by its revolutionary illusions, had a post-tragic sensibility. He refers to the present literary era as "a moment of gentle apocalypse." Happy indeed the writer who can pronounce such a phrase.

Much of Barthes's work is devoted to the repertoire of pleasure—"the great adventure of desire," as he calls it in the essay on Brillat-Savarin's *Physiology of Taste*. Collecting a model of felicity from each thing he examines, he assimilates intellectual practice itself to the erotic. Barthes called the life of the mind desire, and was concerned to defend "the plurality of desire." Meaning is never monogamous. His joyful wisdom or gay science offers the ideal of a free yet capacious, satisfied consciousness; of a condition in which one does not have to choose between good and bad, true and false, in which it is not necessary to justify. The texts and enterprises that engaged Barthes tend to be those in which he could read a defiance of these antitheses. For example, this is how Barthes construes fashion: as a domain, like eros, where contraries do not exist ("Fashion seeks equivalences, validities—not verities"); where one can allow oneself to be gratified; where meaning—and pleasure—is profuse.

To construe in this way, Barthes requires a master category through which everything can be refracted, which makes possible the maximum number of intellectual moves. That most inclusive category is language, the widest sense of language—meaning form itself. Thus, the subject of *Système de la mode* (1967) is not fashion but the language of fashion. Barthes assumes, of course, that the language of fashion *is* fashion; that, as he said in an interview, "fashion exists only through the discourse on it." Assumptions of this sort (myth is a language, fashion is a language) have become a leading, often reductive convention of contemporary intellectual endeavor. In Barthes's work the assumption is less a reductive one than it is proliferative—embarrassment of riches for the critic as artist. To stipulate that there is no understanding outside of language is to assert that there is meaning *everywhere*.

By so extending the reach of meaning, Barthes takes the notion over the top, to arrive at such triumphant paradoxes as the empty subject that contains everything, the empty sign to which all meaning can be attributed. With this euphoric sense of how meaning proliferates, Barthes reads that "zero degree of the monument," the Eiffel Tower, as "this pure—virtually empty—sign" that (his italics) *"means everything."* (The characteristic point of Barthes's arguments-by-paradox is to vindicate subjects untrammeled by utility: it is the uselessness of the Eiffel Tower that makes it infinitely useful as a sign, just as the uselessness of genuine literature is what makes it morally useful.) Barthes found a world of such liberating absences of meaning, both modernist and simply non-Western, in Japan; Japan, he noted, was full of empty signs. In place of moralistic antitheses—true versus false, good versus bad—Barthes offers complementary extremes. "Its form is empty but present, its meaning absent but full," he writes about myth in an essay in the 1950s. Arguments about many subjects have this identical climax: that absence is really presence, emptiness repletion, impersonality the highest achievement of the personal.

Like that euphoric register of religious understanding which discerns treasures of meaning in the most banal and meaningless, which designates as the richest carrier of meaning one vacant of meaning, the brilliant descriptions in Barthes's work bespeak an ecstatic experience of understanding; and ecstasy—whether religious, aesthetic, or sexual—has perennially been described by the metaphors of being empty and being full, the zero state and the state of maximal plenitude: their alternation, their equivalence. The very transposing of subjects into the discourse about them is the same kind of move: emptying subjects out to fill them up again. It is a method of understanding that, presuming ecstasy, fosters detachment. And his very idea of language also supports both aspects of Barthes's sensibility: while endorsing a profusion of meaning, the Saussurean theory—that language *is* form (rather than substance)—is wonderfully congruent with a taste for elegant, that is, reticent, discourse. Creating meaning through the intellectual equivalent of negative space, Barthes's method has one never talking about subjects in themselves: fashion is the language of fashion, a country (Japan) is "the empire of signs"—the ultimate accolade. For reality to exist *as* signs conforms to a maximum idea of decorum: all meaning is deferred, indirect, elegant.

Barthes's ideals of impersonality, of reticence, of elegance, are set forth most beautifully in his appreciation of Japanese culture: in the book called *The Empire of Signs* (1970) and in his essay on the Bunraku puppets. This essay, "Lesson in Writing," recalls Kleist's "On the Puppet Theater," which similarly celebrates the tranquillity, lightness, and grace of being free of thinking, of meaning—free of "the disorders of consciousness." Like the puppets in Kleist's essay, the Bunraku puppets are seen as incarnating an ideal "impassivity, clarity, agility, subtlety." To be both impassive and fantastic, inane and profound, unspontaneous and supremely sensuous—these qualities that Barthes discerned in various facets of Japanese civilization project an ideal of taste and deportment, the ideal of the aesthete in its larger meaning that has been in general circulation since the dandies of the late eighteenth century. Barthes was hardly the first Western observer for whom Japan has meant an aesthete's utopia, the place where one finds aesthete views everywhere and exercises one's own at liberty. The culture where aesthete goals are central—not, as in the West, eccentric—was bound to elicit a strong response. (Japan is mentioned in the Gide essay written in 1942.)

Of the available models of the aesthetic way of looking at the world, perhaps the most eloquent are French and Japanese. In France it has largely been a literary tradition, though with annexes in two popular arts, gastronomy and fashion. Barthes did take up the subject of food as ideology, as classification, as taste—he talks often of savoring; and it seems inevitable that he found the subject of fashion congenial. Writers from Baudelaire to Cocteau have taken fashion seriously, and one of the founding figures of literary modernism, Mallarmé, edited a fashion magazine. French culture, where aesthete ideals have been more explicit and influential than in any other European culture, allows a link between ideas of vanguard art and of fashion. (The French have never shared the Anglo-American conviction that makes the fashionable the opposite of the serious.) In Japan, aesthete standards appear to imbue the whole culture, and long predate the modern ironies; they were formulated as early as the late tenth century, in Sei Shōnagon's *Pillow Book*, that breviary of consummate dandy attitudes, written in what is for us an astonishingly modern, disjunctive form—notes, anecdotes, and lists. Barthes's interest in Japan expresses the attraction to a less defensive, more innocent, and far more elaborated version of the aesthete sensibility: emptier and prettier than the French, more straightforward (no beauty in ugliness, as in Baudelaire); pre-apocalyptic, refined, serene.

In Western culture, where it remains marginal, the dandy attitude has the character of an exaggeration. In one form, the older one, the aesthete is a willful exclusionist of taste, holding attitudes that make it possible to like, to be comfortable with, to give one's assent to the smallest number of things; reducing things to the smallest expression of them. (When taste distributes its plusses and minuses, it favors diminutive adjectives, such as—for praise—happy, amusing, charming, agreeable, suitable.) Elegance equals the largest amount of refusal. As language, this attitude finds its consummate expression in the rueful quip, the disdainful one-liner. In the other form, the aesthete sustains standards that make it possible to be pleased with the largest number of things; annexing new, unconventional, even illicit sources of pleasure. The literary device that best projects this attitude is the list (*Roland Barthes* has many)—the whimsical aesthete polyphony that juxtaposes things and experiences of a starkly different, often incongruous nature, turning them all, by this technique, into artifacts, aesthetic objects. Here elegance equals the wittiest acceptances. The aesthete's posture alternates between *never* being satisfied and *always* finding a way of being satisfied, being pleased with virtually everything.*

Although both directions of dandy taste presuppose detachment, the exclusivist version is cooler. The inclusivist version can be enthusiastic, even effusive; the adjectives used for praise tend to be over- rather than understatements. Barthes, who had much of the high exclusivist taste of the dandy, was more inclined to its modern, democratizing form: aesthete leveling—hence his willingness to find charm, amusement, happiness, pleasure in so many things. His ac-

---

*The version of the aesthete sensibility I once tried to include under the name "camp" can be regarded as a technique of taste for making the aesthete taste less exclusionary (a way of liking more than one really wants to like) and as part of the democratizing of dandy attitudes. Camp taste, however, still presupposes the older, high standards of discrimination—in contrast to the taste incarnated by, say, Andy Warhol, the franchiser and mass marketer of the dandyism of leveling.

count of Fourier, for example, is finally an aesthete's appraisal. Of the "little details" that, he says, make up the "whole of Fourier," Barthes writes: "I am carried away, dazzled, convinced by a sort of charm of expression. . . . Fourier is swarming with these felicities. . . . I cannot resist these pleasures; they seem 'true' to me." Similarly: what another *flâneur,* less committed to finding pleasure everywhere, might experience as the oppressive overcrowdedness of streets in Tokyo signifies for Barthes "the transformation of quality by quantity," a new relation that is "a source of endless jubilation."

Many of Barthes's judgments and interests are implicitly affirmations of the aesthete's standards. His early essays championing the fiction of Robbe-Grillet, which gave Barthes the misleading reputation as an advocate of literary modernism, were in effect aesthete polemics. The "objective," the "literal"—these austere, minimalist ideas of literature are in fact Barthes's ingenious recycling of one of the aesthete's principal theses: that surface is as telling as depth. What Barthes discerned in Robbe-Grillet in the 1950s was a new, high-tech version of the dandy writer; what he hailed in Robbe-Grillet was the desire "to establish the novel on the surface," thereby frustrating our desire to "fall back on a psychology." The idea that depths are obfuscating, demagogic; that no human essence stirs at the bottom of things, and that freedom lies in staying on the surface, the large glass on which desire circulates—this is the central argument of the modern aesthete position, in the various exemplary forms it has taken over the last hundred years. (Baudelaire. Wilde. Duchamp. Cage.)

Barthes is constantly making an argument against depth, against the idea that the most real is latent, submerged. Bunraku is seen as refusing the antinomy of matter and soul, inner and outer. *"Myth hides nothing,"* he declares in "Myth Today" (1956). The aesthete position not only regards the notion of depths, of hiddenness, as a mystification, a lie, but opposes the very idea of antitheses. Of course, to speak of depths and surfaces is already to misrepresent the aesthetic view of the world—to reiterate a duality, like that of form and content, it precisely denies. The largest statement of this position was made by Nietzsche, whose work constitutes a criticism of fixed antitheses (good versus evil, right versus wrong, true versus false).

But while Nietzsche scorned "depths," he exalted "heights." In the post-Nietzschean tradition, there are neither depths nor heights; there are only various kinds of surface, of spectacle. Nietzsche said that every profound nature needs a mask, and spoke—profoundly—in praise of intellectual ruse; but he was making the gloomiest prediction when he said that the coming century, ours, would be the age of the actor. An ideal of seriousness, of sincerity, underlies all of Nietzsche's work, which makes the overlap of his ideas and those of a true aesthete (like Wilde, like Barthes) so problematic. Nietzsche was a histrionic thinker but not a lover of the histrionic. His ambivalence toward spectacle (after all, his criticism of Wagner's music was finally that it was a seduction), his insistence on the authenticity of spectacle, means that criteria other than the histrionic are in effect. In the aesthete's position, reality and spectacle precisely reinforce and infuse each other, and seduction is always something positive. In this respect, Barthes's ideas have an exemplary coherence. Notions of the theater inform, directly or indirectly, all his work. (Divulging the secret, late, he declares in *Roland Barthes* that there was no single text of his "which did not treat of a certain theater, and the spectacle is the universal category through whose forms the world is seen.") Barthes explains Robbe-Grillet's empty, "anthological" description as a technique of theatrical distancing (presenting an object "as if it were in itself a spectacle"). Fashion is, of course, another casebook of the theatrical. So is Barthes's interest in photography, which he treats as a realm of pure haunted spectatorship. In the account of photography given in *Camera Lucida* there are hardly any photographers—the subject is photographs (treated virtually as found objects) and those who are fascinated by them: as objects of erotic reverie, as *memento mori*.

What he wrote about Brecht, whom he discovered in 1954 (when the Berliner Ensemble visited Paris with their production of *Mother Courage*) and helped make known in France, has less to do with the theatrical than does his treatment of some subjects as *forms* of the theatrical. In his frequent use of Brecht in seminars of the 1970s, he cited the prose writings, which he took as a model of critical acuity; it was not Brecht the maker of didactic spectacles but Brecht the didactic intellectual who finally mattered to Barthes. In contrast, with Bunraku what Barthes valued was the element of theatricality as such. In Barthes's early work, the theatrical is the domain of liberty, the place where identities are only roles and one can *change* roles, a zone where meaning itself may be refused. (Barthes speaks of Bunraku's privileged "exemption from meaning.") Barthes's talk about the theatrical, like his evangelism of pleasure, is a way of proselytizing for the attenuating, lightening, baffling of the Logos, of meaning itself.

To affirm the notion of the spectacle is the triumph of the aesthete's position: the promulgation of the ludic, the refusal of the tragic. All of Barthes's intellectual moves have the effect of voiding work of its "content," the tragic of its finality. That is the sense in which his work is genuinely subversive, liberating—playful. It is outlaw discourse, in the great aesthete tradition, which often assumes the liberty of rejecting the "substance" of discourse in order better to appreciate its "form": outlaw discourse turned respectable, as it were, with the help of various theories known as varieties of formalism. In numerous accounts of his intellectual evolution, Barthes describes himself as the perpetual disciple—but the point that he really wants to make is that he remains, finally, untouched. He spoke of his having worked under the aegis of a succession of theories and masters. In fact, Barthes's work has altogether more coherence, and ambivalence. For all his connection with tutelary doctrines, Barthes's submission to doctrine was superficial. In the end, it was necessary that all intellectual gadgetry be discarded. His last books are a kind of unraveling of his ideas. *Roland Barthes,* he says, is the book of his resistance to his ideas, the dismantling of his own authority. And in the inaugural lecture that marked his acceding to a position of the highest authority—the Chair of Literary Semiology at the Collège de France in 1977—Barthes chooses, characteristically enough, to argue for a soft intellectual authority. He praises teaching as a permissive, not a coercive, space where one can be relaxed, disarmed, floating.

Language itself, which Barthes called a "utopia" in the euphoric formulation that ends *Writing Degree Zero,* now comes under attack, as another form of "power," and his very effort to convey his sensitivity to the ways in which language is "power" gives rise to that instantly notorious hyperbole in his Collège de France lecture: the power of language is "quite simply fascist." To assume that society is ruled by monolithic ideologies and repressive mystifications is necessary to Barthes's advocacy of egoism, post-revolutionary but nevertheless antinomian: his notion that the affirmation of the unremittingly personal is a subversive act. This is a classic extension of the aesthete attitude, in which it becomes a politics: a politics of radical individuality. Pleasure is largely identified with unauthorized pleasure, and the right of individual assertion with the sanctity of the asocial self. In the late writings, the theme of protest against power takes the form of an increasingly private definition of experience (as fetishized involvement) and a ludic definition of thought. "The great problem," Barthes says in a late interview, "is to outplay the signified, to outplay law, to outplay the father, to outplay the repressed—I do not say to explode it, but to outplay it." The aesthete's ideal of detachment, of the selfishness of detachment, allows for avowals of passionate, obsessed involvement: the selfishness of ardor, of fascination. (Wilde speaks of his "curious mixture of ardour and of indifference. . . . I

would go to the stake for a sensation and be a sceptic to the last.")
Barthes has to keep affirming the aesthete's detachment, and undermining it—with passions.

Like all great aesthetes, Barthes was an expert at having it both
ways. Thus he identifies writing both with a generous relation to the
world (writing as "perpetual production") and with a defiant relation
(writing as "a perpetual revolution of language," outside the bounds
of power). He wants a politics and an anti-politics, a critical relation
to the world and one beyond moral considerations. The aesthete's radicalism is the radicalism of a privileged, even a replete, consciousness—but a genuine radicalism nonetheless. All genuine moral views
are founded on a notion of refusal, and the aesthete's view, which
can be conformist, does provide certain potentially powerful, not just
elegant, grounds for a great refusal.

The aesthete's radicalism: to be multiple, to make multiple identi-
fications; to assume fully the privilege of the personal. Barthes's
work—he avows that he writes by obsessions—consists of continuities and detours; the accumulation of points of view; finally, their
disburdenment: a mixture of progress and caprice. For Barthes, liberty is a state that consists in remaining plural, fluid, vibrating with
doctrine; whose price is being indecisive, apprehensive, fearful of
being taken for an impostor. The writer's freedom that Barthes describes is, in part, flight. The writer is the deputy of his own ego—of
that self in perpetual flight before what is fixed by writing, as the
mind is in perpetual flight from doctrine. "Who *speaks* is not who
writes, and who *writes* is not who *is.*" Barthes wants to move on—
that is one of the imperatives of the aesthete's sensibility.

Throughout his work Barthes projects himself into his subject. He
is Fourier: unvexed by the sense of evil, aloof from politics, "that
necessary purge"; he "vomits it up." He is the Bunraku puppet: impersonal, subtle. He is Gide: the writer who is ageless (always young,
always mature); the writer as egoist—a triumphant species of "simultaneous being" or plural desire. He is the subject of all the subjects that he praises. (That he must, characteristically, praise may be
connected with his project of defining, creating standards for himself.) In this sense, much of what Barthes wrote now appears autobiographical.

Eventually, it became autobiographical in the literal sense. A brave
meditation on the personal, on the self, is at the center of his late
writings and seminars. Much of Barthes's work, especially the last
three books with their poignant themes of loss, constitutes a candid

defense of his sensuality (as well as his sexuality)—his flavor, his way of tasting the world. The books are also artfully anti-confessional. *Camera Lucida* is a meta-book: a meditation on the even more personal autobiographical book that he planned to write about photographs of his mother, who died in 1978, and then put aside. Barthes starts from the modernist model of writing that is superior to any idea of intention or mere expressiveness; a mask. "The work," Valéry insists, "should not give the person it affects anything that can be reduced to an idea of the author's person and thinking."* But this commitment to impersonality does not preclude the avowal of the self; it is only another variation on the project of self-examination: the noblest project of French literature. Valéry offers one ideal of self-absorption—impersonal, disinterested. Rousseau offers another ideal—passionate, avowing vulnerability. Many themes of Barthes's work lie in the classic discourse of French literary culture: its taste for elegant abstraction, in particular for the formal analysis of the sentiments; its disdain for mere psychology; and its coquetry about the impersonal (Flaubert declaring *"Madame Bovary, c'est moi"* but also insisting in letters on his novel's "impersonality," its lack of connection with himself).

Barthes is the latest major participant in the great national literary project, inaugurated by Montaigne: the self as vocation, life as a reading of the self. The enterprise construes the self as the locus of all possibilities, avid, unafraid of contradiction (nothing need be lost, everything may be gained), and the exercise of consciousness as a life's highest aim, because only through becoming fully conscious may one be free. The distinctive French utopian tradition is this vision of reality redeemed, recovered, transcended by consciousness; a vision of the life of the mind as a life of desire, of full intelligence and pleasure—so different from, say, the traditions of high moral seriousness of German and of Russian literature.

Inevitably, Barthes's work had to end in autobiography. "One must choose between being a terrorist and being an egoist," he once observed in a seminar. The options seem very French. Intellectual terrorism is a central, respectable form of intellectual practice in France—

*This modernist dictum that writing is, ideally, a form of impersonality or absence underlies Barthes's move to eliminate the "author" when considering a book. (The method of his *S/Z*: an exemplary reading of a Balzac novella as virtually an authorless text.) One of the things Barthes does as a critic is to formulate the mandate for one kind of modernism (Flaubert, Valéry, Eliot) for the writer as a general program for *readers*. Another is to contravene that mandate in practice—for most of Barthes's writing is precisely devoted to personal singularity.

tolerated, humored, rewarded: the "Jacobin" tradition of ruthless assertion and shameless ideological about-faces; the mandate of incessant judgment, opinion, anathematizing, overpraising; the taste for extreme positions, then casually reversed, and for deliberate provocation. Alongside this, how modest egoism is!

Barthes's voice became steadily more intimate, his subjects more inward. An affirmation of his own idiosyncrasy (which he does not "decipher") is the main theme of *Roland Barthes*. He writes about the body, taste, love; solitude; erotic desolation; finally, death, or rather desire and death: the twin subjects of the book on photography. As in the Platonic dialogues, the thinker (writer, reader, teacher) and the lover—the two main figures of the Barthesian self—are joined. Barthes, of course, means his erotics of literature more literally, as literally as he can. (The text *enters, fills,* it *grants* euphoria.) But finally he seems fairly Platonic after all. The monologue of *A Lover's Discourse,* which obviously draws on a story of disappointment in love, ends in a spiritual vision in the classic Platonic way, in which lower loves are transmuted into higher, more inclusive ones. Barthes avows that he "wants to unmask, no longer to interpret, but to make of consciousness itself a drug, and thus accede to a vision of irreducible reality, to the great drama of clarity, to prophetic love."

As he divested himself of theories, he gave less weight to the modernist standard of the intricate. He does not want, he says, to place any obstacles between himself and the reader. The last book is part memoir (of his mother), part meditation on eros, part treatise on the photographic image, part invocation of death—a book of piety, resignation, desire; a certain brilliance is being renounced, and the view itself is of the simplest. The subject of photography provided the great exemption, perhaps release, from the exactions of formalist taste. In choosing to write about photography, Barthes takes the occasion to adopt the warmest kind of realism: photographs fascinate because of what they are about. And they may awaken a desire for a further divestment of the self. ("Looking at certain photographs," he writes in *Camera Lucida,* "I wanted to be a primitive, without culture.") The Socratic sweetness and charm become more plaintive, more desperate: writing is an embrace, a being embraced; every idea is an idea reaching out. There is a sense of disaggregation of his ideas, and of himself—represented by his increasing fascination with what he calls "the detail." In the preface to *Sade / Fourier / Loyola,* Barthes writes: "Were I a writer, and dead, how pleased I would be if my life, through the efforts of some friendly and detached biographer, were to reduce itself to a few details, a few preferences, a few inflections, let us say:

to 'biographemes' whose distinction and mobility might travel beyond the limits of any fate, and come to touch, like Epicurean atoms, some future body, destined to the same dispersion." The need to touch, even in the perspective of his own mortality.

Barthes's late work is filled with signals that he has come to the end of something—the enterprise of the critic as artist—and was seeking to become another kind of writer. (He announced his intention to write a novel.) There were exalted avowals of vulnerability, of being forlorn. Barthes more and more entertained an idea of writing which resembles the mystical idea of *kenosis,* emptying out. He acknowledged that not only systems—his ideas were in a state of melt— but the "I" as well has to be dismantled. (True knowledge, says Barthes, depends on the "unmasking of the 'I.' ") The aesthetics of absence—the empty sign, the empty subject, the exemption from meaning—were all intimations of the great project of depersonalization which is the aesthete's highest gesture of good taste. Toward the close of Barthes's work, this ideal took on another inflection. A spiritual ideal of depersonalization—that is perhaps the characteristic terminus of every serious aesthete's position. (Think of Wilde, of Valéry.) It is the point at which the aesthete's view self-destructs: what follows is either silence—or becoming something else.

Barthes harbored spiritual strivings that could not be supported by his aesthete's position. It was inevitable that he pass beyond it, as he did in his very last work and teaching. At the end, he had done with the aesthetics of absence, and now spoke of literature as the embrace of subject and object. There was an emergence of a vision of "wisdom" of the Platonic sort—tempered, to be sure, by wisdom of a worldly kind: skeptical of dogmatisms, conscientious about gratification, wistfully attached to utopian ideals. Barthes's temperament, style, sensibility, had run its course. And from this vantage point his work now appears to unfold, with more grace and poignancy and with far greater intellectual power than that of any other contemporary, the considerable truths vouchsafed to the aesthete's sensibility, to a commitment to intellectual adventure, to the talent for contradiction and inversion—those "late" ways of experiencing, evaluating, reading the world; and surviving in it, drawing energy, finding consolation (but finally not), taking pleasure, expressing love.

(1981)